PENGUIN BOOKS

THE GREEK MYTHS

VOLUME ONE

Robert Graves was born in 1895 in Wimbledon, son of Alfred Percival Graves, the Irish writer, and Amalia Von Ranke. He went from school to the First World War, where he became a captain in the Royal Welch Fusiliers. His principal calling was poetry, and his *Selected Poems* have been published in Penguin Twentieth-Century Classics. Apart from a year as Professor of English Literature at Cairo University in 1926 he earned his living by writing, mostly historical novels, which include *I, Claudius*; *Claudius the God*; *Sergeant Lamb of the Ninth*; *Count Belisarius*; *Wife to Mr Milton*; *Proceed, Sergeant Lamb*; *The Golden Fleece*; *They Hanged My Saintly Billy*; and *The Isles of Unwisdom*. He wrote his autobiography, *Goodbye to All That*, in 1929 and it rapidly established itself as a modern classic. *The Times Literary Supplement* acclaimed it as 'one of the most candid self-portraits of a poet, warts and all, ever painted', as well as being of exceptional value as a war document. His two most discussed non-fiction books are *The White Goddess*, which presents a new view of the poetic impulse, and *The Nazarine Gospel Restored* (with Joshua Podro), a re-examination of primitive Christianity. He translated Apuleius, Lucan, and Suetonius for the Penguin Classics series, and compiled the first modern dictionary of Greek Mythology, *The Greek Myths*. His translation of *The Rubáiyát of Omar Khayyám* (with Omar Ali-Shah) is also published in Penguin. He was elected Professor of Poetry at Oxford in 1961, and made an Honorary Fellow of St John's College, Oxford, in 1971.

Robert Graves died on 7 December 1985 in Majorca, his home since 1929. On his death *The Times* wrote of him,

'He will be remembered for his achievements as a prose stylist, historical novelist and memorist, but above all as the great paradigm of the dedicated poet, "the greatest love poet in English since Donne".'

ROBERT GRAVES

THE GREEK MYTHS

VOLUME ONE

PENGUIN BOOKS

PENGUIN BOOKS

Published by the Penguin Group
Penguin Books Ltd, 80 Strand, London WC2R ORL, England
Penguin Group (USA) Inc., 375 Hudson Street, New York, New York 10014, USA
Penguin Group (Canada), 90 Eglinton Avenue East, Suite 700, Toronto, Ontario, Canada M4P 2Y3
(a division of Pearson Penguin Canada Inc.)
Penguin Ireland, 25 St Stephen's Green, Dublin 2, Ireland
(a division of Penguin Books Ltd)
Penguin Group (Australia), 250 Camberwell Road, Camberwell, Victoria 3124, Australia
(a division of Pearson Australia Group Pty Ltd)
Penguin Books India Pvt Ltd, 11 Community Centre,
Panchsheel Park, New Delhi – 110 017, India
Penguin Group (NZ), 67 Apollo Drive, Rosedale, Auckland 0632, New Zealand
(a division of Pearson New Zealand Ltd)
Penguin Books (South Africa) (Pty) Ltd, 24 Sturdee Avenue,
Rosebank, Johannesburg 2196, South Africa

Penguin Books Ltd, Registered Offices: 80 Strand, London WC2R ORL, England

www.penguin.com

First published 1955
Reprinted with amendments 1957
Revised edition published 1960
Reissued in this edition 2011

2

Copyright © Robert Graves, 1955, 1960
All rights reserved

Printed in England by Clays Ltd, St Ives plc

ISBN: 978-0-241-95275-7

www.greenpenguin.co.uk

CONTENTS OF VOLUME ONE

CONTENTS

CONTENTS

A complete index to both volumes and a map showing the sites mentioned in the text will be found at the end of Volume 2

The death of the Old Bull of the Year apparently poleaxed, and the birth of the New Year's Bull-Calf from a date cluster; under the supervision of a Cretan priestess, who identifies herself with the palm-tree. From a Middle-Minoan bead-seal in the author's collection (diameter enlarged 1½ times). About 1900 B.C.

FOREWORD

SINCE revising *The Greek Myths* in 1958, I have had second thoughts about the drunken god Dionysus, about the Centaurs with their contradictory reputation for wisdom and misdemeanour, and about the nature of divine ambrosia and nectar. These subjects are closely related, because the Centaurs worshipped Dionysus, whose wild autumnal feast was called 'the Ambrosia'. I no longer believe that when his Maenads ran raging around the countryside, tearing animals or children in pieces (see 27. *f*) and boasted afterwards of travelling to India and back (see 27. *c*), they had intoxicated themselves solely on wine or ivy-ale (see 27. *3*). The evidence, summarized in my *What Food the Centaurs Ate* (*Steps*: Cassell & Co., 1958, pp. 319–343), suggests that Satyrs (goat-totem tribesmen), Centaurs (horse-totem tribesmen), and their Maenad womenfolk, used these brews to wash down mouthfuls of a far stronger drug: namely a raw mushroom, *amanita muscaria*, which induces hallucinations, senseless rioting, prophetic sight, erotic energy, and remarkable muscular strength. Some hours of this ecstasy are followed by complete inertia; a phenomenon that would account for the story of how Lycurgus, armed only with an ox-goad, routed Dionysus's drunken army of Maenads and Satyrs after its victorious return from India (see 27. *e*).

On an Etruscan mirror the *amanita muscaria* is engraved at Ixion's feet; he was a Thessalian hero who feasted on ambrosia among the gods (see 63. *b*). Several myths (see 102, 126, etc.) are consistent with my theory that his descendants, the Centaurs, ate this mushroom; and, according to some historians, it was later employed by the Norse 'berserks' to give them reckless power in battle. I now believe that 'ambrosia' and 'nectar' were intoxicant mushrooms: certainly the *amanita muscaria*; but perhaps others, too, especially a small, slender dung-mushroom named *panaeolus papilionaceus*, which induces harmless and most enjoyable hallucinations. A mushroom not unlike it appears on an Attic vase between the hooves of Nessus the Centaur. The 'gods' for whom, in the myths, ambrosia and nectar were reserved, will have been sacred queens and kings of the pre-Classical era. King Tantalus's crime (see 108. *c*) was that he broke the taboo by inviting commoners to share his ambrosia.

Sacred queenships and kingships lapsed in Greece; ambrosia then became, it seems, the secret element of the Eleusinian, Orphic and other Mysteries associated with Dionysus. At all events, the participants swore to keep silence about what they ate or drank, saw unforgettable visions, and were promised immortality. The 'ambrosia' awarded to winners of the Olympic footrace when victory no longer conferred the sacred kingship on them was clearly a substitute: a mixture of foods the initial letters of which, as I show in *What Food the Centaurs Ate*, spelled out the Greek word 'mushroom'. Recipes quoted by Classical authors for nectar, and for *cecyon*, the mint-flavoured drink taken by Demeter at Eleusis, likewise spell out 'mushroom'.

I have myself eaten the hallucigenic mushroom, *psilocybe*, a divine ambrosia in immemorial use among the Masatec Indians of Oaxaca Province, Mexico; heard the priestess invoke Tlaloc, the Mushroom-god, and seen transcendental visions. Thus I wholeheartedly agree with R. Gordon Wasson, the American discoverer of this ancient rite, that European ideas of heaven and hell may well have derived from similar mysteries. Tlaloc was engendered by lightning; so was Dionysus (see 14. *c*); and in Greek folklore, as in Masatec, so are all mushrooms – proverbially called 'food of the gods' in both languages. Tlaloc wore a serpent-crown; so did Dionysus (see 27. *a*). Tlaloc had an underwater retreat; so had Dionysus (see 27. *e*). The Maenads' savage custom of tearing off their victims' heads (see 27. *f* and 28. *d*) may refer allegorically to tearing off the sacred mushroom's head – since in Mexico its stalk is never eaten. We read that Perseus, a sacred King of Argos, converted to Dionysus worship (see 27. *i*), named Mycenae after a toadstool which he found growing on the site, and which gave forth a stream of water (see 73. *r*). Tlaloc's emblem was a toad; so was that of Argos; and from the mouth of Tlaloc's toad in the Tepentitla fresco issues a stream of water. Yet at what epoch were the European and Central American cultures in contact?

These theories call for further research, and I have therefore not incorporated my findings in the text of the present edition. Any expert help in solving the problem would be greatly appreciated.

R. G.

Deyá, Majorca,
   Spain, 1960.

INTRODUCTION

THE medieval emissaries of the Catholic Church brought to Great Britain, in addition to the whole corpus of sacred history, a Continental university system based on the Greek and Latin Classics. Such native legends as those of King Arthur, Guy of Warwick, Robin Hood, the Blue Hag of Leicester, and King Lear were considered suitable enough for the masses, yet by early Tudor times the clergy and the educated classes were referring far more frequently to the myths in Ovid, Virgil, and the grammar school summaries of the Trojan War. Though official English literature of the sixteenth to the nineteenth centuries cannot, therefore, be properly understood except in the light of Greek mythology, the Classics have lately lost so much ground in schools and universities that an educated person is now no longer expected to know (for instance) who Deucalion, Pelops, Daedalus, Oenone, Laocoön, or Antigone may have been. Current knowledge of these myths is mostly derived from such fairy-story versions as Kingsley's *Heroes* and Hawthorne's *Tanglewood Tales*; and at first sight this does not seem to matter much, because for the last two thousand years it has been the fashion to dismiss the myths as bizarre and chimerical fancies, a charming legacy from the childhood of the Greek intelligence, which the Church naturally depreciates in order to emphasize the greater spiritual importance of the Bible. Yet it is difficult to overestimate their value in the study of early European history, religion, and sociology.

'Chimerical' is an adjectival form of the noun *chimaera*, meaning 'she-goat'. Four thousand years ago the Chimaera can have seemed no more bizarre than any religious, heraldic, or commercial emblem does today. She was a formal composite beast with (as Homer records) a lion's head, a goat's body, and a serpent's tail. A Chimaera has been found carved on the walls of a Hittite temple at Carchemish and, like such other composite beasts as the Sphinx and the Unicorn, will originally have been a calendar symbol: each component represented a season of the Queen of Heaven's sacred year – as, according to Diodorus Siculus, the three strings of her tortoise-shell lyre also did. This ancient three-season year is discussed by Nilsson in his *Primitive Time Reckoning* (1920).

Only a small part, however, of the huge, disorganized corpus of Greek mythology, which contains importations from Crete, Egypt,

Palestine, Phrygia, Babylonia, and elsewhere, can properly be classified with the Chimaera as true myth. True myth may be defined as the reduction to narrative shorthand of ritual mime performed on public festivals, and in many cases recorded pictorially on temple walls, vases, seals, bowls, mirrors, chests, shields, tapestries, and the like. The Chimaera and her fellow calendar-beasts must have figured prominently in these dramatic performances which, with their iconographic and oral records, became the prime authority, or charter, for the religious institutions of each tribe, clan, or city. Their subjects were archaic magic-makings that promoted the fertility or stability of a sacred queendom, or kingdom – queendoms having, it seems, preceded kingdoms throughout the Greek-speaking area – and amendments to these, introduced as circumstances required. Lucian's essay *On the Dance* lists an imposing number of ritual mimes still performed in the second century A.D.; and Pausanias's description of the temple paintings at Delphi and the carvings on Cypselus's Chest, suggests that an immense amount of miscellaneous mythological records, of which no trace now remains, survived into the same period.

True myth must be distinguished from:

(1) Philosophical allegory, as in Hesiod's cosmogony.
(2) 'Aetiological' explanation of myths no longer understood, as in Admetus's yoking of a lion and a boar to his chariot.
(3) Satire or parody, as in Silenus's account of Atlantis.
(4) Sentimental fable, as in the story of Narcissus and Echo.
(5) Embroidered history, as in Arion's adventure with the dolphin.
(6) Minstrel romance, as in the story of Cephalus and Procris.
(7) Political propaganda, as in Theseus's Federalization of Attica.
(8) Moral legend, as in the story of Eriphyle's necklace.
(9) Humorous anecdote, as in the bedroom farce of Heracles, Omphale, and Pan.
(10) Theatrical melodrama, as in the story of Thestor and his daughters.
(11) Heroic saga, as in the main argument of the *Iliad*.
(12) Realistic fiction, as in Odysseus's visit to the Phaeacians.[1]

Yet genuine mythic elements may be found embedded in the least promising stories, and the fullest or most illuminating version of a

1. See 4; 69; 83; 84; 87; 89; 99; 106; 136; 161; 162–5; 170.

given myth is seldom supplied by any one author; nor, when searching for its original form, should one assume that the more ancient the written source, the more authoritative it must be. Often, for instance, the playful Alexandrian Callimachus, or the frivolous Augustan Ovid, or the dry-as-dust late-Byzantine Tzetzes, gives an obviously earlier version of a myth than do Hesiod or the Greek tragedians; and the thirteenth-century *Excidium Troiae* is, in parts, mythically sounder than the *Iliad*. When making prose sense of a mythological or pseudo-mythological narrative, one should always pay careful attention to the names, tribal origin, and fates of the characters concerned; and then restore it to the form of dramatic ritual, whereupon its incidental elements will sometimes suggest an analogy with another myth which has been given a wholly different anecdotal twist, and shed light on both.

A study of Greek mythology should begin with a consideration of what political and religious systems existed in Europe before the arrival of Aryan invaders from the distant North and East. The whole of neolithic Europe, to judge from surviving artifacts and myths, had a remarkably homogeneous system of religious ideas, based on worship of the many-titled Mother-goddess, who was also known in Syria and Libya.

Ancient Europe had no gods. The Great Goddess was regarded as immortal, changeless, and omnipotent; and the concept of fatherhood had not been introduced into religious thought. She took lovers, but for pleasure, not to provide her children with a father. Men feared, adored, and obeyed the matriarch; the hearth which she tended in a cave or hut being their earliest social centre, and motherhood their prime mystery. Thus the first victim of a Greek public sacrifice was always offered to Hestia of the Hearth. The goddess's white aniconic image, perhaps her most widespread emblem, which appears at Delphi as the *omphalos*, or navel-boss, may originally have represented the raised white mound of tightly-packed ash, enclosing live charcoal, which is the easiest means of preserving fire without smoke. Later, it became pictorially identified with the lime-whitened mound under which the harvest corn-doll was hidden, to be removed sprouting in the spring; and with the mound of sea-shells, or quartz, or white marble, underneath which dead kings were buried. Not only the moon, but (to judge from Hemera of Greece and Grainne of Ireland) the sun, were the goddess's celestial symbols. In earlier Greek myth, however, the sun yields precedence to the moon – which inspires the greater superstitious fear, does not grow dimmer as the year wanes, and is credited with the power to grant or deny water to the fields.

The moon's three phases of new, full, and old recalled the matriarch's three phases of maiden, nymph (nubile woman), and crone. Then, since the sun's annual course similarly recalled the rise and decline of her physical powers – spring a maiden, summer a nymph, winter a crone – the goddess became identified with seasonal changes in animal and plant life; and thus with Mother Earth who, at the beginning of the vegetative year, produces only leaves and buds, then flowers and fruits, and at last ceases to bear. She could later be conceived as yet another triad: the maiden of the upper air, the nymph of the earth or sea, the crone of the underworld – typified respectively by Selene, Aphrodite, and Hecate. These mystical analogues fostered the sacredness of the number three, and the Moon-goddess became enlarged to nine when each of the three persons – maiden, nymph, and crone – appeared in triad to demonstrate her divinity. Her devotees never quite forgot that there were not three goddesses, but one goddess; though, by Classical times, Arcadian Stymphalus was one of the few remaining shrines where they all bore the same name: Hera.

Once the relevance of coition to child-bearing had been officially admitted – an account of this turning-point in religion appears in the Hittite myth of simple-minded Appu (H. G. Güterbock: *Kumarbi*, 1946) – man's religious status gradually improved, and winds or rivers were no longer given credit for impregnating women. The tribal Nymph, it seems, chose an annual lover from her entourage of young men, a king to be sacrificed when the year ended; making him a symbol of fertility, rather than the object of her erotic pleasure. His sprinkled blood served to fructify trees, crops, and flocks, and his flesh was torn and eaten raw by the Queen's fellow-nymphs – priestesses wearing the masks of bitches, mares, or sows. Next, in amendment to this practice, the king died as soon as the power of the sun, with which he was identified, began to decline in the summer; and another young man, his twin, or supposed twin – a convenient ancient Irish term is 'tanist' – then became the Queen's lover, to be duly sacrificed at midwinter and, as a reward, reincarnated in an oracular serpent. These consorts acquired executive power only when permitted to deputize for the Queen by wearing her magical robes. Thus kingship developed, and though the Sun became a symbol of male fertility once the king's life had been identified with its seasonal course, it still remained under the

Moon's tutelage; as the king remained under the Queen's tutelage, in theory at least, long after the matriarchal phase had been outgrown. Thus the witches of Thessaly, a conservative region, would threaten the Sun, in the Moon's name, with being engulfed by perpetual night.

There is, however, no evidence that, even when women were sovereign in religious matters, men were denied fields in which they might act without female supervision, though it may well be that they adopted many of the 'weaker-sex' characteristics hitherto thought functionally peculiar to man. They could be trusted to hunt, fish, gather certain foods, mind flocks and herds, and help defend the tribal territory against intruders, so long as they did not transgress matriarchal law. Leaders of totem clans were chosen and certain powers awarded them, especially in times of migration or war. Rules for determining who should act as male commander-in-chief varied, it appears, in different matriarchies: usually the queen's maternal uncle, or her brother, or the son of her maternal aunt was chosen. The most primitive tribal commander-in-chief also had authority to act as judge in personal disputes between men, in so far as the queen's religious authority was not thereby impaired. The most primitive matrilineal society surviving today is that of the Nayars of Southern India, where the princesses, though married to child-husbands whom they immediately divorce, bear children to lovers of no particular rank; and the princesses of several matrilineal tribes of West Africa marry foreigners or commoners. The royal women of pre-Hellenic Greece also thought nothing of taking lovers from among their serfs, if the Hundred Houses of Locris and Epizephyrian Locri were not exceptional.

Time was first reckoned by lunations, and every important ceremony took place at a certain phase of the moon; the solstices and equinoxes not being exactly determined but approximated to the nearest new or full moon. The number seven acquired peculiar sanctity, because the king died at the seventh full moon after the shortest day. Even when, after careful astronomical observation, the solar year proved to have 364 days, with a few hours left over, it had to be divided into months – that is, moon-cycles – rather than into fractions of the solar cycle. These months later became what the English-speaking world still calls 'common-law months', each of twenty-eight days; which was a sacred number, in the sense that the moon could be worshipped as a woman, whose menstrual cycle is normally twenty-eight days, and that this is also the true period of the moon's revolutions in

terms of the sun. The seven-day week was a unit of the common-law
month, the character of each day being deduced, it seems, from the
quality attributed to the corresponding month of the sacred king's life.
This system led to a still closer identification of woman with moon and,
since the 364-day year is exactly divisible by twenty-eight, the annual
sequence of popular festivals could be geared to these common-law
months. As a religious tradition, the thirteen-month years survived
among European peasants for more than a millennium after the adoption of the Julian Calendar; thus Robin Hood, who lived at the time of
Edward II, could exclaim in a ballad celebrating the May Day festival:

> How many merry months be in the year?
> There are thirteen, I say . . .

which a Tudor editor has altered to '. . . There are but twelve, I say . . .'
Thirteen, the number of the sun's death-month, has never lost its evil
reputation among the superstitious. The days of the week lay under the
charge of Titans: the genii of sun, moon, and the five hitherto discovered planets, who were responsible for them to the goddess as
Creatrix. This system had probably been evolved in matriarchal
Sumeria.

Thus the sun passed through thirteen monthly stages, beginning at
the winter solstice when the days lengthen again after their long
autumnal decline. The extra day of the sidereal year, gained from the
solar year by the earth's revolution around the sun's orbit, was intercalated between the thirteenth and the first month, and became the most
important day of the 365, the occasion on which the tribal Nymph chose
the sacred king, usually the winner of a race, a wrestling match, or an
archery contest. But this primitive calendar underwent modifications:
in some regions the extra day seems to have been intercalated, not at
the winter solstice, but at some other New Year – at the Candlemas
cross-quarter day, when the first signs of spring are apparent; or at the
spring equinox, when the sun is regarded as coming to maturity; or at
midsummer; or at the rising of the Dog Star, when the Nile floods;
or at the autumnal equinox, when the first rains fall.

Early Greek mythology is concerned, above all else, with the changing relations between the queen and her lovers, which begin with
their yearly, or twice-yearly sacrifices; and end, at the time when
the *Iliad*, was composed and kings boasted: 'We are far better than our
fathers!', with her eclipse by an unlimited male monarchy. Num-

erous African analogues illustrate the progessive stages of this change.

A large part of Greek myth is politico-religious history. Bellerophon masters winged Pegasus and kills the Chimaera. Perseus, in a variant of the same legend, flies through the air and beheads Pegasus's mother, the Gorgon Medusa; much as Marduk, a Babylonian hero, kills the she-monster Tiamat, Goddess of the Sea. Perseus's name should properly be spelled *Pterseus*, 'the destroyer'; and he was not, as Professor Kerenyi has suggested, an archetypal Death-figure but, probably, represented the patriarchal Hellenes who invaded Greece and Asia Minor early in the second millennium B.C., and challenged the power of the Triple-goddess. Pegasus had been sacred to her because the horse with its moon-shaped hooves figured in the rain-making ceremonies and the instalment of sacred kings; his wings were symbolical of a celestial nature, rather than speed. Jane Harrison has pointed out (*Prolegomena to the Study of Greek Religion*, chapter v) that Medusa was once the goddess herself, hiding behind a prophylactic Gorgon mask: a hideous face intended to warn the profane against trespassing on her Mysteries. Perseus beheads Medusa: that is, the Hellenes overran the goddess's chief shrines, stripped her priestesses of their Gorgon masks, and took possession of the sacred horses – an early representation of the goddess with a Gorgon's head and a mare's body has been found in Boeotia. Bellerophon, Perseus's double, kills the Lycian Chimaera: that is, the Hellenes annulled the ancient Medusan calendar, and replaced it with another.

Again, Apollo's destruction of the Python at Delphi seems to record the Achaeans' capture of the Cretan Earth-goddess's shrine; so does his attempted rape of Daphne, whom Hera thereupon metamorphosed into a laurel. This myth has been quoted by Freudian psychologists as symbolizing a girl's instinctive horror of the sexual act; yet Daphne was anything but a frightened virgin. Her name is a contraction of *Daphoene*, 'the bloody one', the goddess in orgiastic mood, whose priestesses, the Maenads, chewed laurel-leaves as an intoxicant and periodically rushed out at the full moon, assaulted unwary travellers, and tore children or young animals in pieces; laurel contains cyanide of potassium. These Maenad colleges were suppressed by the Hellenes, and only the laurel grove testified to Daphoene's former occupancy of the shrines: the chewing of laurel by anyone except the prophetic Pythian Priestess, whom Apollo retained in his service at Delphi, was tabooed in Greece until Roman times.

The Hellenic invasions of the early second millennium B.C., usually called the Aeolian and Ionian, seem to have been less destructive than the Achaean and Dorian ones, which they preceded. Small armed bands of herdsmen, worshipping the Aryan trinity of gods – Indra, Mitra, and Varuna – crossed the natural barrier of Mount Othrys, and attached themselves peacefully enough to the pre-Hellenic settlements in Thessaly and Central Greece. They were accepted as children of the local goddess, and provided her with sacred kings. Thus a male military aristocracy became reconciled to female theocracy, not only in Greece, but in Crete, where the Hellenes also gained a foothold and exported Cretan civilization to Athens and the Peloponnese. Greek was eventually spoken throughout the Aegean and, by the time of Herodotus, one oracle alone spoke a pre-Hellenic language (Herodotus: viii. 134–5). The king acted as the representative of Zeus, or Poseidon, or Apollo, and called himself by one or other of their names, though even Zeus was for centuries a mere demi-god, not an immortal Olympian deity. All early myths about the gods' seduction of nymphs refer apparently to marriages between Hellenic chieftains and local Moon-priestesses; bitterly opposed by Hera, which means by conservative religious feeling.

When the shortness of the king's reign proved irksome, it was agreed to prolong the thirteen-month year to a Great Year of one hundred lunations, in the last of which occurs a near-coincidence of solar and lunar time. But since the fields and crops still needed to be fructified, the king agreed to suffer an annual mock death and yield his sovereignty for one day – the intercalated one, lying outside the sacred sidereal year – to the surrogate boy-king, or *interrex*, who died at its close, and whose blood was used for the sprinkling ceremony. Now the sacred king either reigned for the entire period of a Great Year, with a tanist as his lieutenant; or the two reigned for alternate years; or the Queen let them divide the queendom into halves and reign concurrently. The king deputized for the Queen at many sacred functions, dressed in her robes, wore false breasts, borrowed her lunar axe as a symbol of power, and even took over from her the magical art of rain-making. His ritual death varied greatly in circumstance; he might be torn in pieces by wild women, transfixed with a sting-ray spear, felled with an axe, pricked in the heel with a poisoned arrow, flung over a cliff, burned to death on a pyre, drowned in a pool, or killed in a pre-arranged chariot crash. But die he must. A new stage was reached when animals came to be substituted for boys at the sacrificial altar, and the king refused death after his lengthened reign ended. Dividing the realm into three parts, and awarding one part to each of his successors, he would reign for another term; his excuse being that a closer approximation of solar and lunar time had now been found, namely nineteen years, or 325 lunations. The Great Year had become a Greater Year.

Throughout these successive stages, reflected in numerous myths, the sacred king continued to hold his position only by right of marriage to the tribal Nymph, who was chosen either as a result of a foot race between her companions of the royal house or by ultimogeniture – that is to say, by being the youngest nubile daughter of the junior branch. The throne remained matrilineal, as it theoretically did even in Egypt, and the sacred king and his tanist were therefore always chosen from outside the royal female house; until some daring king at last decided to commit incest with the heiress, who ranked as his daughter, and thus gain a new title to the throne when his reign needed renewal.

Achaean invasions of the thirteenth century B.C. seriously weakened the matrilineal tradition. It seems that the king now contrived to reign for the term of his natural life; and when the Dorians arrived, towards the close of the second millennium, patrilineal succession became the rule. A prince no longer left his father's house and married a foreign princess; she came to him, as Odysseus persuaded Penelope to do. Genealogy became patrilineal, though a Samian incident mentioned in the Pseudo-Herodotus's *Life of Homer* shows that for some time after the Apatoria, or Festival of Male Kinship, had replaced that of Female Kinship, the rites still consisted of sacrifices to the Mother Goddess which men were not eligible to attend.

The familiar Olympian system was then agreed upon as a compromise between Hellenic and pre-Hellenic views: a divine family of six gods and six goddesses, headed by the co-sovereigns Zeus and Hera and forming a Council of Gods in Babylonian style. But after a rebellion of the pre-Hellenic population, described in the *Iliad* as a conspiracy against Zeus, Hera became subservient to him. Athene avowed herself 'all for the Father' and, in the end, Dionysus assured male preponderance in the Council by displacing Hestia. Yet the goddesses, though left in a minority, were never altogether ousted – as they were at Jerusalem – because the revered poets Homer and Hesiod had 'given the deities their titles and distinguished their several provinces and special powers' (Herodotus: ii. 53), which could not be easily expropriated. Moreover, though the system of gathering all the women of royal blood together under the king's control, and thus discouraging outsiders from attempts on a matrilineal throne, was adopted at Rome when the Vestal College was founded, and in Palestine when King David formed his royal harem, it never reached Greece. Patrilineal descent, succession, and inheritance discourage further myth-making; historical legend then begins and fades into the light of common history.

The lives of such characters as Heracles, Daedalus, Teiresias, and Phineus span several generations, because these are titles rather than names of particular heroes. Yet myths, though difficult to reconcile with chronology, are always practical: they insist on some point of tradition, however distorted the meaning may have become in the telling. Take, for instance, the confused story of Aeacus's dream, where ants, falling from an oracular oak, turn into men and colonize the island of Aegina after Hera has depopulated it. Here the main points of interest are: that the oak had grown from a Dodonian acorn; that the ants were Thessalian ants; and that Aeacus was a grandson of the River Asopus. These elements combined to give a concise account of immigrations into Aegina towards the end of the second millennium B.C.

Despite a sameness of pattern in Greek myths, all detailed interpretations of particular legends are open to question until archaeologists can provide a more exact tabulation of tribal movements in Greece, and their dates. Yet the historical and anthropological approach is the only reasonable one: the theory that Chimaera, Sphinx, Gorgon, Centaurs, Satyrs and the like are blind uprushes of the Jungian collective unconscious, to which no precise meaning had ever, or could ever, have been attached, is demonstrably unsound. The Bronze and early Iron Ages in Greece were not the childhood of mankind, as Dr Jung suggests. That Zeus swallowed Metis, for instance, and subsequently gave birth to Athene, through an orifice in his head, is not an irrepressible fancy, but an ingenious theological dogma which embodies at least three conflicting views:

(1) Athene was the parthenogenous daughter of Metis; i.e. the youngest person of the Triad headed by Metis, Goddess of Wisdom.

(2) Zeus swallowed Metis; i.e. the Achaeans suppressed her cult and arrogated all wisdom to Zeus as their patriarchal god.

(3) Athene was the daughter of Zeus; i.e. the Zeus-worshipping Achaeans spared Athene's temples on condition that her votaries accepted his paramount sovereignty.

Zeus's swallowing of Metis, with its sequel, will have been represented graphically on the walls of a temple; and as the erotic Dionysus – once a parthenogenous son of Semele – was reborn from his thigh, so the intellectual Athene was reborn from his head.

If some myths are baffling at first sight, this is often because the mythographer has accidentally or deliberately misinterpreted a sacred picture or dramatic rite. I have called such a process 'iconotropy', and examples of it can be found in every body of sacred literature which sets the seal upon a radical reform of ancient beliefs. Greek myth teems with iconotropic instances. Hephaestus's three-legged workshop tables, for example, which ran by themselves to assemblies of the gods, and back again (*Iliad* xviii. 368 ff.), are not, as Dr Charles Seltman archly suggests in his *Twelve Olympian Gods,* anticipations of automobiles; but golden Sun-disks with three legs apiece (like the emblem of the Isle of Man), apparently representing the number of three-season years for which a 'son of Hephaestus' was permitted to reign in the island of Lemnos. Again, the so-called 'Judgement of Paris', where a hero is called upon to decide between the rival charms of three goddesses and awards his apple to the fairest, records an ancient ritual situation, outgrown by the time of Homer and Hesiod. These three goddesses are one goddess in triad: Athene the maiden, Aphrodite the nymph, and Hera the crone – and Aphrodite is presenting Paris with the apple, rather than receiving it from him. This apple, symbolizing her love bought at the price of his life, will be Paris's passport to the Elysian Fields, the apple orchards of the west, to which only the souls of heroes are admitted. A similar gift is frequently made in Irish and Welsh myth; as well as by the Three Hesperides, to Heracles; and by Eve, 'the Mother of All Living', to Adam. Thus Nemesis, goddess of the sacred grove who, in late myth, became a symbol of divine vengeance on proud kings, carries an apple-hung branch, her gift to heroes. All neolithic and Bronze Age paradises were orchard-islands; *paradise* itself means 'orchard'.

A true science of myth should begin with a study of archaeology, history, and comparative religion, not in the psycho-therapist's consulting-room. Though the Jungians hold that 'myths are original revelations of the pre-conscious psyche, involuntary statements about unconscious psychic happenings', Greek mythology was no more mysterious in content than are modern election cartoons, and for the most part formulated in territories which maintained close political relations with Minoan Crete – a country sophisticated enough to have written archives, four-storey buildings with hygienic plumbing, doors with modern-looking locks, registered trademarks, chess, a central system of weights and measures, and a calendar based on patient astronomic observation.

My method has been to assemble in harmonious narrative all the scattered elements of each myth, supported by little-known variants which may help to determine the meaning, and to answer all questions that arise, as best I can, in anthropological or historical terms. This is, I am well aware, much too ambitious a task for any single mythologist to undertake, however long or hard he works. Errors must creep in. Let me emphasize that any statement here made about Mediterranean religion or ritual before the appearance of written records is conjectural. Nevertheless, I have been heartened, since this book first appeared in 1955, by the close analogues which E. Meyrowitz's *Akan Cosmological Drama* (Faber & Faber) offers to the religious and social changes here presumed. The Akan people result from an ancient southward emigration of Libyo-Berbers – cousins to the pre-Hellenic population of Greece – from the Sahara desert oases (see 3. 3) and their intermarriage at Timbuctoo with Niger River negroes. In the eleventh century A.D. they moved still farther south to what is now Ghana. Four different cult-types persist among them. In the most primitive, the Moon is worshipped as the supreme Triple-goddess Ngame, clearly identical with the Libyan Neith, the Carthaginian Tanit, the Canaanite Anatha, and the early Greek Athene (see 8. 1). Ngame is said to have brought forth the heavenly bodies by her own efforts (see 1. 1), and then to have vitalized men and animals by shooting magical arrows from her new-moon bow into their inert bodies. She also, it is said, takes life in her killer aspect; as did her counterpart, the Moon-goddess Artemis (see 22. 1). A princess of royal line is judged capable, in unsettled times, of being overcome by Ngame's lunar magic and bearing a tribal deity which takes up its residence in a shrine and leads a group of emigrants to some new region. This woman becomes queen-mother, war-leader, judge, and priestess of the settlement she founds. The deity has meanwhile revealed itself as a totem animal which is protected by a close *tabu,* apart from the yearly chase and sacrifice of a single specimen; this throws light on the yearly owl-hunt made by the Pelasgians at Athens (see 97. *4*). States, consisting of tribal federations, are then formed, the most powerful tribal deity becoming the State-god.

The second cult-type marks Akan coalescence with Sudanese worshippers of a Father-god, Odomankoma, who claimed to have made the universe single-handedly (see 4. *c*); they were, it seems, led by elected male chieftains, and had adopted the Sumerian seven-day week. As a compromise myth, Ngame is now said to have vitalized Odomankoma's lifeless creation; and each tribal deity becomes one of the seven planetary powers. These planetary powers – as I have presumed also happened in Greece when Titan-worship came in from the East (see 11. *3*) – form male-and-female pairs. The queen-mother of the state, as Ngame's representative, performs an annual sacred marriage with Odomankoma's representative: namely her chosen lover whom, at the close of the year, the priests murder, skin, and flay. The same practice seems to have obtained among the Greeks (see 9. *a* and 21. *5*).

In the third cult-type, the queen-mother's lover becomes a king, and is venerated as the male aspect of the Moon, corresponding with the Phoenician god Baal Haman; and a boy dies vicariously for him every year as a mock-king (see 30. *1*). The queen-mother now delegates the chief executive powers to a vizier, and concentrates on her ritual fertilizing functions.

In the fourth cult-type, the king, having gained the homage of several petty kings, abrogates his Moon-god aspect and proclaims himself Sun-king in Egyptian style (see 67. *1* and *2*). Though continuing to celebrate the annual sacred marriage, he frees himself from dependence on the Moon. At this stage, patrilocal supersedes matrilocal marriage, and the tribes are supplied with heroic male ancestors to worship, as happened in Greece – though sun-worship there never displaced thunder-god worship.

Among the Akan, every change in court-ritual is marked by an addition to the accepted myth of events in Heaven. Thus, if the king has appointed a royal porter and given his office lustre by marrying him to a princess, a divine porter in Heaven is announced to have done the same. It is likely that Heracles's marriage to the Goddess Hebe and his appointment as porter to Zeus (see 145. *i* and *j*) reflected a similar event at the Mycenaean Court; and that the divine feastings on Olympus reflected similar celebrations at Olympia under the joint presidency of the Zeus-like High King of Mycenae and Hera's Chief Priestess from Argos.

I am deeply grateful to Janet Seymour-Smith and Kenneth Gay for helping me to get this book into shape, to Peter and Lalage Green for proof-reading the first few chapters, to Frank Seymour-Smith for sending scarce Latin and Greek texts from London, and to the many friends who have helped me to amend the first edition.

R. G.

Deyá, Majorca,
    Spain.

NOTE

Each myth is first recounted as a narrative, the paragraphs being identified by italic letters (*a*, *b*, *c*, . . .). Next follows a list of sources, numbered in accordance with the references in the text. Then comes an explanatory comment, divided into paragraphs identified by italic numbers (*1*, *2*, *3*, . . .). Cross-references from one explanatory section to another are made by giving the myth number and paragraph number, thus: (43. 4) directs the reader to par. 4 of the third (explanatory) section of myth 43.

THE GREEK MYTHS

VOLUME ONE

I

THE PELASGIAN CREATION MYTH

IN the beginning, Eurynome, the Goddess of All Things, rose naked from Chaos, but found nothing substantial for her feet to rest upon, and therefore divided the sea from the sky, dancing lonely upon its waves. She danced towards the south, and the wind set in motion behind her seemed something new and apart with which to begin a work of creation. Wheeling about, she caught hold of this north wind, rubbed it between her hands, and behold! the great serpent Ophion. Eurynome danced to warm herself, wildly and more wildly, until Ophion, grown lustful, coiled about those divine limbs and was moved to couple with her. Now, the North Wind, who is also called Boreas, fertilizes; which is why mares often turn their hind-quarters to the wind and breed foals without aid of a stallion.[1] So Eurynome was likewise got with child.

b. Next, she assumed the form of a dove, brooding on the waves and, in due process of time, laid the Universal Egg. At her bidding, Ophion coiled seven times about this egg, until it hatched and split in two. Out tumbled all things that exist, her children: sun, moon, planets, stars, the earth with its mountains and rivers, its trees, herbs, and living creatures.

c. Eurynome and Ophion made their home upon Mount Olympus, where he vexed her by claiming to be the author of the Universe. Forthwith she bruised his head with her heel, kicked out his teeth, and banished him to the dark caves below the earth.[2]

d. Next, the goddess created the seven planetary powers, setting a Titaness and a Titan over each. Theia and Hyperion for the Sun; Phoebe and Atlas for the Moon; Dione and Crius for the planet Mars; Metis and Coeus for the planet Mercury; Themis and Eurymedon for the planet Jupiter; Tethys and Oceanus for Venus; Rhea and Cronus for the planet Saturn.[3] But the first man was Pelasgus, ancestor of the Pelasgians; he sprang from the soil of Arcadia, followed by certain others, whom he taught to make huts and feed upon acorns, and sew pig-skin tunics such as poor folk still wear in Euboea and Phocis.[4]

1. Pliny: *Natural History* iv. 35 and viii. 67; Homer: *Iliad* xx, 223.
2. Only tantalizing fragments of this pre-Hellenic myth survive in Greek literature, the largest being Apollonius Rhodius's *Argo-*

nautica i. 496–505 and Tzetzes: *On Lycophron* 1191; but it is implicit in the Orphic Mysteries, and can be restored, as above, from
the *Berossian Fragment* and the Phoenician cosmognies quoted by
Philo Byblius and Damascius; from the Canaanitish elements in
the Hebrew Creation story; from Hyginus (*Fabula* 197 – see
62. *a*); from the Boeotian legend of the dragon's teeth (see 58. 5);
and from early ritual art. That all Pelasgians were born from
Ophion is suggested by their common sacrifice, the Peloria
(Athenaeus: xiv. 45. 639–40), Ophion having been a *Pelor*, or
'prodigious serpent'.

3. Homer: *Iliad* v. 898; Apollonius Rhodius: ii. 1232; Apollodorus:
   i. 1. 3; Hesiod: *Theogony* 113; Stephanus of Byzantium *sub* Adana;
   Aristophanes: *Birds* 692 ff.; Clement of Rome: *Homilies* vi. 4. 72;
   Proclus on Plato's *Timaeus* ii. p. 307.

4. Pausanias: viii. 1. 2.

*

1. In this archaic religious system there were, as yet, neither gods nor
priests, but only a universal goddess and her priestesses, women being
the dominant sex and man her frightened victim. Fatherhood was not
honoured, conception being attributed to the wind, the eating of beans,
or the accidental swallowing of an insect; inheritance was matrilineal and
snakes were regarded as incarnations of the dead. Eurynome ('wide
wandering') was the goddess's title as the visible moon; her Sumerian
name was Iahu ('exalted dove'), a title which later passed to Jehovah as
the Creator. It was as a dove that Marduk symbolically sliced her in two
at the Babylonian Spring Festival, when he inaugurated the new world
order.

2. Ophion, or Boreas, is the serpent demiurge of Hebrew and Egyptian
myth – in early Mediterranean art, the Goddess is constantly shown in his
company. The earth-born Pelasgians, whose claim seems to have been
that they sprang from Ophion's teeth, were originally perhaps the neolithic 'Painted Ware' people; they reached the mainland of Greece from
Palestine about 3500 B.C., and the early Hellads – immigrants from Asia
Minor by way of the Cyclades – found them in occupation of the Peloponnese seven hundred years later. But 'Pelasgians' became loosely
applied to all pre-Hellenic inhabitants of Greece. Thus Euripides (quoted
by Strabo v. 2. 4) records that the Pelasgians adopted the name 'Danaans'
on the coming to Argos of Danaus and his fifty daughters (see 60. *f*).
Strictures on their licentious conduct (Herodotus: vi. 137) refer probably
to the pre-Hellenic custom of erotic orgies. Strabo says in the same
passage that those who lived near Athens were known as Pelargi ('storks');
perhaps this was their totem bird.

3. The Titans ('lords') and Titanesses had their counterparts in early

Babylonian and Palestinian astrology, where they were deities ruling the seven days of the sacred planetary week; and may have been introduced by the Canaanite, or Hittite, colony which settled the Isthmus of Corinth early in the second millennium B.C. (see 67. 2), or even by the Early Hellads. But when the Titan cult was abolished in Greece, and the seven-day week ceased to figure in the official calender, their number was quoted as twelve by some authors, probably to make them correspond with the signs of the Zodiac. Hesiod, Apollodorus, Stephanus of Byzantium, Pausanias, and others give inconsistent lists of their names. In Babylonian myth the planetary rulers of the week, namely Samas, Sin, Nergal, Bel, Beltis, and Ninib, were all male, except Beltis, the Love-goddess; but in the Germanic week, which the Celts had borrowed from the Eastern Mediterranean, Sunday, Tuesday, and Friday were ruled by Titanesses, as opposed to Titans. To judge from the divine status of Aeolus's paired-off daughters and sons (see 43. 4), and the myth of Niobe (see 77. 1), it was decided, when the system first reached pre-Hellenic Greece from Palestine, to pair a Titaness with each Titan, as a means of safeguarding the goddess's interests. But before long the fourteen were reduced to a mixed company of seven. The planetary powers were as follows: Sun for illumination; Moon for enchantment; Mars for growth; Mercury for wisdom; Jupiter for law; Venus for love; Saturn for peace. Classical Greek astrologers conformed with the Babylonians, and awarded the planets to Helius, Selene, Ares, Hermes (or Apollo), Zeus, Aphrodite, Cronus – whose Latin equivalents, given above, still name the French, Italian, and Spanish weeks.

4. In the end, mythically speaking, Zeus swallowed the Titans, including his earlier self – since the Jews of Jerusalem worshipped a transcendent God, composed of all the planetary powers of the week: a theory symbolized in the seven-branched candlestick, and in the Seven Pillars of Wisdom. The seven planetary pillars set up near the Horse's Tomb at Sparta were said by Pausanias (ii. 20. 9) to be adorned in ancient fashion, and may have been connected with the Egyptian rites introduced by the Pelasgians (Herodotus: ii. 57). Whether the Jews borrowed the theory from the Egyptians, or contrariwise, is uncertain; but the so-called Heliopolitan Zeus, whom A. B. Cook discusses in his Zeus (i. 570–76), was Egyptian in character, and bore busts of the seven planetary powers as frontal ornaments on his body sheath; usually, also, busts of the remaining Olympians as rear ornaments. One bronze statuette of this god was found at Tortosa in Spain, another at Byblos in Phoenicia; and a marble stele from Marseilles displays six planetary busts and one full-length figure of Hermes – who is also given greatest prominence in the statuettes – presumably as the inventor of astronomy. At Rome, Jupiter was similarly claimed to be a transcendent god by Quintis Valerius Soranus,

though the week was not observed there, as it was at Marseilles, Byblos, and (probably) Tortosa. But planetary powers were never allowed to influence the official Olympian cult, being regarded as un-Greek (Herodotus: i. 131), and therefore unpatriotic: Aristophanes (*Peace* 403 ff.) makes Trygalus say that the Moon and 'that old villain the Sun' are hatching a plot to betray Greece into the hands of the Persian barbarians.

5. Pausanias's statement that Pelasgus was the first of men records the continuance of a neolithic culture in Arcadia until Classical times.

2

THE HOMERIC AND ORPHIC CREATION MYTHS

SOME say that all gods and all living creatures originated in the stream of Oceanu which girdles the world, and that Tethys was the mother of all his children.[1]

b. But the Orphics say that black-winged Night, a goddess of whom even Zeus stands in awe,[2] was courted by the Wind and laid a silver egg in the womb of Darkness; and that Eros, whom some call Phanes, was hatched from this egg and set the Universe in motion. Eros was double-sexed and golden-winged and, having four heads, sometimes roared like a bull or a lion, sometimes hissed like a serpent or bleated like a ram. Night, who named him Ericepaius and Protogenus Phaëthon,[3] lived in a cave with him, displaying herself in triad: Night, Order, and Justice. Before this cave sat the inescapable mother Rhea, playing on a brazen drum, and compelling man's attention to the oracles of the goddess. Phanes created earth, sky, sun, and moon, but the triple-goddess ruled the universe, until her sceptre passed to Uranus.[4]

1. Homer: *Iliad* xvi. 201.
2. *Ibid.*: xiv. 261.
3. *Orphic Fragments* 60, 61, and 70.
4. *Ibid.*: 86.

*

1. Homer's myth is a version of the Pelasgian creation story (see 1. 2), since Tethys reigned over the sea like Eurynome, and Oceanus girdled the Universe like Ophion.

2. The Orphic myth is another version, but influenced by a late mystical doctrine of love (*Eros*) and theories about the proper relations

of the sexes. Night's silver egg means the moon, silver being the lunar metal. As Ericepaius ('feeder upon heather'), the love-god Phanes ('revealer'), is a loudly-buzzing celestial bee, son of the Great Goddess (see 18. 4). The beehive was studied as an ideal republic, and confirmed the myth of the Golden Age, when honey dropped from the trees (see 5. b). Rhea's brazen drum was beaten to prevent bees from swarming in the wrong place, and to ward off evil influences, like the bull-roarers used in the Mysteries. As Phaëthon Protogenus ('first-born shiner'), Phanes is the Sun, which the Orphics made a symbol of illumination (see 28. d), and his four heads correspond with the symbolic beasts of the four seasons. According to Macrobius, the Oracle of Colophon identified this Phanes with the transcendent god Iao: Zeus (ram), Spring; Helius (lion), Summer; Hades (snake), Winter; Dionysus (bull), New Year. Night's sceptre passed to Uranus with the advent of patriarchalism.

3

THE OLYMPIAN CREATION MYTH

At the beginning of all things Mother Earth emerged from Chaos and bore her son Uranus as she slept. Gazing down fondly at her from the mountains, he showered fertile rain upon her secret clefts, and she bore grass, flowers, and trees, with the beasts and birds proper to each. This same rain made the rivers flow and filled the hollow places with water, so that lakes and seas came into being.

b. Her first children of semi-human form were the hundred-handed giants Briareus, Gyges, and Cottus. Next appeared the three wild, one-eyed Cyclopes, builders of gigantic walls and master-smiths, formerly of Thrace, afterwards of Crete and Lycia,[1] whose sons Odysseus encountered in Sicily.[2] Their names were Brontes, Steropes, and Arges, and their ghosts have dwelt in the caverns of the volcano Aetna since Apollo killed them in revenge for the death of Asclepius.

c. The Libyans, however, claim that Garamas was born before the Hundred-handed Ones and that, when he rose from the plain, he offered Mother Earth a sacrifice of the sweet acorn.[3]

1. Apollodorus: i. 1–2; Euripides: *Chrysippus*, quoted by Sextus Empiricus, p. 751; Lucretius: i. 250 and ii. 991 ff.

2. Homer: *Odyssey* ix. 106–566; Apollodorus: iii. 10. 4.
3. Apollonius Rhodius: iv. 1493 ff.; Pindar: *Fragment 84*, ed. Bergk.

*

1. This patriarchal myth of Uranus gained official acceptance under the Olympian religious system. Uranus, whose name came to mean 'the sky', seems to have won his position as First Father by being identified with the pastoral god Varuna, one of the Aryan male trinity; but his Greek name is a masculine form of *Ur-ana* ('queen of the mountains', 'queen of summer', 'queen of the winds', or 'queen of wild oxen') – the goddess in her orgiastic midsummer aspect. Uranus's marriage to Mother Earth records an early Hellenic invasion of Northern Greece, which allowed Varuna's people to claim that he had fathered the native tribes he found there, though acknowledging him to be Mother Earth's son. An emendation to the myth, recorded by Apollodorus, is that Earth and Sky parted in deadly strife and were then reunited in love: this is mentioned by Euripides (*Melanippe the Wise*, fragment 484, ed. Nauck) and Apollonius Rhodius (*Argonautica* i. 494). The deadly strife must refer to the clash between the patriarchal and matriarchal principles which the Hellenic invasions caused. Gyges ('earth-born') has another form, *gigas* ('giant'), and giants are associated in myth with the mountains of Northern Greece. Briareus ('strong') was also called Aegaeon (*Iliad* i. 403), and his people may therefore be the Libyo-Thracians, whose Goat-goddess Aegis (see 8. *1*) gave her name to the Aegean Sea. Cottus was the eponymous (name-giving) ancestor of the Cottians who worshipped the orgiastic Cotytto, and spread her worship from Thrace throughout North-western Europe. These tribes are described as 'hundred-handed', perhaps because their priestesses were organized in colleges of fifty, like the Danaids and Nereids; perhaps because the men were organized in war-bands of one hundred, like the early Romans.

2. The Cyclopes seem to have been a guild of Early Helladic bronzesmiths. *Cyclops* means 'ring-eyed', and they are likely to have been tattooed with concentric rings on the forehead, in honour of the sun, the source of their furnace fires; the Thracians continued to tattoo themselves until Classical times (see 28. *2*). Concentric circles are part of the mystery of smith-craft: in order to beat out bowls, helmets, or ritual masks, the smith would guide himself with such circles, described by compass around the centre of the flat disk on which he was working. The Cyclopes were one-eyed also in the sense that smiths often shade one eye with a patch against flying sparks. Later, their identity was forgotten, and the mythographers fancifully placed their ghosts in the caverns of Aetna, to explain the fire and smoke issuing from its crater (see 35. *1*). A close cultural connexion existed between Thrace, Crete, and Lycia; the

Cyclopes will have been at home in all these countries. Early Helladic culture also spread to Sicily; but it may well be (as Samuel Butler first suggested) that the Sicilian composition of the *Odyssey* explains the Cyclopes' presence there (see 170. *b*). The names Brontes, Steropes, and Arges ('thunder,' 'lightning', and 'brightness') are late inventions.

3. Garamas is the eponymous ancestor of the Libyan Garamantians who occupied the Oasis of Djado, south of the Fezzan, and were conquered by the Roman General Balbus in 19 B.C. They are said to have been of Cushite-Berber stock, and in the second century A.D. were subdued by the matrilineal Lemta Berbers. Later they fused with the Negro aboriginals on the south bank of the Upper Niger, and adopted their language. They survive today in a single village under the name of Koromantse. *Garamante* is derived from the words *gara*, *man*, and *te*, meaning, 'Gara's state people'. Gara seems to be the Goddess Ker, or Q're, or Car (see 82. *6* and 86. *2*), who gave her name to the Carians, among other people, and was associated with apiculture. Esculent acorns, a staple food of the ancient world before the introduction of corn, grew in Libya; and the Garamantian settlement of Ammon was joined with the Northern Greek settlement of Dodona in a religious league which, according to Sir Flinders Petrie, may have originated as early as the third millennium B.C. Both places had an ancient oak-oracle (see 51. *a*). Herodotus describes the Garamantians as a peaceable but very powerful people, who cultivate the date-palm, grow corn, and herd cattle (iv. 174 and 183).

4

TWO PHILOSOPHICAL CREATION MYTHS

SOME say that Darkness was first, and from Darkness sprang Chaos. From a union between Darkness and Chaos sprang Night, Day, Erebus, and the Air.

From a union between Night and Erebus sprang Doom, Old Age, Death, Murder, Continence, Sleep, Dreams, Discord, Misery, Vexation, Nemesis, Joy, Friendship, Pity, the Three Fates, and the Three Hesperides.

From a union between Air and Day sprang Mother Earth, Sky, and Sea.

From a union between Air and Mother Earth sprang Terror, Craft, Anger, Strife, Lies, Oaths, Vengeance, Intemperance, Altercation, Treaty, Oblivion, Fear, Pride, Battle; also Oceanus, Metis, and the other Titans, Tartarus, and the Three Erinnyes, or Furies.

From a union between Earth and Tartarus sprang the Giants.

b. From a union between the Sea and its Rivers sprang the Nereids. But, as yet, there were no mortal men until, with the consent of the goddess Athene, Prometheus, son of Iapetus, formed them in the likeness of gods. He used clay and water of Panopeus in Phocis, and Athene breathed life into them.[1]

*

c. Others say that the God of All Things – whoever he may have been, for some call him Nature – appearing suddenly in Chaos, separated earth from the heavens, the water from the earth, and the upper air from the lower. Having unravelled the elements, he set them in due order, as they are now found. He divided the earth into zones, some very hot, some very cold, others temperate; moulded it into plains and mountains; and clothed it with grass and trees. Above it he set the rolling firmament, spangling it with stars, and assigned stations to the four winds. He also peopled the waters with fish, the earth with beasts, and the sky with the sun, the moon, and the five planets. Lastly, he made man – who, alone of all beasts, raises his face to heaven and observes the sun, the moon, and the stars – unless it be indeed true that Prometheus, son of Iapetus, made man's body from water and clay, and that his soul was supplied by certain wandering divine elements, which had survived from the First Creation.[2]

1. Hesiod: *Theogony* 211–32; Hyginus: *Fabulae, Proem*; Apollodorus: i. 7. 1; Lucian: *Prometheus on Caucasus* 13; Pausanias: x. 4. 3.
2. Ovid: *Metamorphoses* i–ii.

*

1. In Hesiod's *Theogony* – on which the first of these philosophical myths is based –the list of abstractions is confused by the Nereids, the Titans and the Giants, whom he feels bound to include. Both the Three Fates and the Three Hesperides are the Triple Moon-goddess in her death aspect.

2. The second myth, found only in Ovid, was borrowed by the later Greeks from the Babylonian Gilgamesh epic, the introduction to which records the goddess Aruru's particular creation of the first man, Eabini, from a piece of clay; but although Zeus had been the Universal Lord for many centuries, the mythographers were forced to admit that the Creator of all things might possibly have been a Creatrix. The Jews, as inheritors

of the 'Pelasgian', or Canaanitish, creation myth, had felt the same embarrassment; in the *Genesis* account, a female 'Spirit of the Lord' broods on the face of the waters, though she does not lay the world egg; and Eve, 'the Mother of All Living', is ordered to bruise the Serpent's head, though he is not destined to go down to the Pit until the end of the world.

3. Similarly, in the Talmudic version of the Creation, the archangel Michael – Prometheus's counterpart – forms Adam from dust at the order, not of the Mother of All Living, but of Jehovah. Jehovah then breathes life into him and gives him Eve who, like Pandora, brings mischief on mankind (see 39. *j*).

4. Greek philosophers distinguished Promethean man from the imperfect earth-born creation, part of which was destroyed by Zeus, and the rest washed away in the Deucalionian Flood (see 38. *c*). Much the same distinction is found in *Genesis* vi. 2–4 between the 'sons of God' and the 'daughters of men', whom they married.

5. The Gilgamesh tablets are late and equivocal; there the 'Bright Mother of the Hollow' is credited with having formed everything – 'Aruru' is only one of this goddess's many titles – and the principal theme is a revolt against her matriarchal order, described as one of utter confusion, by the gods of the new patriarchal order. Marduk, the Babylonian city-god, eventually defeats the goddess in the person of Tiamat the Sea-serpent; and it is then brazenly announced that he, not anyone else, created herbs, lands, rivers, beasts, birds, and mankind. This Marduk was an upstart godling whose claim to have defeated Tiamat and created the world had previously been made by the god Bel – Bel being a masculine form of Belili, the Sumerian Mother-goddess. The transition from matriarchy to patriarchy seems to have come about in Mesopotamia, as elsewhere, through the revolt of the Queen's consort to whom she had deputed executive power by allowing him to adopt her name, robes, and sacred instruments (see 136. 4).

5

THE FIVE AGES OF MAN

SOME deny that Prometheus created men, or that any man sprang from a serpent's teeth. They say that Earth bore them spontaneously, as the best of her fruits, especially in the soil of Attica,[1] and that Alalcomeneus was the first man to appear, by Lake Copais in Boeotia, before even the Moon was. He acted as Zeus's counsellor on the occasion of his quarrel with Hera, and as tutor to Athene while she was still a girl.[2]

b. These men were the so-called golden race, subjects of Cronus, who lived without cares or labour, eating only acorns, wild fruit, and honey that dripped from the trees, drinking the milk of sheep and goats, never growing old, dancing, and laughing much; death, to them, was no more terrible than sleep. They are all gone now, but their spirits survive as genii of happy music retreats, givers of good fortune, and upholders of justice.

c. Next came a silver race, eaters of bread, likewise divinely created. The men were utterly subject to their mothers and dared not disobey them, although they might live to be a hundred years old. They were quarrelsome and ignorant, and never sacrificed to the gods but, at least, did not make war on one another. Zeus destroyed them all.

d. Next came a brazen race, who fell like fruits from the ash-trees, and were armed with brazen weapons. They ate flesh as well as bread, and delighted in war, being insolent and pitiless men. Black Death has seized them all.

e. The fourth race of man was brazen too, but nobler and more generous, being begotten by the gods on mortal mothers. They fought gloriously in the siege of Thebes, the expedition of the Argonauts, and the Trojan War. These became heroes, and dwell in the Elysian Fields.

f. The fifth race is the present race of iron, unworthy descendants of the fourth. They are degenerate, cruel, unjust, malicious, libidinous, unfilial, treacherous.[3]

1. Plato: *Menexenus* 6–7.
2. Hippolytus: *Refutation of All Heresies* v. 6. 3; Eusebius: *Preparation for the Gospel* iii. 1. 3.
3. Hesiod: *Works and Days* 109–201, with scholiast.

*

1. Though the myth of the Golden Age derives eventually from a tradition of tribal subservience to the Bee-goddess, the savagery of her reign in pre-agricultural times had been forgotten by Hesiod's day, and all that remained was an idealistic conviction that men had once lived in harmony together like bees (see 2. 2). Hesiod was a small farmer, and the hard life he lived made him morose and pessimistic. The myth of the silver race also records matriarchal conditions – such as those surviving in Classical times among the Picts, the Moesynoechians of the Black Sea

(see 151. *e*), and some tribes in the Baleares, Galicia, and the Gulf of Sirté – under which men were still the despised sex, though agriculture had been introduced and wars were infrequent. Silver is the metal of the Moon-goddess. The third race were the earliest Hellenic invaders: Bronze Age herdsmen, who adopted the ash-tree cult of the Goddess and her son Poseidon (see 6. 4 and 57. 1). The fourth race were the warrior-kings of the Mycenaean Age. The fifth were the Dorians of the twelfth century B.C., who used iron weapons and destroyed the Mycenaean civilization.

Alalcomeneus ('guardian') is a fictitious character, a masculine form of Alalcomeneïs, Athene's title (*Iliad* iv. 8) as the guardian of Boeotia. He serves the patriarchal dogma that no woman, even a goddess, can be wise without male instruction, and that the Moon-goddess and the Moon itself were late creations of Zeus.

6

THE CASTRATION OF URANUS

URANUS fathered the Titans upon Mother Earth, after he had thrown his rebellious sons, the Cyclopes, into Tartarus, a gloomy place in the Underworld, which lies as far distant from the earth as the earth does from the sky; it would take a falling anvil nine days to reach its bottom. In revenge, Mother Earth persuaded the Titans to attack their father; and they did so, led by Cronus, the youngest of the seven, whom she armed with a flint sickle. They surprised Uranus as he slept, and it was with the flint sickle that the merciless Cronus castrated him, grasping his genitals with the left hand (which has ever since been the hand of ill-omen) and afterwards throwing them, and the sickle too, into the sea by Cape Drepanum. But drops of blood flowing from the wound fell upon Mother Earth, and she bore the Three Erinnyes, furies who avenge crimes of parricide and perjury – by name Alecto, Tisiphone, and Megaera. The nymphs of the ash-tree, called the Meliae, also sprang from that blood.

b. The Titans then released the Cyclopes from Tartarus, and awarded the sovereignty of the earth to Cronus.

However, no sooner did Cronus find himself in supreme command than he confined the Cyclopes to Tartarus again together with the

Hundred-handed Ones and, taking his sister Rhea to wife, ruled in Elis.[1]

> 1. Hesiod: *Theogony* 133–87 and 616–23; Apollodorus: i. 1. 4–5; Servius on Virgil's *Aeneid* v. 801.

*

1. Hesiod, who records this myth, was a Cadmeian, and the Cadmeians came from Asia Minor (see 59. 5), probably on the collapse of the Hittite Empire, bringing with them the story of Uranus's castration. It is known, however, that the myth was not of Hittite composition, since an earlier Hurrian (Horite) version has been discovered. Hesiod's version may reflect an alliance between the various pre-Hellenic settlers in Southern and Central Greece, whose dominant tribes favoured the Titan cult, against the early Hellenic invaders from the north. Their war was successful, but they thereupon claimed suzerainty over the northern natives, whom they had freed. The castration of Uranus is not necessarily metaphorical if some of the victors had originated in East Africa where, to this day, Galla warriors carry a miniature sickle into battle to castrate their enemies; there are close affinities between East African religious rites and those of early Greece.

2. The later Greeks read 'Cronus' as *Chronos*, 'Father Time' with his relentless sickle. But he is pictured in the company of a crow, like Apollo, Asclepius, Saturn, and the early British god Bran; and *cronos* probably means 'crow', like the Latin *cornix* and the Greek *corōne*. The crow was an oracular bird, supposed to house the soul of a sacred king after his sacrifice (see 25. 5 and 50. 1).

3. Here the three Erinnyes, or Furies, who sprang from the drops of Uranus's blood, are the Triple-goddess herself; that is to say, during the king's sacrifice, designed to fructify the cornfields and orchards, her priestesses will have worn menacing Gorgon masks to frighten away profane visitors. His genitals seem to have been thrown into the sea, to encourage fish to breed. The vengeful Erinnyes are understood by the mythographer as warning Zeus not to emasculate Cronus with the same sickle; but it was their original function to avenge injuries inflicted only on a mother, or a suppliant who claimed the protection of the Hearth-goddess (see 105. k, 107. d, and 113. a), not on a father.

4. The ash-nymphs are the Three Furies in more gracious mood: the sacred king was dedicated to the ash-tree, originally used in rain-making ceremonies (see 57. 1). In Scandinavia it became the tree of universal magic; the Three Norns, or Fates, dispensed justice under an ash which Odin, on claiming the fatherhood of mankind, made his magical steed. Women must have been the first rain-makers in Greece as in Libya.

5. Neolithic sickles of bone, toothed with flint or obsidian, seem to

have continued in ritual use long after their supersession as agricultural instruments by sickles of bronze and iron.

6. The Hittites make Kumarbi (Cronus) bite off the genitals of the Sky-god Anu (Uranus), swallow some of the seed, and spit out the rest on Mount Kansura where it grows into a goddess; the God of Love thus conceived by him is cut from his side by Anu's brother Ea. These two births have been combined by the Greeks into a tale of how Aphrodite rose from a sea impregnated by Uranus's severed genitals (see 10. b). Kumarbi is subsequently delivered of another child drawn from his thigh – as Dionysus was reborn from Zeus (see 27. b) – who rides a storm-chariot drawn by a bull, and comes to Anu's help. The 'knife that separated the the earth from the sky' occurs in the same story, as the weapon with which Kumarbi's son, the earth-born giant Ullikummi, is destroyed (see 35. 4).

7

THE DETHRONEMENT OF CRONUS

CRONUS married his sister Rhea, to whom the oak is sacred.[1] But it was prophesied by Mother Earth, and by his dying father Uranus, that one of his own sons would dethrone him. Every year, therefore, he swallowed the children whom Rhea bore him: first Hestia, then Demeter and Hera, then Hades, then Poseidon.[2]

b. Rhea was enraged. She bore Zeus, her third son, at dead of night on Mount Lycaeum in Arcadia, where no creature casts a shadow[3] and, having bathed him in the River Neda, gave him to Mother Earth; by whom he was carried to Lyctos in Crete, and hidden in the cave of Dicte on the Aegean Hill. Mother Earth left him there to be nursed by the Ash-nymph Adrasteia and her sister Io, both daughters of Melisseus, and by the Goat-nymph Amaltheia. His food was honey, and he drank Amaltheia's milk, with Goat-Pan, his foster-brother. Zeus was grateful to these three nymphs for their kindness and, when he became Lord of the Universe, set Amaltheia's image among the stars, as Capricorn.[4] He also borrowed one of her horns, which resembled a cow's, and gave it to the daughters of Melisseus; it became the famous Cornucopia, or horn of plenty, which is always filled with whatever food or drink its owner may desire. But some say that Zeus was suckled by a sow, and rode on her back, and that he lost his navel-string at Omphalion near Cnossus.[5]

c. Around the infant Zeus's golden cradle, which was hung upon a tree (so that Cronus might find him neither in heaven, not on earth, nor in the sea) stood the armed Curetes, Rhea's sons. They clashed their spears against their shields, and shouted to drown the noise of his wailing, lest Cronus might hear it from far off. For Rhea had wrapped a stone in swaddling clothes, which she gave to Cronus on Mount Thaumasium in Arcadia; he swallowed it, believing that he was swallowing the infant Zeus. Nevertheless, Cronus got wind of what had happened and pursued Zeus, who transformed himself into a serpent and his nurses into bears: hence the constellations of the Serpent and the Bears.[6]

d. Zeus grew to manhood among the shepherds of Ida, occupying another cave; then sought out Metis the Titaness, who lived beside the Ocean stream. On her advice he visited his mother Rhea, and asked to be made Cronus's cup-bearer. Rhea readily assisted him in his task of vengeance; she provided the emetic potion, which Metis had told him to mix with Cronus's honeyed drink. Cronus, having drunk deep, vomited up first the stone, and then Zeus's elder brothers and sisters. They sprang out unhurt and, in gratitude, asked him to lead them in a war against the Titans, who chose the gigantic Atlas as their leader; for Cronus was now past his prime.[7]

e. The war lasted ten years but, at last, Mother Earth prophesied victory to her grandson Zeus, if he took as allies those whom Cronus had confined in Tartarus; so he came secretly to Campe, the old gaoleress of Tartarus, killed her, took her keys and, having released the Cyclopes and the Hundred-handed Ones, strengthened them with divine food and drink. The Cyclopes thereupon gave Zeus the thunderbolt as a weapon of offence; and Hades, a helmet of darkness; and Poseidon, a trident. After the three brothers had held a counsel of war, Hades entered unseen into Cronus's presence, to steal his weapons; and, while Poseidon threatened him with the trident and thus diverted his attention, Zeus struck him down with the thunderbolt. The three Hundred-handed Ones now took up rocks and pelted the remaining Titans, and a sudden shout from Goat-Pan put them to flight. The gods rushed in pursuit. Cronus, and all the defeated Titans, except Atlas, were banished to a British island in the farthest west (or, some say, confined in Tartarus), and guarded there by the Hundred-handed Ones; they never troubled Hellas again. Atlas, as their war-leader, was awarded an exemplary punishment, being ordered to carry the sky on his shoulders; but the Titanesses were spared, for the sake of Metis and Rhea.[8]

f. Zeus himself set up at Delphi the stone which Cronus had disgorged. It is still there, constantly anointed with oil, and strands of unwoven wool are offered upon it.[9]

g. Some say that Poseidon was neither eaten nor disgorged, but that Rhea gave Cronus a foal to eat in his stead, and hid him among the horseherds.[10] And the Cretans, who are liars, relate that Zeus is born every year in the same cave with flashing fire and a stream of blood; and that every year he dies and is buried.[11]

1. Scholiast on Apollonius Rhodius: i. 1124.
2. Apollodorus: i. 1. 5; Hesiod: *Theogony* 453–67.
3. Polybius: xvi. 12. 6 ff.; Pausanias: viii. 38. 5.
4. Hyginus: *Poetic Astronomy* ii. 13; Aratus: *Phenomena* 163; Hesiod: *loc. cit.*
5. Philemon: *Pterygium Fragment* i.1 ff.; Apollodorus: i. 1. 6; Athenaeus: 375f. and 376a; Callimachus: *Hymn to Zeus* 42.
6. Hesiod: 485 ff.; Apollodorus: i. 1. 7; First Vatican Mythographer: 104; Callimachus: *Hymn to Zeus* 52 ff.; Lucretius: ii. 633–9; Scholiast on Aratus: v. 46; Hyginus: *Fabula* 139 .
7. Hyginus: *loc. cit.*; Apollodorus: *loc. cit.*; Hesiod: *loc. cit.*
8. Hesiod: *loc. cit.*; Hyginus: *Fabula* 118; Apollodorus: i. 1. 7 and i. 2. 1; Callimachus: *Hymn to Zeus* 52 ff.; Diodorus Siculus: v. 70; Eratosthenes: *Catasterismoi* 27; Pausanias: viii. 8. 2; Plutarch: *Why Oracles Are Silent* 16.
9. Pausanias: x. 24. 5.
10. *Ibid.*: viii. 8. 2.
11. Antoninus Liberalis: *Transformations* 19; Callimachus: *Hymn to Zeus* 8.

*

1. Rhea, paired with Cronus as Titaness of the seventh day, may be equated with Dione, Diana, the Triple-goddess of the Dove and Oak cult (see 11. 2). The bill-hook carried by Saturn, Cronus's Latin counterpart, was shaped like a crow's bill and apparently used in the seventh month of the sacred thirteen-month year to emasculate the oak by lopping off the mistletoe (see 50. 2), just as a ritual sickle was used to reap the first ear of corn. This gave the signal for the sacred Zeus-king's sacrifice; and at Athens, Cronus, who shared a temple with Rhea, was worshipped as the Barley-god Sabazius, annually cut down in the cornfield and bewailed like Osiris or Lityerses or Maneros (see 136. e). But, by the times to which these myths refer, kings had been permitted to prolong

their reigns to a Great Year of one hundred lunations, and offer annual boy victims in their stead; hence Cronus is pictured as eating his own sons to avoid dethronement. Porphyry (*On Abstinence* ii. 56) records that the Cretan Curetes used to offer child sacrifices to Cronus in ancient times.

2. In Crete a kid was early substituted for a human victim; in Thrace, a bull-calf; among the Aeolian worshippers of Poseidon, a foal; but in backward districts of Arcadia boys were still sacrificially eaten even in the Christian era. It is not clear whether the Elean ritual was cannibalistic or whether, Cronus being a Crow-Titan, sacred crows fed on the slaughtered victim.

3. Amaltheia's name, 'tender', shows her to have been a maiden-goddess; Io was an orgiastic nymph-goddess (see 56. *1*); Adrasteia means 'the Inescapable One', the oracular Crone of autumn. Together they formed the usual Moon-triad. The later Greeks identified Adrasteia with the pastoral goddess Nemesis, of the rain-making ash-tree, who had become a goddess of vengeance (see 32. *2*). Io was pictured at Argos as a white cow in heat – some Cretan coins from Praesus show Zeus suckled by her – but Amaltheia, who lived on 'Goat Hill', was always a she-goat; and Melisseus ('honey-man'), Adrasteia and Io's reputed father, is really their mother – Melissa, the goddess as Queen-bee, who annually killed her male consort. Diodorus Siculus (v. 70) and Callimachus (*Hymn to Zeus* 49) both make bees feed the infant Zeus. But his foster-mother is sometimes also pictured as a sow, because that was one of the Crone-goddesses's, emblems (see 74. *4* and 96. *2*); and on Cydonian coins she is a bitch, like the one that suckled Neleus (see 68. *d*). The she-bears are Artemis's beasts (see 22. *4* and 80. *c*) – the Curetes attended her holocausts – and Zeus as serpent is Zeus Ctesius, protector of store-houses, because snakes got rid of mice.

4. The Curetes were the sacred king's armed companions, whose weapon-clashing was intended to drive off evil spirits during ritual performances (see 30. *a*). Their name, understood by the later Greeks as 'young men who have shaved their hair', probably meant 'devotees of Ker, or Car', a widespread title of the Triple-goddess (see 57. *2*). Heracles won his cornucopia from the Achelous bull (see 142. *d*), and the enormous size of the Cretan wild-goat's horns have led mythographers unacquainted with Crete to give Amaltheia an anomalous cow's horn.

5. Invading Hellenes seem to have offered friendship to the pre-Hellenic people of the Titan-cult, but gradually detached their subject-allies from them, and overrun the Peloponnese. Zeus's victory in alliance with the Hundred-handed Ones over the Titans of Thessaly is said by Thallus, the first-century historian, quoted by Tatian in his *Address to the Greeks*, to have taken place '322 years before the seige of Troy': that is to say 1505 B.C., a plausible date for an extension of Hellenic power in Thes-

saly. The bestowal of sovereignty on Zeus recalls a similar event in the Babylonian Creation Epic, when Marduk was empowered to fight Tiamat by his elders Lahmu and Lahamu.

6. The brotherhood of Hades, Poseidon, and Zeus recalls that of the Vedic male trinity – Mitra, Varuna, and Indra – (see 3. *1* and 132. *5*) who appear in a Hittite treaty dated to about 1380 B.C. – but in this myth they seem to represent three successive Hellenic invasions, commonly known as Ionian, Aeolian, and Achaean. The pre-Hellenic worshippers of the Mother-goddess assimilated the Ionians, who became children of Io; tamed the Aeolians; but were overwhelmed by the Achaeans. Early Hellenic chieftains who became sacred kings of the oak and ash cults took the titles 'Zeus' and 'Poseidon', and were obliged to die at the end of their set reigns (see 45. *2*). Both these trees tend to attract lightning, and therefore figure in popular rain-making and fire-making ceremonies throughout Europe.

7. The victory of the Achaeans ended the tradition of royal sacrifices. They ranked Zeus and Poseidon as immortals; picturing both as armed with the thunderbolt – a flint double-axe, once wielded by Rhea, and in the Minoan and Mycenaean religions withheld from male use (see 131. *6*). Later, Poseidon's thunderbolt was converted into a three-pronged fish-spear, his chief devotees having turned seafarers; whereas Zeus retained his as a symbol of supreme sovereignty. Poseidon's name, which was sometimes spelt *Potidan*, may have been borrowed from that of his goddess-mother, after whom the city Potidaea was called: 'the water-goddess of Ida' – Ida meaning any wooded mountain. That the Hundred-handed Ones guarded the Titans in the Far West may mean that the Pelasgians, among whose remnants were the Centaurs of Magnesia – *centaur* is perhaps cognate with the Latin *centuria*, 'a war-band of one hundred' – did not abandon their Titan cult, and continued to believe in a Far Western Paradise, and in Atlas's support of the firmament.

8. Rhea's name is probably a variant of *Era*, 'earth'; her chief bird was the dove, her chief beast the mountain-lion. Demeter's name means 'Barley-mother'; Hestia (see 20. *c*) is the goddess of the domestic hearth. The stone at Delphi, used in rain-making ceremonies, seems to have been a large meteorite.

9. Dicte and Mount Lycaeum were ancient seats of Zeus worship. A fire sacrifice was probably offered on Mount Lycaeum, when no creature cast a shadow – that is to say, at noon on midsummer day; but Pausanias adds that though in Ethiopia while the sun is in Cancer men do not throw shadows, this is invariably the case on Mount Lycaeum. He may be quibbling: nobody who trespassed in this precinct was allowed to live (Aratus: *Phenomena* 91), and it was well known that the dead cast no shadows (Plutarch: *Greek Questions* 39). The cave of Psychro, usually

regarded as the Dictaean Cave, is wrongly sited to be the real one, which has not yet been discovered. Omphalion ('little navel') suggests the site of an oracle (see 20. 2).

10. Pan's sudden shout which terrified the Titans became proverbial and has given the word 'panic' to the English language (see 26. c).

8

THE BIRTH OF ATHENE

ACCORDING to the Pelasgians, the goddess Athene was born beside Lake Tritonis in Libya, where she was found and nurtured by the three nymphs of Libya, who dress in goat-skins.[1] As a girl she killed her playmate, Pallas, by accident, while they were engaged in friendly combat with spear and shield and, in token of grief, set Pallas's name before her own. Coming to Greece by way of Crete, she lived first in the city of Athenae by the Boeotian River Triton.[2]

1. Apollonius Rhodius: iv. 1310.
2. Apollodorus: iii. 12. 3; Pausanias: ix. 33. 5.

*

1. Plato identified Athene, patroness of Athens, with the Libyan goddess Neith, who belonged to an epoch when fatherhood was not recognized (see 1. 1). Neith had a temple at Saïs, where Solon was treated well merely because he was an Athenian (Plato: *Timaeus* 5). Virgin-priestesses of Neith engaged annually in armed combat (Herodotus: iv. 180), apparently for the position of High-priestess. Apollodorus's account (iii. 12. 3) of the fight between Athene and Pallas is a late patriarchal version: he says that Athene, born of Zeus and brought up by the River-god Triton, accidentally killed her foster-sister Pallas, the River Triton's daughter, because Zeus interposed his aegis when Pallas was about to strike Athene, and so distracted her attention. The aegis, however, a magical goat-skin bag containing a serpent and protected by a Gorgon mask, was Athene's long before Zeus claimed to be her father (see 9. d). Goat-skin aprons were the habitual costume of Libyan girls, and *Pallas* merely means 'maiden', or 'youth'. Herodotus writes (iv. 189): 'Athene's garments and aegis were borrowed by the Greeks from the Libyan women, who are dressed in exactly the same way, except that their leather garments are fringed with thongs, not serpents.' Ethiopian girls still wear this costume, which is sometimes ornamented with cowries, a yonic symbol. Herodotus adds here that the loud cries of triumph, *olulu, ololu*, uttered in honour of Athene above (*Iliad* vi. 297–301) were of Libyan origin. *Tritone* means 'the third queen': that is, the eldest member of the triad – mother of the maiden who fought Pallas, and of the nymph into which she grew – just as Core-Persephone was Demeter's daughter (see 24. 3).

2. Pottery finds suggest a Libyan immigration into Crete as early as 4000 B.C.; and a large number of goddess-worshipping Libyan refugees from the Western Delta seem to have arrived there when Upper and Lower Egypt were forcibly united under the First Dynasty about the year 3000 B.C. The First Minoan Age began soon afterwards, and Cretan culture spread to Thrace and Early Helladic Greece.

3. Among other mythological personages named Pallas was the Titan who married the River Styx and fathered on her Zelus ('zeal'), Cratus ('strength'), Bia ('force'), and Nicë ('victory') (Hesiod: *Theogony* 376 and 383; Pausanias: vii. 26. 5; Apollodorus; 2. 2–4); he was perhaps an allegory of the Pelopian dolphin sacred to the Moon-goddess (see 108. 5). Homer calls another Pallas 'the father of the moon' (*Homeric Hymn to Hermes* 100). A third begot the fifty Pallantids, Theseus's enemies (see 97. g and 99. a), who seem to have been originally fighting priestesses of Athene. A fourth was described as Athene's father (see 9. a).

9

ZEUS AND METIS

SOME Hellenes say that Athene had a father named Pallas, a winged goatish giant, who later attempted to outrage her, and whose name she added to her own after stripping him of his skin to make the aegis, and of his wings for her own shoulders;[1] if, indeed, the aegis was not the skin of Medusa the Gorgon, whom she flayed after Perseus had decapitated her.[2]

b. Others say that her father was one Itonus, a king of Iton in Phthiotis, whose daughter Iodama she killed by accidentally letting her see the Gorgon's head,[3] and so changing her into a block of stone, when she trespassed in the precinct at night.

c. Still others say that Poseidon was her father, but that she disowned him and begged to be adopted by Zeus, which he was glad to do.[4]

d. But Athene's own priests tell the following story of her birth. Zeus lusted after Metis the Titaness, who turned into many shapes to escape him until she was caught at last and got with child. An oracle of Mother Earth then declared that this would be a girl-child and that, if Metis conceived again, she would bear a son who was fated to depose Zeus, just as Zeus had deposed Cronus, and Cronus had deposed Uranus. Therefore, having coaxed Metis to a couch with honeyed words, Zeus suddenly opened his mouth and swallowed her, and that was the end of Metis, though he claimed afterwards that she gave him counsel from inside his belly. In due process of time, he was seized by a raging headache as he walked by the shores of Lake Triton, so that his skull seemed about to burst, and he howled for rage until the whole firmament echoed. Up ran Hermes, who at once divined the cause of Zeus's discomfort. He persuaded Hephaestus, or some say Prometheus, to fetch his wedge and beetle and make a breach in Zeus's skull, from which Athene sprang, fully armed, with a mighty shout.[5]

1. Tzetzes: *On Lycophron* 355.
2. Euripides: *Ion* 995.
3. Pausanias: ix. 34. 1.
4. Herodotus: iv. 180.
5. Hesiod: *Theogony* 886–900; Pindar: *Olympian Odes* vii. 34 ff.; Apollodorus: i. 3. 6.

*

1. J. E. Harrison rightly described the story of Athene's birth from Zeus's head as 'a desperate theological expedient to rid her of her matriarchal conditions.' It is also a dogmatic insistence on wisdom as a male prerogative; hitherto the goddess alone had been wise. Hesiod has, in fact, managed to reconcile three conflicting views in his story:

1. Athene, the Athenians' city-goddess, was the parthenogenous daughter of the immortal Metis, Titaness of the fourth day and of the planet Mercury, who presided over all wisdom and knowledge.

2. Zeus swallowed Metis, but did not thereby lose wisdom (i.e. the Achaeans suppressed the Titan cult, and ascribed all wisdom to their god Zeus).

3. Athene was the daughter of Zeus (i.e. the Achaeans insisted that the Athenians must acknowledge Zeus's patriarchal overlordship).

He has borrowed the mechanism of his myth from analogous examples:

Zeus pursuing Nemesis (see 32. b); Cronus swallowing his sons and daughters (see 7. a); Dionysus's rebirth from Zeus's thigh (see 14. c); and the opening of Mother Earth's head by two men with axes, apparently in order to release Core (see 24. 3) – as shown for instance, on a black-figured oil-jar in the Bibliothèque Nationale at Paris. Thereafter, Athene is Zeus's obedient mouthpiece, and deliberately suppresses her ante-cedents. She employs priests, not priestesses.

2. Pallas, meaning 'maiden', is an inappropriate name for the winged giant whose attempt on Athene's chastity is probably deduced from a picture of her ritual marriage, as Athene Laphria, to a goat-king (see 89. 4) after an armed contest with her rival (see 8. 1). This Libyan custom of goat-marriage spread to Northern Europe as part of the May Eve merry-makings. The Akan, a Libyan people, once flayed their kings.

3. Athene's repudiation of Poseidon's fatherhood concerns an early change in the overlordship of the city of Athens (see 16. 3).

4. The myth of Itonus ('willow-man') represents a claim by the Itonians that they worshipped Athene even before the Athenians did; and his name shows that she had a willow cult in Phthiotis – like that of her counterpart, the goddess Anatha, at Jerusalem until Jehovah's priests ousted her and claimed the rain-making willow as his tree at the Feast of Tabernacles.

5. It will have been death for a man to remove an aegis – the goat-skin chastity-tunic worn by Libyan girls – without the owner's consent; hence the prophylactic Gorgon mask set above it, and the serpent con-cealed in the leather pouch, or bag. But since Athene's aegis is described as a shield, I suggest in *The White Goddess* (p. 279) that it was a bag-cover for a sacred disk, like the one which contained Palamedes's alphabetical secret, and which he is said to have invented (see 52. a and 162. 5). Cyrian figurines holding disks of the same proportionate size as the famous Phaestos one, which is spirally marked with a sacred legend, are held by Professor Richter to anticipate Athene and her aegis. The heroic shields so carefully described by Homer and Hesiod seem to have borne pictographs engraved on a spiral band.

6. Iodama, probably meaning 'heifer calf of Io', will have been an antique stone image of the Moon-goddess (see 56. 1), and the story of her petrification is a warning to inquisitive girls against violating the Mysteries (see 25. d).

7. It would be a mistake to think of Athene as solely or predominantly the goddess of Athens. Several ancient acropolises were sacred to her, including Argos (Pausanias: ii. 24. 3), Sparta (*ibid.*: 3. 17. 1), Troy (*Iliad* vi. 88), Smyrna (Strabo: iv. 1. 4), Epidaurus (Pausanias: ii. 32. 5), Troezen (Pausanias: iii. 23. 10), and Pheneus (Pausanias: x. 38. 5). All these are pre-Hellenic sites.

THE FATES

THERE are three conjoined Fates, robed in white, whom Erebus begot on Night: by name Clotho, Lachesis, and Atropos. Of these, Atropos is the smallest in stature, but the most terrible.[1]

b. Zeus, who weighs the lives of men and informs the Fates of his decisions can, it is said, change his mind and intervene to save whom he pleases, when the thread of life, spun on Clotho's spindle, and measured by the rod of Lachesis, is about to be snipped by Atropos's shears. Indeed, men claim that they themselves can, to some degree, control their own fates by avoiding unnecessary dangers. The younger gods, therefore, laugh at the Fates, and some say that Apollo once mischievously made them drunk in order to save his friend Admetus from death.[2]

c. Others hold, on the contrary, that Zeus himself is subject to the Fates, as the Pythian priestess once confessed in an oracle; because they are not his children, but parthenogenous daughters of the Great Goddess Necessity, against whom not even the gods contend, and who is called 'The Strong Fate'.[3]

d. At Delphi only two Fates are worshipped, those of Birth and Death; and at Athens Aphrodite Urania is called the eldest of the three.[4]

1. Homer: *Iliad* xxiv. 49; *Orphic Hymn* xxxiii; Hesiod: *Theogony* 217 ff. and 904, *Shield of Heracles* 259.
2. Homer: *Iliad* viii. 69 and xxii. 209; xvi. 434 and 441-3; Virgil: *Aeneid* x. 814; Homer: *Odyssey* i. 34; *Iliad* ix. 411.
3. Aeschylus: *Prometheus* 511 and 515; Herodotus: i. 91; Plato: *Republic* x. 14-16; Simonides: viii. 20.
4. Pausanias: x. 24. 4 and i. 19. 2.

*

1. This myth seems to be based on the custom of weaving family and clan marks into a newly-born child's swaddling bands, and so allotting him his place in society (see 60. 2); but the Moerae, or Three Fates, are the Triple Moon-goddess – hence their white robes, and the linen thread which is sacred to her as Isis. Clotho is the 'spinner', Lachesis the 'measurer', Atropos is 'she who cannot be turned, or avoided'. *Moera* means

'a share' or 'a phase', and the moon has three phases and three persons: the new, the Maiden-goddess of the spring, the first period of the year; the full moon, the Nymph-goddess of the summer, the second period; and the old moon, the Crone-goddess of autumn, the last period (see 60. *2*).

2. Zeus called himself 'The Leader of the Fates' when he assumed supreme sovereignty and the prerogative of measuring man's life; hence, probably, the disappearance of Lachesis, 'the measurer', at Delphi. But his claim to be their father was not taken seriously by Aeschylus, Herodotus, or Plato.

3. The Athenians called Aphrodite Urania 'the eldest of the Fates' because she was the Nymph-goddess, to whom the sacred king had, in ancient times, been sacrificed at the summer solstice. 'Urania' means 'queen of the mountains' (see 19. *3*).

II

THE BIRTH OF APHRODITE

APHRODITE, Goddess of Desire, rose naked from the foam of the sea and, riding on a scallop shell, stepped ashore first on the island of Cythera; but finding this only a small island, passed on to the Peloponnese, and eventually took up residence at Paphos, in Cyprus, still the principal seat of her worship. Grass and flowers sprang from the soil wherever she trod. At Paphos, the Seasons, daughters of Themis, hastened to clothe and adorn her.

b. Some hold that she sprang from the foam which gathered about the genitals of Uranus, when Cronus threw them into the sea; others, that Zeus begot her on Dione, daughter either of Oceanus and Tethys the sea-nymph, or of Air and Earth. But all agree that she takes the air accompanied by doves and sparrows.[1]

> 1. Hesiod: *Theogony* 188–200 and 353; Festus Grammaticus: iii. 2; *Homeric Hymn to Aphrodite* ii. 5; Apollodorus: i. 1. 3.

*

1. Aphrodite ('foam-born') is the same wide-ruling goddess who rose from Chaos and danced on the sea, and who was worshipped in Syria and Palestine as Ishtar, or Ashtaroth (see 1. *1*). Her most famous centre of

worship was Paphos, where the original white aniconic image of the goddess is still shown in the ruins of a grandiose Roman temple; there every spring her priestess bathed in the sea, and rose again renewed.

2. She is called daughter of Dione, because Dione was the goddess of the oak-tree, in which the amorous dove nested (see 51. *a*). Zeus claimed to be her father after seizing Dione's oracle at Dodona, and Dione therefore became her mother. 'Tethys' and 'Thetis' are names of the goddess as Creatrix (formed, like 'Themis' and 'Theseus', from *tithenai*, 'to dispose' or 'to order'), and as Sea-goddess, since life began in the sea (see 2. *a*). Doves and sparrows were noted for their lechery; and sea food is still regarded as aphrodisiac throughout the Mediterranean.

3. Cythera was an important centre of Cretan trade with the Peloponnese, and it will have been from here that her worship first entered Greece. The Cretan goddess had close associations with the sea. Shells carpeted the floor of her palace sanctuary at Cnossus; she is shown on a gem from the Idean Cave blowing a triton-shell, with a sea-anemone lying beside her altar; the sea-urchin and cuttle-fish (see 81. *1*) were sacred to her. A triton-shell was found in her early sanctuary at Phaestus, and many more in late Minoan tombs, some of these being terracotta replicas.

12

HERA AND HER CHILDREN

HERA, daughter of Cronus and Rhea, having been born on the island of Samos or, some say, at Argos, was brought up in Arcadia by Temenus, son of Pelasgus. The Seasons were her nurses.[1] After banishing their father Cronus, Hera's twin-brother Zeus sought her out at Cnossus in Crete or, some say, on Mount Thornax (now called Cuckoo Mountain) in Argolis, where he courted her, at first unsuccessfully. She took pity on him only when he adopted the disguise of a bedraggled cuckoo, and tenderly warmed him in her bosom. There he at once resumed his true shape and ravished her, so that she was shamed into marrying him.[2]

b. All the gods brought gifts to the wedding; notably Mother Earth gave Hera a tree with golden apples, which was later guarded by the Hesperides in Hera's orchard on Mount Atlas. She and Zeus spent their wedding night on Samos, and it lasted three hundred years. Hera bathes regularly in the spring of Canathus, near Argos, and thus renews her virginity.[3]

c. To Hera and Zeus were born the deities Ares, Hephaestus, and Hebe, though some say that Ares and his twin-sister Eris were conceived when Hera touched a certain flower, and Hebe when she touched a lettuce,[4] and that Hephaestus also was her parthenogenous child – a wonder which he would not believe until he had imprisoned her in a mechanical chair with arms that folded about the sitter, thus forcing her to swear by the River Styx that she did not lie. Others say that Hephaestus was her son by Talos, the nephew of Daedalus.[5]

1. Pausanias: vii. 4. 4 and viii. 22. 2; Strabo: ix. 2. 36; Olen, quoted by Pausanias: ii. 13. 3.
2. Diodorus Siculus: v. 72; Pausanias ii. 36. 2 and 17. 4.
3. Scholiast on Homer's *Iliad* i. 609; Pausanias: ii. 38. 2.
4. Homer: *Iliad* iv. 441; Ovid: *Fasti* v. 255; First Vatican Mythographer: 204.
5. Servius on Virgil's *Eclogues* iv. 62; Cinaethon, quoted by Pausanias: viii. 53. 2.

*

1. Hera's name, usually taken to be a Greek word for 'lady', may represent an original Herwā ('Protectress'). She is the pre-Hellenic Great Goddess. Samos and Argos were the chief seats of her worship in Greece, but the Arcadians claimed that their cult was the earliest, and made it contemporary with their earth-born ancestor Pelasgus ('ancient'). Hera's forced marriage to Zeus commemorates conquests of Crete and Mycenaean – that is to say Cretanized – Greece, and the overthrow of her supremacy in both countries. He probably came to her disguised as a bedraggled cuckoo, in the sense that certain Hellenes who came to Crete as fugitives accepted employment in the royal guard, made a palace conspiracy and seized the kingdom. Cnossus was twice sacked, apparently by Hellenes; about 1700 B.C., and about 1400 B.C.; and Mycenae fell to the Achaeans a century later. The God Indra in the Ramayana had similarly wooed a nymph in cuckoo disguise; and Zeus now borrowed Hera's sceptre, which was surmounted with the cuckoo. Gold-leaf figurines of a naked Argive goddess holding cuckoos have been found at Mycenae; and cuckoos perch on a gold-leaf model temple from the same site. In the well-known Cretan sarcophagus from Hagia Triada a cuckoo perches on a double-axe.

2. Hebe, the goddess as child, was made cup-bearer to the gods in the Olympian cult. She eventually married Heracles (see 145. *i* and *5*), after Ganymedes had usurped her office (see 29. *c*). 'Hephaestus' seems to have

been a title of the sacred king as solar demi-god; 'Ares', a title of his war-chief, or tanist, whose emblem was the wild boar. Both became divine names when the Olympian cult was established and they were chosen to fill the roles, respectively, of War-god and Smith-god. The 'certain flower' is likely to have been the may-blossom: Ovid makes the goddess Flora – with whose worship the may-blossom was associated – point it out to Hera. The may, or whitethorn, is connected with miraculous conception in popular European myth: in Celtic literature its 'sister' is the blackthorn, a symbol of Strife – Ares's twin, Eris.

3. Talos, the smith, was a Cretan hero born to Daedalus's sister Perdix ('partridge'), with whom the mythographer is identifying Hera. Par-tridges, sacred to the Great Goddess, figured in the spring equinox orgies of the Eastern Mediterranean, when a hobbling dance was performed in imitation of cock-partridges. The hens were said by Aristotle, Pliny, and Aelian to conceive merely by hearing the cock's voice. Hobbling Hephae-stus and Talos seem to be the same parthenogenous character; and both were cast down from a height by angry rivals (see 23. b and 92. b) – originally in honour of their goddess-mother.

4. In Argos, Hera's famous statue was seated on a throne of gold and ivory; the story of her imprisonment in a chair may have arisen from the Greek custom of chaining divine statues to their thrones 'to prevent escape'. By losing an ancient statue of its god or goddess, a city might forfeit divine protection, and the Romans, therefore, made a practice of what was politely called 'enticing' gods to Rome – which by Imperial times had become a jackdaw's nest of stolen images. 'The Seasons were her nurses' is one way of saying that Hera was a goddess of the calendar year. Hence the spring cuckoo on her sceptre, and the ripe pomegranate of late autumn, which she carried in her left hand to symbolize the death of the year.

5. A hero, as the word indicates, was a sacred king who had been sacrificed to Hera, whose body was safely under the earth, and whose soul had gone to enjoy her paradise at the back of the North Wind. His golden apples, in Greek and Celtic myth, were passports to this paradise (see 53. 7, 133. 4, and 159. 3).

6. The annual bath with which Hera renewed her virginity was also taken by Aphrodite at Paphos; it seems to have been the purification ceremony prescribed to a Moon-priestess after the murder of her lover, the sacred king (see 22. 1 and 150. 1). Hera, being the goddess of the vegetative year, spring, summer and autumn (also symbolized by the new, full, and old moon) was worshipped at Stymphalus as Child, Bride, and Widow (Pausanias: vii. 22. 2 – see 128. d).

7. The wedding-night on Samos lasted for three hundred years: per-haps became the Samian sacred year, like the Etruscan one, consisted of

ten thirty-day months only: with January and February omitted (Macrobius: i. 13). Each day was lengthened to a year. But the mythographer may here be hinting that it took the Hellenes three hundred years before they forced monogamy on Hera's people.

13

ZEUS AND HERA

ONLY Zeus, the Father of Heaven, might wield the thunderbolt; and it was with the threat of its fatal flash that he controlled his quarrelsome and rebellious family of Mount Olympus. He also ordered the heavenly bodies, made laws, enforced oaths, and pronounced oracles. When his mother Rhea, foreseeing what trouble his lust would cause, forbade him to marry, he angrily threatened to violate her. Though she at once turned into a menacing serpent, this did not daunt Zeus, who became a male serpent and, twining about her in an indissoluble knot, made good his threat.[1] It was then that he began his long series of adventures in love. He fathered the Seasons and the Three Fates on Themis; the Charites on Eurynome; the Three Muses on Mnemosyne, with whom he lay for nine nights; and, some say, Persephone, the Queen of the Underworld, whom his brother Hades forcibly married, on the nymph Styx.[2] Thus he lacked no power either above or below earth; and his wife Hera was equal to him in one thing alone: that she could still bestow the gift of prophecy on any man or beast she pleased.[3]

b. Zeus and Hera bickered constantly. Vexed by his infidelities, she often humiliated him by her scheming ways. Though he would confide his secrets to her, and sometimes accept her advice, he never fully trusted Hera, and she knew that if offended beyond a certain point he would flog or even hurl a thunderbolt at her. She therefore resorted to ruthless intrigue, as in the matter of Heracles's birth; and sometimes borrowed Aphrodite's girdle, to excite his passion and thus weaken his will. He now claimed to be Cronus's first-born son.[4]

c. A time came when Zeus's pride and petulance became so intolerable that Hera, Poseidon, Apollo, and all the other Olympians, except Hestia, surrounded him suddenly as he lay asleep on his couch and bound him with rawhide thongs, knotted into a hundred knots, so that he could not move. He threatened them with instant death, but they had placed his thunderbolt out of reach and laughed insultingly at him. While they were celebrating their victory, and jealously discussing who was to be his successor, Thetis the Nereid, foreseeing a civil war on Olympus, hurried in search of the hundred-handed Briareus, who swiftly untied the thongs, using every hand at once, and released his master. Because it was Hera who had led the conspiracy against him, Zeus hung her up from the sky with a golden bracelet about either wrist and an anvil fastened to either ankle. The other deities were vexed beyond words, but dared attempt no rescue for all her piteous cries. In the end Zeus undertook to free her if they swore never more to rebel against him; and this each in turn grudgingly did. Zeus punished Poseidon and Apollo by sending them as bond-servants to King Laomedon, for whom they built the city of Troy; but he pardoned the others as having acted under duress.[5]

1. *Orphic Fragment* 58; Hesiod: *Theogony* 56.
2. Apollodorus: i. 3. 1–2.
3. Homer: *Iliad* xix. 407.
4. *Ibid.*: i. 547; xvi. 458; viii. 407–8; xv. 17; viii. 397–404; xiv. 197–223; xv. 166.
5. Scholiast on Homer's *Iliad* xxi. 444; Tzetzes: *On Lycophron* 34; Homer: *Iliad* i. 399 ff. and xv. 18–22.

*

1. The marital relations of Zeus and Hera reflect those of the barbarous Dorian Age, when women had been deprived of all their magical power, except that of prophecy, and come to be regarded as chattels. It is possible that the occasion on which the power of Zeus was saved only by Thetis and Briareus, after the other Olympians had conspired against him, was a palace revolution by vassal princes of the Hellenic High King, who nearly succeeded in dethroning him; and that help came from a company of loyal non-Hellenic household troops, recruited in Macedonia, Briareus's home, and from a detachment of Magnesians, Thetis's people. If so, the conspiracy will have been instigated by the High-priestess of Hera, whom the High King subsequently humiliated, as the myth describes.

2. Zeus's violation of the Earth-goddess Rhea implies that the Zeus-worshipping Hellenes took over all agricultural and funerary ceremonies. She had forbidden him to marry, in the sense that hitherto monogamy had been unknown; women took whatever lovers they pleased. His fatherhood of the Seasons, on Themis, means that the Hellenes also assumed control of the calendar: Themis ('order') was the Great Goddess who ordered the year of thirteen months, divided by the summer and winter solstices into two seasons. At Athens these seasons were personified

as Thallo and Carpo (originally 'Carpho'), which mean respectively
'sprouting' and 'withering', and their temple contained an altar to the
phallic Dionysus (see 27. 5). They appear in a rock-carving at Hattusas, or
Pteria, where they are twin aspects of the Lion-goddess Hepta, borne on
the wings of a double-headed Sun-eagle.

3. Charis ('grace') had been the Goddess in the disarming aspect she
presented when the High-priestess chose the sacred king as her lover.
Homer mentions two Charites – Pasithea and Cale, which seems to be a
forced separation of three words: *Pasi thea cale*, 'the Goddess who is
beautiful to all men'. The two Charites, Auxo ('increase') and Hege-
mone ('mastery'), whom the Athenians honoured, corresponded with
the two Seasons. Later, the Charites were worshipped as a triad, to match
the Three Fates – the Triple-goddess in her most unbending mood (see
106. 3). That they were Zeus's children, born to Eurynome the Creatrix,
implies that the Hellenic overlord had power to dispose of all marriage-
able young women.

4. The Muses ('mountain goddesses'), originally a triad (Pausanias: ix.
19. 2), are the Triple-goddess in her orgiastic aspect. Zeus's claim to be
their father is a late one; Hesiod calls them daughters of Mother Earth
and Air.

14

BIRTHS OF HERMES, APOLLO, ARTEMIS,
AND DIONYSUS

AMOROUS Zeus lay with numerous nymphs descended from the
Titans or the gods and, after the creation of man, with mortal women
too; no less than four great Olympian deities were born to him out of
wedlock. First, he begat Hermes on Maia, daughter of Atlas, who bore
him in a cave on Mount Cyllene in Arcadia. Next, he begat Apollo and
Artemis on Leto, daughter of the Titans Coeus and Phoebe, transform-
ing himself and her into quails when they coupled;[1] but jealous Hera
sent the serpent Python to pursue Leto all over the world, and decreed
that she should not be delivered in any place where the sun shone.
Carried on the wings of the South Wind, Leto at last came to Ortygia,
close to Delos, where she bore Artemis, who was no sooner born than
she helped her mother across the narrow straits, and there, between an
olive-tree and a date-palm growing on the north side of Delian Mount

Cynthus, delivered her of Apollo on the ninth day of labour. Delos, hitherto a floating island, became immovably fixed in the sea and, by decree, no one is now allowed either to be born or to die there: sick folk and pregnant women are ferried over to Ortygia instead.[2]

b. The mother of Zeus's son Dionysus is variously named: some say that she was Demeter, or Io;[3] some name her Dione; some, Persephone, with whom Zeus coupled in the likeness of a serpent; and some, Lethe.[4]

c. But the common story runs as follows. Zeus, disguised as a mortal, had a secret love affair with Semele ('moon'), daughter of King Cadmus of Thebes, and jealous Hera, disguising herself as an old neighbour, advised Semele, then already six months with child, to make her mysterious lover a request: that he would no longer deceive her, but reveal himself in his true nature and form. How, otherwise, could she know that he was not a monster? Semele followed this advice and, when Zeus refused her plea, denied him further access to her bed. Then, in anger, he appeared as thunder and lightning, and she was consumed. But Hermes saved her six-months son; sewed him up inside Zeus's thigh, to mature there for three months longer; and, in due course of time, delivered him. Thus Dionysus is called 'twice-born', or 'the child of the double door'.[5]

1. Hesiod: *Theogony* 918; Apollodorus: i. 4. 1; Aristophanes: *Birds* 870; Servius on Virgil's *Aeneid* iii. 72.
2. *Homeric Hymn to Apollo* 14 ff.; Hyginus: *Fabula* 140; Aelian: *Varia Historia* v. 4; Thucydides: iii. 104; Strabo: x. 5.5.
3. Diodorus Siculus: iii. 67 and 74; iv. 4.
4. Scholiast on Pindar's *Pythian Odes* iii. 177; *Orphic Fragment* 59; Plutarch: *Symposiacs* vii. 5.
5. Apollodorus: iii. 4. 3; Apollonius Rhodius: iv. 1137.

*

1. Zeus's rapes apparently refer to Hellenic conquests of the goddess's ancient shrines, such as that on Mount Cyllene; his marriages, to an ancient custom of giving the title 'Zeus' to the sacred king of the oak cult. Hermes, his son by the rape of Maia – a title of the Earth-goddess as Crone – was originally not a god, but the totemistic virtue of a phallic pillar, or cairn. Such pillars were the centre of an orgiastic dance in the goddess's honour.

2. One component in Apollo's godhead seems to have been an oracular mouse – Apollo Smintheus ('Mouse-Apollo') is among his earliest titles (see 158. 2) – consulted in a shrine of the Great Goddess, which perhaps

explains why he was born where the sun never shone, namely underground. Mice were associated with disease and its cure, and the Hellenes therefore worshipped Apollo as a god of medicine and prophecy; afterwards saying that he was born under an olive-tree and a date-palm on the north side of a mountain. They called him a twin-brother of Artemis Goddess of Childbirth, and made his mother Leto – the daughter of the Titans Phoebe ('moon') and Coeus ('intelligence') – who was known in Egypt and Palestine as Lat, fertility-goddess of the date-palm and olive: hence her conveyance to Greece by a South Wind. In Italy she became Latona ('Queen Lat'). Her quarrel with Hera suggests a conflict between early immigrants from Palestine and native tribes who worshipped a different Earth-goddess; the mouse cult, which she seems to have brought with her, was well established in Palestine (1 *Samuel* vi. 4 and *Isaiah* lxvi. 17). Python's pursuit of Apollo recalls the use of snakes in Greek and Roman houses to keep down mice. But Apollo was also the ghost of the sacred king who had eaten the apple – the word *Apollo* may be derived from the root *abol*, 'apple', rather than from *apollunai*, 'destroy', which is the usual view.

3. Artemis, originally an orgiastic goddess, had the lascivious quail as her sacred bird. Flocks of quail will have made Ortygia a resting-place on their way north during the spring migration. The story that Delos, Apollo's birthplace, had hitherto been a floating island (see 43. 4) may be a misunderstanding of a record that his birthplace was now officially fixed: since in Homer (*Iliad* iv. 101) he is called Lycegenes, 'born in Lycia'; and the Ephesians boasted that he was born at Ortygia near Ephesus (Tacitus: *Annals* iii. 61). Both the Boeotian Tegyrans and the Attic Zosterans also claimed him as a native son (Stephanus of Byzantium *sub* Tegyra).

4. Dionysus began, probably, as a type of sacred king whom the goddess ritually killed with a thunderbolt in the seventh month from the winter solstice, and whom her priestesses devoured (see 27. 3). This explains his mothers: Dione, the Oak-goddess; Io and Demeter, Corn-goddesses; and Persephone, Death-goddess. Plutarch, when calling him 'Dionysus, a son of Lethe ("forgetfulness")', refers to his later aspect as God of the Vine.

5. The story of Semele, daughter of Cadmus, seems to record the summary action taken by Hellenese of Boeotia in ending the tradition of royal sacrifice: Olympian Zeus asserts his power, takes the doomed king under his own protection, and destroys the goddess with her own thunderbolt. Dionysus thus becomes an immortal, after rebirth from his immortal father. Semele was worshipped at Athens during the *Lenaea*, the Festival of the Wild Women, when a yearly bull, representing Dionysus, was cut into nine pieces and sacrificed to her: one piece being burned, the

remainder eaten raw by the worshippers. *Semele* is usually explained as a form of Selene ('moon'), and nine was the traditional number of orgiastic moon-priestesses who took part in such feasts – nine such are shown dancing around the sacred king in a cave painting at Cogul, and nine more killed and devoured St Samson of Dol's acolyte in medieval times.

15

THE BIRTH OF EROS

SOME argue that Eros, hatched from the world-egg, was the first of the gods since, without him, none of the rest could have been born; they make him coeval with Mother Earth and Tartarus, and deny that he had any father or mother, unless it were Eileithyia, Goddess of Childbirth.[1]

b. Others hold that he was Aphrodite's son by Hermes, or by Ares, or by her own father, Zeus; or the son of Iris by the West Wind. He was a wild boy, who showed no respect for age or station but flew about on golden wings, shooting barbed arrows at random or wantonly setting hearts on fire with his dreadful torches.[2]

1. *Orphic Hymn* v; Aristotle: *Metaphysics* i. 4; Hesiod: *Theogony* 120; Meleager: *Epigrams* 50; Olen, quoted by Pausanias: ix. 27. 2.
2. Cicero: *On the Nature of the Gods* iii. 23; Virgil: *Ciris* 134; Alcaeus, quoted by Plutarch: *Amatorius* 20.

*

1. Eros ('sexual passion') was a mere abstraction to Hesiod. The early Greeks pictured him as a *Ker*, or winged 'Spite', like Old Age, or Plague, in the sense that uncontrolled sexual passion could be disturbing to ordered society. Later poets, however, took a perverse pleasure in his antics and, by the time of Praxiteles, he had become sentimentalized as a beautiful youth. His most famous shrine was at Thespiae, where the Boeotians worshipped him as a simple phallic pillar – the pastoral Hermes, or Priapus, under a different name (see 150. *a*). The various accounts of his parentage are self-explanatory. Hermes was a phallic god; and Ares, as a god of war, increased desire in the warrior's womenfolk. That Aphrodite was Eros's mother and Zeus his father is a hint that sexual passion does not stop short at incest; his birth from the Rainbow and the West Wind is a lyrical fancy. Eileithyia, 'she who comes to the aid of women in

childbed', was a title of Artemis; the meaning being that there is no love so strong as mother-love.

2. Eros was never considered a sufficiently responsible god to figure among the ruling Olympian family of Twelve.

16

POSEIDON'S NATURE AND DEEDS

WHEN Zeus, Poseidon, and Hades, after deposing their father Cronus, shook lots in a helmet for the lordship of the sky, sea, and murky underworld, leaving the earth common to all, Zeus won the sky, Hades the underworld, and Poseidon the sea. Poseidon, who is equal to his brother Zeus in dignity, though not in power, and of a surly, quarrelsome nature, at once set about building his under-water palace off Aegae in Euboea. In its spacious stables he keeps white chariot horses with brazen hooves and golden manes, and a golden chariot at the approach of which storms instantly cease and sea-monsters rise, frisking, around it.[1]

b. Needing a wife who would be at home in the sea-depths, he courted Thetis the Nereid; but when it was prophesied by Themis that any son born to Thetis would be greater than his father, he desisted, and allowed her to marry a mortal named Peleus. Amphitrite, another Nereid, whom he next approached, viewed his advances with repugnance, and fled to the Atlas Mountains to escape him; but he sent messengers after her, among them one Delphinus, who pleaded Poseidon's cause so winningly that she yielded, and asked him to arrange the marriage. Gratefully, Poseidon set Delphinus's image among the stars as a constellation, the Dolphin.[2]

Amphitrite bore Poseidon three children: Triton, Rhode, and Benthesicyme; but he caused her almost as much jealousy as Zeus did Hera by his love affairs with goddesses, nymphs, and mortals. Especially she loathed his infatuation with Scylla, daughter of Phorcys, whom she changed into a barking monster with six heads and twelve feet by throwing magical herbs into her bathing pool.[3]

c. Poseidon is greedy of earthly kingdoms, and once claimed possession of Attica by thrusting his trident into the acropolis at Athens, where a well of sea-water immediately gushed out and is still to be seen; when the South Wind blows you may hear the sound of the surf far below. Later, during the reign of Cecrops, Athene came and took possession in a gentler manner, by planting the first olive-tree beside the well. Poseidon, in a fury, challenged her to single combat, and Athene would have accepted had not Zeus interposed and ordered them to submit the dispute to arbitration. Presently, then, they appeared before a divine court, consisting of their supernal fellow-deities, who called on Cecrops to give evidence. Zeus himself expressed no opinion, but while all the other gods supported Poseidon, all the goddesses supported Athene. Thus, by a majority of one, the court ruled that Athene had the better right to the land, because she had given it the better gift.

d. Greatly vexed, Poseidon sent huge waves to flood the Thriasian Plain, where Athene's city of Athenae stood, whereupon she took up her abode in Athens instead, and called that too after herself. However, to appease Poseidon's wrath, the women of Athens were deprived of their vote, and the men forbidden to bear their mothers' names as hitherto.[4]

e. Poseidon also disputed Troezen with Athene; and on this occasion Zeus issued an order for the city to be shared equally between them – an arrangement disagreeable to both. Next, he tried unsuccessfully to claim Aegina from Zeus, and Naxos from Dionysus; and in a claim for Corinth with Helius received the Isthmus only, while Helius was awarded the Acropolis. In fury, he tried to seize Argolis from Hera, and was again ready to fight, refusing to appear before his Olympian peers who, he said, were prejudiced against him. Zeus, therefore, referred the matter to the River-gods Inachus, Cephissus, and Asterion, who judged in Hera's favour. Since he had been forbidden to revenge himself with a flood as before, he did exactly the opposite: he dried up his judges' streams so that they now never flow in summer. However, for the sake of Amymone, one of the Danaids who were distressed by this drought, he caused the Argive river of Lerna to flow perpetually.[5]

f. He boasts of having created the horse, though some say that, when he was newly born, Rhea gave one to Cronus to eat; and of having invented the bridle, though Athene had done so before him; but his claim to have instituted horse-racing is not disputed. Certainly, horses are sacred to him, perhaps because of his amorous pursuit of Demeter, when she was tearfully seeking her daughter Persephone. It is said that

Demeter, wearied and disheartened by her search, and disinclined for passionate dalliance with any god or Titan, transformed herself into a mare, and began to graze with the herd of one Oncus, a son of Apollo's who reigned in Arcadian Onceium. She did not, however, deceive Poseidon, who transformed himself into a stallion and covered her, from which outrageous union sprang the nymph Despoena and the wild horse Arion. Demeter's anger was so hot that she is still worshipped locally as 'Demeter the Fury'.[6]

1. Homer: *Iliad* xv. 187–93; viii. 210–11; xiii. 21–30; *Odyssey* v. 381; Apollonius Rhodius: iii. 1240.
2. Apollonius: iii. 13. 5; Hyginus: *Poetic Astronomy* ii. 17.
3. Tzetzes: *On Lycophron* 45 and 50.
4. Herodotus: viii. 55; Apollodorus: iii. 14. 1; Pausanias: 24. 3; Augustine: *On the City of God* xviii. 9; Hyginus: *Fabula* 164.
5. Pausanias: ii. 30. 6; Plutarch: *Symposiacs* ix. 6; Pausanias: ii. 1. 6; ii. 15.5; ii. 22. 5.
6. Pindar: *Pythian Odes* vi. 50; Pausanias: viii. 25. 3–5; Apollodorus: iii. 6. 8.

*

1. Thetis, Amphitrite, and Nereis were different local titles of the Triple Moon-goddess as ruler of the sea; and since Poseidon was the Father-god of the Aeolians, who had taken to the sea, he claimed to be her husband wherever she found worshippers. Peleus married Thetis on Mount Pelion (see 81. *l*). Nereis means 'the wet one', and Amphitrite's name refers to the 'third element', the sea, which is cast about earth, the first element, and above which rises the second element, air. In the Homeric poems Amphitrite means simply 'the sea'; she is not personified as Poseidon's wife. Her reluctance to marry Poseidon matches Hera's reluctance to marry Zeus, and Persephone's to marry Hades; the marriage involved the interference of male priests with female control of the fishing industry. The fable of Delphinus is sentimental allegory: dolphins appear when the sea grows calm. Amphitrite's children were herself in triad: Triton, lucky new moon; Rhode, full harvest-moon; and Benthesicyme, dangerous old moon. But Triton has since become masculinized. Aegae stood on the sheltered Boeotian side of Euboea and served as a port for Orchomenus; and it was hereabouts that the naval expedition mustered against Troy.

2. The story of Amphitrite's vengeance on Scylla is paralleled in that of Pasiphaë's vengeance on another Scylla (see 91. *2*). Scylla ('she who rends' or 'puppy') is merely a disagreeable aspect of herself: the dog-headed Death-goddess Hecate (see 31. *f*), who was at home both on land and in the waves. A seal impression from Cnossus shows her threatening

a man in a boat, as she threatened Odysseus in the Straits of Messina (see 170. t). The account quoted by Tzetzes seems to have been mistakenly deduced from an ancient vase-painting in which Amphitrite stands beside a pool occupied by a dog-headed monster; on the other side of the vase is a drowned hero caught between two dog-headed triads of goddesses at the entrance to the Underworld (see 31. a and 134. 1).

3. Poseidon's attempts to take possession of certain cities are political myths. His dispute over Athens suggests an unsuccessful attempt to make him the city's tutelary deity in place of Athene. Yet her victory was impaired by a concession to patriarchy: the Athenians abandoned the Cretan custom which prevailed in Caria until Classical times (Herodotus: i. 173) when they ceased to take their mother's names. Varro, who gives this detail, represents the trial as a plebiscite of all the men and women of Athens.

It is plain that the Ionian Pelasgians of Athens were defeated by the Aeolians, and that Athene regained her sovereignty only by alliance with Zeus's Achaeans, who later made her disown Poseidon's paternity and admit herself reborn from Zeus's head.

4. The cultivated olive was originally imported from Libya, which supports the myth of Athene's Libyan origin; but what she brought will have been only a cutting – the cultivated olive does not breed true, but must always be grafted on the oleaster, or wild olive. Her tree was still shown at Athens during the second century A.D. The flooding of the Thriasian Plain is likely to be a historical event, but cannot be dated. It is possible that early in the fourteenth century B.C., which meteorologists reckon to have been a period of maximum rainfall, the rivers of Arcadia never ran dry, and that their subsequent shrinking was attributed to the vengeance of Poseidon. Pre-Hellenic Sun-worship at Corinth is well established (Pausanias: ii. 4. 7 – see 67. 2).

5. The myth of Demeter and Poseidon records a Hellenic invasion of Arcadia. Demeter was pictured at Phigalia as the mare-headed patroness of the pre-Hellenic horse cult. Horses were sacred to the moon, because their hooves make a moon-shaped mark, and the moon was regarded as the source of all water; hence the association of Pegasus with springs of water (see 75. b). The early Hellenes introduced a larger breed of horse into Greece from Trans-Caspia, the native variety having been about the size of a Shetland pony and unsuitable for chariotry. They seem to have seized the centres of the horse cult, where their warrior-kings forcibly married the local priestesses and thus won a title to the land; incidentally suppressing the wild-mare orgies (see 72. 4). The sacred horses Arion and Despoena (this being a title of Demeter herself) were then claimed as Poseidon's children. Amymone may have been a name for the goddess at Lerna, the centre of the Danaid water cult (see 60. g and 4).

6. Demeter as Fury, like Nemesis as Fury (see 32. *3*), was the goddess in her annual mood of murder; and the story also told of Poseidon and Demeter at Thelpusia (Pausanias; viii. 42), and of Poseidon and an un-named Fury at the fountain of Tilphusa in Boeotia (Scholiast on Homer's *Iliad* xxiii. 346) was already old when the Hellenes came. It appears in early Indian sacred literature, where Saranyu turns herself into a mare, Vivaswat becomes a stallion and covers her; and the fruit of this union are the two heroic Asvins. 'Demeter Erinnys' may, in fact, have stood not for 'Demeter the Fury', but for 'Demeter Saranyu' – an attempted reconciliation of the two warring cultures; but to the resentful Pelasgians Demeter was, and remained, outraged.

17

HERMES'S NATURE AND DEEDS

W HEN Hermes was born on Mount Cyllene his mother Maia laid him in swaddling bands on a winnowing fan, but he grew with astonishing quickness into a little boy, and as soon as her back was turned, slipped off and went looking for adventure. Arrived at Pieria, where Apollo was tending a fine herd of cows, he decided to steal them. But, fearing to be betrayed by their tracks, he quickly made a number of shoes from the bark of a fallen oak and tied them with plaited grass to the feet of the cows, which he then drove off by night along the road. Apollo dis-covered the loss, but Hermes's trick deceived him, and though he went as far as Pylus in his westward search, and to Onchestus in his eastern, he was forced, in the end, to offer a reward for the apprehension of the thief. Silenus and his satyrs, greedy of reward, spread out in different directions to track him down but, for a long while, without success. At last, as a party of them passed through Arcadia, they heard the muffled sound of music such as they had never heard before, and the nymph Cyllene, from the mouth of a cave, told them that a most gifted child had recently been born there, to whom she was acting as nurse: he had constructed an ingenious musical toy from the shell of a tortoise and some cow-gut, with which he had lulled his mother to sleep.

b. 'And from whom did he get the cow-gut?' asked the alert satyrs, noticing two hides stretched outside the cave. 'Do you charge the poor child with theft?' asked Cyllene. Harsh words were exchanged.

c. At that moment Apollo came up, having discovered the thief's identity by observing the suspicious behaviour of a long-winged bird. Entering the cave, he awakened Maia and told her severely that Hermes must restore the stolen cows. Maia pointed to the child, still wrapped in his swaddling bands and feigning sleep. 'What an absurd charge!' she cried. But Apollo had already recognized the hides. He picked up Hermes, carried him to Olympus, and there formally accused him of theft, offering the hides as evidence. Zeus, loth to believe that his own new-born son was a thief, encouraged him to plead not guilty, but Apollo would not be put off and Hermes, at last, weakened and confessed.

'Very well, come with me,' he said, 'and you may have your herd. I slaughtered only two, and those I cut up into twelve equal portions as a sacrifice to the twelve gods.'

'*Twelve* gods?' asked Apollo. 'Who is the twelfth?'

'Your servant, sir,' replied Hermes modestly. 'I ate no more than my share, though I was very hungry, and duly burned the rest.'

Now, this was the first flesh-sacrifice ever made.

d. The two gods returned to Mount Cyllene, where Hermes greeted his mother and retrieved something that he had hidden underneath a sheepskin.

'What have you there?' asked Apollo.

In answer, Hermes showed his newly-invented tortoise-shell lyre, and played such a ravishing tune on it with the plectrum he had also invented, at the same time singing in praise of Apollo's nobility, intelligence, and generosity, that he was forgiven at once. He led the surprised and delighted Apollo to Pylus, playing all the way, and there gave him the remainder of the cattle, which he had hidden in a cave.

'A bargain!' cried Apollo. 'You keep the cows, and I take the lyre.'

'Agreed,' said Hermes, and they shook hands on it.

e. While the hungry cows were grazing, Hermes cut reeds, made them into a shepherd's pipe, and played another tune. Apollo, again delighted, cried: 'A bargain! If you give me that pipe, I will give you this golden staff with which I herd my cattle; in future you shall be the god of all herdsmen and shepherds.'

'My pipe is worth more than your staff,' replied Hermes. 'But I will make the exchange, if you teach me augury too, because it seems to be a most useful art.'

'I cannot do that,' Apollo said, 'but if you go to my old nurses, the Thriae who live on Parnassus, they will teach you how to divine from pebbles.'

f. They again shook hands and Apollo, taking the child back to Olympus, told Zeus all that had happened. Zeus warned Hermes that henceforth he must respect the rights of property and refrain from telling downright lies; but he could not help being amused. 'You seem to be a very ingenious, eloquent, and persuasive godling,' he said.

'Then make me your herald, Father,' Hermes answered, 'and I will be responsible for the safety of all divine property, and never tell lies, though I cannot promise always to tell the whole truth.'

'That would not be expected of you,' said Zeus, with a smile. 'But your duties would include the making of treaties, the promotion of commerce, and the maintenance of free rights of way for travellers on any road in the world.' When Hermes agreed to these conditions, Zeus gave him a herald's staff with white ribbons, which everyone was ordered to respect; a round hat against the rain, and winged golden sandals which carried him about with the swiftness of wind. He was at once welcomed into the Olympian family, whom he taught the art of making fire by the rapid twirling of the fire-stick.

g. Afterwards, the Thriae showed Hermes how to foretell the future from the dance of pebbles in a basin of water; and he himself invented both the game of knuckle-bones and the art of divining by them. Hades also engaged him as his herald, to summon the dying gently and eloquently, by laying the golden staff upon their eyes.[1]

h. He then assisted the Three Fates in the composition of the Alphabet, invented astronomy, the musical scale, the arts of boxing and gymnastics, weights and measures (which some attribute to Palamedes), and the cultivation of the olive-tree.[2]

i. Some hold that the lyre invented by Hermes had seven strings; others, that it had three only, to correspond with the seasons, or four to correspond with the quarters of the year, and that Apollo brought the number up to seven.[3]

j. Hermes had numerous sons, including Echion the Argonauts' herald; Autolycus the thief; and Daphnis the inventor of bucolic poetry. This Daphnis was a beautiful Sicilian youth whom his mother, a nymph, exposed in a laurel grove on the Mountain of Hera; hence the name given him by the shepherds, his foster parents. Pan taught him to play the pipes; he was beloved by Apollo, and used to hunt with Artemis, who took pleasure in his music. He lavished great care on his many herds of cattle, which were of the same stock as Helius's. A nymph named Nomia made him swear never to be unfaithful to her, on pain of being blinded; but her rival, Chimaera, contrived to seduce him when he was drunk, and Nomia blinded him in fulfilment of her threat. Daphnis consoled himself for a while with sad lays about the loss of sight, but he did not live long. Hermes turned him into a stone, which is still shown at the city of Cephalenitanum; and caused a fountain called Daphnis to gush up at Syracuse, where annual sacrifices are offered.[4]

1. *Homeric Hymn to Hermes* 1–543; Sophocles: *Fragments of The Trackers*; Apollodorus: iii. 10. 2.
2. Diodorus Siculus: v. 75; Hyginus: *Fabula* 277; Plutarch: *Symposiacs* ix. 3.
3. *Homeric Hymn to Hermes* 51; Diodorus Siculus: i. 16; Macrobius: *Saturnaliorum Conviviorum* i. 19; Callimachus: *Hymn to Delos* 253.
4. Diodorus Siculus: iv. 84; Servius on Virgil's *Eclogues* v. 20; viii. 68; x. 26; Philargyrius on Virgil's *Eclogues* v. 20; Aelian: *Varia Historia* x. 18.

*

1. The myth of Hermes's childhood has been preserved in a late literary form only. A tradition of cattle raids made by the crafty Messenians on their neighbours (see 74. *g* and 171. *h*), and of a treaty by which these were discontinued, seems to have been mythologically combined with an account of how the barbarous Hellenes took over and exploited, in the name of their adopted god Apollo, the Creto-Helladic civilization which they found in Central and Southern Greece – boxing, gymnastics, weights and measures, music, astronomy, and olive culture were all pre-Hellenic (see 162. 6) – and learned polite manners.

2. Hermes was evolved as a god from the stone phalli which were local centres of a pre-Hellenic fertility cult (see 15. *1*) – the account of his rapid growth may be Homer's playful obscenity – but also from the Divine Child of the pre-Hellenic Calendar (see 24. 6, 44. 1, 105. 1, 171. 4, etc.); from the Egyptian Thoth, God of Intelligence; and from Anubis, conductor of souls to the Underworld.

3. The heraldic white ribbons on Hermes's staff were later mistaken for serpents, because he was herald to Hades; hence Echion's name. The Thriae are the Triple-Muse ('mountain goddess') of Parnassus, their divination by means of dancing pebbles was also practised at Delphi

(Mythographi Graeci: *Appendix Narrationum* 67). Athene was first credited with the invention of divinatory dice made from knuckle-bones (Zenobius: *Proverbs* v. 75), and these came into popular use; but the art of augury remained an aristocratic prerogative both in Greece and at Rome. Apollo's 'long-winged bird' was probably Hermes's own sacred crane; for the Apollonian priesthood constantly trespassed on the territory of Hermes, an earlier patron of soothsaying, literature, and the arts; as did the Hermetic priesthood on that of Pan, the Muses, and Athene. The invention of fire-making was ascribed to Hermes, because the twirling of the male drill in the female stock suggested phallic magic.

4. Silenus and his sons, the satyrs,, were conventional comic characters in the Attic drama (see 83. 5); originally they had been primitive mountaineers of Northern Greece. He was called an autochthon, or a son of Pan by one of the nymphs (Nonnus; *Dionysiaca* xiv. 97; xxix. 262; Aelian: *Varia Historia* iii. 18).

5. The romantic story of Daphnis has been built around a phallic pillar at Cephalenitanum, and a fountain at Syracuse, each probably surrounded by a laurel grove, where songs were sung in honour of the sightless dead. Daphnis was said to be beloved by Apollo because he had taken the laurel from the orgiastic goddess of Tempe (see 21. 6).

18

APHRODITE'S NATURE AND DEEDS

APHRODITE could seldom be persuaded to lend the other goddesses her magic girdle which made everyone fall in love with its wearer; for she was jealous of her position. Zeus had given her in marriage to Hephaestus, the lame Smith-god; but the true father of the three children with whom she presented him – Phobus, Deimus, and Harmonia – was Ares, the straight-limbed, impetuous, drunken, and quarrelsome God of War. Hephaestus knew nothing of the deception until, one night, the lovers stayed too long together in bed at Ares's Thracian palace; then Helius, as he rose, saw them at their sport and told tales to Hephaestus.

b. Hephaestus angrily retired to his forge, and hammered out a bronze hunting-net, as fine as gossamer but quite unbreakable, which he secretly attached to the posts and sides of his marriage-bed. He told Aphrodite who returned from Thrace, all smiles, explaining that she had been away on business at Corinth: 'Pray excuse me, dear wife, I am taking a short holiday on Lemnos, my favourite island.' Aphrodite did not offer to accompany him and, when he was out of sight, sent hurriedly for Ares, who soon arrived. The two went merrily to bed but, at dawn, found themselves entangled in the net, naked and unable to escape. Hephaestus, turning back from his journey, surprised them there, and summoned all the gods to witness his dishonour. He then announced that he would not release his wife until the valuable marriage-gifts which he had paid her adoptive father, Zeus, were restored to him.

c. Up ran the gods, to watch Aphrodite's embarrassment; but the goddesses, from a sense of delicacy, stayed in their houses. Apollo, nudging Hermes, asked: 'You would not mind being in Ares's position, would you, net and all?'

Hermes swore by his own head, that he would not, even if there were three times as many nets, and all the goddesses were looking on with disapproval. At this, both gods laughed uproariously, but Zeus was so disgusted that he refused to hand back the marriage-gifts, or to interfere in a vulgar dispute between a husband and wife, declaring that Hephaestus was a fool to have made the affair public. Poseidon who, at sight of Aphrodite's naked body, had fallen in love with her, concealed his jealousy of Ares, and pretended to sympathize with Hephaestus. 'Since Zeus refuses to help,' he said, 'I will undertake that Ares, as a fee for his release, pays the equivalent of the marriage-gifts in question.'

'That is all very well,' Hephaestus replied gloomily. 'But if Ares defaults, you will have to take his place under the net.'

'In Aphrodite's company?' Apollo asked, laughing.

'I cannot think that Ares will default,' Poseidon said nobly. 'But if he should do so, I am ready to pay the debt and marry Aphrodite myself.'

So Ares was set at liberty, and returned to Thrace; and Aphrodite went to Paphos, where she renewed her virginity in the sea.[1]

d. Flattered by Hermes's frank confession of his love for her, Aphrodite presently spent a night with him, the fruit of which was Hermaphroditus, a double-sexed being; and, equally pleased by Poseidon's intervention on her behalf, she bore him two sons, Rhodus and Herophilus.[2] Needless to say, Ares defaulted, pleading that if Zeus would not pay, why should he? In the end, nobody paid, because Hephaestus was madly in love with Aphrodite and had no real intention of divorcing her.

e. Later, Aphrodite yielded to Dionysus, and bore him Priapus; an ugly child with enormous genitals – it was Hera who had given him this obscene appearance, in disapproval of Aphrodite's promiscuity. He is a gardener and carries a pruning-knife.[3]

f. Though Zeus never lay with his adopted daughter Aphrodite, as some say that he did, the magic of her girdle put him under constant temptation, and at last he decided to humiliate her by making her fall desperately in love with a mortal. This was the handsome Anchises, King of the Dardanians, a grandson of Ilus and, one night, when he was asleep in his herdsman's hut on Trojan Mount Ida, Aphrodite visited him in the guise of a Phrygian princess, clad in a dazzlingly red robe, and lay with him on a couch spread with the skins of bears and lions, while bees buzzed drowsily about them. When they parted at dawn, she revealed her identity, and made him promise not to tell anyone that she had slept with him. Anchises was horrified to learn that he had uncovered the nakedness of a goddess, and begged her to spare his life. She assured him that he had nothing to fear, and that their son would be famous.[4] Some days later, while Anchises was drinking with his companions, one of them asked: 'Would you not rather sleep with the daughter of So-and-so than with Aphrodite herself?' 'No,' he replied unguardedly. 'Having slept with both, I find the question inept.'

g. Zeus overheard this boast, and threw a thunderbolt at Anchises, which would have killed him outright, had not Aphrodite interposed her girdle, and thus diverted the bolt into the ground at his feet. Nevertheless, the shock so weakened Anchises that he could never stand upright again, and Aphrodite, after bearing his son Aeneas, soon lost her passion for him.[5]

h. One day, the wife of King Cinyras the Cyprian – but some call him King Phoenix of Byblus, and some King Theias the Assyrian – foolishly boasted that her daughter Smyrna was more beautiful even than Aphrodite. The goddess avenged this insult by making Smyrna fall in love with her father and climb into his bed one dark night, when her nurse had made him too drunk to realize what he was doing. Later, Cinyras discovered that he was both the father and grandfather of Smyrna's unborn child and, wild with wrath, seized a sword and chased her from the palace. He overtook her on the brow of a hill, but Aphrodite hurriedly changed Smyrna into a myrrh-tree, which the descending sword split in halves. Out tumbled the infant Adonis. Aphrodite, already repenting of the mischief that she had made, concealed Adonis in a chest, which she entrusted to Persephone, Queen of the Dead, asking her to stow it away in a dark place.

i. Persephone had the curiosity to open the chest, and found Adonis inside. He was so lovely that she lifted him out and brought him up in her own palace. The news reached Aphrodite, who at once visited Tartarus to claim Adonis; and when Persephone would not assent, having by now made him her lover, she appealed to Zeus. Zeus, well aware that Aphrodite also wanted to lie with Adonis, refused to judge so unsavoury a dispute; and transferred it to a lower court, presided over by the Muse Calliope. Calliope's verdict was that Persephone and Aphrodite had equal claims on Adonis – Aphrodite for arranging his birth, Persephone for rescuing him from the chest – but that he should be allowed a brief annual holiday from the amorous demands of both these insatiable goddesses. She therefore divided the year into three equal parts, of which he was to spend one with Persephone, one with Aphrodite, and the third by himself.

Aphrodite did not play fair: by wearing her magic girdle all the time, she persuaded Adonis to give her his own share of the year, grudge the share due to Persephone, and disobey the court-order.[6]

j. Persephone, justly aggrieved, went to Thrace, where she told her benefactor Ares that Aphrodite now preferred Adonis to himself. 'A mere mortal,' she cried, 'and effeminate at that!' Ares grew jealous and, disguised as a wild boar, rushed at Adonis who was out hunting on Mount Lebanon, and gored him to death before Aphrodite's eyes. Anemones sprang from his blood, and his soul descended to Tartarus. Aphrodite went tearfully to Zeus, and pleaded that Adonis should not have to spend more than the gloomier half of the year with Persephone, but might be her companion for the summer months. This Zeus magnanimously granted. But some say that Apollo was the boar, and revenged himself for an injury Aphrodite had done him.[7]

k. Once, to make Adonis jealous, Aphrodite spent several nights at Lilybaeum with Butes the Argonaut; and by him became the mother of Eryx, a king of Sicily. Her children by Adonis were one son, Golgos, founder of Cyprian Golgi, and a daughter, Beroë, founder of Beroea in Thrace; and some say that Adonis, not Dionysus, was the father of her son Priapus.[8]

l. The Fates assigned to Aphrodite one divine duty only, namely to make love; but one day, Athene catching her surreptitiously at work on a loom, complained that her own prerogatives had been infringed and threatened to abandon them altogether. Aphrodite apologized profusely, and has never done a hand's turn of work since.[9]

1. Homer: *Odyssey* viii. 266–367.
2. Diodorus Siculus: iv. 6; Scholiast on Pindar's *Pythian Odes* viii. 24.
3. Pausanias: ix. 31. 2; Scholiast on Apollonius Rhodius: i. 932.
4. *Homeric Hymn to Aphrodite* 45–200; Theocritus: *Idylls* i. 105–7; Hyginus: *Fabula* 94.
5. Servius on Virgil's *Aeneid* ii. 649.
6. Apollodorus: iii. 14. 3–4; Hyginus: *Poetic Astronomy* ii. 7 and *Fabulae* 58, 164, 251; Fulgentius: *Mythology* iii. 8.
7. Servius on Virgil's *Eclogues* x. 18; *Orphic Hymn* lv. 10; Ptolemy Hephaestionos: i. 306.
8. Apollonius Rhodius: iv. 914–19; Diodorus Siculus: iv. 83; Scholiast on Theocruitus's *Idylls* xv. 100; Tzetzes: *On Lycophron* 831.
9. Hesiod: *Theogony* 203–4; Nonnus: *Dionysiaca* xxiv. 274–81.

*

1. The later Hellenes belittled the Great Goddess of the Mediterranean who had long been supreme at Corinth, Sparta, Thespiae, and Athens, by placing her under male tutelage and regarding her solemn sex-orgies as adulterous indiscretions. The net in which Homer represents Aphrodite as caught by Hephaestus was, originally, her own as Goddess of the Sea (see 89. 2), and her priestess seems to have worn it during the spring carnival; the priestess of the Norse Goddess Holle, or Gode, did the same on May Eve.

2. Priapus originated in the rude wooden phallic images which presided over Dionysian orgies. He is made a son of Adonis because of the miniature 'gardens' offered at his festivals. The pear-tree was sacred to Hera as prime goddess of the Peloponnese, which was therefore called Apia (see 64. 4 and 74. 6).

3. Aphrodite Urania ('queen of the mountain') or Erycina ('of the heather') was the nymph-goddess of midsummer. She destroyed the sacred king, who mated with her on a mountain top, as a queen-bee destroys the drone: by tearing out his sexual organs. Hence the heather-loving bees and the red robe in her mountain-top affair with Anchises; hence also the worship of Cybele, the Phrygian Aphrodite of Mount Ida, as a queen-bee, and the ecstatic self-castration of her priests in memory of her lover Attis (see 79. 1). Anchises was one of the many sacred kings who were struck with a ritual thunderbolt after consorting with the Death-in-Life Goddess (see 24. a). In the earliest version of the myth he was killed, but in later ones he escaped: to make good the story of how pious Aeneas, who brought the sacred Palladium to Rome, carried his father away from burning Troy (see 168. c). His name identifies Aphrodite with Isis, whose

husband Osiris, was castrated by Set disguised as a boar; 'Anchises' is, in fact, a synonym of Adonis. He had a shrine at Aegesta near Mount Eryx (Dionysius of Halicarnassus: i. 53) and was therefore said by Virgil to have died at Drepanum, a neighbouring town, and been buried on the mountain (*Aeneid* iii. 710, 759, etc.). Other shrines of Anchises were shown in Arcadia and the Troad. At Aphrodite's shrine on Mount Eryx a golden honeycomb was displayed, said to have been a votive offering presented by Daedalus when he fled to Sicily (see 92. *h*).

4. As Goddess of Death-in-Life, Aphrodite earned many titles which seem inconsistent with her beauty and complaisance. At Athens, she was called the Eldest of the Fates and sister of the Erinnyes: and elsewhere Melaenis ('black one'), a name ingeniously explained by Pausanias as meaning that most love-making takes place at night; Scotia ('dark one'); Androphonos ('man-slayer'); and even, according to Plutarch, Epitymbria ('of the tombs').

5. The myth of Cinyras and Smyrna evidently records a period in history when the sacred king in a matrilineal society decided to prolong his reign beyond the customary length. He did so by celebrating a marriage with the young priestess, nominally his daughter, who was to be queen for the next term, instead of letting another princeling marry her and take away his kingdom (see 65. *1*).

6. Adonis (Phoenician: *adon*, 'lord') is a Greek version of the Syrian demi-god Tammuz, the spirit of annual vegetation. In Syria, Asia Minor and Greece, the goddess's sacred year was at one time divided into three parts, ruled by the Lion, Goat, and Serpent (see 75. *2*). The Goat, emblem of the central part, was the Love-goddess Aphrodite's; the Serpent, emblem of the last part, was the Death-goddess Persephone's; the Lion, emblem of the first part, was sacred to the Birth-goddess, here named Smyrna, who had no claim on Adonis. In Greece, this calendar gave place to a two-season year, bisected either by the equinoxes in the Eastern style, as at Sparta and Delphi, or by the solstices in the Northern style, as at Athens and Thebes; which explains the difference between the respective verdicts of the Mountain-goddess Calliope and Zeus.

7. Tammuz was killed by a boar, like many similar mythical characters – Osiris, Cretan Zeus, Ancaeus of Arcadia (see 157. *e*), Carmanor of Lydia (see 136. *b*), and the Irish hero Diarmuid. This boar seems once to have been a sow with crescent-shaped tusks, the goddess herself as Persephone; but when the year was bisected, the bright half ruled by the sacred king, and the dark half ruled by his tanist, or rival, this rival came in wild-boar disguise – like Set when he killed Osiris, or Finn mac Cool when he killed Diarmuid. Tammuz's blood is allegorical of the anemones that redden the slopes of Mount Lebanon after the winter rains; the Adonia, a mourning festival in honour of Tammuz, was held at Byblus

every spring. Adonis's birth from a myrrh-tree – myrrh being a well-known aphrodisiac – shows the orgiastic character of his rites. The drops of gum which the myrrh-tree shed were supposed to be tears shed for him (Ovid: *Metamorphoses* x. 500 ff.). Hyginus makes Cinyras King of Assyria (*Fabula* 58), perhaps because Tammuz-worship seemed to have originated there.

8. Aphrodite's son Hermaphroditus was a youth with womanish breasts and long hair. Like the *androgyne*, or bearded woman, the hermaphrodite had, of course, its freakish physical counterpart, but as religious concepts both originated in the transition from matriarchy to patriarchy. Hermaphroditus is the sacred king deputizing for the Queen (see 136. 4), and wearing artificial breasts. Androgyne is the mother of a pre-Hellenic clan which has avoided being patriarchalized; in order to keep her magistratal powers or to ennoble children born to her from a slave-father, she assumes a false beard, as was the custom at Argos. Bearded goddesses like the Cyprian Aphrodite, and womanish gods like Dionysus, correspond with these transitional social stages.

9. Harmonia, is, at first sight, a strange name for a daughter borne by Aphrodite to Ares; but, then as now, more than usual affection and harmony prevailed in a state which was at war.

19
ARES'S NATURE AND DEEDS

THRACIAN Ares loves battle for its own sake, and his sister Eris is always stirring up occasions for war by the spread of rumour and the inculcation of jealousy. Like her, he never favours one city or party more than another, but fights on this side or that, as inclination prompts him, delighting in the slaughter of men and the sacking of towns. All his fellow-immortals hate him, from Zeus and Hera downwards, except Eris, and Aphrodite who nurses a perverse passion for him, and greedy Hades who welcomes the bold young fighting-men slain in cruel wars.

b. Ares has not been consistently victorious. Athene, a much more skilful fighter than he, has twice worsted him in battle; and once, the gigantic sons of Aloeus conquered and kept him imprisoned in a brazen vessel for thirteen months until, half dead, he was released by Hermes; and, on another occasion, Heracles sent him running in fear back to Olympus. He professes too deep a contempt for litigation ever to appear in court as a plantiff, and has only once done so as a defendant: that was when his fellow-deities charged him with the wilful murder of Poseidon's son Halirrhothius. He pleaded justification, claiming to have saved his daughter Alcippe, of the House of Cecrops, from being violated by the said Halirrhothius. Since no one had witnessed the incident, except Ares himself, and Alcippe, who naturally confirmed her father's evidence, the court acquitted him. This was the first judgement ever pronounced in a murder trial; and the hill on which the proceedings took place became known as the Areiopagus, a name it still bears.[1]

    1. Apollodorus: iii. 14. 2; Pausanias: i. 21. 7.

*

    1. The Athenians disliked war, except in defence of liberty, or for some other equally cogent reason, and despised the Thracians as barbarous because they made it a pastime.

    2. In Pausanias's account of the murder, Halirrhothius had already succeeded in violating Alcippe. But Halirrhothius can only be a synonym for Poseidon; and Alcippe a synonym for the mare-headed goddess. The myth, in fact, recalls Poseidon's rape of Demeter, and refers to a conquest of Athens by Poseidon's people and the goddess's humiliation at their hands (see 16. *3*). But it has been altered for patriotic reasons, and combined with a legend of some early murder trial. 'Areiopagus' probably means 'the hill of the propitiating Goddess', *areia* being one of Athene's titles.

20

HESTIA'S NATURE AND DEEDS

IT is Hestia's glory that, alone of the great Olympians, she never takes part in wars or disputes. Like Artemis and Athene, moreover, she has always resisted every amorous invitation offered her by gods, Titans, or others; for, after the dethronement of Cronus, when Poseidon and Apollo came forward as rival suitors, she swore by Zeus's head to remain a virgin for ever. At that, Zeus gratefully awarded her the first victim of every public sacrifice,[1] because she had preserved the peace of Olympus.

    b. Drunken Priapus once tried to violate her at a rustic feast attended by the gods, when everyone had fallen asleep from repletion; but an ass brayed aloud, Hestia awoke, screamed to find Priapus about to straddle her, and sent him running off in comic terror.[2]

c. She is the Goddess of the Hearth and in every private house and city hall protects suppliants who flee to her for protection. Universal reverence is paid Hestia, not only as the mildest, most upright and most charitable of all the Olympians, but as having invented the art of building houses; and her fire is so sacred that, if ever a hearth goes cold, either by accident or in token of mourning, it is kindled afresh with the aid of a fire-wheel.[3]

1. *Homeric Hymn to Aphrodite* 21–30.
2. Ovid: *Fasti* vi. 319 ff.
3. Diodorus Siculus: v. 68.

*

1. The centre of Greek life – even at Sparta, where the family had been subordinated to the State – was the domestic hearth, also regarded as a sacrificial altar; and Hestia, as its goddess, represented personal security and happiness, and the sacred duty of hospitality. The story of her marriage-offers from Poseidon and Apollo has perhaps been deduced from the joint worship of these three deities at Delphi. Priapus's attempt to violate her is an anecdotal warning against sacrilegious ill-treatment of women-guests who have come under the protection of the domestic or public hearth: even the ass, a symbol of lust (see 35. *4*), proclaims Priapus's criminal folly.

2. The archaic white aniconic image of the Great Goddess, in use throughout the Eastern Mediterranean, seems to have represented a heap of glowing charcoal, kept alive by a covering of white ash, which was the most cosy and economical means of heating in ancient times; it gave out neither smoke nor flame, and formed the natural centre of family or clan gatherings. At Delphi the charcoal-heap was translated into limestone for out-of-doors use, and became the *omphalos*, or navel-boss, frequently shown in Greek vase-paintings, which marked the supposed centre of the world. This holy object, which has survived the ruin of the shrine, is inscribed with the name of Mother Earth, stands $11\frac{1}{4}$ inches high, and measures $15\frac{1}{2}$ inches across; about the size and shape of a charcoal fire needed to heat a large room. In Classical times the Pythoness had an attendant priest who induced her trance by burning barley grains, hemp, and laurel over an oil lamp in an enclosed space, and then interpreted what she said. But it is likely that the hemp, laurel, and barley were once laid on the hot ashes of the charcoal mound, which is a simpler and more effective way of producing narcotic fumes (see 51. *b*). Numerous tri-

angular or leaf-shaped ladles in stone or clay have been found in Cretan and Mycenaean shrines – some of them showing signs of great heat – and seem to have been used for tending the sacred fire. The charcoal mound was sometimes built on a round, three-legged clay table, painted red, white, and black, which are the moon's colours (see 90. 3); examples have been found in the Peloponnese, Crete, and Delos – one of them, from a chamber tomb at Zafer Papoura near Cnossus, had the charcoal still piled on it.

21

APOLLO'S NATURE AND DEEDS

APOLLO, Zeus's son by Leto, was a seven-months' child, but gods grow up swiftly. Themis fed him on nectar and ambrosia, and when the fourth day dawned he called for bow and arrows, with which Hephaestus at once provided him. On leaving Delos he made straight for Mount Parnassus, where the serpent Python, his mother's enemy, was lurking; and wounded him severely with arrows. Python fled to the Oracle of Mother Earth at Delphi, a city so named in honour of the monster Delphyne, his mate; but Apollo dared follow him into the shrine, and there despatched him beside the sacred chasm.[1]

b. Mother Earth reported this outrage to Zeus, who not only ordered Apollo to visit Tempe for purification, but instituted the Pythian Games, in honour of Python, over which he was to preside penitentially. Quite unabashed, Apollo disregarded Zeus's command to visit Tempe. Instead, he went to Aigialaea for purification, accompanied by Artemis; and then, disliking the place, sailed to Tarrha in Crete, where King Carmanor performed the ceremony.[2]

c. On his return to Greece, Apollo sought out Pan, the disreputable old goat-legged Arcadian god and, having coaxed him to reveal the art of prophecy, seized the Delphic Oracle and retained its priestess, called the Pythoness, in his own service.

d. Leto, on hearing the news, came with Artemis to Delphi, where she turned aside to perform some private rite in a sacred grove. The giant Tityus interrupted her devotions, and was trying to violate her, when Apollo and Artemis, hearing screams, ran up and killed him with a volley of arrows – a vengeance which Zeus, Tityus's father, was pleased to consider a pious one. In Tartarus, Tityus was stretched out for torment, his arms and legs securely pegged to the ground; the area covered was no less than nine acres, and two vultures ate his liver.[3]

e. Next, Apollo killed the satyr Marsyas, a follower of the goddess Cybele. This was how it came about. One day, Athene made a double-flute from stag's bones, and played on it at a banquet of the gods. She could not understand, at first, why Hera and Aphrodite were laughing silently behind their hands, although her music seemed to delight the other deities; she therefore went away by herself into a Phrygian wood, took up the flute again beside a stream, and watched her image in the water, as she played. Realizing at once how ludicrous that bluish face and those swollen cheeks made her look, she threw down the flute, and laid a curse on anyone who picked it up.

f. Marsyas was the innocent victim of this curse. He stumbled upon the flute, which he had no sooner put to his lips than it played of itself, inspired by the memory of Athene's music; and he went about Phrygia in Cybele's train, delighting the ignorant peasants. They cried out that Apollo himself could not have made better music, even on his lyre, and Marsyas was foolish enough not to contradict them. This, of course, provoked the anger of Apollo, who invited him to a contest, the winner of which should inflict whatever punishment he pleased on the loser. Marsyas consented, and Apollo impanelled the Muses as a jury. The contest proved an equal one, the Muses being charmed by both instruments, until Apollo cried out to Marsyas: 'I challenge you to do with your instrument as much as I can do with mine. Turn it upside down, and both play and sing at the same time.'

g. This, with a flute, was manifestly impossible, and Marsyas failed to meet the challenge. But Apollo reversed his lyre, and sang such delightful hymns in honour of the Olympian gods that the Muses could not do less than give the verdict in his favour. Then, for all his pretended sweetness, Apollo took a most cruel revenge on Marsyas: flaying him alive and nailing his skin to a pine (or, some say, to a plane-tree), near the source of the river which now bears his name.[4]

h. Afterwards, Apollo won a second musical contest, at which King Midas presided; this time he beat Pan. Becoming the acknowledged god of Music, he has ever since played on his seven-stringed lyre while the gods banquet. Another of his duties was once to guard the herds and flocks which the gods kept in Pieria; but he later delegated this task to Hermes.[5]

i. Though Apollo refuses to bind himself in marriage, he has got many nymphs and mortal women with child; among them, Phthia, on whom he fathered Dorus and his brothers; and Thalia the Muse, on whom he fathered the Corybantes; and Coronis, on whom he fathered Asclepius; and Aria, on whom he fathered Miletus; and Cyrene, on whom he fathered Aristaeus.[6]

j. He also seduced the nymph Dryope, who was tending her father's flocks on Mount Oeta in the company of her friends, the Hamadryads. Apollo disguised himself as a tortoise, with which they all played and, when Dryope put him into her bosom, he turned into a hissing serpent, scared away the Hamadryads, and enjoyed her. She bore him Amphissus, who founded the city of Oeta and built a temple to his father; there Dryope served as priestess until, one day, the Hamadryads stole her away, and left a poplar in her place.[7]

k. Apollo was not invariably successful in love. On one occasion he tried to steal Marpessa from Idas, but she remained true to her husband. On another, he pursued Daphne, the mountain nymph, a priestess of Mother Earth, daughter of the river Peneius in Thessaly; but when he overtook her, she cried out to Mother Earth who, in the nick of time, spirited her away to Crete, where she bcame known as Pasiphaë. Mother Earth left a laurel-tree in her place, and from its leaves Apollo made a wreath to console himself.[8]

l. His attempt on Daphne, it must be added, was no sudden impulse. He had long been in love with her, and had brought about the death of his rival, Leucippus, son of Oenomaus, who disguised himself as a girl and joined Daphne's mountain revels. Apollo, knowing of this by divination, advised the mountain nymphs to bathe naked, and thus make sure that everyone in their company was a woman; Leucippus's imposture was at once discovered, and the nymphs tore him to pieces.[9]

m. There was also the case of the beautiful youth Hyacinthus, a Spartan prince, with whom not only the poet Thamyris fell in love – the first man who ever wooed one of his own sex – but Apollo himself, the first god to do so. Apollo did not find Thamyris a serious rival; having overheard his boast that he could surpass the Muses in song, he maliciously reported it to them, and they at once robbed Thamyris of his sight, his voice, and his memory for harping. But the West Wind had also taken a fancy to Hyacinthus, and became insanely jealous of Apollo, who was one day teaching the boy how to hurl a discus, when the West Wind caught it in mid-air, dashed it against Hyacinthus's skull, and killed him. From his blood sprang the hyacinth flower, on which his initial letters are still to be traced.[10]

n. Apollo earned Zeus's anger only once after the famous conspiracy to dethrone him. This was when his son Asclepius, the physician, had the temerity to resurrect a dead man, and thus rob Hades of a subject; Hades naturally lodged a complaint on Olympus, Zeus killed Asclepius with a thunderbolt, and Apollo in revenge killed the Cyclopes. Zeus was enraged at the loss of his armourers, and would have banished Apollo to Tartarus for ever, had not Leto pleaded for his forgiveness and undertaken that he would mend his ways. The sentence was reduced to one year's hard labour, which Apollo was to serve in the sheep-folds of King Admetus of Therae. Obeying Leto's advice, Apollo not only carried out the sentence humbly, but conferred great benefits on Admetus.[11]

o. Having learned his lesson, he thereafter preached moderation in all things: the phrases 'Know thyself!' and 'Nothing in excess!' were always on his lips. He brought the Muses down from their home on Mount Helicon to Delphi, tamed their wild frenzy, and led them in formal and decorous dances.[12]

1. Hyginus: *Fabula* 140; Apollodorus: i. 4. 1; *Homeric Hymn to Apollo* 300–306; Scholiast on Apollonius Rhodius: ii. 706.
2. Aelian: *Varia Historia* iii. 1; Plutarch: *Greek Questions* 12; *Why Oracles Are Silent* 15; Pausanias: ii. 7. 7; x. 16. 3.
3. Apollodorus: i. 4. 1; Pausanias: ii. 30.3 and x. 6. 5; Plutarch: *Greek Questions* 12; Hyginus: *Fabula* 55; Homer: *Odyssey* xi. 576 ff.; Pindar: *Pythian Odes* iv. 90 ff.
4. Diodorus Siculus: iii. 58–9; Hyginus: *Fabula* 165; Apollodorus: i. 4. 2; Second Vatican Mythographer: 115; Pliny: *Natural History* xvi. 89.
5. Hyginus: *Fabula* 191; Homer: *Iliad* i. 603.
6. Apollodorus: i. 7. 6; i. 3. 4; iii. 10. 3; iii. 1. 2; Pausanias: x. 17. 3.
7. Antoninus Liberalis: 32; Stephanus of Byzantium *sub* Dryope; Ovid: *Metamorphoses* ix. 325 ff.
8. Apollodorus: i. 7. 9; Plutarch: *Agis* 9.
9. Hyginus: *Fabula* 203; Pausanias: viii. 20. 2; x. 5. 3; Parthenius: *Erotica* 15; Tzetzes: *On Lycophron* 6.
10. Homer: *Iliad* ii. 595–600; Lucian: *Dialogues of the Gods* 14; Apollodorus: i. 3.3; Pausanias: iii. 1. 3.
11. Apollodorus: iii. 10. 4; Diodorus Siculus: iv. 71.
12. Homer: *Iliad* i. 603–4; Plutarch: *On the Pythian Oracles* 17.

*

1. Apollo's history is a confusing one. The Greeks made him the son of Leto, a goddess known as Lat in Southern Palestine (see 14. *2*), but he was also a god of the Hyperboreans ('beyond-the-North-Wind-men'), whom Hecataeus (Diodorus Siculus: ii. 47) clearly identified with the British, though Pindar (*Pythian Odes* x. 50–55) regarded them as Libyans. Delos was the centre of this Hyperborean cult which, it seems, extended south-eastward to Nabataea and Palestine, north-westward to Britain, and included Athens. Visits were constantly exchanged between the states united in this cult (Diodorus Siculus: *loc cit.*).

2. Apollo, among the Hyperboreans, sacrificed hetacombs of asses (Pindar: *loc. cit.*), which identifies him with the 'Child Horus', whose defeat of his enemy Set the Egyptians annually celebrated by driving wild asses over a precipice (Plutarch: *On Isis and Osiris* 30). Horus was avenging Set's murder of his father Osiris – the sacred king, beloved of the Triple Moon-goddess Isis, or Lat, whom his tanist sacrificed at midsummer and midwinter, and of whom Horus was himself the reincarnation. The myth of Leto's pursuit by Python corresponds with the myth of Isis's pursuit by Set (during the seventy-two hottest days of the year). Moreover, Python is identified with Typhon, the Greek Set (see 36. *1*), in the *Homeric Hymn to Apollo*, and by the scholiast on Apollonius Rhodius. The Hyperborean Apollo is, in fact, a Greek Horus.

3. But the myth has been given a political turn: Python is said to have been sent against Leto by Hera, who had borne him parthenogenetically to spite Zeus (*Homeric Hymn to Apollo* 305); and Apollo, after killing Python (and presumably also his mate Delphyne), seizes the oracular shrine of Mother Earth at Delphi – for Hera was Mother Earth, or Delphyne in her prophetic aspect. It seems that certain Northern Hellenes, allied with Thraco-Libyans, invaded Central Greece and the Peloponnese, where they were opposed by the pre-Hellenic worshippers of the Earth-goddess, but captured her chief oracular shrines. At Delphi, they destroyed the sacred oracular serpent – a similar serpent was kept in the Erechtheum at Athens (see 25. *2*) – and took over the oracle in the name of their god Apollo Smintheus. Smintheus ('mousy'), like Esmun the Canaanite god of healing, had a curative mouse for his emblem. The invaders agreed to identify him with Apollo, the Hyperborean Horus, worshipped by their allies. To placate local opinion at Delphi, regular funeral games were instituted in honour of the dead hero Python, and his priestess was retained in office.

4. The Moon-goddess Brizo ('soother') of Delos, indistinguishable from Leto, may be identified with the Hyperborean Triple-goddess Brigit, who became Christianized as St Brigit, or St Bride. Brigit was patroness of all the arts, and Apollo followed her example. The attempt on Leto by the giant Tityus suggests an abortive rising by the mountain-eers of Phocis against the invaders.

5. Apollo's victories over Marsyas and Pan commemorate the Hellenic conquests of Phrygia and Arcadia, and the consequent supersession in those regions of wind instruments by stringed ones, except among the peasantry. Masyas's punishment may refer to the ritual flaying of a sacred king – as Athene stripped Pallas of his magical aegis (see 9. *a*) – or the removal of the entire bark from an alder-shoot, to make a shepherd's pipe, the alder being personified as a god or demi-god (see 28. *1* and 57. *1*). Apollo was claimed as an ancestor of the Dorian Greeks, and of the Milesians, who paid him especial honours. The Corybantes, dancers at the Winter Solstice festival, were called his children by Thalia the Muse, because he was god of Music.

6. His pursuit of Daphne the Mountain-nymph, daughter of the river Peneius, and priestess of Mother Earth, refers apparently to the Hellenic capture of Tempe, where the goddess Daphoene ('bloody one') was worshipped by a college of orgiastic laurel-chewing Maenads (see 46. *2* and 51. *2*). After suppressing the college – Plutarch's account sug-gests that the priestesses fled to Crete, where the Moon-goddess was called Pasiphaë (see 88. *e*) – Apollo took over the laurel which, after-wards, only the Pythoness might chew. Daphoene will have been mare-headed at Tempe, as at Phigalia (see 16. *5*); Leucippus ('white horse') was the sacred king of the local horse cult, annually torn in pieces by the wild women, who bathed after his murder to purify themselves, not before (see 22. *1* and 150. *1*).

7. Apollo's seduction of Dryope on Oeta perhaps records the local supersession of an oak cult by a cult of Apollo, to whom the poplar was sacred (see 42. *d*); as does his seduction of Aria. His tortoise disguise is a reference to the lyre he had bought from Hermes (see 17. *d*). Phthia's name suggests that she was an autumnal aspect of the goddess. The unsuccessful attempt on Marpessa ('snatcher'), seems to record Apollo's failure to seize a Messenian shrine: that of the Grain-goddess as Sow (see 74. *4*). Apollo's servitude to Admetus of Pherae may recall a historical event: the humiliation of the Apollonian priesthood in punishment for their massacre of a pre-Hellenic smith-guild which had enjoyed Zeus's protection.

8. The myth of Hyacinthus, which seems at first sight no more than a sentimental fable told to explain the mark on the Greek hyacinth (see 165. *j* and *2*) concerns the Cretan Flower-hero Hyacinthus (see 159. *4*), also apparently called Narcissus (see 85. *2*), whose worship was intro-duced into Mycenaean Greece, and who named the later summer month of Hyacinthius in Crete, Rhodes, Cos, Thera, and at Sparta. Dorian Apollo usurped Hyacinthus's name at Tarentum, where he had a hero

tomb (Polybius: viii. 30); and at Amyclae, a Mycenaean city, another 'tomb of Hyacinthus' became the foundation of Apollo's throne. Apollo was an immortal by this time, Hyacinthus reigned only for a season: his death by a discus recalls that of his nephew Acrisius (see 73. 3).

9. Coronis ('crow'), mother of Asclepius by Apollo, was probably a title of Athene's (see 25. 5); but the Athenians always denied that she had children, and disguised the myth (see 50. b).

10. In Classical times, music, poetry, philosophy, astronomy, mathematics, medicine, and science came under Apollo's control. As the enemy of barbarism, he stood for moderation in all things, and the seven strings of his lute were connected with the seven vowels of the later Greek alphabet (see 52. 8), given mystical significance, and used for therapeutic music. Finally, because of his identification with the Child Horus, a solar concept, he was worshipped as the sun, whose Corinthian cult had been taken over by Solar Zeus; and his sister Artemis was, rightly, identified with the moon.

11. Cicero, in his essay On the Nature of the Gods (iii. 23), makes Apollo son of Leto only the fourth of an ancient series: he distinguishes Apollo son of Hephaestus, Apollo the father of the Cretan Corybantes, and the Apollo who gave Arcadia its laws.

12. Apollo's killing of the Python is not, however, so simple a myth as at first appears, because the stone omphalos on which the Pythoness sat was traditionally the tomb of the hero incarnate in the serpent, whose oracles she delivered (Hesychius sub Archus's Mound; Varro: On the Latin Languages vii. 17). The Hellenic priest of Apollo usurped the functions of the sacred king who, legitimately and ceremonially, had always killed his predecessor, the hero. This is proved by the Stepteria rite recorded in Plutarch's Why Oracles Are Silent (15). Every ninth year a hut representing a king's dwelling was built on the threshing floor at Delphi and a night attack suddenly made on it by . . . [here there is a gap in the account] . . . The table of first-fruits was overturned, the hut set on fire, and the torchmen fled from the sanctuary without looking behind them. Afterwards the youth who had taken part in the deed went to Tempe for purification, whence he returned in triumph, crowned and carrying a laurel branch.

13. The sudden concerted assault on the inmate of the hut recalls the mysterious murder of Romulus by his companions. It also recalls the yearly Buphonia sacrifice at Athens when the priests who had killed the Zeus-ox with a double-axe, fled without looking behind them; then ate the flesh at a communal feast (see 53. 7), staged a mimic resurrection of the ox, and brought up the axe for trial on a charge of sacrilege.

14. At Delphi, as at Cnossus, the sacred king must have reigned until the ninth year (see 88. 6). The boy went to Tempe doubtless because the Apollo cult had originated there.

ARTEMIS'S NATURE AND DEEDS

ARTEMIS, Apollo's sister, goes armed with bow and arrows and, like him, has the power both to send plagues or sudden death among mortals, and to heal them. She is the protectress of little children, and of all sucking animals, but she also loves the chase, especially that of stags.

b. One day, while she was still a three-year-old child, her father Zeus, on whose knees she was sitting, asked her what presents she would like. Artemis answered at once: 'Pray give me eternal virginity; as many names as my brother Apollo; a bow and arrows like his; the office of bringing light; a saffron hunting tunic with a red hem reaching to my knees; sixty young ocean nymphs, all of the same age, as my maids of honour; twenty river nymphs from Amnisus in Crete, to take care of my buskins and feed my hounds when I am not out shooting; all the mountains in the world; and, lastly, any city you care to choose for me, but one will be enough, because I intend to live on mountains most of the time. Unfortunately, women in labour will often be invoking me, since my mother Leto carried and bore me without pains, and the Fates have therefore made me patroness of childbirth.'[1]

c. She stretched up for Zeus's beard, and he smiled proudly, saying: 'With children like you, I need not fear Hera's jealous anger! You shall have all this, and more besides: not one, but thirty cities, and a share in many others, both on the mainland and in the archipelago; and I appoint you guardian of their roads and harbours.'[2]

d. Artemis thanked him, sprang from his knee, and went first to Mount Leucus in Crete, and next to the Ocean stream, where she chose numerous nine-year-old nymphs for her attendants; their mothers were delighted to let them go.[3] On Hephaestus's invitation, she then visited the Cyclopes on the Island of Lipara, and found them hammering away at a horse-trough for Poseidon. Brontes, who had been instructed to make whatever she wanted, took her on his knee; but, disliking his endearments, she tore a handful of hair from his chest, where a bald patch remained to the day of his death; anyone might have supposed that he had the mange. The nymphs were terrified at the wild appearance of the Cyclopes, and at the din of their smithy – well they might be, for whenever a little girl is disobedient her mother threatens her with Brontes, Arges, or Steropes. But Artemis boldly told them to abandon Poseidon's trough for a while, and make her a silver bow, with a quiverful of arrows, in return for which they should eat the first prey she brought down.[4] With these weapons she went to Arcadia, where Pan was engaged in cutting up a lynx to feed his bitches and their whelps. He gave her three lop-eared hounds, two parti-coloured and one spotted, together capable of dragging live lions back to their kennels; and seven swift hounds from Sparta.[5]

e. Having captured alive two couple of horned hinds, she harnessed them to a golden chariot with golden bits, and drove north over Thracian Mount Haemus. She cut her first pine torch on Mysian Olympus, and lit it at the cinders of a lightning-struck tree. She tried her silver bow four times: her first two targets were trees; her third, a wild beast; her fourth, a city of unjust men.[6]

f. Then she returned to Greece, where the Amnisian nymphs unyoked her hinds, rubbed them down, fed them on the same quick-growing trefoil, from Hera's pasture, which the steeds of Zeus eat, and watered them from golden troughs.[7]

g. Once the River-god Alpheius, son of Thetis, dared fall in love with Artemis and pursue her across Greece; but she came to Letrini in Elis (or, some say, as far as the island of Ortygia near Syracuse), where she daubed her face, and those of all her nymphs, with white mud, so that she became indistinguishable from the rest of the company. Alpheius was forced to retire, pursued by mocking laughter.[8]

h. Artemis requires the same perfect chastity from her companions as she practises herself. When Zeus had seduced one of them, Callisto, daughter of Lycaon, Artemis noticed that she was with child. Changing her into a bear, she shouted to the pack, and Callisto would have been hunted to death had she not been caught up to Heaven by Zeus who, later, set her image among the stars. But some say that Zeus himself changed Callisto into a bear, and that jealous Hera arranged for Artemis to chase her in error. Callisto's child, Arcas, was saved, and became the ancestor of the Arcadians.[9]

i. On another occasion, Actaeon, son of Aristaeus, stood leaning against a rock near Orchomenus when he happened to see Artemis bathing in a stream not far off, and stayed to watch. Lest he should afterwards dare boast to his companions that she had displayed herself naked in his presence, she changed him into a stag and, with his own pack of fifty hounds, tore him to pieces.[10]

1. Callimachus: *Hymn to Artemis* 1 ff.
2. *Ibid.*: 26 ff.
3. *Ibid.*: 40 ff.
4. *Ibid.*: 47 ff.
5. *Ibid.*: 69 ff.
6. *Ibid.*: 110 ff.
7. *Ibid.*: 162 ff.
8. Pausanias: vi. 22. 5; Scholiast on Pindar's *Pythian Odes* ii. 12.
9. Hyginus: *Poetic Astronomy* ii. 1; Apollodorus: iii. 8. 2.
10. Hyginus: *Fabula* 181; Pausanias: ix. 2. 3.

*

1. The Maiden of the Silver Bow, whom the Greeks enrolled in the Olympian family, was the youngest member of the Artemis Triad, 'Artemis' being one more title of the Triple Moon-goddess; and had a right therefore to feed her hinds on trefoil, a symbol of trinity. Her silver bow stood for the new moon. Yet the Olympian Artemis was more than a Maiden. Elsewhere, at Ephesus, for instance, she was worshipped in her second person, as Nymph, an orgiastic Aphrodite with a male consort, and the date-palm (see 14. *a*), stag, and bee (see 18. *3*) for her principal emblems. Her midwifery belongs, rather, to the Crone, as do her arrows of death; and the nine-year-old priestesses are a reminder that the moon's death number is three times three. She recalls the Cretan 'Lady of the Wild Things', apparently the supreme Nymph-goddess of archaic totem societies; and the ritual bath in which Actaeon surprised her, like the horned hinds of her chariot (see 125. *a*) and the quails of Ortygia (see 14. *3*), seems more appropriate to the Nymph than the Maiden. Actaeon was, it seems, a sacred king of the pre-Hellenic stag cult, torn to pieces at the end of his reign of fifty months, namely half a Great Year; his co-king, or tanist, reigning for the remainder. The Nymph properly took her bath after, not before, the murder. There are numerous parallels to this ritual custom in Irish and Welsh myth, and as late as the first century A.D. a man dressed in a stag's skin was periodically chased and killed on the Arcadian Mount Lycaeum (Plutarch: *Greek Questions* 39). The hounds will have been white with red ears, like the 'hounds of Hell' in Celtic mythology. There was a fifth horned hind which escaped Artemis (see 125. *a*).

2. The myth of her pursuit by Alpheius seems modelled on that of his hopeless pursuit of Arethusa which turned her into a spring and him into a river (Pausanias: v. 7. 2), and may have been invented to account for the gypsum, or white clay, with which the priestesses of

Artemis Alpheia at Letrini and Ortygia daubed their faces in honour of
the White Goddess. *Alph* denotes both whiteness and cereal produce:
alphos is leprosy; *alphe* is gain; *alphiton* is pearl barley; *Alphito* was the
White Grain-goddess as Sow. Artemis's most famous statue at Athens
was called 'the White-browed' (Pausanias: i. 26. 4). The meaning of
Artemis is doubtful: it may be 'strong-limbed', from *artemes*; or 'she who
cuts up', since the Spartans called her *Artamis*, from *artao*; or 'the lofty
convener', from *airo* and *themis*; or the 'themis' syllable may mean
'water', because the moon was regarded as the source of all water.

3. Ortygia, 'Quail Island', near Delos, was also sacred to Artemis
(see 14. *a*).

4. The myth of Callisto has been told to account for the two small
girls, dressed as she-bears, who appeared in the Attic festival of Brau-
ronian Artemis, and for the traditional connexion between Artemis and
the Great Bear. But an earlier version of the myth may be presumed, in
which Zeus seduced Artemis, although she first transformed herself into
a bear and then daubed her face with gypsum, in an attempt to escape
him. Artemis was, originally, the ruler of the stars, but lost them to Zeus.

5. Why Brontes had his hair plucked out is doubtful; Callimachus may
be playfully referring to some well-known picture of the event, in which
the paint had worn away from the Cyclops' chest.

6. As 'Lady of Wild Things', or patroness of all the totem clans,
Artemis had been annually offered a living holocaust of totem beasts,
birds, and plants, and this sacrifice survived in Classical time at Patrae, a
Calydonian city (Pausanias: iv. 32. 6); she was there called Artemis
Laphria. At Messene a similar burnt sacrifice was offered to her by the
Curetes, as totem-clan representatives (iv. 32. 9); and another is recorded
from Hierapolis, where the victims were hung to the trees of an artificial
forest inside the goddess's temple (Lucian: *On the Syrian Goddess* 41).

7. The olive-tree was sacred to Athene, the date-palm to Isis and Lat.
A Middle Minoan bead-seal in my possession shows the goddess standing
beside a palm, dressed in a palm-leaf skirt, and with a small palm-tree held
in her hand; she watches a New Year bull-calf being born from a date-
cluster. On the other side of the tree is a dying bull, evidently the royal
bull of the Old Year.

23

HEPHAESTUS'S NATURE AND DEEDS

HEPHAESTUS, the Smith-god, was so weakly at birth that his disgusted
mother, Hera, dropped him from the height of Olympus, to rid herself

of the embarrassment that his pitiful appearance caused her. He survived this misadventure, however, without bodily damage, because he
fell into the sea, where Thetis and Eurynome were at hand to rescue
him. These gentle goddesses kept him with them in an underwater
grotto, where he set up his first smithy and rewarded their kindness by
making them all sorts of ornamental and useful objects.[1]

One day, when nine years had passed, Hera met Thetis, who happened to be wearing a brooch of his workmanship, and asked: 'My
dear, where in the world did you find that wonderful jewel?'

Thetis hesitated before replying, but Hera forced the truth from her.
At once she fetched Hephaestus back to Olympus, where she set him
up in a much finer smithy, with twenty bellows working day and night,
made much of him, and arranged that he should marry Aphrodite.

b. Hephaestus became so far reconciled with Hera that he dared
reproach Zeus himself for hanging her by the wrists from Heaven
when she rebelled against him. But silence would have been wiser,
because angry Zeus only heaved him down from Olympus a second
time. He was a whole day falling. On striking the earth of the island of
Lemnos, he broke both legs and, though immortal, had little life left in
his body when the islanders found him. Afterwards pardoned and restored to Olympus, he could walk only with golden leg-supports.[2]

c. Hephaestus is ugly and ill-tempered, but has great power in his
arms and shoulders, and all his work is of matchless skill. He once made
a set of golden mechanical women to help him in his smithy; they can
even talk, and undertake the most difficult tasks he entrusts to them.
And he owns a set of three-legged tables with golden wheels, ranged
around his workshop, which can run by themselves to a meeting of the
gods, and back again.[3]

1. Homer: *Iliad* xviii. 394–409.
2. *Ibid.*: i. 586–94.
3. *Ibid.*: xviii. 368 ff.

*

1. Hephaestus and Athene shared temples at Athens, and his name
may be a worn-down form of *hemero-phaistos*, 'he who shines by day'
(i.e. the sun), whereas Athene was the moon-goddess, 'she who shines by
night', patroness of smithcraft and of all mechanical arts. It is not generally
recognized that every Bronze Age tool, weapon, or utensil had magical
properties, and that the smith was something of a sorcerer. Thus, of the

three persons of the Brigit Moon-triad (see 21. 4), one presided over poets, another over smiths, the third over physicians. When the goddess has been dethroned the smith is elevated to godhead. That the Smith-god hobbles is a tradition found in regions as far apart as West Africa and Scandinavia; in primitive times smiths may have been purposely lamed to prevent them from running off and joining enemy tribes. But a hobbling partridge-dance was also performed in erotic orgies connected with the mysteries of smithcraft (see 92. 2) and, since Hephaestus had married Aphrodite, he may have been hobbled only once a year: at the Spring Festival.

Metallurgy first reached Greece from the Aegean Islands. The importation of finely worked Helladic bronze and gold perhaps accounts for the myth that Hephaestus was guarded in a Lemnian grotto by Thetis and Eurynome, titles of the Sea-goddess who created the universe. The nine years which he spent in the grotto show his subservience to the moon. His fall, like that of Cephalus (see 89. *j*), Talos (see 92. *b*) Sciron (see 96. *f*), Iphitus (see 135. *b*), and others, was the common fate of the sacred king in many parts of Greece when their reigns ended. The golden leg-supports were perhaps designed to raise his sacred heel from the ground.

2. Hephaestus's twenty three-legged tables have, it seems, much the same origin as the Gasterocheires who built Tiryns (see 73. *3*), being golden sun-disks with three legs, like the heraldic device of the Isle of Man doubtless bordering some early icon which showed Hephaestus being married to Aphrodite. They represent three-season years, and denote the length of his reign; he dies at the beginning of the twentieth year, when a close approximation of solar and lunar time occurs; this cycle was officially recognized at Athens only towards the close of the fifth century B.C., but had been discovered several hundred years before (*White Goddess*, pp. 284 and 291). Hephaestus was connected with Vulcan's forges in the volcanic Lipari islands because Lemnos, a seat of his worship, is volcanic and a jet of natural asphaltic gas which issued from the summit of Mount Moschylus had burned steadily for centuries (Tzetzes: *On Lycophron* 227; Heyschius *sub* Moschylus). A similar jet, described by Bishop Methodius in the fourth century A.D., burned on Mount Lemnos in Lycia and was still alight in 1801. Hephaestus had a shrine on both these mountains. Lemnos (probably from *leibein*, 'she who pours out') was the name of the Great Goddess of this matriarchal island (Hecataeus, quoted by Stephanus of Byzantium *sub* Lemnos – see 149. *1*).

24

DEMETER'S NATURE AND DEEDS

THOUGH the priestesses of Demeter, goddess of the cornfield, initiate brides and bridegrooms into the secrets of the couch, she has no husband of her own. While still young and gay, she bore Core and the lusty Iacchus to Zeus, her brother, out of wedlock.[1] She also bore Plutus to the Titan Iasius, or Iasion, with whom she fell in love at the wedding of Cadmus and Harmonia. Inflamed by the nectar which flowed like water at the feast, the lovers slipped out of the house and lay together openly in a thrice-ploughed field. On their return, Zeus guessing from their demeanour and the mud on their arms and legs what they had been at, and enraged that Iasius should have dared to touch Demeter, struck him dead with a thunderbolt. But some say that Iasius was killed by his brother Dardanus, or torn to pieces by his own horses.[2]

b. Demeter herself has a gentle soul, and Erysichthon, son of Tropias, was one of the few men with whom she ever dealt harshly. At the head of twenty companions, Erysichthon dared invade a grove which the Pelasgians had planted for her at Dotium, and began cutting down the sacred trees, to provide timber for his new banqueting hall. Demeter assumed the form of Nicippe, priestess of the grove, and mildly ordered Erysichthon to desist. It was only when he threatened her with his axe that she revealed herself in splendour and condemned him to suffer perpetual hunger, however much he might eat. Back he went to dinner, and gorged all day at his parents' expense, growing hungrier and thinner the more he ate, until they could no longer afford to keep him supplied with food, and he became a beggar in the streets, eating filth. Contrariwise, on Pandareus the Cretan, who stole Zeus's golden dog and thus avenged her for the killing of Iasius, Demeter bestowed the royal gift of never suffering from the belly-ache.[3]

c. Demeter lost her gaiety for ever when young Core, afterwards called Persephone, was taken from her. Hades fell in love with Core, and went to ask Zeus's leave to marry her. Zeus feared to offend his eldest brother by a downright refusal, but knew also that Demeter would not forgive him if Core were committed to Tartarus; he therefore answered politically that he could neither give nor withhold his consent. This emboldened Hades to abduct the girl, as she was picking flowers in a meadow – it may have been at Sicilian Enna; or at Attic Colonus; or at Hermione; or somewhere in Crete, or near Pisa, or near Lerna; or beside Arcadian Pheneus, or at Boeotian Nysa, or anywhere else in the widely separated regions which Demeter visited in her wandering search for Core. But her own priests say that it was at Eleusis. She sought Core without rest for nine days and nights, neither eating nor drinking, and calling fruitlessly all the while. The only news she could get came from old Hecate, who early one morning had heard Core crying 'A rape! A rape!' but, on hurrying to the rescue, found no sign of her.[4]

d. On the tenth day, after a disagreeable encounter with Poseidon among the herds of Oncus, Demeter came in disguise to Eleusis, where King Celeus and his wife Metaneira entertained her hospitably; and she was invited to remain as wet-nurse to Demophoön, the newly-born prince. Their lame daughter Iambe tried to console Demeter with comically lascivious verses, and the dry-nurse, old Baubo, persuaded her to drink barley-water by a jest: she groaned as if in travail and, unexpectedly, produced from beneath her skirt Demeter's own son Iacchus, who leaped into his mother's arms and kissed her.

e. 'Oh, how greedily you drink!' cried Abas, an elder son of Celeus's, as Demeter gulped the pitcherful of barley-water, which was flavoured with mint. Demeter threw him a grim look, and he was metamorphosed into a lizard. Somewhat ashamed of herself, Demeter now decided to do Celeus a service, by making Demophoön immortal. That night she held him over the fire, to burn away his mortality. Metaneira, who was the daughter of Amphictyon, happened to enter the hall before the process was complete, and broke the spell; so Demophoön died. 'Mine is an unlucky house!' Celeus complained, weeping at the fate of his two sons, and thereafter was called Dysaules. 'Dry your tears, Dysaules,' said Demeter. 'You still have three sons, including Triptolemus on whom I intend to confer such great gifts that you will forget your double loss.'

f. For Triptolemus, who herded his father's cattle, had recognized Demeter and given her the news she needed: ten days before this his brothers Eumolpus, a shepherd, and Eubuleus, a swineherd, had been out in the fields, feeding their beasts, when the earth suddenly gaped open, engulfing Eubuleus's swine before his very eyes; then, with a heavy thud of hooves, a chariot drawn by black horses appeared, and dashed down the chasm. The chariot-driver's face was invisible, but his right arm was tightly clasped around a shrieking girl. Eumolpus had been told of the event by Eubuleus, and made it the subject for a lament.

g. Armed with this evidence, Demeter summoned Hecate. Together they approached Helius, who sees everything, and forced him to admit that Hades had been the villain, doubtless with the connivance of his brother Zeus. Demeter was so angry that, instead of returning to Olympus, she continued to wander about the earth, forbidding the trees to yield fruit and the herbs to grow, until the race of men stood in danger of extinction. Zeus, ashamed to visit Demeter in person at Eleusis, sent her first a message by Iris (of which she took no notice), and then a deputation of the Olympian gods, with conciliatory gifts, begging her to be reconciled to his will. But she would not return to Olympus, and swore that the earth must remain barren until Core had been restored.

h. Only one course of action remained for Zeus. He sent Hermes with a message to Hades: 'If you do not restore Core, we are all un-done!' and with another to Demeter: 'You may have your daughter again, on the single condition that she has not yet tasted the food of the dead.'

i. Because Core had refused to eat so much as a crust of bread ever since her abduction, Hades was obliged to cloak his vexation, telling her mildly: 'My child, you seem to be unhappy here, and your mother weeps for you. I have therefore decided to send you home.'

j. Core's tears ceased to flow, and Hermes helped her to mount his chariot. But, just as she was setting off for Eleusis, one of Hades's gardeners, by name Ascalaphus, began to cry and hoot derisively. 'Having seen the Lady Core,' he said, 'pick a pomegranate from a tree in your orchard, and eat seven seeds, I am ready to bear witness that she has tasted the food of the dead!' Hades grinned, and told Ascalaphus to perch on the back of Hermes's chariot.

k. At Eleusis, Demeter joyfully embraced Core; but, on hearing about the pomegranate, grew more dejected than ever, and said again: 'I will neither return to Olympus, nor remove my curse from the land.' Zeus then persuaded Rhea, the mother of Hades, Demeter, and himself, to plead with her; and a compromise was at last reached. Core should spend three months of the year in Hades's company, as Queen of Tartarus, with the title of Persephone, and the remaining nine in Demeter's. Hecate offered to make sure that this arrangement was kept, and to keep constant watch on Core.

l. Demeter finally consented to return home. Before leaving Eleusis,
she instructed Triptolemus, Eumolpus, and Celeus (together with
Diocles, King of Pherae, who had been assiduously searching for Core
all this while) in her worship and mysteries. But she punished Ascalaphus for his tale-bearing by pushing him down a hole and covering it
with an enormous rock, from which he was finally released by Heracles;
and then she changed him into a short-eared owl.[5] She also rewarded
the Pheneations of Arcadia, in whose house she rested after Poseidon
had outraged her, with all kinds of grain, but forbade them to sow
beans. One Cyamites was the first who dared do so; he has a shrine by
the river Cephissus.[6]

m. Triptolemus she supplied with seed-corn, a wooden plough, and
a chariot drawn by serpents; and sent him all over the world to teach
mankind the art of agriculture. But first she gave him lessons on the
Rarian Plain, which is why some call him the son of King Rarus. And
to Phytalus, who had treated her kindly on the banks of the Cephissus,
she gave a fig-tree, the first ever seen in Attica, and taught him how to
cultivate it.[7]

1. Aristophanes: *Frogs* 338; *Orphic Hymn* li.
2. Homer: *Odyssey* v. 125–8; Diodorus Siculus: v. 49; Hesiod:
   Theogony 969 ff.
3. Servius on Virgil's *Aeneid* iii. 167; Hyginus: *Fabula* 250; Callimachus: *Hymn to Demeter* 34 ff.; Antoninus Liberalis: *Transformations* 11,; Pausanias: x. 30. 1.
4. Hyginus: *Fabula* 146; Diodorus Siculus: v. 3; Scholiast on
   Sophocles's *Oedipus at Colonus* 1590; Apollodorus: i. 5. 1; Scholiast on Hesiod's *Theogony* 914; Pausanias: vi. 21. 1 and i. 38. 5;
   Conon: *Narrations* 15; *Homeric Hymn to Demeter* 17.
5. Apollodorus: i. 5. 1–3 and 12; *Homeric Hymn to Demeter* 398 ff. and
   445 ff.
6. Pausanias: viii. 15. 1 and i. 37. 3.
7. *Homeric Hymn to Demeter* 231–74; Apollodorus: i. 5. 2; *Orphic
   Fragment* 50; Hyginus: *Fabula* 146; Ovid: *Metamorphoses* v. 450–
   563 and *Fasti* iv. 614; Nicander: *Theriaca*; Pausanias: i. 14. 2 and
   37. 2.

*

1. Core, Persephone, and Hecate were, clearly, the Goddess in Triad as
Maiden, Nymph, and Crone, at a time when only women practised the
mysteries of agriculture. Core stands for the green corn, Persephone for
the ripe ear, and Hecate for the harvested corn – the 'carline wife' of the
English countryside. But Demeter was the goddess's general title, and

Persephone's name has been given to Core, which confuses the story. The myth of Demeter's adventure in the thrice-ploughed fields points to a fertility rite, which survived until recently in the Balkans: the corn-priestess will have openly coupled with the sacred king at the autumn sowing in order to ensure a good harvest. In Attica the field was first ploughed in spring; then, after the summer harvest, cross-ploughed with a lighter share; finally, when sacrifices had been offered to the Tillage-gods, ploughed again in the original direction during the autumn month of Pyanepsion, as a preliminary to sowing (Hesiod: *Works and Days* 432–3, 460, 462; Plutarch: *On Isis and Osiris* 69; *Against Colotes* 22).

2. Persephone (from *phero* and *phonos*, 'she who brings destruction'), also called Persephatta at Athens (from *ptersis* and *ephapto*, 'she who fixes destruction') and Proserpina ('the fearful one') at Rome, was, it seems, a title of the Nymph when she sacrificed the sacred king. The title 'Hecate' ('one hundred') apparently refers to the hundred lunar months of his reign, and to the hundredfold harvest. The king's death by a thunderbolt, or by the teeth of horses, or at the hands of the tanist, was his common fate in primitive Greece.

3. Core's abduction by Hades forms part of the myth in which the Hellenic trinity of gods forcibly marry the pre-Hellenic Triple-goddess – Zeus, Hera; Zeus or Poseidon, Demeter; Hades, Core – as in Irish myth Brian, Iuchar, and Iucharba marry the Triple-goddess Eire, Fodhla, and Banbha (see 7. 6 and 16. 1). It refers to male usurpation of the female agricultural mysteries in primitive times. Thus the incident of Demeter's refusal to provide corn for mankind is only another version of Ino's con-spiracy to destroy Athamas's harvest (see 70. c). Further, the Core myth accounts for the winter burial of a female corn-puppet, which was un-covered in the early spring and found to be sprouting; this pre-Hellenic custom survived in the countryside in Classical times, and is illustrated by vase-paintings of men freeing Core from a mound of earth with mattocks, or breaking open Mother Earth's head with axes.

4. The story of Erysichthon, son of Tropias, is moral anecdote: among the Greeks, as among the Latins and early Irish, the felling of a sacred grove carried the death penalty. But a desperate and useless hunger for food, which the Elizabethans called 'the wolf', would not be an appro-priate punishment for tree-felling, and Erysichthon's name – also borne by a son of Cecrops the patriarchalist and introducer of barley-cakes (see 25. d) – means 'earth-tearer', which suggests that his real crime was daring to plough without Demeter's consent, like Athamas. Pandareus's stealing of the golden dog suggests Cretan intervention in Greece, when the Achaeans tried to reform agricultural ritual. This dog, taken from the Earth-goddess, seems to have been the visible proof of the Achaean High King's independence of her (see 124. 1).

5. The myths of Hylas ('of the woodland' – see 150. *1*), Adonis (see 18. *7*), Lityerses (see 136. *e*), and Linus (see 147. *1*) describes the annual mourning for the sacred king, or his boy-surrogate, sacrificed to placate the goddess of vegetation. This same surrogate appears in the legend of Triptolemus, who rode in a serpent-drawn chariot and carried sacks of corn, to symbolize that his death brought wealth. He was also Plutus ('wealthy'), begotten in the ploughed field, from whom Hades's euphemistic title 'Pluto' is borrowed. Triptolemus (*triptolmaios*, 'thrice daring') may be a title awarded the sacred king for having three times dared to plough the field and couple with the corn-priestess. Celeus, Diocles, and Eumolpus, whom Demeter taught the art of agriculture, represent priestly heads of the Amphictyonic League – Metaneira is described as Amphictyon's daughter – who honoured her at Eleusis.

6. It was at Eleusis ('advent'), a Mycenaean city, that the great Eleusinian Mysteries were celebrated, in the month called Boedromion ('running for help'). Demeter's ecstatic initiates symbolically consummated her love affair with Iasius, or Triptolemus, or Zeus, in an inner recess of the shrine, by working a phallic object up and down a woman's top-boot; hence Eleusis suggests a worn-down derivative of *Eilythuies*, '[the temple] of her who rages in a lurking place'. The mystagogues, dressed as shepherds, then entered with joyful shouts, and displayed a winnowing-fan, containing the child Brimus, son of Brimo ('angry one'), the immediate fruit of this ritual marriage. Brimo was a title of Demeter's, and Brimus a synonym for Plutus; but his celebrants knew him best as Iacchus – from the riotuous hymn, the *Iacchus*, which was sung on the sixth day of the Mysteries during a torchlight procession from Demeter's temple.

7. Eumolpus represents the singing shepherds who brought in the child; Triptolemus is a cowherd, in service to Io the Moon-goddess as cow (see 56. *1*), who watered the seed-corn; and Eubuleus a swineherd, in service to the goddess Marpessa (see 74. *4* and 96. *2*), Phorcis, Choere, or Cerdo, the Sow-goddess, who made the corn sprout. Eubuleus was the first to reveal Core's fate, because 'swineherd', in early European myth, means soothsayer, or magician. Thus Eumaeus ('searching well'), Odysseus's swineherd (see 171. *a*), is addressed as *dios* ('god-like'); and though, by Classical times, swineherds had long ceased to exercise their prophetic art, swine were still sacrificed to Demeter and Persephone by being thrown down natural chasms. Eubuleus is not said to have benefited from Demeter's instruction, probably because her cult as Sow-goddess had been suppressed at Eleusis.

8. 'Rarus', whether it means 'an abortive child', or 'a womb', is an inappropriate name for a king, and will have referred to the womb of the Corn-mother from which the corn sprang.

9. Iambe and Baubo personify the obscene songs, in iambic metre, which were sung to relieve emotional tension at the Eleusinian Mysteries; but Iambe, Demeter, and Baubo form the familiar triad of maiden, nymph, and crone. Old nurses in Greek myth nearly always stand for the goddess as Crone. Abas was turned into a lizard, because lizards are found in the hottest and driest places, and can live without water; this is a moral anecdote told to teach children respect for their elders and reverence for the gods.

10. The story of Demeter's attempt to make Demophoön immortal is paralleled in the myths of Medea (see 156. *a*) and Thetis (see 181. *r*). It refers, partly, to the widespread primitive custom of 'saining' children against evil spirits with sacred fire carried around them at birth, or with a hot griddle set under them; partly to the custom of burning boys to death, as a vicarious sacrifice for the sacred king (see 92. *7*), and so conferring immortality on them. Celeus, the name of Demophoön's father, can mean 'burner' as well as 'woodpecker' or 'sorcerer'.

11. A primitive taboo rested on red-coloured food, which might be offered to the dead only (see 170. *5*); and the pomegranate was supposed to have sprung – like the eight-petalled scarlet anemone – from the blood of Adonis, or Tammuz (see 18. *7*). The seven pomegranate seeds represent, perhaps, the seven phases of the moon during which farmers wait for the green corn-shoots to appear. But Persephone eating the pomegranate is originally Sheol, the Goddess of Hell, devouring Tammuz; while Ishtar (Sheol herself in a different guise) weeps to placate his ghost. Hera, as a former Death-goddess, also held a pomegranate.

12. The *ascalaphos*, or short-eared owl, was a bird of evil omen; and the fable of his tale-bearing is told to account for the noisiness of owls in November, before the three winter months of Core's absence begin. Heracles released Ascalaphus (see 134. *d*).

13. Demeter's gift of the fig to Phytalus, whose family was a leading one in Attica (see 97. *a*), means no more than that the practice of fig-caprification – pollenizing the domestic tree with a branch of the wild one – ceased to be a female prerogative at the same time as agriculture. The taboo on the planting of beans by men seems to have survived later than that on grain, because of the close connexion between beans and ghosts. In Rome beans were thrown to ghosts at the All Souls' festival, and if a plant grew from one of these, and a woman ate its beans, she would be impregnated by a ghost. Hence the Pythagoreans abstained from beans lest they might deny an ancestor his chance of reincarnation.

14. Demeter is said to have reached Greece by way of Crete, landing at Thoricus in Attica (*Hymn to Demeter* 123). This is probable: the Cretans had established themselves in Attica, where they first worked the silver mines at Laureium. Moreover, Eleusis is a Mycenaean site, and Diodorus

Siculus (v. 77) says that rites akin to the Eleusinian were performed at Cnossus for all who cared to attend, and that (v. 79) according to the Cretans all rites of initiation were invented by their ancestors. But Demeter's origin is to be looked for in Libya.

15. The flowers which, according to Ovid, Core was picking were poppies. An image of a goddess with poppy-heads in her headdress was found at Gazi in Crete; another goddess on a mould from Palaiokastro holds poppies in her hand; and on the gold ring from the Acropolis Treasure at Mycenae a seated Demeter gives three poppy-heads to a standing Core. Poppy-seeds were used as a condiment on bread, and poppies are naturally associated with Demeter, since they grow in corn-fields; but Core picks or accepts poppies because of the soporific qualities, and because of their scarlet colour which promises resurrection after death (see 27. 12). She is about to retire for her annual sleep.

25

ATHENE'S NATURE AND DEEDS

ATHENE invented the flute, the trumpet, the earthenware pot, the plough, the rake, the ox-yoke, the horse-bridle, the chariot, and the ship. She first taught the science of numbers, and all women's arts, such as cooking, weaving, and spinning. Although a goddess of war, she gets no pleasure from battle, as Ares and Eris do, but rather from settling disputes, and upholding the law by pacific means. She bears no arms in time of peace and, if ever she needs any, will usually borrow a set from Zeus. Her mercy is great: when the judges' votes are equal in a criminal trial at the Areiopagus, she always gives a casting vote to liberate the accused. Yet, once engaged in battle, she never loses the day, even against Ares himself, being better grounded in tactics and strategy than he; and wise captains always approach her for advice.[1]

b. Many gods, Titans, and giants would gladly have married Athene, but she has repulsed all advances. On one occasion, in the course of the Trojan War, not wishing to borrow arms from Zeus, who had declared himself neutral, she asked Hephaestus to make her a set of her own. Hephaestus refused payment, saying coyly that he would undertake the work for love; and when, missing the implication of these words, she entered the smithy to watch him beat out the red-hot metal, he suddenly turned about and tried to outrage her. Hephaestus, who does not often behave so grossly, was the victim of a malicious joke: Poseidon had just informed him that Athene was on her way to the smithy, with Zeus's consent, hopefully expecting to have violent love made to her. As she tore herself away, Hephaestus ejaculated against her thigh, a little above the knee. She wiped off the seed with a handful of wool, which she threw away in disgust; it fell to the ground near Athens, and accidentally fertilized Mother Earth, who was on a visit there. Revolted at the prospect of bearing a child which Hephaestus had tried to father on Athene, Mother Earth declared that she would accept no responsibility for its upbringing.

c. 'Very well,' said Athene, 'I will take care of it myself.' So she took charge of the infant as soon as he was born, called him Erichthonius and, not wishing Poseidon to laugh at the success of his practical joke, hid him in a sacred basket; this she gave to Aglauros, eldest daughter of the Athenian King Cecrops, with orders to guard it carefully.[2]

d. Cecrops, a son of Mother Earth and, like Erichthonius – whom some suppose to have been his father – part man, part serpent, was the first king to recognize paternity. He married a daughter of Actaeus, the earliest King of Attica. He also instituted monogamy, divided Attica into twelve communities, built temples to Athene, and abolished certain bloody sacrifices in favour of sober barley-cake offerings.[3] His wife was named Agraulos; and his three daughters, Aglauros, Herse, and Pandrosos, lived in a three-roomed house on the Acropolis. One evening, when the girls had returned from a festival, carrying Athene's sacred baskets on their heads, Hermes bribed Aglauros to give him access to Herse, the youngest of the three, with whom he had fallen violently in love. Aglauros kept Hermes's gold, but did nothing to earn it, because Athene had made her jealous of Herse's good fortune; so Hermes strode angrily into the house, turned Aglauros to stone, and had his will of Herse. After Herse had borne Hermes two sons, Cephalus, the beloved of Eos, and Ceryx, the first herald of the Eleusinian Mysteries, she and Pandrosos and their mother Agraulos were curious enough to peep beneath the lid of the basket which Aglauros had carried. Seeing a child with a serpent's tail for legs, they screamed in fear and, headed by Agraulos, leaped from the Acropolis.[4]

e. On learning of this fatality, Athene was so grieved that she let fall the enormous rock which she had been carrying to the Acropolis as an additional fortification, and it became Mount Lycabettus. As for the crow that had brought her the news, she changed its colour from white to black, and forbade all crows ever again to visit the Acropolis. Erichthonius then took refuge in Athene's aegis, where she reared him so tenderly that some mistook her for his mother. Later, he became King of Athens, where he instituted the worship of Athene, and taught his fellow-citizens the use of silver. His image was set among the stars as the constellation Auriga, since he had introduced the four-horse chariot.[5]

f. Another, very different, account of Agraulos's death is current: namely that once, when an assault was being launched against Athens, she threw herself from the Acropolis, in obedience to an oracle, and so saved the day. This version purports to explain why all young Athenians, on first taking up arms, visit the temple of Agraulos and there dedicate their lives to the city.[6]

g. Athene, though as modest as Artemis, is far more generous. When Teiresias, one day, accidentally surprised her in a bath, she laid her hands over his eyes and blinded him, but gave him inward sight by way of a compensation.[7]

h. She is not recorded to have shown petulant jealousy on more than a single occasion. This is the story. Arachne, a princess of Lydian Colophon – famed for its purple dye – was so skilled in the art of weaving that Athene herself could not compete with her. Shown a cloth into which Arachne had woven illustrations of Olympian love affairs, the goddess searched closely to find a fault but, unable to do so, tore it up in a cold, vengeful rage. When the terrified Arachne hanged herself from a rafter, Athene turned her into a spider – the insect she hates most – and the rope into a cobweb, up which Arachne climbed to safety.[8]

1. Tzetzes: *On Lycophron* 520; Hesychius *sub* Hippia; Servius on Virgil's *Aeneid* iv. 402; Pindar: *Olympian Odes* xiii. 79; Livy: vii. 3; Pausanias: i. 24. 3, etc.; Homer: *Iliad* i. 199 ff.; v. 736; v. 840–863; xxi. 391–422; Aeschylus: *Eumenides* 753.

2. Hyginus: *Poetic Astronomy* ii. 13; Apollodorus: iii. 14. 6; Hyginus: *Fabula* 166.

3. Pausanias: i. 5. 3; viii. 2. 1; Apollodorus: iii. 14. 1; Strabo: ix. 1. 20; Aristophanes: *Plutus* 773; Athenaeus: p. 555c; Eustathius: *On Homer* p. 1156; Parian Marble: lines 2–4.

4. Apollodorus: iii. 14. 3 and 6; *Inscriptiones Graecae* xiv. 1389; Hyginus: *Fabula* 166.

5. Antigonus Carystius: 12; Callimachus: *Hecale* i. 2. 3; Philostratus: *Life of Apollonius of Tyana* vii. 24; Hyginus: *Poetic Astronomy* ii. 13; *Fabula* 274; Apollodorus: iii. 14. 1.

6. Suidas and Hesychius *sub* Agraulos; Plutarch: *Alcibiades* 15.

7. Callimachus: *The Bathing of Pallas*.
8. Ovid: *Metamorphoses* vi. 1–145; Virgil: *Georgics* iv. 246.

*

1. The Athenians made their goddess's maidenhood symbolic of the city's invincibility; and therefore disguised early myths of her outrage by Poseidon (see 19. 2), and Boreas (see 48. 1); and denied that Erichthonius, Apollo, and Lychnus ('lamp') were her sons by Hephaestus. They derived 'Erichthonius' from either *erion*, 'wool', or *eris*, 'strife', and *chthonos*, 'earth', and invented the myth of his birth to explain the presence, in archaic pictures, of a serpent-child peeping from the goddess's aegis. Poseidon's part in the birth of Erichthonius may originally have been a simpler and more direct one; why else should Erichthonius introduce the Poseidonian four-horse chariot into Athens?

2. Athene had been the Triple-goddess, and when the central person, the Goddess as Nymph, was suppressed and myths relating to her transferred to Aphrodite, Oreithyia (see 48. b), or Alcippe (see 19. b), there remained the Maiden clad in goat-skins, who specialized in war (see 8. 1), and the Crone, who inspired oracles and presided over all the arts. *Erichthonius* is perhaps an expanded form of *Erechtheus* (see 47. 1), meaning 'from the land of heather' (see 18. 1) rather than 'much earth', as is usually said; the Athenians represented him as a serpent with a human head, because he was the hero, or ghost, of the sacrificed king who made the Crone's wishes known. In this Crone-aspect, Athene was attended by an owl and a crow. The ancient royal family of Athens claimed descent from Erichthonius and Erechtheus, and called themselves Erechtheids; they used to wear golden serpents as amulets and kept a sacred serpent in the Erechtheum. But Erichthonius was also a procreative wind from the heather-clad mountains, and Athene's aegis (or a replica) was taken to all newly married couples at Athens, to ensure their fertility (Suidas *sub* Aegis).

3. Some of the finest Cretan pots are known to have been made by women, and so originally, no doubt, were all the useful instruments invented by Athene; but in Classical Greece an artisan had to be a man. Silver was at first a more valuable metal than gold, since harder to refine, and sacred to the moon; Periclean Athens owed her pre-eminence largely to the rich silver mines at Laureium first worked by the Cretans, which allowed her to import food and buy allies.

4. The occasion on which Cecrops's daughters leaped from the Acropolis may have been a Hellenic capture of Athens, after which an attempt was made to force monogamy on Athene's priestesses, as in the myth of Halirrhothius (see 19. b). They preferred death to dishonour – hence the oath taken by the Athenian youths at Agraulos's shrine. The other story of Agraulos's death is merely a moral anecdote: a warning against

the violation of Athene's mysteries. 'Agraulos' was one more title of the Moon-goddess; *agraulos* and its transliteration *aglauros* mean much the same thing, *agraulos* being a Homeric epithet for shepherds, and *aglauros* (like *herse* and *pandrosos*) referring to the moon as the reputed source of the dew which refreshed the pastures. At Athens girls went out under the full moon at midsummer to gather dew – the same custom survived in England until the last century – for sacred purposes. The festival was called the Hersephoria, or 'dew-gathering'; Agraulos or Agraule was, in fact, a title of Athene herself, and Agraule is said to have been worshipped in Cyprus until late times (Porphyry: *On Vegetarianism* 30) with human sacrifices. A gold ring from Mycenae shows three priestesses advancing towards a temple; the two leaders scatter dew, the third (presumably Agraulos) has a branch tied to her elbow. The ceremony perhaps originated in Crete. Hermes's seduction of Herse, for which he paid Aglauros in gold, must refer to the ritual prostitution of priestesses before an image of the goddess – Aglauros turned to stone. The sacred baskets carried on such occasions will have contained phallic snakes and similar orgiastic objects. Ritual prostitution by devotees of the Moon-goddess was practised in Crete, Cyprus, Syria, Asia Minor, and Palestine.

5. Athene's expulsion of the crow is a mythic variant of Cronus's banishment – *Cronus* means 'crow' (see 6. 2) – the triumph, in fact, of Olympianism, with the introduction of which Cecrops, who is really Ophion-Boreas the Pelasgian demiurge (see 1. 1), has here been wrongly credited. The crow's change of colour recalls the name of Athene's Welsh counterpart: Branwen, 'white crow', sister to Bran (see 57. 1). Athene was, it seems, titled 'Coronis'.

6. Her vengeance on Arachne may be more than just a pretty fable, if it records an early commercial rivalry between the Athenians and the Lydio-Carian thalassocrats, or sea-rulers, who were of Cretan origin. Numerous seals with a spider emblem which have been found at Cretan Miletus – the mother city of Carian Miletus and the largest exporter of dyed woollens in the ancient world – suggest a public textile industry operated there at the beginning of the second millennium B.C. For a while the Milesians controlled the profitable Black Sea trade, and had an *entrepôt* at Naucratis in Egypt. Athene had good reason to be jealous of the spider.

7. An apparent contradiction occurs in Homer. According to the *Catalogue of the Ships* (*Iliad* ii. 547 ff.), Athene set Erechtheus down in her rich temple at Athens; but, according to the *Odyssey* (vii. 80), she goes to Athens and enters his strong house. The fact was that the sacred king had his own quarters in the Queen's palace where the goddess's image was kept. There were no temples in Crete or Mycenaean Greece, only domestic shrines or oracular caves.

PAN'S NATURE AND DEEDS

SEVERAL powerful gods and goddesses of Greece have never been enrolled among the Olympian Twelve. Pan, for instance, a humble fellow, now dead, was content to live on earth in rural Arcadia; and Hades, Persephone, and Hecate know that their presence is unwelcome on Olympus; and Mother Earth is far too old and set in her ways to accommodate herself to the family life of her grandchildren and great-grandchildren.

b. Some say that Hermes fathered Pan on Dryope, daughter of Dryops; or on the nymph Oeneis; or on Penelope, wife of Odysseus, whom he visited in the form of a ram; or on Amaltheia the Goat.[1] He is said to have been so ugly at birth, with horns, beard, tail, and goat-legs, that his mother ran away from him in fear, and Hermes carried him up to Olympus for the gods' amusement. But Pan was Zeus's foster-brother, and therefore far older than Hermes, or than Penelope, on whom (others say) he was fathered by all the suitors who wooed her during Odysseus's absence. Still others make him the son of Cronus and Rhea; or of Zeus by Hybris, which is the least improbable account.[2]

c. He lived in Arcadia, where he guarded flocks, herds, and bee-hives, took part in the revels of the mountain-nymphs, and helped hunters to find their quarry. He was, on the whole, easy-going and lazy, loving nothing better than his afternoon sleep, and revenged himself on those who disturbed him with a sudden loud shout from a grove, or grotto, which made the hair bristle on their heads. Yet the Arcadians paid him so little respect that, if ever they returned empty-handed after a long day's hunting, they dared scourge him with squills.[3]

d. Pan seduced several nymphs, such as Echo, who bore him Iynx and came to an unlucky end for love of Narcissus; and Eupheme, nurse of the Muses, who bore him Crotus, the Bowman in the Zodiac. He also boasted that he had coupled with all Dionysus's drunken Maenads.[4]

e. Once he tried to violate the chaste Pitys, who escaped him only by being metamorphosed into a fir-tree, a branch of which he afterwards wore as a chaplet. On another occasion he pursued the chaste Syrinx from Mount Lycaeum to the River Ladon, where she became a reed; there, since he could not distinguish her from among all the rest, he cut

several reeds at random, and made them into a Pan-pipe. His greatest
success in love was the seduction of Selene, which he accomplished by
disguising his hairy black goatishness with well-washed white fleeces.
Not realizing who he was, Selene consented to ride on his back, and let
him do as he pleased with her.[5]

f. The Olympian gods, while despising Pan for his simplicity and
love of riot, exploited his powers. Apollo wheedled the art of prophecy
from him, and Hermes copied a pipe which he had let fall, claimed it as
his own invention, and sold it to Apollo.

g. Pan is the only god who has died in our time. The news of his
death came to one Thamus, a sailor in a ship bound for Italy by way of
the island of Paxi. A divine voice shouted across the sea: 'Thamus, are
you there? When you reach Palodes, take care to proclaim that the
great god Pan is dead!', which Thamus did; and the news was greeted
from the shore with groans and laments.[6]

1. *Homeric Hymn to Pan* 34 ff.; Scholiast on Theocritus's *Idylls* i. 3;
   Herodotus: ii. 145; Eratosthenes: *Catasterismoi* 27.
2. *Homeric Hymn to Pan*: *loc. cit.*; Servius on Virgil's *Georgics* i. 16;
   Duris, quoted by Tzetzes: *On Lycophron* 772; Apollodorus: 1. 4. 1;
   Scholiast on Aeschylus's *Rhesus* 30.
3. Theocritus: *Idylls* i. 16; Euripides: *Rhesus* 36; Hesychius *sub*
   Agreus Theocritus: *Idylls* vii. 107.
4. Ovid: *Metamorphoses* iii. 356–401; Hyginus: *Fabula* 224; *Poetic
   Astronomy* ii. 27.
5. Lucian: *Dialogues of the Gods* xxii. 4; Ovid: *Metamorphoses* i.
   694–712; Philargyrius on Virgil's *Georgics* iii. 392.
6. Plutarch: *Why Oracles Are Silent* 17.

*

1. Pan, whose name is usually derived from *paein*, 'to pasture', stands
for the 'devil', or 'upright man', of the Arcadian fertility cult, which
closely resembled the witch cult of North-western Europe. This man,
dressed in a goat-skin, was the chosen lover of the Maenads during their
drunken orgies on the high mountains, and sooner or later paid for his
privilege with death.

2. The accounts of Pan's birth vary greatly. Since Hermes was the
power resident in a phallic stone which formed the centre of these orgies
(see 14. 1), the shepherds described their god Pan as his son by a woodpecker, a bird whose tapping is held to portend the welcome summer
rain. The myth that he fathered Pan on Oeneis is self-explanatory, though
the original Maenads used other intoxicants than wine (see 27. 2); and

the name of his reputed mother, Penelope ('with a web over her face'), suggests that the Maenads wore some form of war paint for their orgies, recalling the stripes of the *penelope*, a variety of duck. Plutarch says (*On the Delays of Divine Punishment* 12) that the Maenads who killed Orpheus were tattooed by their husbands as a punishment (see 28. *f*); and a Maenad whose legs and arms are tattooed with a webbed pattern appears on a vase at the British Museum (Catalogue E. 301). Hermes's visit to Penelope in the form of a ram – the ram devil is as common in the North-western witch cult as the goat – her impregnation by all the suitors (see 171. *l*), and the claim that Pan had coupled with every one of the Maenads refers to the promiscuous nature of the revels in honour of the Fir-goddess Pitys or Elate (see 78. *1*). The Arcadian mountaineers were the most primitive in Greece (see 1. *5*), and their more civilized neighbours professed to despise them.

3. Pan's son, the wryneck; or snake-bird, was a spring migrant employed in erotic charms (see 56. *1* and 152. *2*). Squills contain an irritant poison – valuable against mice and rats – and were used as a purge and diuretic before taking part in a ritual act; thus squill came to symbolize the removal of evil influences (Pliny: *Natural History* xx. 39), and Pan's image was scourged with squill if game were scarce (see 108. *10*).

4. His seduction of Selene must refer to a moonlight May Eve orgy, in which the young Queen of the May rode upon her upright man's back before celebrating a greenwood marriage with him. By this time the ram cult had superseded the goat cult in Arcadia (see 27. *2*).

5. The Egyptian Thamus apparently misheard the ceremonial lament *Thamus Pan-megas Tethnēce* ('the all-great Tammuz is dead!') for the message: 'Thamus, Great Pan is dead!' At any rate, Plutarch, a priest at Delphi in the latter half of the first century A.D., believed and published it; yet when Pausanias made his tour of Greece, about a century later, he found Pan's shrines, altars, sacred caves, and sacred mountains still much frequented.

27

DIONYSUS'S NATURE AND DEEDS

AT Hera's orders the Titans seized Zeus's newly-born son Dionysus, a horned child crowned with serpents and, despite his transformations, tore him into shreds. These they boiled in a cauldron, while a pomegranate-tree sprouted from the soil where his blood had fallen; but, rescued and reconstituted by his grandmother Rhea, he came to life again. Persephone, now entrusted with his charge by Zeus, brought him to King Athamas of Orchomenus and his wife Ino, whom she persuaded to rear the child in the women's quarters, disguised as a girl. But Hera could not be deceived, and punished the royal pair with madness, so that Athamas killed their son Learches, mistaking him for a stag.[1]

b. Then, on Zeus's instructions, Hermes temporarily transformed Dionysus into a kid or a ram, and presented him to the nymphs Macris, Nysa, Erato, Bromie, and Bacche, of Heliconian Mount Nysa. They tended Dionysus in a cave, cosseted him, and fed him on honey, for which service Zeus subsequently placed their images among the stars, naming them the Hyades. It was on Mount Nysa that Dionysus invented wine, for which he is chiefly celebrated.[2]

When he grew to manhood Hera recognized him as Zeus's son, despite the effeminacy to which his education had reduced him, and drove him mad also. He went wandering all over the world, accompanied by his tutor Silenus and a wild army of Satyrs and Maenads, whose weapons were the ivy-twined staff tipped with a pine-cone, called the *thyrsus,* and swords and serpents and fear-imposing bull-roarers. He sailed to Egypt, bringing the vine with him; and at Pharos King Proteus received him hospitably. Among the Libyans of the Nile Delta, opposite Pharos, were certain Amazon queens whom Dionysus invited to march with him against the Titans and restore King Ammon to the kingdom from which he had been expelled. Dionysus's defeat of the Titans and restoration of King Ammon was the earliest of his many military successes.[3]

c. He then turned east and made for India. Coming to the Euphrates, he was opposed by the King of Damascus, whom he flayed alive, but built a bridge across the river with ivy and vine; after which a tiger, sent by his father Zeus, helped him across the river Tigris. He reached India, having met with much opposition by the way, and conquered the whole country, which he taught the art of viniculture, also giving it laws and founding great cities.[4]

d. On his return he was opposed by the Amazons, a horde of whom he chased as far as Ephesus. A few took sanctuary in the Temple of Artemis, where their descendants are still living; others fled to Samos and Dionysus followed them in boats, killing so many that the battlefield is called Panhaema. Near Phloeum some of the elephants which he had brought from India died, and their bones are still pointed out.⁵

e. Next, Dionysus returned to Europe by way of Phrygia, where his grandmother Rhea purified him of the many murders he had committed during his madness, and initiated him into her Mysteries. He then invaded Thrace; but no sooner had his people landed at the mouth of the river Strymon than Lycurgus, King of the Edonians, opposed them savagely with an ox-goad, and captured the entire army, except Dionysus himself, who plunged into the sea and took refuge in Thetis's grotto. Rhea, vexed by this reverse, helped the prisoners to escape, and drove Lycurgus mad: he struck his own son Dryas dead with an axe, in the belief that he was cutting down a vine. Before recovering his senses he had begun to prune the corpse of its nose and ears, fingers and toes; and the whole land of Thrace grew barren in horror of his crime. When Dionysus, returning from the sea, announced that this barrenness would continue unless Lycurgus were put to death, the Edonians led him to Mount Pangaeum, where wild horses pulled his body apart.⁶

f. Dionysus met with no further opposition in Thrace, but travelled on to his well-beloved Boeotia, where he visited Thebes, and invited the women to join his revels on Mount Cithaeron. Pentheus, King of Thebes, disliking Dionysus's dissolute appearance, arrested him, together with all his Maenads, but went mad and, instead of shackling Dionysus, shackled a bull. The Maenads escaped again, and went raging out upon the mountains, where they tore calves in pieces. Pentheus attempted to stop them; but, inflamed by wine and religious ecstasy, they rent him limb from limb. His mother Agave led the riot, and it was she who wrenched off his head.⁷

g. At Orchomenus the three daughters of Minyas, by name Alcithoë, Leucippe, and Arsippe, or Aristippe, or Arsinoë, refused to join in the revels, though Dionysus himself invited them, appearing in the form of a girl. He then changed his shape, becoming successively a lion, a bull, and a panther, and drove them insane. Leucippe offered her own son Hippasus as a sacrifice – he had been chosen by lot – and the three sisters, having torn him to pieces and devoured him, skimmed the mountains in a frenzy until at last Hermes changed them into birds, though some say that Dionysus changed them into bats.⁸ The murder of Hippasus is annually atoned at Orchomenus, in a feast called Agrionia ('provocation to savagery'), when the women devotees pretend to seek Dionysus and then, having agreed that he must be away with the Muses, sit in a circle and ask riddles, until the priest of Dionysus rushes from his temple, with a sword, and kills the one whom he first catches.[9]

h. When all Boeotia had acknowledged Dionysus's divinity, he made a tour of the Aegean Islands, spreading joy and terror wherever he went. Arriving at Icaria, he found that his ship was unseaworthy, and hired another from certain Tyrrhenian sailors who claimed to be bound for Naxos. But they proved to be pirates and, unaware of his godhead, steered for Asia, intending to sell him there as a slave. Dionysus made a vine grow from the deck and enfold the mast, while ivy twined about the rigging; he also turned the oars into serpents, and became a lion himself, filling the vessel with phantom beasts and the sound of flutes, so that the terrified pirates leaped overboard and became dolphins.[10]

i. It was at Naxos that Dionysus met the lovely Ariadne whom Theseus had deserted, and married her without delay. She bore him Oenopion, Thoas, Staphylus, Latromis, Euanthes, and Tauropolus. Later, he placed her bridal chaplet among the stars.[11]

j. From Naxos he came to Argos and punished Perseus, who at first opposed him and killed many of his followers, by inflicting a madness on the Argive women: they began devouring their own infants raw. Perseus hastily admitted his error, and appeased Dionysus by building a temple in his honour.

k. Finally, having established his worship throughout the world, Dionysus ascended to Heaven, and now sits at the right hand of Zeus as one of the Twelve Great Ones. The self-effacing goddess Hestia resigned her seat at the high table in his favour; glad of any excuse to escape the jealous wranglings of her family, and knowing that she could always count on a quiet welcome in any Greek city which it might please her to visit. Dionysus then descended, by way of Lerna, to Tartarus where he bribed Persephone with a gift of myrtle to release his dead mother, Semele. She ascended with him into Artemis's temple at Troezen; but, lest other ghosts should be jealous and aggrieved, he changed her name and introduced her to his fellow-Olympians as Thyone. Zeus placed an apartment at her disposal, and Hera preserved an angry but resigned silence.[12]

1. Euripides: *Bacchae* 99–102; Onomacritus, quoted by Pausanias: viii. 37. 3; Diodorus Siculus: iii. 62; *Orphic Hymn* xlv. 6; Clement of Alexandria: *Address to the Greeks* ii. 16.

2. Apollodorus: iii. 4. 3; Hyginus: *Fabula* 182; Theon on Aratus's *Phenomena* 177; Diodorus Siculus: iii. 68–69; Apollonius Rhodius: iv. 1131; Servius on Virgil's *Eclogues* vi. 15.

3. Apollodorus: iii. 5. 1; Aeschylus: *The Edonians, a Fragment*; Diodorus Siculus: iii. 70–71.

4. Euripides: *Bacchae* 13; Theophilus, quoted by Plutarch: *On Rivers* 24; Pausanias: x. 29. 2; Diodorus Siculus: ii. 38; Strabo: xi. 5. 5; Philostratus: *Life of Apollonius of Tyana* ii. 8–9; Arrian: *Indica* 5.

5. Pausanias: vii. 2. 4–5; Plutarch: *Greek Questions* 56.

6. Apollodorus: iii. 5. 1; Homer: *Iliad* vi. 130–40.

7. Theocritus: *Idylls* xxvi.; Ovid: *Metamorphoses* iii. 714 ff.; Euripides: *Bacchae, passim*.

8. Ovid: *Metamorphosis* iv. 1–40; 390–415; Antoninus Liberalis: 10; Aelian: *Varia Historia* iii. 42; Plutarch: *Greek Questions* 38.

9. Plutarch: *loc. cit.*

10. *Homeric Hymn to Dionysus* 6 ff.; Apollodorus: iii. 5. 3; Ovid: *Metamorphoses* iii. 577–699.

11. Scholiast on Apollonius Rhodius: iii. 996; Hesiod: *Theogony* 947; Hyginus: *Poetic Astronomy* ii. 5.

12. Apollodorus: iii. 5. 3; Pausanias: ii. 31. 2.

*

1. The main clue to Dionysus's mystic history is the spread of the vine cult over Europe, Asia and North Africa. Wine was not invented by the Greeks: it seems to have been first imported in jars from Crete. Grapes grew wild on the southern coast of the Black Sea, whence their cultivation spread to Mount Nysa in Libya, by way of Palestine, and so to Crete; to India, by way of Persia; and to Bronze Age Britain, by way of the Amber Route. The wine orgies of Asia Minor and Palestine – the Canaanite Feast of Tabernacles was, originally, a Bacchanal orgy – were marked by much the same ecstasies as the beer orgies of Thrace and Phrygia. Dionysus's triumph was that wine everywhere superseded other intoxicants (see 38. *3*). According to Pherecydes (178) *Nysa* means 'tree'.

2. He had once been subservient to the Moon-goddess Semele (see 14. *5*) – also called Thyone, or Cotytto (see 3. *1*) – and the destined victim of her orgies. His being reared as a girl, as Achilles also was (see 160. *5*), recalls the Cretan custom of keeping boys 'in darkness'(*scotioi*), that is to say, in the women's quarters, until puberty. One of his titles was *Dendrites*, 'tree-youth', and the Spring Festival, when the trees suddenly burst into leaf and the whole world is intoxicated with desire, celebrated his emancipation. He is described as a horned child in order not to particularize the horns, which were goat's, stag's, bull's, or ram's according to the place of his worship. When Apollodorus says that he was disguised as a kid to save him from the wrath of Hera – 'Eriphus' ('kid') was one of his titles

(Hesychius *sub* Eriphos) – this refers to the Cretan cult of Dionysus-Zagreus, the wild goat with the enormous horns. Virgil (*Georgics* ii. 380–84) wrongly explains that the goat was the animal most commonly sacrificed to Dionysus 'because goats injure the vine by gnawing it.' Dionysus as a stag is Learchus, whom Athamas killed when driven mad by Hera. In Thrace he was a white bull. But in Arcadia Hermes disguised him as a ram, because the Arcadians were shepherds, and the Sun was entering the Ram at their Spring Festival. The Hyades ('rain-makers') into whose charge he gave Dionysus, were renamed 'the tall', 'the lame', 'the passionate', 'the roaring', and 'the raging' Ones, to describe his ceremonies. Hesiod (quoted by Theon: *On Aratus* 171) records the Hyades' earlier names as Phaesyle (? 'filtered light'), Coronis ('crow'), Cleia ('famous'), Phaeo ('dim'), and Eudore ('generous'); and Hyginus's list (*Poetis Astronomy* ii. 21) is somewhat similar. *Nysus* means 'lame', and in these beer orgies on the mountain the sacred king seems to have hobbled like a partridge – as in the Canaanite Spring Festival called the *Pesach* ('hobbling' – see 23. *1*). But that Macris fed Dionysus on honey, and that the Maenads used ivy-twined fir-branches as thyrsi, records an earlier form of intoxicant: spruce-beer, laced with ivy, and sweetened with mead. Mead was 'nectar', brewed from fermented honey, which the gods continued to drink in the Homeric Olympus.

3. J. E. Harrison, who first pointed out (*Prolegomena* ch. viii) that Dionysus the Wine-god is a late superimposition on Dionysus the Beer-god also called Sabazius, suggests that *tragedy* may be derived not from *tragos*, 'a goat', as Virgil suggests (*loc. cit.*), but from *tragos*, 'spelt' – a grain used in Athens for beer-brewing. She adds that, in early vase-paintings, horse-men, not goat-men, are pictured as Dionysus's companions; and that his grape-basket is, at first, a winnowing fan. In fact, the Libyan or Cretan goat was associated with wine; the Helladic horse with beer and nectar. Thus Lycurgus, who opposes the later Dionysus, is torn to pieces by wild horses – priestesses of the Mare-headed goddess – which was the fate of the earlier Dionysus. Lycurgus's story has been confused by the irrelevant account of the curse that overtook his land after the murder of Dryas ('oak'); Dryas was the oak-king, annually killed. The trimming of his extremities served to keep his ghost at bay (see 153. *b* and 171. *i*), and the wanton felling of a sacred oak carried the death penalty. Cotytto was the name of the goddess in whose honour the Edonian Rites were performed (Strabo: x. 3. 16).

4. Dionysus had epiphanies as Lion, Bull, and Serpent, because these were Calendar emblems of the tripartite year (see 31. *7*; 75. *2*, and 123. *1*). He was born in winter as a serpent (hence his serpent crown); became a lion in the spring; and was killed and devoured as a bull, goat, or stag at midsummer. These were his transformations when the Titans set on him

(see 30. *a*). Among the Orchomenans a panther seems to have taken the serpent's place. His Mysteries resembled Osiris's; hence his visit to Egypt.

5. Hera's hatred of Dionysus and his wine-cup, like the hostility shown by Pentheus and Perseus, reflects conservative opposition to the ritual use of wine and to the extravagant Maenad fashion, which had spread from Thrace to Athens, Corinth, Sicyon, Delphi, and other civilized cities. Eventually, in the late seventh and early sixth centuries B.C., Periander, tyrant of Corinth, Cleisthenes, tyrant of Sicyon, and Peisistratus, tyrant of Athens, deciding to approve the cult, founded official Dionysiac feasts. Thereupon Dionysus and his vine were held to have been accepted in Heaven – he ousted Hestia from her position as one of the Twelve Olympians at the close of the fifth century B.C. – though some gods continued to exact 'sober sacrifices'. But, although one of the recently deciphered tablets from Nestor's palace at Pylus shows that he had divine status even in the thirteenth century B.C., Dionysus never really ceased to be a demi-god, and the tomb of his annual resurrection continued to be shown at Delphi (Plutarch: *On Isis and Osiris* 35), where the priests regarded Apollo as his immortal part (see 28. *3*). The story of his rebirth from Zeus's thigh, as the Hittite god of the Winds had been born from Kumabi's (see 6. *6*), repudiates his original matriarchal setting. Ritual rebirth from a man was a well-known Jewish adoption ceremony (*Ruth* iii. 9), a Hittite borrowing.

6. Dionysus voyaged in a new-moon boat, and the story of his conflict with the pirates seems to have been based on the same icon which gave rise to the legend of Noah and the beasts in the Ark: the lion, serpent, and other creatures are his seasonal epiphanies. Dionysus is, in fact, Deucalion (see 38. *3*). The Laconians of Brasiae preserved an uncanonical account of his birth: how Cadmus shut Semele and her child in an ark, which drifted to Brasiae, where Semele died and was buried, and how Ino reared Dionysus (Pausanias: iii. 24. 3).

7. Pharos, a small island off the Nile Delta, on the shore of which Proteus went through the same transformations as Dionysus (see 169. *a*), had the greatest harbour of Bronze Age Europe (see 39. *2* and 169. *6*). It was the depôt for traders from Crete, Asia Minor, the Aegean Islands, Greece, and Palestine. From here the vine cult will have spread in every direction. The account of Dionysus's campaign in Libya may record military aid sent to the Garamantians by their Greek allies (see 3. *3*); that of his Indian campaign has been taken for a fanciful history of Alexander's drunken progress to the Indus, but is earlier in date and records the eastward spread of the vine. Dionysus's visit to Phrygia, where Rhea initiated him, suggests that the Greek rites of Dionysus as Sabazius, or Bromius, were of Phrygian origin.

8. The Corona Borealis, Ariadne's bridal chaplet, was also called 'the

Cretan Crown'. She was the Cretan Moon-goddess, and her vinous children by Dionysus – Oenopion, Thoas, Staphylus, Tauropolus, Latromis, and Euanthes – were the eponymous ancestors of Helladic tribes living in Chios, Lemnos, the Thracian Chersonese, and beyond (see 98. *o*). Because the vine cult reached Greece and the Aegean by way of Crete – *oinos*, 'wine', is a Cretan word – Dionysus has been confused with Cretan Zagreus, who was similarly torn to pieces at birth (see 30. *a*).

9. Agave, mother of Pentheus, is the Moon-goddess who ruled the beer revels. The tearing to pieces of Hippasus by the three sisters, who are the Triple-goddess as Nymph, is paralleled in the Welsh tale of Pwyll Prince of Dyffed where, on May Eve, Rhiannon, a corruption of Rigantona ('great queen'), devours a foal who is really her son Pryderi ('anxiety'). Poseidon was also eaten in the form of a foal by his father Cronus; but probably in an earlier version by his mother Rhea (see 7. *g*). The meaning of the myth is that the ancient rite in which mare-headed Maenads tore the annual boy victim – Sabazius, Bromius, or whatever he was called – to pieces and ate him raw, was superseded by the more orderly Dionysian revels; the change being signalized by the killing of a foal instead of the usual boy.

10. The pomegranate which sprouted from Dionysus's blood was also the tree of Tammuz-Adonis-Rimmon; its ripe fruit splits open like a wound and shows the red seeds inside. It symbolizes death and the promise of resurrection when held in the hand of the goddess Hera or Persephone (see 24. *11*).

11. Dionysus's rescue of Semele, renamed Thyone ('raging queen'), has been deduced from pictures of a ceremonial held at Athens on the dancing floor dedicated to the Wild Women. There to the sound of singing, piping, and dancing, and with the scattering of flower petals from baskets, a priest summoned Semele to emerge from an *omphalos*, or artificial mound, and come attended by 'the spirit of Spring', the young Dionysus (Pindar: *Fragment* 75. 3). At Delphi a similar ascension ceremony conducted wholly by women was called the *Herois*, or 'feast of the heroine' (Plutarch: *Greek Questions* 12; Aristophanes: *Frogs* 373–96, with scholiast). Still another may be presumed in Artemis's temple at Troezen. The Moon-goddess, it must be remembered, had three different aspects – in the words of John Skelton:

> Diana in the leavës green;
> Luna who so bright doth sheen;
> Persephone in Hell.

Semele was, in fact, another name for Core, or Persephone, and the ascension scene is painted on many Greek vases, some of which show Satyrs assisting the heroine's emergence with mattocks; their presence

indicates that this was a Pelasgian rite. What they disinterred was probably a corn-doll buried after the harvest and now found to be sprouting
green. Core, of course, did not ascend to Heaven; she wandered about on
earth with Demeter until the time came for her to return to the Underworld. But soon after the award of Olympic status to Dionysus the
Assumption of his virgin-mother became dogmatic and, once a goddess,
she was differentiated from Core, who continued heroine-like to ascend
and descend.

12. The vine was the tenth tree of the sacral tree-year and its month
corresponded with September, when the vintage feast took place. Ivy,
the eleventh tree, corresponded with October, when the Maenads
revelled and intoxicated themselves by chewing ivy leaves; and was
important also because, like four other sacred trees – El's prickly oak on
which the cochineal insects fed, Phoroneus's alder, and Dionysus's own
vine and pomegranate – it provided a red dye (see 52. 3). Theophilus,
the Byzantine monk (Rugerus: *On Handicrafts*, ch. 98), says that 'poets
and artists loved ivy because of the secret powers it contained . . .one of
which I will tell you. In March, when the sap rises, if you perforate the
stems of ivy with an auger in a few places, a gummy liquid will exude
which, when mixed with urine and boiled, turns a blood colour called
"lake", useful for painting and illumination.' Red dye was used to colour
the faces of male fertility images (Pausanias: ii. 2. 5), and of sacred kings
(see 170. 11); at Rome this custom survived in the reddening of the
triumphant general's face. The general represented the god Mars, who
was a Spring-Dionysus before he specialized as the Roman God of War,
and who gave his name to the month of March. English kings still have
their faces slightly rouged on State occasions to make them look healthy
and prosperous. Moreover, Greek ivy, like the vine and plane-tree, has a
five-pointed leaf, representing the creative hand of the Earth-goddess
Rhea (see 53. *a*). The myrtle was a death tree (see 109. 4).

28

ORPHEUS

ORPHEUS, son of the Thracian King Oeagrus and the Muse Calliope,
was the most famous poet and musician who ever lived. Apollo presented him with a lyre, and the Muses taught him its use, so that he not
only enchanted wild beasts, but made the trees and rocks move from
their places to follow the sound of his music. At Zone in Thrace a
number of ancient mountain oaks are still standing in the pattern of
one of his dances, just as he left them.[1]

b. After a visit to Egypt, Orpheus joined the Argonauts, with whom he sailed to Colchis, his music helping them to overcome many difficulties – and, on his return, married Eurydice, whom some called Agriope, and settled among the savage Cicones of Thrace.[2]

c. One day, near Tempe, in the valley of the river Peneius, Eurydice met Aristaeus, who tried to force her. She trod on a serpent as she fled, and died of its bite; but Orpheus boldly descended into Tartarus, hoping to fetch her back. He used the passage which opens at Aornum in Thesprotis and, on his arrival, not only charmed the ferryman Charon, the Dog Cerberus, and the three Judges of the Dead with his plaintive music, but temporarily suspended the tortures of the damned; and so far soothed the savage heart of Hades that he won leave to restore Eurydice to the upper world. Hades made a single condition: that Orpheus might not look behind him until she was safely back under the light of the sun. Eurydice followed Orpheus up through the dark passage, guided by the sounds of his lyre, and it was only when he reached the sunlight again that he turned to see whether she were still behind him, and so lost her for ever.[3]

d. When Dionysus invaded Thrace, Orpheus neglected to honour him, but taught other sacred mysteries and preached the evil of sacrificial murder to the men of Thrace, who listened reverently. Every morning he would rise to greet the dawn on the summit of Mount Pangaeum, preaching that Helius, whom he named Apollo, was the greatest of all gods. In vexation, Dionysus set the Maenads upon him at Deium in Macedonia. First waiting until their husbands had entered Apollo's temple, where Orpheus served as priest, they seized the weapons stacked outside, burst in, murdered their husbands, and tore Orpheus limb from limb. His head they threw into the river Hebrus, but it floated, still singing, down to the sea, and was carried to the island of Lesbos.[4]

e. Tearfully, the Muses collected his limbs and buried them at Leibethra, at the foot of Mount Olympus, where the nightingales now sing sweeter than anywhere else in the world. The Maenads had attempted to cleanse themselves of Orpheus's blood in the river Helicorn; but the River-god dived under the ground and disappeared for the space of nearly four miles, emerging with a different name, the Baphyra. Thus he avoided becoming an accessory to the murder.[5]

f. It is said that Orpheus had condemned the Maenads' promiscuity and preached homosexual love; Aphrodite was therefore no less angered than Dionysus. Her fellow-Olympians, however, could not agree that his murder had been justified, and Dionysus saved the Maenad's lives by turning them into oak-trees, which remained rooted to the ground. The Thracian men who had survived the massacre decided to tattoo their wives as a warning against the murder of priests; and the custom survives to this day.[6]

g. As for Orpheus's head: after being attacked by a jealous Lemnian serpent (which Apollo at once changed into a stone) it was laid to rest in a cave at Antissa, sacred to Dionysus. There it prophesied day and night until Apollo, finding that his oracles at Delphi, Gryneium, and Clarus were deserted, came and stood over the head, crying: 'Cease from interference in my business; I have borne long enough with you and your singing!' Thereupon the head fell silent.[7] Orpheus's lyre had likewise drifted to Lesbos and been laid up in a temple of Apollo, at whose intercession, and that of the Muses, the Lyre was placed in heaven as a Constellation.[8]

h. Some give a wholly different account of how Orpheus died: they say that Zeus killed him with a thunderbolt for divulging divine secrets. He had, indeed, instituted the Mysteries of Apollo in Thrace; those of Hecate in Aegina; and those of Subterrene Demeter at Sparta.[9]

1. Pindar: *Pythian Odes* iv. 176, with scholiast; Aeschylus: *Agamemnon* 1629–30; Euripides: *Bacchae* 561–4; Apollonius Rhodius: i. 28–31.
2. Diodorus Siculus: iv. 25; Hyginus: *Fabula* 164; Athenaeus: xiii. 7.
3. Hyginus: *loc. cit.*; Diodorus Siculus: *loc. cit.*; Pausanias: ix. 30. 3; Euripides: *Alcestis* 357, with scholiast.
4. Aristophanes: *Frogs* 1032; Ovid: *Metamorphoses* xi. 1–85; Conon: *Narrations* 45.
5. Aeschylus: *Bassarids*, quoted by Eratosthenes: *Catasterismoi* 24; Pausanias: ix. 30. 3–4.
6. Ovid: *loc. cit.*; Conon: *loc. cit.*; Plutarch: *On the Slowness of Divine Vengeance* 12.
7. Lucian: *Against the Unlearned* ii; Philostratus: *Heroica* v. 704; *Life of Apollonius of Tyana* iv. 14.
8. Lucian: *loc. cit.*; Eratosthenes: *Catasterismoi* 24; Hyginus: *Poetic Astronomy* ii. 7.
9. Pausanias: ix. 30. 3; ii. 30. 2; iii. 14. 5.

*

1. Orpheus's singing head recalls that of the decapitated Alder-god Bran which, according to the *Mabinogion*, sang sweetly on the rock at Harlech in North Wales; a fable, perhaps, of funerary pipes made from

alder-bark. Thus the name Orpheus, if it stands for *ophruoeis*, 'on the river bank', may be a title of Bran's Greek counterpart, Phoroneus (see 57. *1*), or Cronus, and refer to the alders 'growing on the banks of' the Peneius and other rivers. The name of Orpheus's father, Oeagrus ('of the wild sorb-apple'), points to the same cult, since the sorb-apple (French = *alisier*) and the alder (Spanish = *aliso*) both bear the name of the pre-Hellenic River-goddess Halys, or Alys, or Elis, queen of the Elysian Islands, where Phoroneus, Cronus, and Orpheus went after death. Aornum is Avernus, an Italic variant of the Celtic Avalon ('apple-tree island' – see 31. *2*).

2. Orpheus is said by Diodorus Siculus to have used the old thirteen-consonant alphabet; and the legend that he made the trees move and charmed wild beasts apparently refers to its sequence of seasonal trees and symbolic animals (see 52. *3*; 132. *3* and *5*). As sacred king he was struck by a thunderbolt – that is, killed with a double-axe – in an oak grove at the summer solstice, and then dismembered by the Maenads of the bull cult, like Zagreus (see 30. *a*); or of the stag cult, like Actaeon (see 22. *i*); the Maenads in fact, represented the Muses. In Classical Greece the practice of tattooing was confined to Thracians, and in a vase-painting of Orpheus's murder a Maenad has a small stag tattooed on her forearm. This Orpheus did not come in conflict with the cult of Dionysus; he *was* Dionysus, and he played the rude alder-pipe, not the civilized lyre. Thus Proclus (Commentary on Plato's *Politics*: p. 398) writes:

> Orpheus, because he was the principal in the Dionysian rites, is said to have suffered the same fate as the god.

and Apollodorus (i. 3. 2) credits him with having invented the Mysteries of Dionysus.

3. The novel worship of the Sun as All-father seems to have been brought to the Northern Aegean by the fugitive priesthood of the mono-theistic Akhenaton, in the fourteenth century B.C., and grafted upon the local cults; hence Orpheus's alleged visit to Egypt. Records of this faith are found in Sophocles (*Fragments* 523 and 1017), where the sun is referred to as 'the eldest flame, dear to the Thracian horsemen', and as 'the sire of the gods, and father of all things.' It seems to have been forcefully resisted by the more conservative Thracians, and bloodily suppressed in some parts of the country. But later Orphic priests, who wore Egyptian costume, called the demi-god whose raw bull's flesh they ate 'Dionysus', and reserved the name Apollo for the immortal Sun: distinguishing Dionysus, the god of the senses, from Apollo, the god of the intellect. This explains why the head of Orpheus was laid up in Dionysus's sanc-tuary, but the lyre in Apollo's. Head and lyre are both said to have drifted to Lesbos, which was the chief seat of lyric music; Terpander, the earliest

historical musician, came from Antissa. The serpent's attack on Orpheus's head represents either the protest of an earlier oracular hero against Orpheus's intrusion at Antissa, or that of Pythian Apollo which Philostratus recorded in more direct language.

4. Eurydice's death by snake-bite and Orpheus's subsequent failure to bring her back into the sunlight, figure only in late myth. They seem to be mistakenly deduced from pictures which show Orpheus's welcome in Tartarus, where his music has charmed the Snake goddess Hecate, or Agriope ('savage face'), into giving special privileges to all ghosts initiated into the Orphic Mysteries, and from other pictures showing Dionysus, whose priest Orpheus was, descending to Tartarus in search of his mother Semele (see 27. *k*). Eurydice's victims died of snake-bite, not herself (see 33. *1*).

5. The alder-month is the fourth of the sacral tree-sequence, and it precedes the willow-month, associated with the water magic of the goddess Helice ('willow' – see 44. *1*); willows also gave their name to the river Helicon, which curves around Parnassus and is sacred to the Muses – the Triple Mountain-goddess of inspiration. Hence Orpheus was shown in a temple-painting at Delphi (Pausanias: x. 30. 3) leaning against a willow-tree and touching its branches. The Greek alder cult was suppressed in very early times, yet vestiges of it remain in Classical literature: alders enclose the death-island of the witch-goddess Circe (Homer: *Odyssey* v. 64 and 239) – she also had a willow-grove cemetery at Colchis (Apollonius Rhodius: iii. 220 – see 152. *b*) and, according to Virgil the sisters of Phaëthon were metamorphosed into an alder thicket (see 42. *3*).

6. This is not to suggest that Orpheus's decapitation was never more than a metaphor applied to the lopped alder-bough. A sacred king necessarily suffered dismemberment, and the Thracians may well have had the same custom as the Iban Dayaks of modern Sarawak. When the men come home from a successful head-hunting expedition the Iban women use the trophy as a means of fertilizing the rice crop by invocation. The head is made to sing, mourn, and answer questions and nursed tenderly in every lap until it finally consents to enter an oracular shrine, where it gives advice on all important occasions and, like the heads of Eurystheus, Bran, and Adam, repels invasions (see 146. *2*).

29

GANYMEDES

GANYMEDES, the son of King Tros who gave his name to Troy, was the most beautiful youth alive and therefore chosen by the gods to be

Zeus's cup-bearer. It is said that Zeus, desiring Ganymedes also as his
bedfellow, disguised himself in eagle's feathers and abducted him from
the Trojan plain.[1]

b. Afterwards, on Zeus's behalf, Hermes presented Tros with a
golden vine, the work of Hephaestus, and two fine horses, in compensation for his loss, assuring him at the same time that Ganymedes had
become immortal, exempt from the miseries of old age, and was now
smiling, golden bowl in hand, as he dispensed bright nectar to the
Father of Heaven.[2]

c. Some say that Eos had first abducted Ganymedes to be her para-
mour, and that Zeus took him from her. Be that as it may, Hera certainly deplored the insult to herself, and to her daughter Hebe, until
then the cup-bearer of the gods; but she succeeded only in vexing
Zeus, who set Ganymedes's image among the stars as Aquarius, the
water-carrier.[3]

1. Homer: *Iliad* xx. 231–5; Apollodorus: iii. 12. 2; Virgil: *Aeneid*
   v. 252 ff.; Ovid: *Metamorphoses* x. 155 ff.
2. Scholiast on Euripides's *Orestes* 1391; Homer: *Iliad* v. 266;
   Homeric Hymn to Aphrodite 202–17; Apollodorus: ii. 5. 9; Pausanias: v. 24. 1.
3. Scholiast on Apollonius Rhodius: iii. 115; Virgil: *Aeneid* i. 32,
   with scholiast; Hyginus: *Fabula* 224; Virgil: *Georgics* iii. 304.

*

1. Ganymedes's task as wine-pourer to all the gods – not merely Zeus
in early accounts – and the two horses, given to King Tros as compensation for his death, suggest the misreading of an icon which showed the
new king preparing for his sacred marriage. Ganymedes's bowl will have
contained a libation, poured to the ghost of his royal predecessor; and the
officiating priest in the picture, to whom he is making a token resistance,
has apparently been misread as amorous Zeus. Similarly, the waiting
bride has been misread as Eos by a mythographer who recalled Eos's
abduction of Tithonus, son of Laomedon – because Laomedon is also
said, by Euripides (*Trojan Women* 822), to have been Ganymedes's
father. This icon would equally illustrate Peleus's marriage to Thetis,
which the gods viewed from their twelve thrones; the two horses were
ritual instruments of his rebirth as king, after a mock-death (see 81. *4*).
The eagle's alleged abduction of Ganymedes is explained by a Caeretan
black-figured vase: an eagle darting at the thighs of a newly enthroned
king named Zeus typifies the divine power conferred upon him – his
ka, or other self – just as a solar hawk descended on the Pharoahs at their
coronation. Yet the tradition of Ganymedes's youth suggests that the

king shown in the icon was the royal surrogate, or *interrex*, ruling only for a single day: like the Phaëthon (see 42. 2), Zagreus (see 30. 1), Chrysippus (see 105. 2), and the rest. Zeus's eagle may therefore be said not only to have enroyalled him, but to have snatched him up to Olympus.

2. A royal ascent to Heaven on eagle-back, or in the form of an eagle, is a widespread religious fancy. Aristophanes caricatures it in *Peace* (1 ff.) by sending his hero up on the back of a dung-beetle. The soul of the Celtic hero Lugh – Llew Llaw in the *Mabinogion* – flew up to Heaven as an eagle when the tanist killed him at midsummer. Etana, the Babylonian hero, after his sacred marriage at Kish, rode on eagle-back towards Ishtar's heavenly courts, but fell into the sea and was drowned. Etana's death, by the way, was not the usual end-of-the-year sacrifice, as in the case of Icarus (see 92. 3), but a punishment for the bad crops which had characterized his reign – he was flying to discover a magical herb of fertility. His story is woven into an account of the continuous struggle between Eagle and Serpent – waxing and waning year, King and Tanist – and as in the myth of Llew Llaw, the Eagle, reduced to his last gasp at the winter solstice, has its life and strength magically renewed. Thus we find in *Psalm* ciii. 5: 'Thy youth is renewed, as the eagle's.'

3. The Zeus-Ganymedes myth gained immense popularity in Greece and Rome because it afforded religious justification for grown man's passionate love of a boy. Hitherto, sodomy had been tolerated only as an extreme form of goddess-worship: Cybele's male devotees tried to achieve ecstatic unity with her by emasculating themselves and dressing like women. Thus a sodomistic priesthood was a recognized institution in the Great Goddess's temples at Tyre, Joppa, Hierapolis, and at Jerusalem (1 *Kings* xv. 12 and 2 *Kings* xxiii. 7) until just before the Exile. But this new passion, for the introduction of which Thamyris (see 21. *m*) has been given the credit by Apollodorus, emphasized the victory of patriarchy over matriarchy. It turned Greek philosophy into an intellectual game that men could play without the assistance of women, now that they had found a new field of homosexual romance. Plato exploited this to the full, and used the myth of Ganymedes to justify his own sentimental feelings towards his pupils (*Phaedrus* 79); though elsewhere (*Laws* i. 8) he denounced sodomy as against nature, and called the myth of Zeus's indulgence in it 'a wicked Cretan invention'. (Here he has the support of Stephanus of Byzantium [*sub* Harpagia], who says that King Minos of Crete carried off Ganymedes to be his bedfellow, 'having received the laws from Zeus'.) With the spread of Platonic philosophy the hitherto intellectually dominant Greek woman degenerated into an unpaid worker and breeder of children wherever Zeus and Apollo were the ruling gods.

4. Ganymedes's name refers, properly, to the joyful stirring of his own

desire at the prospect of marriage, not to that of Zeus when refreshed by nectar from his bedfellow's hand; but, becoming *catamitus* in Latin, it has given English the word 'catamite', meaning the passive object of male homosexual lust.

5. The constellation Aquarius, identified with Ganymedes, was originally the Egyptian god, presiding over the source of the Nile, who poured water, not wine, from a flagon (Pindar: *Fragment* 110); but the Greeks took little interest in the Nile.

6. Zeus's nectar, which the later mythographers described as a supernatural red wine, was, in fact, a primitive brown mead (see 27. 2); and ambrosia, the delectable food of the gods, seems to have been a porridge of barley, oil, and chopped fruit (see 98. 7), with which kings were pampered when their poorer subjects still subsisted on asphodel (see 31. 2), mallow, and acorns.

30

ZAGREUS

ZEUS secretly begot his son Zagreus on Persephone, before she was taken to the Underworld by her uncle Hades. He set Rhea's sons, the Cretan Curetes or, some say, the Corybantes, to guard his cradle in the Idaean Cave, where they leaped about him, clashing their weapons, as they had leaped about Zeus himself at Dicte. But the Titans, Zeus's enemies, whitening themselves with gypsum until they were unrecognizable, waited until the Curetes slept. At midnight they lured Zagreus away, by offering him such childish toys as a cone, a bull-roarer, golden apples, a mirror, a knuckle-bone, and a tuft of wool. Zagreus showed courage when they murderously set upon him, and went through several transformations in an attempt to delude them: he became successively Zeus in a goat-skin coat, Cronus making rain, a lion, a horse, a horned serpent, a tiger, and a bull. At that point the Titans seized him firmly by the horns and feet, tore him apart with their teeth, and devoured his flesh raw.

b. Athene interrupted this grisly banquet shortly before its end and, rescuing Zagreus's heart, enclosed it in a gypsum figure, into which she breathed life; so that Zagreus became an immortal. His bones were

collected and buried at Delphi, and Zeus struck the Titans dead with
thunderbolts.[1]

> 1. Diodorus Siculus: v. 75. 4; Nonnus: *Dionysiaca* vi. 296 and xxvii.
> 228; Harpocration *sub* apomatton; Tzetzes: *On Lycophron* 355;
> Eustathius on Homer's *Iliad* ii. 735; Firmicus Maternus: *Concern-
> ing the Errors of Profane Religions* vi; Euripides: *The Cretans*,
> *Fragment* 475. Orphic Fragments (*Kern*, 34).

*

1. This myth concerns the annual sacrifice of a boy which took place
in ancient Crete: a surrogate for Minos the Bull-king. He reigned for a
single day, went through a dance illustrative of the five seasons – lion,
goat, horse, serpent, and bull-calf – and was then eaten raw. All the toys
with which the Titans lured him away were objects used by the philosophical Orphics, who inherited the tradition of this sacrifice but devoured
a bull-calf raw, instead of a boy. The bull-roarer was a pierced stone or
piece of pottery, which when whirled at the end of a cord made a noise
like a rising gale; and the tuft of wool may have been used to daub the
Curetes with the wet gypsum – these being youths who had cut and dedicated their first hair to the goddess Car (see 95. 5). They were also called
Corybantes, or crested dancers. Zagreus's other gifts served to explain
the nature of the ceremony by which the participants became one
with the god: the cone was an ancient emblem of the goddess, in whose
honour the Titans sacrificed him (see 20. 2); the mirror represented
each initiate's other self, or ghost; the golden apples, his passport to
Elysium after a mock-death; the knuckle-bone, his divinatory powers
(see 17. 3).

2. A Cretan hymn discovered a few years ago at Palaiokastro, near the
Dictaean Cave, is addressed to the Cronian One, greatest of youths, who
comes dancing at the head of his demons and leaps to increase the fertility
of soil and flocks, and for the success of the fishing fleet. Jane Harrison in
Themis suggests that the shielded tutors there mentioned, who 'took thee,
immortal child, from Rhea's side,' merely pretended to kill and eat the
victim, an initiate into their secret society. But all such mock-deaths at
initiation ceremonies, reported from many parts of the world, seem
ultimately based on a tradition of actual human sacrifice; and Zagreus's
calendar changes distinguish him from an ordinary member of a totemistic fraternity.

3. The uncanonical tiger in the last of Zagreus's transformations is
explained by his identity with Dionysus (see 27. *c*), of whose death and
resurrection the same story is told, although with cooked flesh instead of
raw, and Rhea's name instead of Athene's. Dionysus, too, was a horned
serpent – he had horns and serpent locks at birth (see 27. *a*) – and his

Orphic devotees ate him sacramentally in bull form. Zagreus became
'Zeus in a goat-skin coat', because Zeus or his child surrogate had
ascended to Heaven wearing a coat made from the hide of the goat
Amaltheia (see 7. b). 'Cronus making rain' is a reference to the use of the
bull-roarer in rain-making ceremonies. In this context the Titans were
Titanoi, 'white-chalk men', the Curetes themselves disguised so that the
ghost of the victim would not recognize them. When human sacrifices
went out of fashion, Zeus was represented as hurling his thunderbolt at
the cannibals; and the *Titanes*, 'lords of the seven-day week', became
confused with the *Titanoi*, 'the white-chalk men', because of their hostility to Zeus. No Orphic, who had once eaten the flesh of his god, ever
again touched meat of any kind.

4. Zagreus-Dionysus was also known in Southern Palestine. According to the Ras Shamra tablets, Ashtar temporarily occupied the throne of
Heaven while the god Baal languished in the Underworld, having eaten
the food of the dead. Ashtar was only a child and when he sat on the
throne, his feet did not reach the footstool; Baal presently returned and
killed him with a club. The Mosaic Law prohibited initiation feasts in
Ashtar's honour: 'Thou shalt not seethe a kid in his mother's milk' – an
injunction three times repeated (*Exodus* xxiii. 19; xxxiv. 26; *Deuteronomy*
xiv. 21).

31

THE GODS OF THE UNDERWORLD

When ghosts descend to Tartarus, the main entrance to which lies in a
grove of black poplars beside the Ocean stream, each is supplied by
pious relatives with a coin laid under the tongue of its corpse. They are
thus able to pay Charon, the miser who ferries them in a crazy boat
across the Styx. This hateful river bounds Tartarus on the western
side,[1] and has for its tributaries Acheron, Phlegethon, Cocytus, Aornis,
and Lethe. Penniless ghosts must wait for ever on the near bank; unless
they have evaded Hermes, their conductor, and crept down by a back
entrance, such as at Laconian Taenarus,[2] or Thesprotian Aornum. A
three-headed or, some say, fifty-headed dog named Cerberus, guards
the opposite shore of Styx, ready to devour living intruders or ghostly
fugitives.[3]

b. The first region of Tartarus contains the cheerless Asphodel

Fields, where souls of heroes stay without purpose among the throngs of less distinguished dead that twitter like bats, and where only Orion still has the heart to hunt the ghostly deer.[4] None of them but would rather live in bondage to a landless peasant than rule over all Tartarus. Their one delight is in libations of blood poured to them by the living: when they drink they feel themselves almost men again. Beyond these meadows lie Erebus and the palace of Hades and Persephone. To the left of the palace, as one approaches it, a white cypress shades the pool of Lethe, where the common ghosts flock down to drink. Initiated souls avoid this water, choosing to drink instead from the pool of Memory, shaded by a white poplar [?], which gives them a certain advantage over their fellows.[5] Close by, newly arrived ghosts are daily judged by Minos, Rhadamanthys, and Aeacus at a place where three roads meet. Rhadamanthys tries Asiatics and Aeacus tries Europeans; but both refer the difficult cases to Minos. As each verdict is given the ghosts are directed along one of the three roads; that leading back to the Asphodel Meadows, if they are neither virtuous nor evil; that leading to the punishment-field of Tartarus, if they are evil; that leading to the orchards of Elysium, if they are virtuous.

c. Elysium, ruled over by Cronus, lies near Hades's dominions, its entrance close to the pool of Memory, but forms no part of them; it is a happy land of perpetual day, without cold or snow, where games, music, and revels never cease, and where the inhabitants may elect to be reborn on earth whenever they please. Near by are the Fortunate Islands, reserved for those who have been three times born, and three times attained Elysium.[6] But some say that there is another Fortunate Isle called Leuce in the Black Sea, opposite the mouths of the Danube, wooded and full of beasts, wild and tame, where the ghosts of Helen and Achilles hold high revelry and declaim Homer's verses to heroes who have taken part in the events celebrated by him.[7]

d. Hades, who is fierce and jealous of his rights, seldom visits the upper air, except on business or when he is overcome by sudden lust. Once he dazzled the Nymph Minthe with the splendour of his golden chariot and its four black horses, and would have seduced her without difficulty had not Queen Persephone made a timely appearance and metamorphosed Minthe into sweet-smelling mint. On another occasion Hades tried to violate the Nymph Leuce, who was similarly metamorphosed into the white poplar standing by the pool of Memory.[8] He willingly allows none of his subjects to escape, and few who visit

Tartarus return alive to describe it, which makes him the most hated of the gods.

e. Hades never knows what is happening in the world above, or in Olympus,[9] except for fragmentary information which comes to him when mortals strike their hands upon the earth and invoke him with oaths and curses. His most prized possession is the helmet of invisibility, given him as a mark of gratitude by the Cyclopes when he consented to release them at Zeus's order. All the riches of gems and precious metals hidden beneath the earth are his, but he owns no property above ground, except for certain gloomy temples in Greece and, possibly, a herd of cattle in the island of Erytheia which, some say, really belong to Helius.[10]

f. Queen Persephone, however, can be both gracious and merciful. She is faithful to Hades, but has had no children by him and prefers the company of Hecate, goddess of witches, to his.[11] Zeus himself honours Hecate so greatly that he never denies her the ancient power which she has always enjoyed: of bestowing on mortals, or withholding from them, any desired gift. She has three bodies and three heads – lion, dog, and mare.[12]

g. Tisiphone, Alecto, and Megaera, the Erinnyes or Furies, live in Erebus, and are older than Zeus or any of the other Olympians. Their task is to hear complaints brought by mortals against the insolence of the young to the aged, of children to parents, of hosts to guests, and of householders or city councils to suppliants – and to punish such crimes by hounding the culprits relentlessly, without rest or pause, from city to city and from country to country. These Erinnyes are crones, with snakes for hair, dogs' heads, coal-black bodies, bats' wings, and blood-shot eyes. In their hands they carry brass-studded scourges, and their victims die in torment.[13] It is unwise to mention them by name in conversation; hence they are usually styled the Eumenides, which means 'The Kindly Ones' – as Hades is styled Pluton, or Pluto, 'The Rich One'.

1. Pausanias: x. 28. 1.
2. Apollodorus: ii. 5. 2; Strabo: viii. 5. 1.
3. Homer: *Iliad* viii. 368; Hesiod: *Theogony* 311; Apollodorus: *loc. cit.*; Euripides: *Heracles* 24.
4. Homer: *Odyssey* xi. 539; xi. 572–5; xi. 487–91.
5. *Petelia Orphic Tablet.*
6. Plato: *Gorgias* 168; Pindar: *Olympian Odes* ii. 68–80; Hesiod: *Works and Days* 167 ff.

7. Pausanias: iii. 19. 11; Philostratus: *Heroica* x. 32–40.
8. Strabo: viii. 3. 14; Servius on Virgil's *Eclogue* vii. 61.
9. Homer: *Iliad* ix. 158–9; xx. 61.
10. Homer: *Iliad* ix. 567 ff.; Apollodorus: ii. 5. 10; Scholiast on Pindar's *Isthmian Odes* vi. 32.
11. Apollonius Rhodius: iii. 529; Ovid: *Metamorphoses* xiv. 405; Scholiast on Theocritus's *Idylls* ii. 12.
12. Hesiod: *Theogony* 411–52.
13. Apollodorus: i. 1. 4; Homer: *Iliad* ix. 453–7; xv. 204; xix. 259; *Odyssey* ii. 135 and xvii. 475; Aeschylus: *Eumenides* 835 and *Libation Bearers* 290 and 924; Euripides: *Orestes* 317 ff.; *Orphic Hymn* lxviii. 5.

*

1. The mythographers made a bold effort to reconcile the conflicting views of the afterworld held by the primitive inhabitants of Greece. One view was that ghosts lived in their tombs, or underground caverns or fissures, where they might take the form of serpents, mice, or bats, but never be reincarnate as human beings. Another was that the souls of sacred kings walked visibly on the sepulchral islands where their bodies had been buried. A third was that ghosts could become men again by entering beans, nuts, or fish, and being eaten by their prospective mothers. A fourth was that they went to the Far North, where the sun never shines, and returned, if at all, only as fertilizing winds. A fifth was that they went to the Far West, where the sun sets in the ocean, and a spirit world much like the present. A sixth was that a ghost received punishment according to the life he had led. To this the Orphics finally added the theory of metempsychosis, the transmigration of souls: a process which could be to some degree controlled by the use of magical formulas.

2. Persephone and Hecate stood for the pre-Hellenic hope of regeneration; but Hades, a Hellenic concept for the ineluctability of death. Cronus, despite his bloody record, continued to enjoy the pleasures of Elysium, since that had always been the privilege of a sacred king, and Menelaus (*Odyssey* iv. 561) was promised the same enjoyment, not because he had been particularly virtuous or courageous but because he had married Helen, the priestess of the Spartan Moon-goddess (see 159. 1). The Homeric adjective *asphodelos*, applied only to *leimōnes* ('meadows'), probably means 'in the valley of that which is not reduced to ashes' (from *a* = not, *spodos* = ash, *elos* = valley) – namely the hero's ghost after his body has been burned; and, except in acorn-eating Arcadia, asphodel roots and seeds, offered to such ghosts, made the staple Greek diet before the introduction of corn. Asphodel grows freely even on waterless islands and ghosts, like gods, are conservative in their diet. Elysium seems to mean 'apple-land' – *alisier* is a pre-Gallic word for

sorb-apple – as do the Arthurian 'Avalon' and the Latin 'Avernus', or 'Avolnus', both formed from the Indo-European root *abol*, meaning apple.

3. Cerberus was the Greek counterpart of Anubis, the dog-headed son of the Libyan Death-goddess Nephthys, who conducted souls to the Underworld. In European folklore, which is partly of Libyan origin, the souls of the damned were hunted to the Northern Hell by a yelling pack of hounds – the hounds of Annwm, Herne, Arthur, or Gabriel – a myth derived from the noisy summer migration of wild geese to their breeding places in the Arctic circle. Cerberus was, at first, fifty-headed, like the spectral pack that destroyed Actaeon (see 22. 1); but afterwards three-headed, like his mistress Hecate (see 134. 1).

4. Styx ('hated'), a small stream in Arcadia, the waters of which were supposed to be deadly poison, was located in Tartarus only by late mythographers. Acheron ('stream of woe') and Cocytus ('wailing') are fanciful names to describe the misery of death. Aornis ('birdless') is a Greek mistranslation of the Italic 'Avernus'. Lethe means 'forgetfulness'; and Erebus 'covered'. Phlegethon ('burning') refers to the custom of cremation but also, perhaps, to the theory that sinners were burned in streams of lava. Tartarus seems to be a reduplication of the pre-Hellenic word *tar*, which occurs in the names of places lying to the West; its sense of infernality comes late.

5. Black poplars were sacred to the Death-goddess (see 51. 7 and 170. *l*); and white poplars, or aspens, either to Persephone as Goddess of Regeneration, or to Heracles because he harrowed Hell (see 134. *f*) – golden head-dresses of aspen leaves have been found in Mesopotamian burials of the fourth millennium B.C. The Orphic tablets do not name the tree by the pool of Memory; it is probably the white poplar into which Leuce was transformed, but possibly a nut-tree, the emblem of Wisdom (see 86. 1). White-cypress wood, regarded as an anti-corruptive, was used for household chests and coffins.

6. Hades had a temple at the foot of Mount Menthe in Elis, and his rape of Minthe ('mint') is probably deduced from the use of mint in funerary rites, together with rosemary and myrtle, to offset the smell of decay. Demeter's barley-water drink at Eleusis was flavoured with mint (see 24. *e*). Though awarded the sun-cattle of Erytheia ('red land'), because that was where the Sun met his nightly death, Hades is more usually called Cronus, or Geryon, in this context (see 132. 4).

7. Hesiod's account of Hecate shows her to have been the original Triple-goddess, supreme in Heaven, on earth, and in Tartarus; but the Hellenes emphasized her destructive powers at the expense of her creative ones until, at last, she was invoked only in clandestine rites of black magic, especially at places where three roads met. That Zeus did not deny her

the ancient power of granting every mortal his heart's desire is a tribute to the Thessalian witches, of whom everyone stood in dread. Lion, dog, and horse, her heads, evidently refer to the ancient tripartite year, the dog being the Dog-star Sirius; as do also Cerberus's heads.

8. Hecate's companions, the Erinnyes, were personified pangs of conscience after the breaking of a taboo – at first only the taboo of insult, disobedience, or violence to a mother (see 105. k and 114. 1). Suppliants and guests came under the protection of Hestia, Goddess of the Hearth (see 20. c), and to ill-treat them would be to disobey and insult her.

9. Leuce, the largest island in the Black Sea, but very small at that, is now a treeless Rumanian penal colony (see 164. 3).

32

TYCHE AND NEMESIS

TYCHE is a daughter of Zeus, to whom he has given power to decide what the fortune of this or that mortal shall be. On some she heaps gifts from a horn of plenty, others she deprives of all that they have. Tyche is altogether irresponsible in her awards, and runs about juggling with a ball to exemplify the uncertainty of chance: sometimes up, sometimes down. But if it ever happens that a man, whom she has favoured, boasts of his abundant riches and neither sacrifices a part of them to the gods, nor alleviates the poverty of his fellow-citizens, then the ancient goddess Nemesis steps in to humiliate him.[1] Nemesis, whose home is at Attic Rhamnus, carries an apple-bough in one hand, and a wheel in the other, and wears a silver crown adorned with stags; the scourge hangs at her girdle. She is a daughter of Oceanus and has something of Aphrodite's beauty.

b. Some say that Zeus once fell in love with Nemesis, and pursued her over the earth and through the sea. Though she constantly changed her shape, he violated her at last by adopting the form of a swan, and from the egg she laid came Helen, the cause of the Trojan War.[2]

1. Pindar: *Olympian Odes* xii. 1–2; Herodotus: i. 34 and iii. 40; Apollonius Rhodius: iv. 1042–3; Sophocles: *Philoctetes* 518.
2. Pausanias: i. 33. 3; Homer's *Cypria*, quoted by Athenaeus p. 334b; Apollodorus: iii. 10. 7.

*

1. Tyche ('fortune'), like Dice and Aedos (personifications of Natural Law, or Justice, and Shame), was an artificial deity invented by the early

philosophers; whereas Nemesis ('due enactment') had been the Nymph-goddess of Death-in-Life (see 18. 3) whom they now redefined as a moral control on Tyche. That Nemesis's wheel was originally the solar year is suggested by the name of her Latin counterpart, Fortuna (from *vortumna*, 'she who turns the year about'). When the wheel had turned half circle, the sacred king, raised to the summit of his fortune, was fated to die – the Actaeon stags on her crown (see 22. i) announce this – but when it came full circle, he revenged himself on the rival who had supplanted him. Her scourge was formerly used for ritual flogging, to fructify the trees and crops, and the apple-bough was the king's passport to Elysium (see 53. 5; 80. 4; and 133. 4).

2. The Nemesis whom Zeus chased (see 62. b), is not the philosophical concept of divine vengeance on overweening mortals, but the original Nymph-goddess, whose usual name was Leda. In pre-Hellenic myth, the goddess chases the sacred king and, although he goes through his seasonal transformations (see 30. 1), counters each of them in turn with her own, and devours him at the summer solstice. In Hellenic myth the parts are reversed: the goddess flees, changing shape, but the king pursues and finally violates her, as in the story of Zeus and Metis (see 9. d), or Peleus and Thetis (see 81. k). The required seasonal transformations will have been indicated on the spokes of Nemesis's wheel; but in Homer's *Cypria* only a fish and 'various beasts' are mentioned (see 89. 2). 'Leda' is another form of Leto, or Latona, whom the Python, not Zeus, chased (see 14. a). Swans were sacred to the goddess (Euripides: *Iphigeneia Among the Taurians* 1095 ff.), because of their white plumage, also because the V-formation of their flight was a female symbol, and because, at mid-summer, they flew north to unknown breeding grounds, supposedly taking the dead king's soul with them (see 33. 5 and 142. 2).

3. The philosophical Nemesis was worshipped at Rhamnus where, according to Pausanias (i. 33. 2–3), the Persian commander-in-chief, who had intended to set up a white marble trophy in celebration of his conquest of Attica, was forced to retire by news of a naval defeat at Salamis; the marble was used instead for an image of the local Nymph-goddess Nemesis. It is supposed to have been from this event that Nemesis came to personify 'Divine vengeance', rather than the 'due enactment' of the annual death drama; since to Homer, at any rate, *nemesis* had been merely a warm human feeling that payment should be duly made, or a task duly performed. But Nemesis the Nymph-goddess bore the title Adrasteia ('inescapable' – Strabo: xiii. 1. 13), which was also the name of Zeus's foster-nurse, an ash-nymph (see 7. b); and since the ash-nymphs and the Erinnyes were sisters, born from the blood of Uranus, this may have been how Nemesis came to embody the idea of vengeance. The ash-tree was one of the goddess's seasonal disguises, and an important one to her

pastoral devotees, because of its association with thunderstorms and with the lambing month, the third of the sacral year (see 52. 3).

4. Nemesis is called a daughter of Oceanus, because as the Nymph-goddess with the apple-bough she was also the sea-born Aphrodite, sister of the Erynnyes (see 18. 4).

33

THE CHILDREN OF THE SEA

THE fifty Nereids, gentle and beneficent attendants on the Sea-goddess Thetis, are mermaids, daughters of the nymph Doris by Nereus, a prophetic old man of the sea, who has the power of changing his shape.[1]

b. The Phorcids, their cousins, children of Ceto by Phorcys, another wise old man of the sea, are Ladon, Echidne, and the three Gorgons, dwellers in Libya; the three Graeae; and, some say, the three Hesperides. The Gorgons were named Stheino, Euryale, and Medusa, all once beautiful. But one night Medusa lay with Poseidon, and Athene, enraged that they had bedded in one of her own temples, changed her into a winged monster with glaring eyes, huge teeth, protruding tongue, brazen claws and serpent locks, whose gaze turned men to stone. When eventually Perseus decapitated Medusa, and Poseidon's children Chrysaor and Pegasus sprang from her dead body, Athene fastened the head to her aegis; but some say that the aegis was Medusa's own skin, flayed from her by Athene.[2]

c. The Graeae are fair-faced and swan-like, but with hair grey from birth, and only one eye and one tooth between the three of them. Their names are Enyo, Pemphredo, and Deino.[3]

d. The three Hesperides, by name Hespere, Aegle, and Erytheis, live in the far-western orchard which Mother Earth gave to Hera. Some call them daughters of Night, others of Atlas and of Hesperis, daughter of Hesperus; sweetly they sing.[4]

e. Half of Echidne was lovely woman, half was speckled serpent. She once lived in a deep cave among the Arimi, where she ate men raw, and raised a brood of frightful monsters to her husband Typhon; but hundred-eyed Argus killed her while she slept.[5]

f. Ladon was wholly serpent, though gifted with the power of human speech, and guarded the golden apples of the Hesperides until Heracles shot him dead.[6]

g. Nereus, Phorcys, Thaumas, Eurybia, and Ceto were all children born to Pontus by Mother Earth; thus the Phorcids and Nereids claim cousinhood with the Harpies. These are the fair-haired and swift-winged daughters of Thaumas by the Ocean-nymph Electra, who snatch up criminals for punishment by the Erinnyes, and live in a Cretan cave.[7]

1. Homer: *Iliad* xviii. 36 ff.; Apollodorus: i. 2. 7.
2. Hesiod: *Theogony* 270 ff. and 333 ff.; Apollodorus: ii. 4. 3; Ovid: *Metamorphoses* iv. 792–802; Scholiast on Apollonius Rhodius iv. 1399; Euripides: *Ion* 989 ff.
3. Hesiod: *Theogony* 270–4; Apollodorus: ii. 4. 2.
4. Hesiod: *Theogony* 215 and 518; Diodorus Siculus: iv. 27. 2; Euripides: *Heracles* 394.
5. Homer: *Iliad* ii, 783; Hesiod: *Theogony* 295 ff.; Apollodorus: ii. 1. 2.
6. Hesiod: *Theogony* 333–5; Apollonius Rhodius: iv. 1397; Apollodorus: ii. 5. 11.
7. Apollodorus: i. 2. 6; Hesiod: *Theogony* 265–9; Homer: *Odyssey* xx. 77–8; Apollonius Rhodius: ii. 298–9.

*

1. It seems that the Moon-goddess's title Eurynome ('wide rule' or 'wide wandering') proclaimed her ruler of heaven and earth; Eurybia ('wide strength'), ruler of the sea; Eurydice ('wide justice') the serpent-grasping ruler of the Underworld. Male human sacrifices were offered to her as Eurydice, their death being apparently caused by viper's venom (see 28. *4*; 154. *b* and 168. *e*). Echidne's death at the hand of Argus probably refers to the suppression of the Serpent-goddess's Argive cult. Her brother Ladon is the oracular serpent who haunts every paradise, his coils embracing the apple-tree (see 133. *4*).

2. Among Eurybia's other sea-titles were Thetis ('disposer'), or its variant Tethys; Ceto, as the sea-monster corresponding with the Hebrew Rahab, or the Babylonian Tiamat (see 73. *7*); Nereis, as the goddess of the wet element. Electra as provider of amber, a sea product highly valued by the ancients (see 148. *11*); Thaumas, as wonderful; and Doris, as bountiful. Nereus – *alias* Proteus ('first man') – the prophetic 'old man of the sea', who took his name from Nereis, not contrariwise, seems to have been an oracular sacred king, buried on a coastal island (see 133. *d*); he is pictured in an early vase-painting as fish-tailed, with a lion, a stag, and a viper emerging from his body. Proteus, in the *Odyssey*, similarly changed shapes, to mark the seasons through which the sacred king moved from birth to death (see 30. 1).

3. The fifty Nereids seem to have been a college of fifty Moon-priestesses, whose magic rites ensured good fishing; and the Gorgons, representatives of the Triple-goddess, wearing prophylactic masks – with scowl, glaring eyes, and protruding tongue between bared teeth – to frighten strangers from her Mysteries (see 73. 9). The Sons of Homer knew only a single Gorgon, who was a shade in Tartarus (*Odyssey* xi. 633–5), and whose head, an object of terror to Odysseus (*Odyssey* xi. 634), Athene wore on her aegis, doubtless to warn people against examining the divine mysteries hidden behind it. Greek bakers used to paint Gorgon masks on their ovens, to discourage busybodies from opening the oven door, peeping in, and thus allowing a draught to spoil the bread. The Gorgons' names – Stheino ('strong'), Euryale ('wide roaming'), and Medusa ('cunning one') – are titles of the Moon-goddess; the Orphics called the moon's face 'the Gorgon's head'.

4. Poseidon's fathering of Pegasus on Medusa recalls his fathering of the horse Arion on Demeter, when she disguised herself as a mare, and her subsequent fury (see 16.*f*); both myths describe how Poseidon's Hellenes forcibly married the Moon-priestesses, disregarding their Gorgon masks, and took over the rain-making rites of the sacred horse cult. But a mask of Demeter was still kept in a stone chest at Pheneus, and the *priest* of Demeter assumed it when he performed the ceremony of beating the Infernal Spirits with rods (Pausanias: viii. 15. 1).

5. Chrysaor was Demeter's new-moon sign, the golden sickle, or falchion; her consorts carried it when they deputized for her. Athene, in this version, is Zeus's collaborator, reborn from his head, and a traitress to the old religion (see 9. 1). The three Harpies, regarded by Homer as personifications of the storm winds (*Odyssey* xx. 66–78), were the earlier Athene, the Triple-goddess, in her capacity of sudden destroyer. So were the Graeae, the Three Grey Ones, as their names Enyo ('warlike'), Pemphredo ('wasp'), and Deino ('terrible') show; their single eye and tooth are misreadings of a sacred picture (see 73. 9), and the swan is a death-bird in European mythology (see 32. 2).

6. Phorcys, a masculine form of Phorcis, the Goddess or Sow (see 74. 4 and 96. 2), who devours corpses, appears in Latin as *Orcus*, a title of Hades, and as *porcus*, hog. The Gorgons and Grey Ones were called Phorcides, because it was death to profane the Goddess's Mysteries; but Phorcys's prophetic wisdom must refer to a sow-oracle (see 24. 7).

7. The names of the Hesperides, described as children either of Ceto and Phorcys, or of Night, or of Atlas the Titan who holds up the heavens in the Far West (see 39. 1 and 133. *e*), refer to the sunset. Then the sky is green, yellow, and red, as if it were an apple-tree in full bearing; and the

Sun, cut by the horizon like a crimson half-apple, meets his death dramatically in the western waves. When the Sun has gone, Hesperus appears.
This star was sacred to the Love-goddess Aphrodite, and the apple was
the gift by which her priestess decoyed the king, the Sun's representative,
to his death with love-songs; if an apple is cut in two transversely, her
five-pointed star appears in the centre of each half.

34

THE CHILDREN OF ECHIDNE

ECHIDNE bore a dreadful brood to Typhon: namely, Cerberus, the
three-headed Hound of Hell; the Hydra, a many-headed water-serpent
living at Lerna; the Chimaera, a fire-breathing goat with lion's head
and serpent's body; and Orthrus, the two-headed hound of Geryon,
who lay with his own mother and begot on her the Sphinx and the
Nemean Lion.[1]

1. Hesiod: *Theogony* 306 ff.

                              *

1. Cerberus (see 31. *a* and 134. *e*), associated by the Dorians with the
dog-headed Egyptian god Anubis who conducted souls to the Underworld, seems to have originally been the Death-goddess Hecate, or
Hecabe (see 168. *1*); she was portrayed as a bitch because dogs eat corpse
flesh and howl at the moon.

2. The Chimaera was, apparently, a calendar-symbol of the tripartite
year (see 75. *2*), of which the seasonal emblems were lion, goat, and
serpent.

3. Orthrus (see 132. *d*), who fathered the Chimaera, the Sphinx (see
105. *e*), the Hydra (see 60. *h* and 124. *c*), and the Nemean Lion (see 123. *b*)
on Echidne was Sirius, the Dog-star, which inaugurated the Athenian
New Year. He had two heads, like Janus, because the reformed year at
Athens had two seasons, not three; Orthrus's son, the Lion, emblemizing
the first half, and his daughter, the Serpent, emblemizing the second.
When the Goat-emblem disappeared, the Chimaera gave place to the
Sphinx, with her winged lion's body and serpent's tail. Since the reformed
New Year began when the Sun was in Leo and the Dog Days had now
begun, Orthrus looked in two directions – forward to the New Year,
backward to the Old – like the Calendar-goddess Cardea, whom the
Romans named Postvorta and Antevorta on that account. Orthrus was
called 'early' presumably because he introduced the New Year.

THE GIANTS' REVOLT

ENRAGED because Zeus had confined their brothers, the Titans, in Tartarus, certain tall and terrible giants, with long locks and beards, and serpent-tails for feet, plotted an assault on Heaven. They had been born from Mother Earth at Thracian Phlegra, twenty-four in number.[1]

b. Without warning, they seized rocks and fire-brands and hurled them upwards from their mountain tops, so that the Olympians were hard pressed. Hera prophesied gloomily that the giants could never be killed by any god, but only by a single, lion-skinned mortal; and that even he could do nothing unless the enemy were anticipated in their search for a certain herb of invulnerability, which grew in a secret place on earth. Zeus at once took counsel with Athene; sent her off to warn Heracles, the lion-skinned mortal to whom Hera was evidently referring, exactly how matters stood; and forbade Eros, Selene, and Helius to shine for a while. Under the feeble light of the stars, Zeus groped about on earth, in the region to which Athene directed him, found the herb, and brought it safely to Heaven.

c. The Olympians could now join battle with the giants. Heracles let loose his first arrow against Alcyoneus, the enemy's leader. He fell to the ground, but sprang up again revived, because this was his native soil of Phlegra. 'Quick, noble Heracles!' cried Athene. 'Drag him away to another country!' Heracles caught Alcyoneus up on his shoulders, and dragged him over the Thracian border, where he despatched him with a club.

d. Then Porphyrion leaped into Heaven from the great pyramid of rocks which the giants had piled up, and none of the gods stood his ground. Only Athene adopted a posture of defence. Rushing by her, Porphyrion made for Hera, whom he tried to strangle; but, wounded in the liver by a timely arrow from Eros's bow, he turned from anger to lust, and ripped off Hera's glorious robe. Zeus, seeing that his wife was about to be outraged, ran forward in jealous wrath, and felled Porphyrion with a thunderbolt. Up he sprang again, but Heracles, returning to Phlegra in the nick of time, mortally wounded him with an arrow. Meanwhile, Ephialtes had engaged Ares and beaten him to his knees; however, Apollo shot the wretch in the left eye and called to Heracles, who at once planted another arrow in the right. Thus died Ephialtes.

e. Now, wherever a god wounded a giant – as when Dionysus felled Eurytus with his thyrsus, or Hecate singed Clytius with her torches, or Hephaestus scalded Mimas with a ladle of red-hot metal, or Athene crushed the lustful Pallas with a stone, it was Heracles who had to deal the death blow. The peace-loving goddesses Hestia and Demeter took no part in the conflict, but stood dismayed, wringing their hands; the Fates, however, swung brazen pestles to good effect.[2]

f. Discouraged, the remaining giants fled back to earth, pursued by the Olympians. Athene threw a vast missile at Enceladus, which crushed him flat and became the island of Sicily. And Poseidon broke off part of Cos with his trident and threw it at Polybutes; this became the nearby islet of Nisyros, beneath which he lies buried.[3]

g. The remaining giants made a last stand at Bathos, near Arcadian Trapezus, where the ground still burns, and giants' bones are sometimes turned up by ploughmen. Hermes, borrowing Hades's helmet of invisibility, struck down Hippolytus, and Artemis pierced Gration with an arrow; while the Fates' pestles broke the heads of Agrius and Thoas. Ares, with his spear, and Zeus, with his thunderbolt, now accounted for the rest, though Heracles was called upon to despatch each giant as he fell. But some say that the battle took place on the Phlegraean Plain, near Cumae in Italy.[4]

h. Silenus the earth-born Satyr claims to have taken part in this battle at the side of his pupil Dionysus, killing Enceladus and spreading panic among the giants by the braying of his old pack-ass; but Silenus is usually drunken and cannot distinguish truth from falsehood.[5]

1. Apollodorus: i. 6. 1; Hyginus: *Fabulae, Proem.*
2. Apollodorus: i. 6. 2.
3. Apollodorus: *loc. cit.*; Strabo: x. 5. 16.
4. Pausanias: viii. 29. 1-2; Apollodorus: *loc. cit.*; Diodorus Siculus: iv. 21.
5. Euripides: *Cyclops* 5 ff.

*

1. This is a post-Homeric story, preserved in a degenerate version: Eros and Dionysus, who take part in the fighting, are late-comers to Olympus (see 15. *1-2* and 27. *5*), and Heracles is admitted there before his apotheosis on Mount Oeta (see 147. *h*). It purports to account for the finding of mammoth bones at Trapezus (where they are still shown in the

local museum); and for the volcanic fires at Bathos near by – also at Arcadian, or Thracian, Pallene, at Cumae, and in the islands of Sicily and Nisyros, beneath which Athene and Poseidon are said to have buried two of the giants.

2. The historical incident underlying the Giants' Revolt – and also the Aloeids' Revolt (see 37. *b*), of which it is usually regarded as a doublet – seems to be a concerted attempt by non-Hellenic mountaineers to storm certain Hellenic fortresses, and their repulse by the Hellenes' subject-allies. But the powerlessness and cowardice of the gods, contrasted with the invincibility of Heracles, and the farcical incidents of the battle, are more characteristic of popular fiction than of myth.

3. There is, however, a hidden religious element in the story. These giants are not flesh and blood, but earth-born spirits, as their serpent-tails prove, and can be thwarted only by the possession of a magical herb. No mythographer mentions the name of the herb, but it was probably the *ephialtion*, a specific against the nightmare. Ephialtes, the name of the giants' leader means literally 'he who leaps upon' (*incubus* in Latin); and the attempts of Porphyrion to strangle and rape Hera, and of Pallas to rape Athene, suggest that the story mainly concerns the wisdom of invoking Heracles the Saviour, when threatened by erotic nightmares at any hour of the twenty-four.

4. Alcyoneus ('mighty ass') is probably the spirit of the sirocco, 'the breath of the Wild Ass, or Typhon' (see 36. *1*), which brings bad dreams, and murderous inclinations, and rapes; and this makes Silenus's claim to have routed the giants with the braying of his pack-ass still more ridiculous (see 20. *b*). Mimas ('mimicry') may refer to the delusive verisimilitude of dreams; and Hippolytus ('stampede of horses') recalls the ancient attribution of terror-dreams to the Mare-headed goddess. In the north, it was Odin whom sufferers from 'the Nightmare and her ninefold' invoked, until his place was taken by St Swithold.

5. What use Heracles made of the herb can be deduced from the Babylonian myth of the cosmic fight between the new gods and the old. There Marduck, Heracles's counterpart, holds a herb to his nostrils against the noxious smell of the goddess Tiamat; here Alcyoneus's breath has to be counteracted.

36

TYPHON

IN revenge for the destruction of the giants, Mother Earth lay with Tartarus, and presently in the Corycian Cave of Cilicia brought forth her youngest child, Typhon: the largest monster ever born.[1] From the thighs downward he was nothing but coiled serpents, and his arms which, when he spread them out, reached a hundred leagues in either direction, had countless serpents' heads instead of hands. His brutish ass-head touched the stars, his vast wings darkened the sun, fire flashed from his eyes, and flaming rocks hurtled from his mouth. When he came rushing towards Olympus, the gods fled in terror to Egypt, where they disguised themselves as animals: Zeus becoming a ram; Apollo, a crow; Dionysus, a goat; Hera, a white cow; Artemis, a cat; Aphrodite, a fish; Ares, a boar; Hermes, an ibis, and so on.

b. Athene alone stood her ground, and taunted Zeus with cowardice until, resuming his true form, he let fly a thunderbolt at Typhon, and followed this up with a sweep of the same flint sickle that had served to castrate his grandfather Uranus. Wounded and shouting, Typhon fled to Mount Casius, which looms over Syria from the north, and there the two grappled. Typhon twined his myriad coils about Zeus, disarmed him of his sickle and, after severing the sinews of his hands and feet with it, dragged him into the Corycian Cave. Zeus is immortal, but now he could not move a finger, and Typhon had hidden the sinews in a bear-skin, over which Delphyne, a serpent-tailed sister-monster, stood guard.

c. The news of Zeus's defeat spread dismay among the gods, but Hermes and Pan went secretly to the cave, where Pan frightened Delphyne with a sudden horrible shout, while Hermes skilfully abstracted the sinews and replaced them on Zeus's limbs.[2]

d. But some say that it was Cadmus who wheedled the sinews from Delphyne, saying that he needed them for lyre-strings on which to play her delightful music; and Apollo who shot her dead.[3]

e. Zeus returned to Olympus and, mounted upon a chariot drawn by winged horses, once more pursued Typhon with thunderbolts. Typhon had gone to Mount Nysa, where the Three Fates offered him ephemeral fruits, pretending that these would restore his vigour though, in reality, they doomed him to certain death. He reached Mount Haemus in Thrace and, picking up whole mountains, hurled them at Zeus, who interposed his thunderbolts, so that they rebounded on the monster, wounding him frightfully. The streams of Typhon's blood gave Mount Haemus its name. He fled towards Sicily, where Zeus ended the running fight by hurling Mount Aetna upon him, and fire belches from its cone to this day.[4]

1. Hesiod: *Theogony* 819 ff.; Pindar: *Pythian Odes* i. 15 ff.; Hyginus: *Fabula* 152.
2. Apollodorus: i. 6. 3.
3. Nonnus: *Dionysiaca* i. 481 ff.; Apollonius Rhodius: ii. 706.
4. Apollodorus: *loc. cit.*; Pindar: *loc. cit.*

*

1. 'Corycian', said to mean 'of the leather sack', may record the ancient custom of confining winds in bags, followed by Aeolus (see 170. *g*), and preserved by medieval witches. In the other Corycian Cave, at Delphi, Delphyne's serpent-mate was called Python, not Typhon. Python ('serpent') personified the destructive North Wind – winds were habitually depicted with serpent tails – which whirls down on Syria from Mount Casius, and on Greece from Mount Haemus (see 21. *2*). Typhon, on the other hand, means 'stupefying smoke', and his appearance describes a volcanic eruption; hence Zeus was said to have buried him at last under Mount Aetna. But the name Typhon also meant the burning Sirocco from the Southern Desert, a cause of havoc in Libya and Greece, which carries a volcanic smell and was pictured by the Egyptians as a desert ass (see 35. *4* and 83. *2*). The god Set, whose breath Typhon was said to be, maimed Osiris in much the same way as Python maimed Zeus, but both were finally overcome; and the parallel has confused Python with Typhon.

2. This divine flight into Egypt, as Lucian observes (*On Sacrifices* 14), was invented to account for the Egyptian worship of gods in animal form – Zeus-Ammon as ram (see 133. *j*), Hermes-Thoth as ibis or crane (see 52. *6*), Hera-Isis as cow (see 56. *2*), Artemis-Pasht as cat, and so on; but it may also refer historically to a frightened exodus of priests and priestesses from the Aegean Archipelago, when a volcanic eruption engulfed half of the large island of Thera, shortly before 2000 B.C. Cats were not domesticated in Classical Greece. A further source of this legend seems to be the Babylonian Creation Epic, the *Enuma Elish*, according to which, in Damascius's earlier version, the goddess Tiamat, her consort Apsu, and their son Mummi ('confusion'), let loose Kingu and a horde of other monsters against the newly-born trinity of gods: Ea, Anu, and Bel. A panic flight follows; but presently Bel rallies his brothers, takes command and defeats Tiamat's forces, crushing her skull with a club and slicing her in two 'like a flat-fish'.

3. The myth of Zeus, Delphyne, and the bear-skin records Zeus's humiliation at the hands of the Great Goddess, worshipped as a She-bear, whose chief oracle was at Delphi; the historical occasion is unknown, but the Cadmeians of Boeotia seem to have been concerned with preserving the Zeus cult. Typhon's 'ephemeral fruits', given him by the Three

Fates, appear to be the usual death-apples (see 18. 4; 32. 4; 33. 7, etc.). In a proto-Hittite version of the myth the serpent Illyunka overcomes the Storm-god and takes away his eyes and heart, which he recovers by a stratagem. The Divine Council then call on the goddess Inara to exact vengeance. Illyunka, invited by her to a feast, eats until gorged; whereupon she binds him with a cord and he is despatched by the Storm-god.

4. Mount Casius (now Jebel-el-Akra) is the Mount Hazzi which figures in the Hittite story of Ullikummi the stone giant, who grew at an enormous rate, and was ordered by his father Kumarbi to destroy the seventy gods of Heaven. The Storm-god, the Sun-god, the Goddess of Beauty and all their fellow-deities failed to kill Ullikummi, until Ea the God of Wisdom, using the knife that originally severed Heaven from Earth, cut off the monster's feet and sent it crashing into the sea. Elements of this story occur in the myth of Typhon, and also in that of the Aloeids, who grew at the same rate and used mountains as a ladder to Heaven (see 37. b). The Cadmeians are likely to have brought these legends into Greece from Asia Minor (see 6. 1).

37

THE ALOEIDS

EPHIALTES and Otus were the bastard sons of Iphimedeia, a daughter of Triops. She had fallen in love with Poseidon, and used to crouch on the seashore, scooping up the waves in her hands and pouring them into her lap; thus she got herself with child. Ephialtes and Otus were, however, called the Aloeids because Iphimedeia subsequently married Aloeus, who had been made king of Boeotian Asopia by his father, Helius. The Aloeids grew one cubit in breadth and one fathom in height every year and, when they were nine years old, being then nine cubits broad and nine fathoms high, declared war on Olympus. Ephialtes swore by the river Styx to outrage Hera, and Otus similarly swore to outrage Artemis.[1]

b. Deciding that Ares the God of War must be their first capture, they went to Thrace, disarmed him, bound him, and confined him in a brazen vessel, which they hid in the house of their stepmother Eriboea, Iphimedeia being now dead. Then their siege of Olympus began: they made a mound for its assault by piling Mount Pelion on Mount Ossa, and further threatened to cast mountains into the sea until it became dry land, though the lowlands were swamped by the waves. Their confidence was unquenchable because it had been prophesied that no other men, nor any gods, could kill them.

c. On Apollo's advice, Artemis sent the Aloeids a message: if they raised their seige, she would meet them on the island of Naxos, and there submit to Otus's embraces. Otus was overjoyed, but Ephialtes, not having received a similar message from Hera, grew jealous and angry. A cruel quarrel broke out on Naxos, where they went together: Ephialtes insisting that the terms should be rejected unless, as the elder of the two, he were the first to enjoy Artemis. The argument had reached its height, when Artemis herself appeared in the form of a white doe, and each Aloeid, seizing his javelin, made ready to prove himself the better marksman by flinging it at her. As she darted between them, swift as the wind, they let fly and each pierced the other through and through. Thus both perished, and the prophecy that they could not be killed by other men, or by gods, was justified. Their bodies were carried back for interment in Boeotian Anthedon; but the Naxians still pay them heroic honours. They are remembered also as the founders of Boeotian Ascra; and as the first mortals to worship the Muses of Helicon.[2]

d. The siege of Olympus being thus raised, Hermes went in search of Ares, and forced Eriboea to release him, half-dead, from the brazen vessel. But the souls of the Aloeids descended to Tartarus, where they were securely tied to a pillar with knotted cords of living vipers. There they sit, back to back and the Nymph Styx perches grimly on the pillar-top, as a reminder of their unfulfilled oaths.[3]

1. Apollodorus: i. 7. 4; Pausanias: ii. 3. 8; Pindar: *Pythian Odes* iv. 88–92.
2. Homer: *Odyssey* xi. 305–20; *Iliad* v. 385–90; Pausanias: ix. 29. 1–2.
3. Apollodorus: i. 7. 4; Hyginus: *Fabula* 28.

*

1. This is another popular version of the Giants' Revolt (see 35. *b*). The name Ephialtes, the assault on Olympus, the threat to Hera, and the prophecy of their invulnerability, occur in both version. Ephialtes and Otus, 'sons of the threshing-floor' by 'her who strengthens the genitals', grandsons of 'Three Face', namely Hecate, and worshippers of the wild Muses, personify the incubus, or orgiastic nightmare, which stifles and outrages sleeping women. Like the Nightmare in British legend, they are associated with the number nine. The myth is confused by a shadowy

historical episode reported by Diodorus Siculus (v. 50 ff.). He says that Aloeus, a Thessalian, sent his sons to liberate their mother Iphimedeia and their sister Pancratis ('all-strength') from the Thracians, who had carried them off to Naxos; their expedition was successful, but they quarrelled about the partition of the island and killed each other. However, though Stephanus of Byzantium records that the city of Aloeium in Thessaly was named after the Aloeids, early mythographers make them Boeotians.

2. The twins' mutual murder recalls the eternal rivalry for the love of the White Goddess between the sacred king and his tanist, who alternately meet death at each other's hands. That they were called 'sons of the threshing-floor' and escaped destruction by Zeus's lightning, connects them with the corn cult, rather than the oak cult. Their punishment in Tartarus, like that of Theseus and Peirithous (see 103. *c*), seems to be deduced from an ancient calendar symbol showing the twins' heads turned back to back, on either side of a column, as they sit on the Chair of Forgetfulness. The column, on which the Death-in-Life Goddess perches, marks the height of summer when the sacred king's reign ends and the tanist's begins. In Italy, this same symbol became two-headed Janus; but the Italian New Year was in January, not at the heliacal rising of two-headed Sirius (see 34. *3*).

3. Ares's imprisonment for thirteen months is an unrelated mythic fragment of uncertain date, referring perhaps to an armistice of one whole year – the Pelasgian year had thirteen months – agreed upon between the Thessalo-Boeotians and Thracians, with war-like tokens of both nations entrusted to a brazen vessel in a temple of Hera Eriboea. Pelion, Ossa, and Olympus are all mountains to the east of Thessaly, with a distant view of the Thracian Chersonese where the war terminated by this armistice may have been fought.

38

DEUCALION'S FLOOD

DEUCALION's Flood, so called to distinguish it from the Ogygian and other floods, was caused by Zeus's anger against the impious sons of Lycaon, the son of Pelasgus. Lycaon himself first civilized Arcadia and instituted the worship of Zeus Lycaeus; but angered Zeus by sacrificing a boy to him. He was therefore transformed into a wolf, and his house struck by lightning. Lycaon's sons were, some say, twenty-two in number; but others say fifty.[1]

b. News of the crimes committed by Lycaon's sons reached Olympus, and Zeus himself visited them, disguised as a poor traveller. They had the effrontery to set umble soup before him, mixing the guts of their brother Nyctimus with the umbles of sheep and goats that it contained. Zeus was undeceived and, thrusting away the table on which they had served the loathsome banquet – the place was afterwards known as Trapezus – changed all of them except Nyctimus, whom he restored to life, into wolves.[2]

c. On his return to Olympus, Zeus in disgust let loose a great flood on the earth, meaning to wipe out the whole race of man; but Deucalion, King of Phthia, warned by his father Prometheus the Titan, whom he had visited in the Caucasus, built an ark, victualled it, and went aboard with his wife Pyrrha, a daughter of Epimetheus. Then the South Wind blew, the rain fell, and the rivers roared down to the sea which, rising with astonishing speed, washed away every city of the coast and plain; until the entire world was flooded, but for a few mountain peaks, and all mortal creatures seemed to have been lost, except Deucalion and Pyrrha. The ark floated about for nine days until, at last, the waters subsided, and it came to rest on Mount Parnassus or, some tell, on Mount Aetna; or Mount Athos; or Mount Othrys in Thessaly. It is said that Deucalion was reassured by a dove which he had sent on an exploratory flight.[3]

d. Disembarking in safety, they offered a sacrifice to Father Zeus, the preserver of fugitives, and went down to pray at the shrine of Themis, beside the river Cephissus, where the roof was now draped with seaweed and the altar cold. They pleaded humbly that mankind should be renewed, and Zeus, hearing their voices from afar, sent Hermes to assure them that whatever request they might make would be granted forthwith. Themis appeared in person, saying: 'Shroud your heads, and throw the bones of your mother behind you!' Since Deucalion and Pyrrha had different mothers, both now deceased, they decided that the Titaness meant Mother Earth, whose bones were the rocks lying on the river bank. Therefore, stooping with shrouded heads, they picked up rocks and threw them over their shoulders; these became either men or women, according as Deucalion or Pyrrha had handled them. Thus mankind was renewed, and ever since a 'people' (laos) and 'a stone' (laas) have been much the same word in many languages.[4]

e. However, as it proved, Deucalion and Pyrrha were not the sole survivors of the Flood, for Megarus, a son of Zeus, had been roused from his couch by the scream of cranes that summoned him to the peak of Mount Gerania, which remained above water. Another who escaped was Cerambus of Pelion, whom the nymphs changed to a scarabaeus, and he flew to the summit of Parnassus.[5]

f. Similarly, the inhabitants of Parnassus – a city founded by Parnasus, Poseidon's son, who invented the art of augury – were awakened by the howling of wolves and followed them to the mountain top. They named their new city Lycorea, after the wolves.[6]

g. Thus the flood proved of little avail, for some of the Parnassians migrated to Arcadia, and revived Lycaon's abominations. To this day a boy is sacrificed to Lycaean Zeus, and his guts mixed with others in an umble soup, which is then served to a crowd of shepherds beside a stream. The shepherd who eats the boy's gut (assigned to him by lot), howls like a wolf, hangs his clothes upon an oak, swims across the stream, and becomes a werewolf. For eight years he herds with wolves, but if he abstains from eating men throughout that period, may return at the close, swim back across the stream and resume his clothes. Not long ago, a Parrhasian named Damarchus spent eight years with the wolves, regained his humanity and, in the tenth year, after hard practice in the gymnasium, won the boxing prize at the Olympic Games.[7]

h. This Deucalion was the brother of Cretan Ariadne and the father of Orestheus, King of the Ozolian Locrians, in whose time a white bitch littered a stick, which Orestheus planted, and which grew into a vine. Another of his sons, Amphictyon, entertained Dionysus, and was the first man to mix wine with water. But his eldest and most famous son was Hellen, father of all Greeks.[8]

1. Apollodorus: iii. 8. 1; Pausanias: viii. 2. 1; Scholiast on Caesar Germanicus's *Aratea* 89; Ovid: *Metamorphoses* i. 230 ff.
2. Apollodorus: *loc. cit.*; Tzetzes: *On Lycophron* 481; Pausanias: viii. 3. 1; Ovid: *Metamorphoses* i. 230 ff.
3. Ovid: *ibid.* i. 317; Scholiast on Euripides's *Orestes* 1095; Hyginus: *Fabula* 153; Servius on Virgil's *Eclogues* vi. 41; Scholiast on Pindar's *Olympian Odes* ix. 42; Plutarch: *Which Animals Are Craftier?* 13.
4. Apollodorus: i. 7. 2; Ovid: *Metamorphoses* i. 260–415.
5. Pausanias: i. 40. 1; Ovid: *Metamorphoses* vii. 352–6.
6. Pausanias x. 6. 1–2.
7. Pausanias: viii. 2. 3 and vi. 8. 2; Pliny: *Natural History* viii. 34; Plato: *Republic* viii. 16.

8. Pausanias: x. 38. 1; Eustathius on Homer: p. 1815; Apollodorus; i. 7. 2.

*

1. The story of Zeus and the boy's guts is not so much a myth as a moral anecdote expressing the disgust felt in more civilized parts of Greece for the ancient cannibalistic practices of Arcadia, which were still performed in the name of Zeus, as 'barbarous and unnatural' (Plutarch: Life of Pelopidas). Lycaon's virtuous Athenian contemporary Cecrops (see 25. d) offered only barley-cakes, abstaining even from animal sacrifices. The Lycaonian rites, which the author denies that Zeus ever countenanced, were apparently intended to discourage the wolves from preying on flocks and herds, by sending them a human king. 'Lycaeus' means 'of the she-wolf', but also 'of the light', and the lightning in the Lycaon myth shows that Arcadian Zeus began as a rain-making sacred king – in service to the divine She-wolf, the Moon, to whom the wolf-pack howls.

2. A Great Year of one hundred months, or eight solar years, was divided equally between the sacred king and his tanist; and Lycaon's fifty sons – one for every month of the sacred king's reign – will have been the eaters of the umble soup. The figure twenty-two, unless it has been arrived at by a count of the families who claimed descent from Lycaon and had to participate in the umble-feast, probably refers to the twenty-two five-year lustra which composed a cycle – the 110-year cycle constituting the reign of a particular line of priestesses.

3. The myth of Deucalion's Flood, apparently brought from Asia by the Hellads, has the same origin as the Biblical legend of Noah. But though Noah's invention of wine is the subject of a Hebrew moral tale, incidentally justifying the enslavement of the Canaanites by their Kassite and Semitic conquerors, Deucalion's claim to the invention has been suppressed by the Greeks in favour of Dionysus. Deucalion is, however, described as the brother of Ariadne, who was the mother, by Dionysus, of various vine-cult tribes (see 27. 8), and has kept his name 'new-wine sailor' (from deucos and halieus). The Deucalion myth records a Mesopotamian flood of the third millenium B.C.; but also the autumnal New Year feast of Babylonia, Syria and Palestine. This feast celebrated Parnapishtim's outpouring of sweet new wine to the builders of the ark, in which (according to the Babylonian Gilgamesh Epic) he and his family survived the Deluge sent by the goddess Ishtar. The ark was a moon-ship (see 123. 5) and the feast was celebrated on the new moon nearest to the autumnal equinox, as a means of inducing the winter rains. Ishtar, in the Greek myth, is called Pyrrha – the name of the goddess-mother of the Puresati (Philistines), a Cretan people who came to Palestine by way of Cilicia about the year 1200 B.C.; in Greek, pyrrha means 'fiery red', and is an adjective applied to wine.

4. Xisuthros was the hero of the Sumerian Flood legend, recorded by Berossus, and his ark came to rest on Mount Ararat. All these arks were built of acacia-wood, a timber also used by Isis for building Osiris's death barge.

5. The myth of an angry god who decides to punish man's wickedness with a deluge seems to be a late Greek borrowing from the Phoenicians, or the Jews; but the number of different mountains, in Greece, Thrace, and Sicily, on which Deucalion is said to have landed, suggests that an ancient Flood myth has been superimposed on a later legend of a flood in Northern Greece. In the earliest Greek version of the myth, Themis renews the race of man without first obtaining Zeus's consent; it is therefore likely that she, not he, was credited with the Flood, as in Babylonia.

6. The transformation of stones into a people is, perhaps, another Helladic borrowing from the East; St John the Baptist referred to a similar legend, in a pun on the Hebrew words *banim* and *abanim*, declaring that God could raise up *children* to Abraham from the desert *stones* (*Matthew* iii. 3–9 and *Luke* iii. 8).

7. That a white bitch, the Moon-goddess Hecate, littered a vine-stock in the reign of Deucalion's son Orestheus is probably the earliest Greek wine myth. The name Ozolian is said to be derived from *ozoi*, 'vine shoots' (see 147. 7). One of the wicked sons of Lycaon was also named Orestheus, which may account for the forced connexion which the mythographers have made between the myth of the umble soup and the Deucalionian Flood.

8. Amphictyon, the name of another of Deucalion's sons, is a male form of Amphictyonis, the goddess in whose name the famous northern confederation, the Amphictyonic League, had been founded; according to Strabo, Callimachus, and the Scholiast on Euripides's *Orestes*, it was regularized by Acrisius of Argos (see 73. *a*). Civilized Greeks, unlike the dissolute Thracians, abstained from neat wine; and its tempering with water at the conference of the member states, which took place in the vintage season at Anthela near Thermopylae, will have been a precaution against murderous disputes.

9. Deucalion's son Hellen was the eponymous ancestor of the entire Hellenic race (see 43. *b*): his name shows that he was a royal deputy for the priestess of Helle, or Hellen, or Helen, or Selene, the Moon; and, according to Pausanias (iii. 20. 6), the first tribe to be called Hellenes came from Thessaly, where Helle was worshipped (see 70. 8).

10. Aristotle (*Meteorologica* i. 14) says that Deucalion's Flood took place 'in ancient Greece (Graecia), namely the district about Dodona and the Achelous River'. *Graeci* means 'worshippers of the Crone', presumably the Earth-goddess of Dodona, who appeared in triad as the Graeae (see 33. *c*); and it has been suggested that the Achaeans were forced to

invade the Peloponnese because unusually heavy rains had swamped their grazing grounds. Helle's worship (see 62. *3*; 70. *8* and 159. *1*) seems to have ousted that of the Graeae.

11. The scarabaeus beetle was an emblem of immortality in Lower Egypt because it survived the flooding of the Nile – the Pharoah as Osiris entered his sun-boat in the form of a scarabaeus – and its sacral use spread to Palestine, the Aegean, Etruria, and the Balearic Islands. Antoninus Liberalis also mentions the myth of Cerambus, or Terambus, quoting Nicander.

39

ATLAS AND PROMETHEUS

PROMETHEUS, the creator of mankind, whom some include among the seven Titans, was the son either of the Titan Eurymedon, or of Iapetus by the nymph Clymene; and his brothers were Epimetheus, Atlas, and Menoetius.[1]

b. Gigantic Atlas, eldest of the brothers, knew all the depths of the sea; he ruled over a kingdom with a precipitous coastline, larger than Africa and Asia put together. This land of Atlantis lay beyond the Pillars of Heracles, and a chain of fruit-bearing islands separated it from a farther continent, unconnected with ours. Atlas's people canalized and cultivated an enormous central plain, fed by water from the hills which ringed it completely, except for a seaward gap. They also built palaces, baths, race-courses, great harbour works, and temples; and carried war not only westwards as far as the other continent, but eastward as far as Egypt and Italy. The Egyptians say that Atlas was the son of Poseidon, whose five pairs of male twins all swore allegiance to their brother by the blood of a bull sacrificed at the pillar-top; and that at first they were extremely virtuous, bearing with fortitude the burden of their great wealth in gold and silver. But one day greed and cruelty overcame them and, with Zeus's permission, the Athenians defeated them single-handed and destroyed their power. At the same time, the gods sent a deluge which, in one day and one night, overwhelmed all Atlantis, so that the harbour works and temples were buried beneath a waste of mud and the sea became unnavigable.[2]

c. Atlas and Menoetius, who escaped, then joined Cronus and the

Titans in their unsuccessful war against the Olympian gods. Zeus killed Menoetius with a thunderbolt and sent him down to Tartarus, but spared Atlas, whom he condemned to support Heaven on his shoulders for all eternity.[3]

d. Atlas was the father of the Pleiades, the Hyades, and the Hesperides; and has held up the Heavens ever since, except on one occasion, when Heracles temporarily relieved him of the task. Some say that Perseus petrified Atlas into Mount Atlas by showing him the Gorgon's head; but they forget that Perseus was reputedly a distant ancestor of Heracles.[4]

e. Prometheus, being wiser than Atlas, foresaw the issue of the rebellion against Cronus, and therefore preferred to fight on Zeus's side, persuading Epimetheus to do the same. He was, indeed, the wisest of his race, and Athene, at whose birth from Zeus's head he had assisted, taught him architecture, astronomy, mathematics, navigation, medicine, metallurgy, and other useful arts, which he passed on to mankind. But Zeus, who had decided to extirpate the whole race of man, and spared them only at Prometheus's urgent plea, grew angry at their increasing powers and talents.[5]

f. One day, when a dispute took place at Sicyon, as to which portions of a sacrificial bull should be offered to the gods, and which should be reserved for men, Prometheus was invited to act as arbiter. He therefore flayed and jointed a bull, and sewed its hide to form two open-mouthed bags, filling these with what he had cut up. One bag contained all the flesh, but this he concealed beneath the stomach, which is the least tempting part of any animal; and the other contained the bones, hidden beneath a rich layer of fat. When he offered Zeus the choice of either, Zeus, easily deceived, chose the bag containing the bones and fat (which are still the divine portion); but punished Prometheus, who was laughing at him behind his back, by withholding fire from mankind. 'Let them eat their flesh raw!' he cried.[6]

g. Prometheus at once went to Athene, with a plea for a backstairs admittance to Olympus, and this she granted. On his arrival, he lighted a torch at the fiery chariot of the Sun and presently broke from it a fragment of glowing charcoal, which he thrust into the pithy hollow of a giant fennel-stalk. Then, extinguishing his torch, he stole away undiscovered, and gave fire to mankind.[7]

h. Zeus swore revenge. He ordered Hephaestus to make a clay woman, and the four Winds to breathe life into her, and all the goddesses of Olympus to adorn her. This woman, Pandora, the most beautiful ever created, Zeus sent as a gift to Epimetheus, under Hermes's escort. But Epimetheus, having been warned by his brother to accept no gift from Zeus, respectfully excused himself. Now even angrier than before, Zeus had Prometheus chained naked to a pillar in the Caucasian mountains, where a greedy vulture tore at his liver all day, year in, year out; and there was no end to the pain, because every night (during which Prometheus was exposed to cruel frost and cold) his liver grew whole again.

i. But Zeus, loth to confess that he had been vindictive, excused his savagery by circulating a falsehood: Athene, he said, had invited Prometheus to Olympus for a secret love affair.

j. Epimetheus, alarmed by his brother's fate, hastened to marry Pandora, whom Zeus had made as foolish, mischievous, and idle as she was beautiful – the first of a long line of such women. Presently she opened a jar, which Prometheus had warned Epimetheus to keep closed, and in which he had been at pains to imprison all the Spites that might plague mankind: such as Old Age, Labour, Sickness, Insanity, Vice, and Passion. Out these flew in a cloud, stung Epimetheus and Pandora in every part of their bodies, and then attacked the race of mortals. Delusive Hope, however, whom Prometheus had also shut in the jar, discouraged them by her lies from a general suicide.[8]

1. Eustathius: *On Homer* p. 987; Hesiod: *Theogony* 507 ff.; Apollodorus: i. 2. 3.
2. Plato: *Timaeus* 6 and *Critias* 9–10.
3. Homer: *Odyssey* i. 52–4; Hesiod: *loc. cit.*; Hyginus: *Fabula* 150.
4. Diodorus Siculus: iv. 27; Apollodorus: ii. 5. 11; Ovid: *Metamorphoses* iv. 630.
5. Aeschylus: *Prometheus Bound* 218, 252, 445 ff., 478 ff., and 228–36.
6. Hesiod: *Theogony* 521–64; Lucian: *Dialogues of the Gods* 1 and *Prometheus on Caucasus* 3.
7. Servius on Virgil's *Eclogues* vi. 42.
8. Hesiod: *Works and Days* 42–105 and *Theogony* 565–619; Scholiast on Apollonius Rhodius ii. 1249.

*

1. Later mythographers understood Atlas as a simple personification of Mount Atlas, in North-western Africa, whose peak seemed to hold up the Heavens; but, for Homer, the columns on which he supported the firmament stood far out in the Atlantic Ocean, afterwards named in his honour by Herodotus. He began, perhaps, as the Titan of the Second Day

of the Week, who separated the waters of the firmament from the waters
of the earth. Most rain comes to Greece from the Atlantic, especially at
the heliacal rising of Atlas's star-daughters, the Hyades; which partly
explains why his home was in the west. Heracles took the Heavens from
his shoulders in two senses (see 133. 3–4 and 123. 4).

2. The Egyptian legend of Atlantis – also current in folk-tale along the
Atlantic seaboard from Gibraltar to the Hebrides, and among the Yorubas
in West Africa – is not to be dismissed as pure fancy, and seems to date
from the third millennium B.C. But Plato's version, which he claims that
Solon learned from his friends the Libyan priests of Saïs in the Delta, has
apparently been grafted on a later tradition: how the Minoan Cretans,
who had extended their influence to Egypt and Italy, were defeated by
a Hellenic confederacy with Athens at its head (see 98. 1); and how,
perhaps as the result of a submarine earthquake, the enormous harbour
works built by the Keftiu ('sea-people', meaning the Cretans and their
allies) on the island of Pharos (see 27. 7 and 169. 6), subsided under several
fathoms of water – where they have lately been rediscovered by divers.
These works consisted of an outer and an inner basin, together covering
some two hundred and fifty acres (Gaston Jondet: *Les Ports submergés de
l'ancienne île de Pharos*, 1916). Such an identification of Atlantis with
Pharos would account for Atlas's being sometimes described as a son of
Iapetus – the Japhet of *Genesis*, whom the Hebrews called Noah's son
and made the ancestor of the Sea-people's confederacy – and sometimes
as a son of Poseidon, patron of Greek seafarers. Noah is Deucalion (see
38. c) and, though in Greek myth Iapetus appears as Deucalion's grandfather, this need mean no more than that he was the eponymous ancestor
of the Canaanite tribe which brought the Mesopotamian Flood legend,
rather than the Atlantian, to Greece. Several details in Plato's account,
such as the pillar-sacrifice of bulls and the hot-and-cold water systems in
Atlas's palace, make it certain that the Cretans are being described, and
no other nation. Like Atlas, the Cretans 'knew all the depths of the sea'.
According to Diodorus (v. 3), when most of the inhabitants of Greece
were destroyed by the great flood, the Athenians forgot that they had
founded Saïs in Egypt. This seems to be a muddled way of saying that
after the submergence of the Pharos harbour-works the Athenians forgot
their religious ties with the city of Saïs, where the same Libyan goddess
Neith, or Athene, or Tanit, was worshipped.

3. Plato's story is confused by his account of the vast numbers of
elephants in Atlantis, which may refer to the heavy import of ivory into
Greece by way of Pharos, but has perhaps been borrowed from the older
legend. The whereabouts of the folk-tale Atlantis has been the subject of
numerous theories, though Plato's influence has naturally concentrated
popular attention on the Atlantic Ocean. Until recently, the Atlantic

Ridge (stretching from Iceland to the Azores and then bending south-eastward to Ascension Island and Tristan da Cunha) was supposed to be its remains; but oceanographic surveys show that apart from these peaks the entire ridge has been under water for at least sixty million years. Only one large inhabited island in the Atlantic is known to have disappeared: the plateau now called the Dogger Bank. But the bones and implements hauled up in cod-nets show that this disaster occurred in paleolithic times; and it is far less likely that the news of its disappearance reached Europe from survivors who drifted across the intervening waste of waters than that the memory of a different catastrophe was brought to the Atlantic seaboard by the highly civilized neolithic immigrants from Libya, usually known as the passage-grave builders.

4. These were farmers and arrived in Great Britain towards the close of the third millennium B.C.; but no explanation has been offered for their mass movement westwards by way of Tunis and Morocco to Southern Spain and then northward to Portugal and beyond. According to the Welsh Atlantis legend of the lost Cantrevs of Dyfed (impossibly located in Cardigan Bay), a heavy sea broke down the sea-walls and destroyed sixteen cities. The Irish Hy Brasil; the Breton City of Ys; the Cornish Land of Lyonesse (impossibly located between Cornwall and the Scilly Isles); the French Île Verte; the Portuguese Ilha Verde: all are variants of this legend. But if what the Egyptian priests really told Solon was that the disaster took place in the Far West, and that the survivors moved 'beyond the Pillars of Heracles', Atlantis can be easily identified.

5. It is the country of the Atlantians, mentioned by Diodorus Siculus (see 131. m) as a most civilized people living to the westward of Lake Tritonis, from whom the Libyan Amazons, meaning the matriarchal tribes later described by Herodotus, seized their city of Cerne. Diodorus's legend cannot be archaeologically dated, but he makes it precede a Libyan invasion of the Aegean Islands and Thrace, an event which cannot have taken place later than the third millennium B.C. If, then, Atlantis was Western Libya, the floods which caused it to disappear may have been due either to a phenomenal rainfall such as caused the famous Mesopotamian and Ogygian Floods (see 38. 3–5), or to a high tide with a strong north-westerly gale, such as washed away a large part of the Netherlands in the twelfth and thirteenth centuries and formed the Zuider Zee,* or to a subsidence of the coastal region. Atlantis may, in fact, have been swamped at the formation of Lake Tritonis (see 8. a), which apparently once covered several thousand square miles of the Libyan lowlands; and perhaps extended northward into the Western Gulf of Sirte, called by the geographer Scylax 'the Gulf of Tritonis', where the dangerous reefs

*Since this was written, history has repeated itself disastrously.

suggest a chain of islands of which only Jerba and the Kerkennahs survive.

6. The island left in the centre of the Lake mentioned by Diodorus (see 131. *l*) was perhaps the Chaamba Bou Rouba in the Sahara. Diodorus seems to be referring to such a catastrophe when he writes in his account of the Amazons and Atlantians (iii. 55): 'And it is said that, as a result of earthquakes, the parts of Libya towards the ocean engulfed Lake Tritonis, making it disappear.' Since Lake Tritonis still existed in his day, what he had probably been told was that 'as a result of earthquakes in the Western Mediterranean the sea engulfed part of Libya and formed Lake Tritonis.' The Zuider Zee and the Copaic Lake have now both been reclaimed; and Lake Tritonis, which, according to Scylax, still covered nine hundred square miles in Classical times, has shrunk to the salt-marshes of Chott Melghir and Chott el Jerid. If this was Atlantis, some of the dispossessed agriculturists were driven west to Morocco, others south across the Sahara, others east to Egypt and beyond, taking their story with them; a few remained by the lakeside. Plato's elephants may well have been found in this territory, though the mountainous coastline of Atlantis belongs to Crete, of which the sea-hating Egyptians knew only by hear-say.

7. The five pairs of Poseidon's twin sons who took the oath of allegiance to Atlas will have been representatives at Pharos of 'Keftiu' kingdoms allied to the Cretans. In the Mycenaean Age double-sovereignty was the rule: Sparta with Castor and Polydeuces, Messenia with Idas and Lynceus, Argos with Proetus and Acrisius, Tiryns with Heracles and Iphicles, Thebes with Eteocles and Polyneices. Greed and cruelty will have been displayed by the Sons of Poseidon only after the fall of Cnossus, when commercial integrity declined and the merchant turned pirate.

8. Prometheus's name, 'forethought', may originate in a Greek misunderstanding of the Sanskrit word *pramantha*, the swastika, or fire-drill, which he had supposedly invented, since Zeus Prometheus at Thurii was shown holding a fire-drill. Prometheus, the Indo-European folk-hero, became confused with the Carian hero Palamedes, the inventor or distributor of all civilized arts (under the goddess's inspiration); and with the Babylonian god Ea, who claimed to have created a splendid man from the blood of Kingu (a sort of Cronus), while the Mother-goddess Aruru created an inferior man from clay. The brothers Pramanthu and Manthu, who occur in the *Bhagavata Purāna*, a Sanskrit epic, may be prototypes of Prometheus and Epimetheus ('afterthought'); yet Hesiod's account of Prometheus, Epimetheus, and Pandora is not a genuine myth, but an antifeminist fable, probably of his own invention, though based on the story of Demophon and Phyllis (see 169. *j*). Pandora ('all-giving') was the Earth-goddess Rhea, worshipped under that title at Athens and elsewhere (Aristophanes: *Birds* 971; Philostratus: *Life of Apollonius of Tyana* vi. 39), whom the pessimistic Hesiod blames for man's mortality and all the ills

which beset life, as well as for the frivolous and unseemly behaviour of wives. His story of the division of the bull is equally unmythical: a comic anecdote, invented to account for Prometheus's punishment, and for the anomaly of presenting the gods only with the thigh-bones and fat cut from the sacrificial beast. In *Genesis* the sanctity of the thigh-bones is explained by Jacob's lameness which an angel inflicted on him during a wrestling match. Pandora's jar (not box) originally contained winged souls.

9. Greek islanders still carry fire from one place to another in the pith of giant fennel, and Prometheus's enchainment on Mount Caucasus may be a legend picked up by the Hellenes as they migrated to Greece from the Caspian Sea: of a frost-giant, recumbent on the snow of the high peaks, and attended by a flock of vultures.

10. The Athenians were at pains to deny that their goddess took Prometheus as her lover, which suggests that he had been locally identified with Hephaestus, another fire-god and inventor, of whom the same story was told (see 25. *b*) because he shared a temple with Athene on the Acropolis.

11. Menoetius ('ruined strength') is a sacred king of the oak cult; the name refers perhaps to his ritual maiming (see 7. *1* and 50. *2*).

12. While the right-handed *swastika* is a symbol of the sun, the left-handed is a symbol of the moon. Among the Akan of West Africa, a people of Libyo-Berber ancestry (see *Introduction, end*), it represents the Triple-goddess Ngame.

40
EOS

AT the close of every night, rosy-fingered, saffron-robed Eos, a daughter of the Titans Hyperion and Theia, rises from her couch in the east, mounts her chariot drawn by the horses Lampus and Phaëthon, and rides to Olympus, where she announces the approach of her brother Helius. When Helius appears, she becomes Hemera, and accompanies him on his travels until, as Hespera, she announces their safe arrival on the western shores of Ocean.[1]

b. Aphrodite was once vexed to find Ares in Eos's bed, and cursed her with a constant longing for young mortals, whom thereupon she secretly and shamefacedly began to seduce, one after the other. First, Orion; next, Cephalus; then Cleitus, a grandson of Melampus; though she was married to Astraeus, who came of Titan stock, and to whom she bore not only the North, West, and South Winds, but also Phosphorus and, some say, all the other stars of Heaven.[2]

c. Lastly, Eos carried off Ganymedes and Tithonus, sons of Tros or Ilus. When Zeus robbed her of Ganymedes she begged him to grant Tithonus immortality, and to this he assented. But she forgot to ask also for perpetual youth, a gift won by Selene for Endymion; and Tithonus became daily older, greyer, and more shrunken, his voice grew shrill, and, when Eos tired of nursing him, she locked him in her bedroom, where he turned into a cicada.[3]

1. Homer: *Odyssey* v. 1 and xxiii. 244–6; Theocritus: *Idylls* ii. 148.
2. Apollodorus: i. 4. 4; Homer *Odyssey* xv. 250; Hesiod: *Theogony* 378–82.
3. Scholiast on Apollonius Rhodius: iii. 115; *Homeric Hymn to Aphrodite* 218–38; Hesiod: *Theogony* 984; Apollodorus: iii. 12. 4; Horace: *Odes* iii. 20; Ovid: *Fasti* i. 461.

*

1. The Dawn-maiden was a Hellenic fancy, grudgingly accepted by the mythographers as a Titaness of the second generation; her two-horse chariot and her announcement of the Sun's advent are allegories rather than myths.

2. Eos's constant love affairs with young mortals are also allegories: dawn brings midnight lovers a renewal of erotic passion, and is the most usual time for men to be carried off by fever. The allegory of her union with Astraeus is a simple one: the stars merge with dawn in the east and Astraeus, the dawn wind, rises as if it were their emanation. Then, because wind was held to be a fertilizing agent, Eos became the mother by Astraeus of the Morning Star left alone in the sky. (Astraeus was another name for Cephalus, also said to have fathered the Morning Star on her.) It followed philosophically that, since the Evening Star is identical with the Morning Star, and since Evening is Dawn's last appearance, all the stars must be born from Eos, and so must every wind but the dawn wind. This allegory, however, contradicted the myth of Boreas's creation by the Moon-goddess Eurynome (see 1. 1).

3. In Greek art, Eos and Hemera are indistinguishable characters. Tithonus has been taken by the allegorist to mean 'a grant of a stretching-out' (from *teinō* and *ōnē*), a reference to the stretching-out of his life, at Eos's plea; but it is likely, rather, to have been a masculine form of Eos's own name, Titonë – from *titō*, 'day' (Tzetzes: *On Lycophron* 941) and *onë*, 'queen' – and to have meant 'partner of the Queen of Day'. Cicadas are active as soon as the day warms up, and the golden cicada was an emblem of Apollo as the Sun-god among the Greek colonists of Asia Minor.

41

ORION

ORION, a hunter of Boeotian Hyria, and the handsomest man alive, was the son of Poseidon and Euryale. Coming one day to Hyria in Chios, he fell in love with Merope, daughter of Dionysus's son Oenopion. Oenopion had promised Merope to Orion in marriage, if he would free the island from the dangerous wild beasts that infested it; and this he set himself to do, bringing the pelts to Merope every evening. But when the task was at last accomplished, and he claimed her as his wife, Oenopion brought him rumours of lions, bears, and wolves still lurking in the hills, and refused to give her up, the fact being that he was in love with her himself.

b. One night Orion, in disgust, drank a skinful of Oenopion's wine, which so inflamed him that he broke into Merope's bedroom, and forced her to lie with him. When dawn came, Oenopion invoked his father, Dionysus, who sent satyrs to ply Orion with still more wine, until he fell fast asleep; whereupon Oenopion put out both his eyes and flung him on the seashore. An oracle announced that the blind man would regain his sight, if he travelled to the east and turned his eye-sockets towards Helius at the point where he first rises from Ocean. Orion at once rowed out to sea in a small boat and, following the sound of a Cyclops's hammer, reached Lemnos. There he entered the smithy of Hephaestus, snatched up an apprentice named Cedalion, and carried him off on his shoulders as a guide. Cedalion led Orion over land and sea, until he came at last to the farthest Ocean, where Eos fell in love with him, and her brother Helius duly restored his sight.

c. After visiting Delos in Eos's company, Orion returned to avenge himself on Oenopion, whom he could not, however, find anywhere in Chios, because he was hiding in an underground chamber made for him by Hephaestus. Sailing on to Crete, where he thought that Oenopion might have fled for protection to his grandfather Minos, Orion met Artemis, who shared his love of the chase. She soon persuaded him to forget his vengeance and, instead, come hunting with her.[1]

d. Now, Apollo was aware that Orion had not refused Eos's invitation to her couch in the holy island of Delos – Dawn still daily blushes to remember this indiscretion – and, further, boasted that he would rid the whole earth of wild beasts and monsters. Fearing, therefore, that his sister Artemis might prove as susceptible as Eos, Apollo went to Mother Earth and, mischievously repeating Orion's boast, arranged for a monstrous scorpion to pursue him. Orion attacked the scorpion, first with arrows, then with his sword, but, finding that its armour was proof against any mortal weapon, dived into the sea and swam away in the direction of Delos where, he hoped, Eos would protect him. Apollo then called to Artemis: 'Do you see that black object bobbing about in the sea, far away, close to Ortygia? It is the head of a villain called Candaon, who has just seduced Opos, one of your Hyperborean priestesses. I challenge you to transfix it with an arrow!' Now, Candaon was Orion's Boeotian nickname, though Artemis did not know this. She took careful aim, let fly, and, swimming out to retrieve her quarry, found that she had shot Orion through the head. In great grief she implored Apollo's son Asclepius to revive him, and he consented; but was destroyed by Zeus's thunderbolt before he could accomplish his task. Artemis then set Orion's image among the stars, eternally pursued by the Scorpion; his ghost had already descended to the Asphodel Fields.

e. Some, however, say that the scorpion stung Orion to death, and that Artemis was vexed with him for having amorously chased her virgin companions, the seven Pleiades, daughters of Atlas and Pleione. They fled across the meadows of Boeotia, until the gods, having changed them into doves, set their images among the stars. But this is a mistaken account, since the Pleiades were not virgins: three of them had lain with Zeus, two with Poseidon, one with Ares, and the seventh married Sisyphus of Corinth, and failed to be included in the constellation, because Sisyphus was a mere mortal.[2]

f. Others tell the following strange story of Orion's birth, to account for his name (which is sometimes written Urion) and for the tradition that he was a son of Mother Earth. Hyrieus, a poor bee-keeper and farmer, had vowed to have no children, and he grew old and impotent. When, one day, Zeus and Hermes visited him in disguise, and were hospitably entertained, they enquired what gift he most desired. Sighing deeply, Hyrieus replied that what he most wanted, namely to have a son, was now impossible. The gods, however, instructed him to sacrifice a bull, make water on its hide, and then bury it in his wife's grave. He did so and, nine months later, a child was born to him, whom

he named Uroin – 'he who makes water' – and, indeed, both the rising
and setting of the constellation Orion bring rain.³

1. Homer: *Odyssey* xi. 310; Apollodorus: i. 4. 3–4; Parthenius;
   Love Stories 20; Lucian: *On the Hall* 28; Theon: *On Aratus* 638;
   Hyginus: *Poetic Astronomy* ii. 34.
2. Apollodorus: *loc. cit.*
3. Servius on Virgil's *Aeneid* i. 539; Ovid: *Fasti* v. 537 ff.; Hyginus:
   Poetic Astronomy ii. 34.

*

1. Orion's story consists of three or four unrelated myths strung
together. The first, confusedly told, is that of Oenopion. This concerns
a sacred king's unwillingness to resign his throne, at the close of his term,
even when the new candidate for kingship had been through his ritual
combats and married the queen with the usual feasting. But the new king
is only an *interrex* who, after reigning for one day, is duly murdered and
devoured by Maenads (see 30. *1*); the old king, who has been shamming
dead in a tomb, then remarries the queen and continues his reign (see
123. *4*).

2. The irrelevant detail of the Cyclop's hammer explains Orion's
blindness: a mythological picture of Odysseus searing the drunken
Cyclops's eye (see 170. *d*) has apparently been combined with a Hellenic
allegory: how the Sun Titan is blinded every evening by his enemies, but
restored to sight by the following Dawn. Orion ('the dweller on the
mountain') and Hyperion ('the dweller on high') are, in fact, identified
here. Orion's boast that he would exterminate the wild beasts not only
refers to his ritual combats (see 123. *1*), but is a fable of the rising Sun, at
whose appearance all wild beasts retire to their dens (compare *Psalm*
civ. 22).

3. Plutarch's account of the scorpion sent by the god Set to kill the
Child Horus, son of Isis and Osiris, in the hottest part of the summer,
explains Orion's death by scorpion-bite and Artemis's appeal to Asclepius
(Plutarch: *On Isis and Osiris* 19). Horus died, but Ra, the Sun-god,
revived him, and later he avenged his father Osiris's death; in the original
myth Orion, too, will have been revived. Orion is also, in part, Gilgamesh,
the Babylonian Heracles, whom Scorpion-men attack in the Tenth
Tablet of the Calendar epic – a myth which concerned the mortal wounding of the sacred king as the Sun rose in Scorpio. Exactly at what
season the wounding took place depends on the antiquity of the myth;
when the Zodiac originated, Scorpio was probably an August sign, but in
Classical times the precession of the equinoxes had advanced it to October.

4. Another version of Orion's death is recorded on one of the Hittite
Ras Shamra tablets. Anat, or Anatha, the Battle-goddess, fell in love with

a handsome hunter named Aqhat, and when he vexatiously refused to give her his bow, asked the murderous Yatpan to steal it from him. To her great grief the clumsy Yatpan not only killed Aqhat, but dropped the bow into the sea. The astronomical meaning of this myth is that Orion and the Bow – a part of the constellation, which the Greeks called 'The Hound' – sink below the southern horizon for two whole months every spring. In Greece this story seems to have been adapted to a legend of how the orgiastic priestesses of Artemis – Opis being a title of Artemis herself – killed an amorous visitor to their islet of Ortygia. And in Egypt, since the return of the constellation Orion introduces the summer heat, it was confusingly identified with Horus's enemy Set, the two bright stars above him being his ass's ears.

5. The myth of Orion's birth is perhaps more than a comic tale, modelled on that of Philemon and Baucis (Ovid: *Metamorphoses* viii. 670–724), and told to account for the first syllable of his ancient name, Urion – as though it were derived from *ourein*, 'to urinate', not from *ouros*, the Homeric form of *oros*, 'mountain', Yet a primitive African rain-producing charm, which consists in making water on a bull's hide, may have been known to the Greeks; and that Orion was a son of Poseidon, the water-god, is a clear allusion to his rain-making powers.

6. The name Pleiades, from the root *plei*, 'to sail', refers to their rising at the season when good weather for sailing approaches. But Pindar's form *Peleiades*, 'flock of doves', was perhaps the original form, since the *Hyades* are piglets. It appears that a seventh star in the group became extinct towards the end of the second millennium B.C. (see 67. *j*); since Hyginus (*Fabula* 192) says that Electra disappeared in grief for the destruction of the House of Dardanus. Orion's vain pursuit of the Pleiades, which occur in the Bull constellation, refers to their rising above the horizon just before the reappearance of Orion.

42

HELIUS

HELIUS, whom the cow-eyed Euryphaessa, or Theia, bore to the Titan Hyperion, is a brother of Selene and Eos. Roused by the crowing of the cock, which is sacred to him, and heralded by Eos, he drives his four-horse chariot daily across the Heavens from a magnificent palace in the far east, near Colchis, to an equally magnificent far-western palace, where his unharnessed horses pasture in the Islands of the

Blessed.[1] He sails home along the Ocean stream, which flows around the world, embarking his chariot and team on a golden ferry-boat made for him by Hephaestus, and sleeps all night in a comfortable cabin.[2]

b. Helius can see everything that happens on earth, but is not particularly observant – once he even failed to notice the robbery of his sacred cattle by Odysseus's companions. He has several herds of such cattle, each consisting of three hundred and fifty head. Those in Sicily are tended by his daughters Phaetusa and Lampetia, but he keeps his finest herd in the Spanish island of Erytheia.[3] Rhodes is his freehold. It happened that, when Zeus was allotting islands and cities to the various gods, he forgot to include Helius among these, and 'Alas!' he said, 'now I shall have to begin all over again'.

'No, Sire,' replied Helius politely, 'today I noticed signs of a new island emerging from the sea, to the south of Asia Minor. I shall be well content with that.'

c. Zeus called the Fate Lachesis to witness that any such new island should belong to Helius;[4] and, when Rhodes had risen well above the waves, Helius claimed it and begot seven sons and a daughter there on the Nymph Rhode. Some say that Rhodes had existed before this time, and was re-emerging from the waves after having been overwhelmed by the great flood which Zeus sent. The Telchines were its aboriginal inhabitants and Poseidon fell in love with one of them, the nymph Halia, on whom he begot Rhode and six sons; which six sons insulted Aphrodite in her passage from Cythera to Paphos, and were struck mad by her; they ravished their mother and committed other outrages so foul that Poseidon sank them underground, and they became the Eastern Demons. But Halia threw herself into the sea and was deified as Leucothea – though the same story is told of Ino, mother of Corinthian Melicertes. The Telchines, foreseeing the flood, sailed away in all directions, especially to Lycia, and abandoned their claims on Rhodes. Rhode was thus left the sole heiress, and her seven sons by Helius ruled in the island after its re-emergence. They became famous astronomers, and had one sister named Electryo, who died a virgin and is now worshipped as a demi-goddess. One of them, by name Actis, was banished for fratricide, and fled to Egypt, where he founded the city of Heliopolis, and first taught the Egyptians astrology, inspired by his father Helius. The Rhodians have now built the Colossus, seventy cubits high, in his honour. Zeus also added to Helius's dominions the new island of Sicily, which had been a missile flung in the battle with the giants.

d. One morning Helius yielded to his son Phaëthon who had been constantly plaguing him for permission to drive the sun-chariot. Phaëthon wished to show his sisters Prote and Clymene what a fine fellow he was: and his fond mother Rhode (whose name is uncertain because she had been called by both her daughters' names and by that of Rhode) encouraged him. But, not being strong enough to check the career of the white horses, which his sisters had yoked for him, Phaëthon drove them first so high above the earth that everyone shivered, and then so near the earth that he scorched the fields. Zeus, in a fit of rage, killed him with a thunderbolt, and he fell into the river Po. His grieving sisters were changed into poplar-trees on its banks, which weep amber tears; or, some say, into alder-trees.[5]

1. *Homeric Hymn to Helius* 2 and 9–16; *Homeric Hymn to Athene* 13; Hesiod: *Theogony* 371–4; Pausanias: v. 25. 5; Nonnus: *Dionysiaca* xii. 1; Ovid: *Metamorphosis* ii. 1 ff. and 106 ff.; Hyginus: *Fabula* 183; Athenaeus: vii. 296.
2. Apollodorus: ii. 5. 10; Athenaeus: xi. 39.
3. Homer: *Odyssey* xii. 323 and 375; Apollodorus: i. 6. 1; Theocritus: *Idylls* xxv. 130.
4. Pindar: *Olympian Odes* vii. 54 ff.
5. Scholiast on Pindar's *Olympian Odes* vi. 78; Tzetzes: *Chiliads* iv. 137; Hyginus: *Fabulae* 52, 152 and 154; Euripides: *Hippolytus* 737; Apollonius Rhodius: iv. 598 ff.; Lucian: *Dialogues of the Gods* 25; Ovid: *Metamorphoses* i. 755 ff.; Virgil: *Eclogues* vi. 62; Diodorus Siculus v. 3; Apollodorus: i. 4. 5.

*

1. The Sun's subordination to the Moon, until Apollo usurped Helius's place and made an intellectual deity of him, is a remarkable feature of early Greek myth. Helius was not even an Olympian, but a mere Titan's son; and, although Zeus later borrowed certain solar characteristics from the Hittite and Corinthian god Tesup (see 67. 1) and other oriental sun-gods, these were unimportant compared with his command of thunder and lightning. The number of cattle in Helius's herds – the *Odyssey* makes him Hyperion (see 170. t) – is a reminder of his tutelage to the Great Goddess: being the number of days covered by twelve complete lunations, as in the Numan year (Censorinus: xx), less the five days sacred to Osiris, Isis, Set, Horus, and Nephthys. It is also a multiple of the Moon-numbers fifty and seven. Helius's so-called daughters are, in fact,

Moon-priestesses – cattle being lunar rather than solar animals in early European myth; and Helius's mother, the cow-eyed Euryphaessa, is the Moon-goddess herself. The allegory of a sun-chariot coursing across the sky is Hellenic in character; but Nilsson in his *Primitive Time Reckoning* (1920) has shown that the ancestral clan cults even of Classical Greece were regulated by the moon alone, as was the agricultural economy of Hesiod's Boeotia. A gold ring from Tiryns and another from the Acropolis at Mycenae prove that the goddess controlled both the moon and the sun, which are placed above her head.

2. In the story of Phaëthon, which is another name for Helius himself (Homer, *Iliad* xi. 735 and *Odyssey* v. 479), an instructive fable has been grafted on the chariot allegory, the moral being that fathers should not spoil their sons by listening to female advice. This fable, however, is not quite so simple as it seems: it has a mythic importance in its reference to the annual sacrifice of a royal prince, on the one day reckoned as belonging to the terrestrial, but not to the sidereal year, namely that which followed the shortest day. The sacred king pretended to die at sunset; the boy *interrex* was at once invested with his titles, dignities, and sacred implements, married to the queen, and killed twenty-four hours later: in Thrace, torn to pieces by women disguised as horses (see 27. *d* and 130. *1*), but at Corinth, and elsewhere, dragged at the tail of a sun-chariot drawn by maddened horses, until he was crushed to death. Thereupon the old king reappeared from the tomb where he had been hiding (see 41. *1*), as the boy's successor. The myths of Glaucus (see 71. *a*), Pelops (see 109. *j*), and Hippolytus ('stampede of horses' – see 101. *g*), refer to this custom, which seems to have been taken to Babylon by the Hittites.

3. Black poplars were sacred to Hecate, but the white gave promise of resurrection (see 31. 5 and 134. *f*); thus the transformation of Phaëthon's sisters into poplars points to a sepulchral island where a college of priestesses officiated at the oracle of a tribal king. That they were also said to have been turned into alders supports this view: since alders fringed Circe's Aeaea ('wailing'), a sepulchral island lying at the head of the Adriatic, not far from the mouth of the Po (Homer: *Odyssey* v. 64 and 239). Alders were sacred to Phoroneus, the oracular hero and inventor of fire (see 57. *1*). The Po valley was the southern terminus of the Bronze Age route down which amber, sacred to the sun, travelled to the Mediterranean from the Baltic (see 148. 9).

4. Rhodes was the property of the Moon-goddess Danaë – called Cameira, Ialysa, and Linda (see 60. 2) – until she was extruded by the Hittite Sun-god Tesup, worshipped as a bull (see 93. *1*). Danaë may be identified with Halia ('of the sea'), Leucothea ('white goddess'), and Electryo ('amber'). Poseidon's six sons and one daughter, and Helius's seven sons, point to a seven-day week ruled by planetary powers, or

Titans (see 1. 3). Actis did not found Heliopolis – Onn, or Aunis – one of the most ancient cities in Egypt; and the claim that he taught the Egyptians astrology is ridiculous. But after the Trojan War the Rhodians were for a while the only sea-traders recognized by the Pharaohs, and seem to have had ancient religious ties with Heliopolis, the centre of the Ra cult. The 'Heliopolitan Zeus', who bears busts of the seven planetary powers on his body sheath, may be of Rhodian inspiration; like similar statues found at Tortosa in Spain, and Byblos in Phoenicia (see 1. 4).

43

THE SONS OF HELLEN

HELLEN, son of Deucalion, married Orseis, and settled in Thessaly, where his eldest son, Aeolus, succeeded him.[1]

b. Hellen's youngest son, Dorus, emigrated to Mount Parnassus, where he founded the first Dorian community. The second son, Xuthus, had already fled to Athens after being accused of theft by his brothers, and there married Creusa, daughter of Erechtheus, who bore him Ion and Achaeus. Thus the four most famous Hellenic nations, namely the Ionians, Aeolians, Achaeans, and Dorians, are all descended from Hellen. But Xuthus did not prosper at Athens: when chosen as arbitrator, upon Erechtheus's death, he pronounced his eldest brother-in-law, Cecrops the Second, to be the rightful heir to the throne. This decision proved unpopular, and Xuthus, banished from the city, died in Aegialus, now Achaia.[2]

c. Aeolus seduced Cheiron's daughter, the prophetess Thea, by some called Thetis, who was Artemis's companion of the chase. Thea feared that Cheiron would punish her severely when he knew of her condition, but dared not appeal to Artemis for assistance; however, Poseidon, wishing to do his friend Aeolus a favour, temporarily disguised her as a mare called Euippe. When she had dropped her foal, Melanippe, which he afterwards transformed into an infant girl, Poseidon set Thea's image among the stars; this is now called the constellation of the Horse. Aeolus took up Melanippe, renamed her Arne, and entrusted her to one Desmontes who, being childless, was glad to adopt her. Cheiron knew nothing of all this.

d. Poseidon seduced Arne, on whom he had been keeping an eye, so soon as she was of age; and Desmontes, discovering that she was with child, blinded her, shut her in an empty tomb, and supplied her with the very least amount of bread and water that would serve to sustain life. There she bore twin sons, whom Desmontes ordered his servants to expose on Mount Pelion, for the wild beasts to devour. But an Icarian herdsman found and rescued the twins, one of whom so closely resembled his maternal grandfather that he was named Aeolus; the other had to be content with the name Boeotus.

e. Meanwhile, Metapontus, King of Icaria, had threatened to divorce his barren wife Theano unless she bore him an heir within the year. While he was away on a visit to an oracle she appealed to the herdsman for help, and he brought her the foundlings whom, on Metapontus's return, she passed off as her own. Later, proving not to be barren after all, she bore him twin sons; but the foundlings, being of divine parentage, were far more beautiful than they. Since Metapontus had no reason to suspect that Aeolus and Boeotus were not his own children, they remained his favourites. Growing jealous, Theano waited until Metapontus left home again, this time for a sacrifice at the shrine of Artemis Metapontina. She then ordered his own sons to go hunting with their elder brothers, and murder them as if by accident. Theano's plot failed, however, because in the ensuing fight Poseidon came to the assistance of his sons. Aeolus and Boeotus were soon carrying their assailants' dead bodies back to the palace, and when Theano saw them approach she stabbed herself to death with a hunting knife.

f. At this, Aeolus and Boeotus fled to their foster-father, the herdsman, where Poseidon in person revealed the secret of their parentage. He ordered them to rescue their mother, who was still languishing in the tomb, and to kill Desmontes. They obeyed without hesitation; Poseidon then restored Arne's sight, and all three went back to Icaria. When Metapontus learned that Theano had deceived him he married Arne and formally adopted her sons as his heirs.[3]

g. All went well for some years, until Metapontus decided to discard Arne and marry again. Aeolus and Boeotus took their mother's side in the ensuing wrangle, and killed Autolyte, the new queen, but were obliged to forfeit their inheritance and flee. Boeotus, with Arne, took refuge in the palace of his grandfather Aeolus, who bequeathed him the southern part of his kingdom, and renamed it Arne; the inhabitants are still called Boeotians. Two Thessalian cities, one of which later became Chaeronaea, also adopted Arne's name.[4]

h. Aeolus, meanwhile, had set sail with a number of friends and, steering west, took possession of the seven Aeolian Islands in the Tyrrhenian Sea, where he became famous as the confidant of the gods and guardian of the winds. His home was on Lipara, a floating island of sheer cliff, within which the winds were confined. He had six sons and six daughters by his wife Enarete, all of whom lived together, well content with one another's company, in a palace surrounded by a brazen wall. It was a life of perpetual feasting, song, and merriment until, one day, Aeolus discovered that the youngest son, Macareus, had been sleeping with his sister Canache. In horror, he threw the fruit of their incestuous love to the dogs, and sent Canache a sword with which she dutifully killed herself. But he then learned that his other sons and daughters, having never been warned that incest among humans was displeasing to the gods, had also innocently paired off, and considered themselves as husbands and wives. Not wishing to offend Zeus, who regards incest as an Olympic prerogative, Aeolus broke up these unions, and ordered four of his remaining sons to emigrate. They visited Italy and Sicily, where each founded a famous kingdom, and rivalled his father in chastity and justice; only the fifth and eldest son stayed at home, as Aeolus's successor to the throne of Lipara. But some say that Macareus and Canache had a daughter, Amphissa, later beloved by Apollo.[5]

i. Zeus had confined the winds because he feared that, unless kept under control, they might one day sweep both earth and sea away into the air, and Aeolus took charge of them at Hera's desire. His task was to let them out, one by one, at his own discretion, or at the considered request of some Olympian deity. If a storm were needed he would plunge his spear into the cliff-side and the winds would stream out of the hole it had made, until he stopped it again. Aeolus was so discreet and capable that, when his death hour approached, Zeus did not commit him to Tartarus, but seated him on a throne within the Cave of the Winds, where he is still to be found. Hera insists that Aeolus's responsibilities entitle him to attend the feasts of the gods; but the other Olympians – especially Poseidon, who claims the sea, and the air above it, as his own property, and grudges anyone the right to raise storms – regard him as an interloper.[6]

1. Apollodorus: i. 7. 3.
2. Herodotus: i. 56; Pausanias: vii. 1. 2.
3. Hyginus: Fabula 186; Poetic Astronomy ii. 18.

4. Diodorus Siculus: iv. 67. 6; Pausanias: ix. 40. 3.
5. Ovid: *Heroides* xi; Homer: *Odyssey* x. 1 ff.; Hyginus: *Fabula* 238; Plutarch: *Parallel Stories* 28; Diodorus Siculus: v. 8; Pausanias: x. 38. 2.
6. Homer: *Odyssey loc. cit.*; Virgil: *Aeneid* i. 142–5.

*

1. The Ionians and Aeolians, the first two waves of patriarchal Hellenes to invade Greece, were persuaded by the Hellads already there to worship the Triple-goddess and change their social customs accordingly, becoming Greeks (*graikoi*, 'worshippers of the Grey Goddess, or Crone'). Later, the Achaeans and Dorians succeeded in establishing patriarchal rule and patrilinear inheritance, and therefore described Achaeus and Dorus as first-generation sons of a common ancestor, Hellen – a masculine form of the Moon-goddess Helle or Helen. The *Parian Chronicle* records that this change from Greeks to Hellenes took place in 1521 B.C., which seems a reasonable enough date. Aeolus and Ion were then relegated to the second generation, and called sons of the thievish Xuthus, this being a way of denouncing the Aeolian and Ionian devotion to the orgiastic Moon-goddess Aphrodite – whose sacred bird was the *xuthos*, or sparrow, and whose priestesses cared nothing for the patriarchal view that women were the property of their fathers and husbands. But Euripides, as a loyal Ionian of Athens, makes Ion elder brother to Dorus and Achaeus, and the son of Apollo as well (see 44. *a*).

2. Poseidon's seduction of Melanippe, his seduction of the Mare-headed Demeter (see 16. *f*), and Aeolus's seduction of Euippe, all refer perhaps to the same event: the seizure of Aeolians of the pre-Hellenic horse-cult centres. The myth of Arne's being blinded and imprisoned in a tomb, where she bore the twins Aeolus and Boeotus, and of their subsequent exposure on the mountain among wild beasts, is apparently deduced from the familiar icon that yielded the myths of Danaë (see 73. 4), Antiope (see 76. *a*), and the rest. A priestess of Mother Earth's is shown crouched in a *tholus* tomb, presenting the New Year twins to the shepherds, for revelation at her Mysteries; *tholus* tombs have their entrances always facing east, as if in promise of rebirth. These shepherds are instructed to report that they found the infants abandoned on the mountainside, being suckled by some sacred animal – cow, sow, she-goat, bitch, or she-wolf. The wild beasts from whom the twins are supposed to have been saved represent the seasonal transformations of the newly-born sacred king (see 30. 1).

3. Except for the matter of the imprisoned winds, and the family incest on Lipara, the remainder of the myth concerns tribal migrations. The mythographers are thoroughly confused between Aeolus the son of Hellen; another Aeolus who, in order to make the Aeolians into third-

generation Greeks, is said to have been the son of Xuthus; and the third Aeolus, grandson of the first.

4. Since the Homeric gods did not regard the incest of Aeolus's sons and daughters as in the least reprehensible, it looks as if both he and Enarete were not mortals and thus bound by the priestly tables of kindred and affinity, but Titans; and that their sons and daughters were the remaining six couples, in charge of the seven celestial bodies and the seven days of the sacred week (see 1. *d*). This would explain their privileged and god-like existence, without problems of either food, drink, or clothing, in an impregnable palace built on a floating island – like Delos before the birth of Apollo (see 14. *3*). 'Macareus' means 'happy', as only gods were happy. It was left for Latin mythographers to humanize Aeolus, and awaken him to a serious view of his family's conduct; their amendment to the myth permitted them to account both for the foundation of Aeolian kingdoms in Italy and Sicily and – because 'Canache' means 'barking' and her child was thrown to the dogs – for the Italian custom of puppy sacrifice. Ovid apparently took this story from the second book of Sostratus's Etruscan History (Plutarch: *Parallel Stories* 28).

5. The winds were originally the property of Hera, and the male gods had no power over them; indeed, in Diodorus's account, Aeolus merely teaches the islanders the use of sails in navigation and foretells, from signs in the fire, what winds will rise. Control of the winds, regarded as the spirits of the dead, is one of the privileges that the Death-goddess's representatives have been most loth to surrender; witches in England, Scotland, and Brittany still claimed to control and sell winds to sailors as late as the sixteenth and seventeenth centuries. But the Dorians had been thorough: already by Homer's time they had advanced Aeolus, the eponymous ancestor of the Aeolians, to the rank of godling, and given him charge of his fellow-winds at Hera's expense – the Aeolian Islands, which bore his name, being situated in a region notorious for the violence and diversity of its winds (see 170. *g*). This compromise was apparently accepted with bad grace by the priests of Zeus and Poseidon, who opposed the creation of any new deities, and doubtless also by Hera's conservative devotees, who regarded the winds as her inalienable property.

44

ION

APOLLO lay secretly with Erechtheus's daughter Creusa, wife to Xuthus, in a cave below the Athenian Propylaea. When her son was born Apollo spirited him away to Delphi, where he became a temple

servant, and the priests named him Ion. Xuthus had no heir and, after
many delays, went at last to ask the Delphic Oracle how he might procure one. To his surprise he was told that the first person to meet him as
he left the sanctuary would be his son; this was Ion, and Xuthus concluded that he had begotten him on some Maenad in the promiscuous
Dionysiac orgies at Delphi many years before. Ion could not contradict this, and acknowledged him as his father. But Creusa was vexed
to find that Xuthus now had a son, while she had none, and tried to
murder Ion by offering him a cup of poisoned wine. Ion, however,
first poured a libation to the gods, and a dove flew down to taste the
spilt wine. The dove died, and Creusa fled for sanctuary to Apollo's
altar. When the vengeful Ion tried to drag her away, the priestess intervened, explaining that he was Creusa's son by Apollo, though Xuthus
must not be undeceived in the belief that he had fathered him on a
Maenad. Xuthus was then promised that he would beget Dorus and
Achaeus on Creusa.

b. Afterwards, Ion married Helice, daughter of Selinus, King of
Aegialus, whom he succeeded on the throne; and, at the death of
Erechtheus, he was chosen King of Athens. The four occupational
classes of Athenians – farmers, craftsmen, priests, and soldiers – are
named after the sons borne to him by Helice.[1]

1. Pausanias: vii. 1. 2; Euripides: *Ion*; Strabo: viii. 7. 1; Conon:
   Narrations 27.

*

1. This theatrical myth is told to substantiate the Ionians' seniority over
Dorians and Achaeans (see 43. *1*), and also to award them divine descent
from Apollo. But Creusa in the cave is perhaps the goddess, presenting the
New Year infant, or infants (see 43. *2*), to a shepherd – mistaken for
Apollo in pastoral dress. Helice, the willow, was the tree of the fifth
month, sacred to the Triple Muse, whose priestess used it in every kind
of witchcraft and water-magic (see 28. *5*); the Ionians seem to have
subordinated themselves willingly to her.

45

ALCYONE AND CEYX

ALCYONE was the daughter of Aeolus, guardian of the winds, and
Aegiale. She married Ceyx of Trachis, son of the Morning-star, and

they were so happy in each other's company that she daringly called
herself Hera, and him Zeus. This naturally vexed the Olympian Zeus
and Hera, who let a thunderstorm break over the ship in which Ceyx
was sailing to consult an oracle, and drowned him. His ghost appeared
to Alcyone who, greatly against her will, had stayed behind in Trachis,
whereupon distraught with grief, she leapt into the sea. Some pitying
god transformed them both into kingfishers.

b. Now, every winter, the hen-kingfisher carries her dead mate with
great wailing to his burial and then, building a closely compacted nest
from the thorns of the sea-needle, launches it on the sea, lays her eggs in
it, and hatches out her chicks. She does all this in the Halcyon Days –
the seven which precede the winter solstice, and the seven which
succeed it – while Aeolus forbids his winds to sweep across the waters.

c. But some say that Ceyx was turned into a seamew.[1]

> 1. Apollodorus: 1. 7. 3; Scholiast on Aristophanes's *Birds* 250;
> Scholiast and Eustathius on Homer's *Iliad* ix. 562; Pliny: *Natural
> History* x. 47; Hyginus: *Fabula* 65; Ovid: *Metamorphoses* xi. 410–
> 748; Lucian: *Halcyon* i.; Plutarch: *Which Animals Are the Craftier?*
> 35.

*

1. The legend of the halcyon's, or kingfisher's, nest (which has no
foundation in natural history, since the halcyon does not build any kind
of nest, but lays eggs in holes by the waterside) can refer only to the birth
of the new sacred king at the winter solstice – after the queen who represents his mother, the Moon-goddess, has conveyed the old king's corpse
to a sepulchral island. But because the winter solstice does not always
coincide with the same phase of the moon, 'every year' must be understood, as 'every Great Year', of one hundred lunations, in the last of
which solar and lunar time were roughly synchronized, and the sacred
king's term ended.

2. Homer connects the halcyon with Alcyone (see 80. *d*), a title of
Meleager's wife Cleopatra (*Iliad* ix. 562), and with a daughter of Aeolus,
guardian of the winds (see 43. *h*). *Halcyon* cannot therefore mean *hal-cyon*,
'sea-hound', as is usually supposed, but must stand for *alcy-one*, 'the
queen who wards off evil'. This derivation is confirmed by the myth of
Alcyone and Ceyx, and the manner of their punishment by Zeus and
Hera. The seamew part of the legend need not be pressed, although this
bird, which has a plaintive cry, was sacred to the Sea-goddess Aphrodite,
or Leucothea (see 170. *y*), like the halcyon of Cyprus (see 160. *g*). It seems
that late in the second millennium B.C. the sea-faring Aeolians, who had

agreed to worship the pre-Hellenic Moon-goddess as their divine ances-
tress and protectress, became tributary to the Zeus-worshipping Achaeans, and were forced to accept the Olympian religion. 'Zeus', which
according to Johannes Tzetzes (*Antehomerica* 102 ff. and *Chiliades* i. 474)
had hitherto been a title borne by petty kings (see 68. 1), was henceforth
reserved for the Father of Heaven alone. But in Crete, the ancient mystical tradition that Zeus was born and died annually lingered on into
Christian times, and tombs of Zeus were shown at Cnossus, on Mount
Ida, and on Mount Dicte, each a different cult-centre. Callimachus was
scandalized, and in his *Hymn to Zeus* wrote: 'The Cretans are always
liars. They have even built thy tomb, O Lord! But thou art not dead, for
thou livest for ever.' This is quoted in *Titus* i. 12 (see 7. 6).

3. Pliny, who describes the halcyon's alleged nest in detail – apparently
the zoöphyte called *halcyoneum* by Linnaeus – reports that the halcyon is
rarely seen, and then only at the two solstices and at the setting of the
Pleiades. This proves her to have originally been a manifestation of the
Moon-goddess, who was alternately the Goddess of Life-in-Death at the
winter solstice, and of Death-in-Life at the summer solstice; and who,
every Great Year, early in November, when the Pleiades set, sent the
sacred king his death summons.

4. Still another Alcyone, daughter of Pleione ('sailing queen') by
Atlas, was the leader of the seven Pleiades (see 39. d). The Pleiades'
heliacal rising in May began the navigational year; their setting marked
its end, when (as Pliny notes in a passage about the halcyon) a remarkably
cold north wind blows. The circumstances of Ceyx's death show that the
Aeolians, who were famous sailors, worshipped the goddess as 'Alcyone'
because she protected them from rocks and rough weather: Zeus wrecked
Ceyx's ship, in defiance of her powers, by hurling a thunderbolt at it.
Yet the halcyon was still credited with the magical power of allaying
storms; and its body, when dried, was used as a talisman against Zeus's
lightning – presumably on the ground that where once it strikes it will
not strike again. The Mediterranean is inclined to be calm about the time
of the winter solstice.

46

TEREUS

TEREUS, a son of Ares, ruled over the Thracians then occupying
Phocian Daulis – though some say that he was King of Pagae in
Megaris[1] – and, having acted as mediator in a boundary dispute for

Pandion, King of Athens and father of the twins Butes and Erechtheus, married their sister Procne, who bore him a son, Itys.

b. Unfortunately Tereus, enchanted by the voice of Procne's younger sister Philomela, had fallen in love with her; and, a year later, concealing Procne in a rustic cabin near his palace at Daulis, he reported her death to Pandion. Pandion, condoling with Tereus, generously offered him Philomela in Procne's place, and provided Athenian guards as her escort when she went to Daulis for the wedding. These guards Tereus murdered and, when Philomela reached the palace, he had already forced her to lie with him. Procne soon heard the news but, as a measure of precaution, Tereus cut out her tongue and confined her to the slaves' quarters, where she could communicate with Philomela only be weaving a secret message into the pattern of a bridal robe intended for her. This ran simply: 'Procne is among the slaves.'

c. Meanwhile, an oracle had warned Tereus that Itys would die by the hand of a blood relative and, suspecting his brother Dryas of a murderous plot to seize the throne, struck him down unexpectedly with an axe. The same day, Philomela read the message woven into the robe. She hurried to the slaves' quarters, found one of the rooms bolted, broke down the door, and released Procne, who was chattering unintelligibly and running around in circles.

'Oh, to be revenged on Tereus, who pretended that you were dead, and seduced me!' wailed Philomela, aghast.

Procne, being tongueless, could not reply, but flew out and, seizing her son Itys, killed him, gutted him, and then boiled him in a copper cauldron for Tereus to eat on his return.

d. When Tereus realized what flesh he had been tasting, he grasped the axe with which he had killed Dryas and pursued the sisters as they fled from the palace. He soon overtook them and was on the point of committing a double murder when the gods changed all three into birds; Procne became a swallow; Philomela, a nightingale; Tereus, a hoopoe. And the Phocians say that no swallow dares nest in Daulis or its environs, and no nightingale sings, for fear of Tereus. But the swallow, having no tongue, screams and flies around in circles; while the hoopoe flutters in pursuit of her, crying 'Pou? Pou?' (where? where?). Meanwhile, the nightingale retreats to Athens, where she mourns without cease for Itys, whose death she inadvertently caused, singing 'Itu! Itu!'[2]

e. But some say that Tereus was turned into a hawk.[3]

1. Apollodorus: iii. 14. 8; Thucydides: ii. 29; Strabo: ix. 3. 13; Pausanias: i. 41. 8

2. Apollodorus: iii. 14. 8; Nonnus: *Dionysiaca* iv. 320; Pausanias: i. 5. 4; i. 41. 8 and x. 4. 6; Hyginus: *Fabula* 45; Fragments of Sophocles's *Tereus*; Eustathius on Homer's *Odyssey* xix. 418; Ovid: *Metamorphoses* vi. 426–674; First Vatican Mythographer: 217.

3. Hyginus: *Fabula* 45.

*

1. This extravagant romance seems to have been invented to account for a series of Thraco-Pelasgian wall-paintings, found by Phocian invaders in a temple at Daulis ('shaggy'), which illustrated different methods of prophecy in local use.

2. The cutting-out of Procne's tongue misrepresents a scene showing a prophetess in a trance, induced by the chewing of laurel-leaves; her face is contorted with ecstasy, not pain, and the tongue which seems to have been cut out is in fact a laurel-leaf, handed her by the priest who interprets her wild babblings. The weaving of the letters into the bridal robe misrepresents another scene: a priestess has cast a handful of oracular sticks on a white cloth, in the Celtic fashion described by Tacitus (*Germania* x), or the Scythian fashion described by Herodotus (iv. 67); they take the shape of letters, which she is about to read. In the so-called eating of Itys by Tereus, a willow-priestess is taking omens from the entrails of a child sacrificed for the benefit of a king. The scene of Tereus and the oracle probably showed him asleep on a sheep-skin in a temple, receiving a dream revelation (see 51. *g*); the Greeks would not have mistaken this. That of Dryas's murder probably showed an oak-tree and priests taking omens beneath it, in Druidic fashion, by the way a man fell when he died. Procne's transformation into a swallow will have been deduced from a scene that showed a priestess in a feathered robe, taking auguries from the flight of a swallow; Philomela's transformation into a nightingale, and Tereus's into a hoopoe, seem to result from similar misreadings. Tereus's name, which means 'watcher', suggests that a male augur figured in the hoopoe picture.

3. Two further scenes may be presumed: a serpent-tailed oracular hero, being offered blood-sacrifices; and a young man consulting a bee-oracle. These are, respectively, Erechtheus and Butes (see 47. *1*) who was the most famous bee-keeper of antiquity, the brothers of Procne and Philomela. Their mother was Zeuxippe, 'she who yokes horses', doubtless a Mare-headed Demeter.

4. All mythographers but Hyginus make Procne a nightingale, and Philomela a swallow. This must be a clumsy attempt to rectify a slip made by some earlier poet; that Tereus cut out Philomela's tongue, not

Procne's. The hoopoe is a royal bird, because it has a crest of feathers; and is particularly appropriate to the story of Tereus, because its nests are notorious for their stench. According to the Koran, the hoopoe told Solomon prophetic secrets.

5. Daulis, afterwards called Phocis, seems to have been the centre of a bird cult. Phocus, the eponymous founder of the new state, was called the son of Ornytion ('moon bird'–see 81.b), and a later king was named Xuthus ('sparrow' – see 43. 1). Hyginus reports that Tereus became a hawk, a royal bird of Egypt, Thrace, and North-western Europe.

47

ERECHTHEUS AND EUMOLPUS

KING PANDION died prematurely of grief when he learned what had befallen Procne, Philomela, and Itys. His twin sons shared the inheritance: Erechtheus becoming King of Athens, while Butes served as priest both to Athene and Poseidon.[1]

b. By his wife Praxithea, Erechtheus had four sons, among them his successor, Cecrops; also seven daughters: namely Protogonia, Pandora, Procnis, wife of Cephalus, Creusa, Oreithyia, Chthonia, who married her uncle Butes, and Otionia, the youngest.[2]

c. Now, Poseidon secretly loved Chione, Oreithyia's daughter by Boreas. She bore him a son, Eumolpus, but threw him into the sea, lest Boreas should be angry. Poseidon watched over Eumolpus, and cast him up on the shores of Ethiopia, where he was reared in the house of Benthesicyme, his half-sister by the Sea-goddess Amphitrite. When Eumolpus came of age, Benthesycime married him to one of her daughters; but he fell in love with another of them, and she therefore banished him to Thrace, where he plotted against his protector, King Tegyrius, and was forced to seek refuge at Eleusis. Here he mended his ways, and became priest of the Mysteries of Demeter and Persephone, into which he subsequently initiated Heracles, at the same time teaching him to sing and play the lyre. With the lyre, Eumolpus had great skill; and was also victorious in the flute contest at Pelias's funeral games. His Eleusinian co-priestesses were the daughters of Celeus; and his well-known piety at last earned him the dying forgiveness of King Tegyrius, who bequeathed him the throne of Thrace.[3]

d. When war broke out between Athens and Eleusis, Eumolpus brought a large force of Thracians to the Eleusinians' assistance, claiming the throne of Attica himself in the name of his father Poseidon. The Athenians were greatly alarmed, and when Erechtheus consulted an oracle he was told to sacrifice his youngest daughter Otionia to Athene, if he hoped for victory. Otionia was willingly led to the altar, whereupon her two eldest sisters, Protogonia and Pandora, also killed themselves, having once vowed that if one of them should die by violence, they would die too.[4]

e. In the ensuing battle, Ion led the Athenians to victory; and Erechtheus struck down Eumolpus as he fled. Poseidon appealed for vengeance to his brother Zeus, who at once destroyed Erechtheus with a thunderbolt; but some say that Poseidon felled him with a trident blow at Macrae, where the earth opened to receive him.

f. By the terms of a peace then concluded, the Eleusinians became subject to the Athenians in everything, except the control of their Mysteries. Eumolpus was succeeded as priest by his younger son Ceryx, whose descendants still enjoy great hereditary privileges at Eleusis.[5]

g. Ion reigned after Erechtheus; and, because of his three daughters' self-sacrifice, wineless libations are still poured to them today.[6]

1. Ovid: *Metamorphoses* vi. 675 ff.; Apollodorus: ii. 15. 1.
2. Ovid: *loc. cit.*; Suidas *sub* Parthenoi; Apollodorus: *loc. cit.*; Hyginus: *Fabula* 46.
3. Plutarch: *On Exile* 17; Apollodorus: ii. 5. 12; Theocritus: *Idyll* xxiv. 110; Hyginus: *Fabula* 273; Pausanias: i. 38. 3.
4. Apollodorus: iii. 15. 4; Hyginus *Fabula* 46; Suidas: *loc. cit.*
5. Pausanias: vii. 1. 2 and i. 38. 3; Euripides: *Ion* 277 ff.
6. Scholiast on Sophocles's *Oedipus at Colonus* 100.

*

1. The myth of Erechtheus and Eumolpus concerns the subjugation of Eleusis by Athens, and the Thraco-Libyan origin of the Eleusinian Mysteries. An Athenian cult of the orgiastic Bee-nymph of Midsummer also enters into the story, since Butes is associated in Greek myth with a bee cult on Mount Eryx (see 154. *d*); and his twin brother Erechtheus ('he who hastens over the heather', rather than 'shatterer') is the husband of the 'Active Goddess', the Queen-bee. The name of King Tegyrius of Thrace, whose kingdom Erechtheus's great-grandson inherited, makes a further association with bees: it means 'beehive coverer'. Athens was famous for its honey.

2. Erechtheus's three noble daughters, like the three daughters of his ancestor Cecrops, are the Pelasgian Triple-goddess, to whom libations were poured on solemn occasions: Otiona ('with the ear-flaps'), who is said to have been chosen as a sacrifice to Athene, being evidently the Owl-goddess Athene herself; Protogonia, the Creatrix Eurynome (see 1. 1); and Pandora, the Earth-goddess Rhea (see 39. 8). At the transition from matriarchy to patriarchy some of Athene's priestesses may have been sacrificed to Poseidon (see 121. 3).

3. Poseidon's trident and Zeus's thunderbolt were originally the same weapon, the sacred *labrys*, or double-axe, but distinguished from each other when Poseidon became god of the sea, and Zeus claimed the sole right to the thunderbolt (see 7. 7).

4. Butes, who was enrolled among the Argonauts (see 148. 1), did not really belong to the Erechtheid family; but his descendants, the Buteids of Athens, forced their way into Athenian society and, by the sixth century, held the priesthoods of Athene Polias and of Poseidon Erechtheus – but was a fusion of the Hellenic Poseidon with the old Pelasgian hero – as a family inheritance (Pausanias: i. 26. 6), and seem to have altered the myth accordingly, as they also altered the Theseus myth (see 95. 3). They combined the Attic Butes with their ancestor, the Thracian son of Boreas, who had colonized Naxos and in a raid on Thessaly violated Coronis (see 50. 5), the Lapith princess (Diodorus Siculus: v. 50).

48

BOREAS

OREITHYIA, daughter of Erechtheus, King of Athens, and his wife Praxithea, was one day whirling in a dance beside the river Ilissus, when Boreas, son of Astraeus and Eos, and brother of the South and West Winds, carried her off to a rock near the river Ergines where, wrapped in a mantle of dark clouds, he ravished her.[1]

b. Boreas had long loved Oreithyia and repeatedly sued for her hand, but Erechtheus put him off with vain promises until at length, complaining that he had wasted too much time in words, he resorted to his natural violence. Some, however, say that Oreithyia was carrying a basket in the annual Thesmophorian procession that winds up the slope of the Acropolis to the temple of Athene Polias, when Boreas tucked her beneath his tawny wings and whirled her away, unseen by the surrounding crowd.

c. He took her to the city of the Thracian Cicones, where she became his wife, and bore him twin sons, Calais and Zetes, who grew wings when they reached manhood; also two daughters, namely Chione, who bore Eumolpus to Poseidon, and Cleopatra, who married King Phineus, the victim of the Harpies.[2]

d. Boreas has serpent-tails for feet, and inhabits a cave on Mount Haemus, in the seven recesses of which Ares stables his horses; but he is also at home beside the river Strymon.[3]

e. Once, disguising himself as a dark-maned stallion, he covered twelve of the three thousand mares belonging to Erichthonius, son of Dardanus, which used to graze in the water-meadows beside the river Scamander. Twelve fillies were born from this union; they could race over ripe ears of standing corn without bending them, or over the crests of waves.[4]

f. The Athenians regard Boreas as their brother-in-law and, having once successfully invoked him to destroy King Xerxes's fleet, they built him a fine temple on the banks of the river Ilissus.[5]

1. Apollodorus: iii. 15. 1–2; Apollonius Rhodius: i. 212 ff.
2. Ovid: *Metamorphoses* vi. 677 ff.; Scholiast on Homer's *Odyssey* xiv. 533; Apollodorus: iii. 15. 3.
3. Pausanias: v. 19. 1; Callimachus: *Hymn to Artemis* 114 and *Hymn to Delos* 26 and 63–5.
4. Homer: *Iliad* xx. 219 ff.
5. Herodotus: vii. 189.

*

1. Serpent-tailed Boreas, the North Wind, was another name for the demiurge Ophion who danced with Eurynome, or Oreithyia, Goddess of Creation (see 1. *a*), and impregnated her. But, as Ophion was to Eurynome, or Boreas to Oreithyia, so was Erechtheus to the original Athene; and Athene Pōlias ('of the city'), for whom Oreithyia danced, may have been Athene Polias – Athene the Filly, goddess of the local horse cult, and beloved by Boreas-Erechtheus, who thus became the Athenians' brother-in-law. The Boreas cult seems to have originated in Libya. It should be remembered that Hermes, falling in love with Oreithyia's predecessor Herse while she was carrying a sacred basket in a similar procession, to the Acropolis, had ravished her without incurring Athene's displeasure. The Thesmophoria seems to have once been an orgiastic

festival in which priestesses publicly prostituted themselves as a means of fertilizing the cornfields (see 24. 1). These baskets contained phallic objects (see 25. 4).

2. A primitive theory that children were the reincarnations of dead ancestors, who entered into women's wombs as sudden gusts of wind, lingered in the erotic cult of the Mare-goddess; and Homer's authority was weighty enough to make educated Romans still believe, with Pliny, that Spanish mares could conceive by turning their hindquarters to the wind (Pliny: *Natural History* iv. 35 and viii. 67). Varro and Columella mention the same phenomenon, and Lactantius, in the late third century A.D., makes it an analogy of the Virgin's impregnation by the *Sanctus Spiritus*.

3. Boreas blows in winter from the Haemus range and the Strymon and, when Spring comes with its flowers, seems to have impregnated the whole land of Attica; but, since he cannot blow backwards, the myth of Oreithyia's rape apparently also records the spread of the North Wind cult from Athens to Thrace. From Thrace, or directly from Athens, it reached the Troad, where the owner of the three thousand mares was Erichthonius, a synonym of Erechtheus (see 158. g). The twelve fillies will have served to draw three four-horse chariots, one for each of the annual triad: Spring, Summer, and Autumn. Mount Haemus was a haunt of the monster Typhon (see 36. e).

4. Socrates, who had no understanding of myths, misses the point of Oreithyia's rape: he suggests that a princess of that name, playing on the cliffs near the Ilissus, or on the Hill of Ares, was accidentally blown over the edge and killed (Plato: *Phaedrus* vi. 229b). The cult of Boreas had recently been revived at Athens to commemorate his destruction of the Persian fleet (Herodotus: vii. 189). He also helped the Megalopolitans against the Spartans and earned annual sacrifices (Pausanias: viii. 36. 3).

49

ALOPE

THE Arcadian King Cercyon, son of Hephaestus, had a beautiful daughter, Alope, who was seduced by Poseidon and, without her father's knowledge, bore a son whom she ordered a nurse to expose on a mountain. A shepherd found him being suckled by a mare, and took him to the sheep-cotes, where his rich robe attracted great interest. A fellow-shepherd volunteered to rear the boy, but insisted on taking the robe too, in proof of his noble birth. The two shepherds began to quarrel, and murder would have been done, had their companions not led them before King Cercyon. Cercyon called for the disputed robe and, when it was brought, recognized it as having been cut from a garment belonging to his daughter. The nurse now took fright, and confessed her part in the affair; whereupon Cercyon ordered Alope to be immured, and the child to be exposed again. He was once more suckled by the mare and, this time, found by the second shepherd who, now satisfied as to his royal parentage, carried him to his own cabin and called him Hippothous.[1]

b. When Theseus killed Cercyon, he set Hippothous on the throne of Arcadia; Alope had meanwhile died in prison, and was buried beside the road leading from Eleusis to Megara, near Cercyon's wrestling ground. But Poseidon transformed her body into a spring, named Alope.[2]

1. Hyginus: *Fabulae* 38 and 187.
2. Pausanias: i. 39. 3; Aristophanes: *Birds* 533; Hyginus: *Fabula* 187.

*

1. This myth is of familiar pattern (see 43. *c*: 68. *d*; 105. *a*, etc.), except that Hippothous is twice exposed and that, on the first occasion, the shepherds come to blows. The anomaly is perhaps due to a misreading of an icon-sequence, which showed royal twins being found by shpeherds, and these same twins coming to blows when grown to manhood – like Pelias and Neleus (see 68. *f*), Proetus and Acrisius (see 73. *a*) or Eteocles and Polyneices (see 106. *b*).

2. Alope is the Moon-goddess as vixen who gave her name to the Thessalian city of Alope (Pherecydes, quoted by Stephanus of Byzantium *sub* Alope); the vixen was also the emblem of Messenia (see 89. *8* and 146. *6*). The mythographer is probably mistaken in recording that the robe worn by Hippothous was cut from Alope's dress; it will have been the swaddling band into which his clan and family marks were woven (see 10. *1* and 60. *2*).

50

ASCLEPIUS

CORONIS, daughter of Phlegyas, King of the Lapiths, Ixion's brother, lived on the shores of the Thessalian Lake Beobeis, in which she used to wash her feet.[1]

b. Apollo became her lover, and left a crow with snow-white feathers to guard her while he went to Delphi on business. But Coronis had long nursed a secret passion for Ischys, the Arcadian son of Elatus, and now admitted him to her couch, though already with child by Apollo. Even before the excited crow had set out for Delphi, to report the scandal and be praised for its vigilance, Apollo had divined Coronis's infidelity, and therefore cursed the crow for not having pecked out Ischys's eyes when he approached Coronis. The crow was turned black by this curse, and all its descendants have been black ever since.[2]

c. When Apollo complained to his sister Artemis of the insult done him, she avenged it by shooting a quiverful of arrows at Coronis. Afterwards, gazing at her corpse, Apollo was filled with sudden remorse, but could not now restore her to life. Her spirit had descended to Tartarus, her corpse had been laid on the funeral pyre, the last perfumes poured over it, and the fire already alight, before Apollo recovered his presence of mind; then he motioned to Hermes, who by the light of the flames cut the still living child from Coronis's womb.[3] It was a boy, whom Apollo named Asclepius, and carried off to the cave of Cheiron the Centaur, where he learned the arts of medicine and the chase. As for Ischys, also called Chylus: some say that he was killed by Zeus with a thunderbolt, others that Apollo himself shot him down.[4]

d. The Epidaurians, however, tell a very different story. They say that Coronis's father, Phlegyas, who founded the city of that name where he gathered together all the best warriors of Greece, and lived by raiding, came to Epidaurus to spy out the land and the strength of the people; and that his daughter Coronis who, unknown to him, was with child by Apollo, came too. In Apollo's shrine at Epidaurus, with the assistance of Artemis and the Fates, Coronis gave birth to a boy, whom she at once exposed on Mount Titthion, now famous for the medicinal virtues of its plants. There, Aresthanas, a goatherd, noticing that his bitch and one of his she-goats were no longer with him, went in search of them, and found them taking turns to suckle a child. He was about to lift the child up, when a bright light all about it deterred him. Loth to meddle with a divine mystery, he piously turned away, thus leaving Asclepius to the protection of his father Apollo.[5]

e. Asclepius, say the Epidaurians, learned the art of healing both from Apollo and from Cheiron. He became so skilled in surgery and the use of drugs that he is revered as the founder of medicine. Not only did he heal the sick, but Athene had given him two phials of the Gorgon

Medusa's blood; with what had been drawn from the veins of her left side, he could raise the dead; with what had been drawn from her right side, he could destroy instantly. Others say that Athene and Asclepius divided the blood between them: he used it to save life, but she to destroy life and instigate wars. Athene had previously given two drops of this same blood to Erichthonius, one to kill, the other to cure, and fastened the phials to his serpent body with golden bands.[6]

f. Among those whom Asclepius raised from the dead were Lycurgus, Capaneus, and Tyndareus. It is not known on which occasion Hades complained to Zeus that his subjects were being stolen from him – whether it was after the resurrection of Tyndareus, or of Glaucus, or of Hippolytus, or of Orion; it is certain only that Asclepius was accused of having been bribed with gold, and that both he and his patient were killed by Zeus's thunderbolt.[7]

g. However, Zeus later restored Asclepius to life; and so fulfilled an indiscreet prophecy made by Cheiron's daughter Euippe, who had declared that Asclepius would become a god, die, and resume godhead – thus twice renewing his destiny. Asclepius's image, holding a curative serpent, was set among the stars by Zeus.[8]

h. The Messenians claim that Asclepius was a native of Tricca in Messene; the Arcadians, that he was born at Thelpusa; and the Thessalians, that he was a native of Tricca in Thessaly. The Spartans call him, Agnitas, because they have carved his image from a willow-trunk; and the people of Sicyon honour him in the form of a serpent mounted on a mule-cart. At Sicyon the left hand of his image holds the cone of a pistachio-pine; but at Epidaurus it rests on a serpent's head; in both cases the right hand holds a sceptre.[9]

i. Asclepius was the father of Podaleirius and Machaon, the physicians who attended the Greeks during the siege of Troy; and of the radiant Hygieia. The Latins call him Aesculapius, and the Cretans say that he, not Polyeidus, restored Glaucus, son of Minos, to life; using a certain herb, shown him by a serpent in a tomb.[10]

1. Strabo: ix. 5. 21 and xiv. 1. 40.
2. Pausanias: ii. 26. 5; Pindar: *Pythian Odes* iii. 25 ff.; Apollodorus: iii. 10. 3.
3. Pindar: *Pythian Odes* iii. 8 ff.; Pausanias: *loc. cit.*; Hyginus: *Fabula* 202; Ovid: *Metamorphoses* ii. 612 ff.
4. Apollodorus: iii. 10. 3; Hyginus: *loc. cit.* and *Poetic Astronomy* ii. 40.
5. Pausanias: ix. 36. 1 and ii. 26. 4; *Inscriptiones Graecae* iv. 1. 28.

6. Diodorus Siculus: v. 74. 6; Apollodorus: iii. 10. 3; Tatian: *Address to the Greeks*; Euripides: *Ion* 999 ff.

7. Apollodorus: iii. 10. 3–4; Lucian: *On the Dance* 45; Hyginus: *Fabula* 49; Eratosthenes, quoted by Hyginus: *Poetic Astronomy* ii. 14; Pindar: *Pythian Odes* iii. 55 ff., with scholiast.

8. Germanicus Caesar: *On Aratus's Phenomena* 77 ff.; Ovid: *Metamorphoses* 642 ff.; Hyginus: *loc. cit.*

9. Pausanias: ii. 26. 6; viii. 25. 6; iii. 14. 7 and ii. 10. 3; Strabo: xiv. 1. 39.

10. Homer: *Iliad* ii. 732; Hyginus: *Poetic Astronomy* ii. 14.

*

1. This myth concerns ecclesiastical politics in Northern Greece, Attica, and the Peloponnese: the suppression, in Apollo's name, of a pre-Hellenic medical cult, presided over by Moon-priestesses at the oracular shrines of local heroes reincarnate as serpents, or crows, or ravens. Among their names were Phoroneus, identifiable with the Celtic Raven-god Bran, or Vron (see 57. 1); Erichthonius the serpent-tailed (see 25. 2); and Cronus (see 7. 1), which is a form of Coronus ('crow' or 'raven'), the name of two other Lapith kings (see 78. a). 'Asclepius' ('unceasingly gentle') will have been a complimentary title given to all physician heroes, in the hope of winning their benevolence.

2. The goddess Athene, patroness of this cult, was not originally regarded as a maiden; the dead hero having been both her son and her lover. She received the title 'Coronis' because of the oracular crow, or raven, and 'Hygieia' because of the cures she brought about. Her all-heal was the mistletoe, *ixias*, a word with which the name Ischys ('strength') and Ixion ('strong native') are closely connected (see 63. 1). The Eastern-European mistletoe, or loranthus, is a parasite of the oak and not, like the Western variety, of the poplar or the apple-tree; and 'Aesculapius', the Latin form of Asclepius – apparently meaning 'that which hangs from the esculent oak', i.e. the mistletoe – may well be the earlier title of the two. Mistletoe was regarded as the oak-tree's genitals, and when the Druids ritually lopped it with a golden sickle, they were performing a symbolic emasculation (see 7. 1). The viscous juice of its berries passed for oak-sperm, a liquid of great regenerative virtue. Sir James Frazer has pointed out in his *Golden Bough* that Aeneas visited the Underworld with mistletoe in his hand, and thus held the power of returning at will to the upper air. The 'certain herb', which raised Glaucus from the tomb, is likely to have been the mistletoe also. Ischys, Asclepius, Ixion and Polyeidus are, in fact, the same mythic character: personifications of the curative power resident in the dismembered genitals of the sacrificed oak-hero. 'Chylus', Ischys's other name, means 'the juice of a plant, or berry'.

3. Athene's dispensation of Gorgon-blood to Asclepius and Erichthonius suggests that the curative rites used in this cult were a secret guarded by priestesses, which it was death to investigate – the Gorgon-head is a formal warning to pryers (see 73. 5). But the blood of the sacrificed oak-king, or of his child surrogate, is likely to have been dispensed on these occasions, as well as mistletoe-juice.

4. Apollo's mythographers have made his sister Artemis responsible for Ischys's murder; and, indeed, she was originally the same goddess as Athene, in whose honour the oak-king met his death. They have also made Zeus destroy both Ischys and Asclepius with thunderbolts; and, indeed, all oak-kings fell beneath the double-axe, later formalized as a thunderbolt, and their bodies were usually roasted in a bonfire.

5. Apollo cursed the crow, burned Coronis to death for her illegitimate love affair with Ischys, and claimed Asclepius as his own son; then Cheiron and he taught him the art of healing. In other words: Apollo's Hellenic priests were helped by their Magnesian allies the Centaurs, who were hereditary enemies of the Lapiths, to take over a Thessalian crow-oracle, hero and all, expelling the college of Moon-priestesses and suppressing the worship of the goddess. Apollo retained the stolen crow, or raven, as an emblem of divination, but his priests found dream-interpretation a simpler and more effective means of diagnosing their patients' ailments than the birds' enigmatic croaking. At the same time, the sacral use of mistletoe was discontinued in Arcadia, Messenia, Thessaly, and Athens; and Ischys became a son of the pine-tree (Elatus), not of the oak – hence the pistachio-cone in the hands of Asclepius's image at Sicyon. There was another Lapith princess named Coronis whom Butes, the ancestor of the Athenian Butadae, violated (see 47. 4).

6. Asclepius's serpent form, like that of Erichthonius – whom Athene also empowered to raise the dead with Gorgon-blood – shows that he was an oracular hero; but several tame serpents were kept in his temple at Epidaurus (Pausanias: ii. 28. 1) as a symbol of renovation: because serpents cast their slough every year (see 160. 11). The bitch who suckled Asclepius, when the goatherd hailed him as the new-born king, must be Hecate, or Hecabe (see 31. 3; 38. 7; 134. 1; 168. n and 1); and it is perhaps to account for this bitch, with whom he is always pictured, that Cheiron has been made to tutor him in hunting. His other foster-mother, the she-goat, must be the Goat-Athene, in whose aegis Erichthonius took refuge (see 25. 2); indeed, if Asclepius originally had a twin – as Pelias was suckled by a mare, and Neleus by a bitch (see 68. d) – this will have been Erichthonius.

7. Athene, when reborn as a loyal virgin-daughter of Olympian Zeus, had to follow Apollo's example and curse the crow, her former familiar (see 25. e).

8. The willow was a tree of powerful moon-magic (see 28. 5; 44. 1 and 116. 4); and the bitter drug prepared from its bark is still a specific against rheumatism – to which the Spartans in their damp valleys will have been much subject. But branches of the particular variety of willow with which the Spartan Asclepius was associated, namely the *agnus castus*, were strewn on the beds of matrons at the Athenian Thesmophoria, a fertility festival (see 48. 1), supposedly to keep off serpents (Arrian: *History of Animals* ix. 26), though really to encourage serpent-shaped ghosts; and Asclepius's priests may therefore have specialized in the cure of barren-ness.

51

THE ORACLES

THE Oracles of Greece and Greater Greece are many; but the eldest is that of Dodonian Zeus. In ages past, two black doves flew from Egyptian Thebes: one to Libyan Ammon, the other to Dodona, and each alighted on an oak-tree, which they proclaimed to be an oracle of Zeus. At Dodona, Zeus's priestesses listen to the cooing of doves, or to the rustling of oak-leaves, or to the clanking of brazen vessels suspended from the branches. Zeus has another famous oracle at Olympia, where his priests reply to questions after inspecting the entrails of sacrificial victims.[1]

b. The Delphic Oracle first belonged to Mother Earth, who appointed Daphnis as her prophetess; and Daphnis, seated on a tripod, drank in the fumes of prophecy, as the Pythian priestess still does. Some say that Mother Earth later resigned her rights to the Titaness Phoebe, or Themis; and that she ceded them to Apollo, who built himself a shrine of laurel-boughs brought from Tempe. But others say that Apollo robbed the oracle from Mother Earth, after killing Python, and that his Hyperborean priests Pagasus and Agyieus established his worship there.

c. At Delphi it is said that the first shrine was made of bees' wax and feathers; the second, of fern-stalks twisted together; the third, of laurel-boughs; that Hephaestus built the fourth of bronze, with golden song-birds perched on the roof, but one day the earth engulfed it; and that the fifth, built of dressed stone, burned down in the year of the fifty-eighth Olympiad [489 B.C.], and was replaced by the present shrine.[2]

d. Apollo owns numerous other oracular shines: such as those in the Lycaeum and on the Acropolis at Argos, both presided over by a priestess. But at Boeotian Ismenium, his oracles are given by priests, after the inspection of entrails; at Clarus, near Colophon, his seer drinks the water of a secret well and pronounces an oracle in verse; while at Telmessus and elsewhere, dreams are interpreted.[3]

e. Demeter's priestesses give oracles to the sick at Patrae, from a mirror lowered into her well by a rope. At Pharae, in return for a copper coin, the sick who consult Hermes are granted their oracular responses in the first chance words that they hear on leaving the market place.[4]

f. Hera has a venerable oracle near Pagae; and Mother Earth is still consulted at Aegeira in Achaea, which means 'The Place of Black Poplars', where her priestess drinks bull's blood, deadly poison to all other mortals.[5]

g. Besides these, there are many other oracles of heroes, the oracle of Heracles, at Achaean Bura, where the answer is given by a throw of four dice;[6] and numerous oracles of Asclepius, where the sick flock for consultation and for cure, and are told the remedy in their dreams after a fast.[7] The oracles of Theban Amphiaraus and Mallian Amphilochus – with Mopsus, the most infallible extant – follow the Asclepian procedure.[8]

h. Moreover, Pasiphaë has an oracle at Laconian Thalamae, patronized by the Kings of Sparta, where answers are also given in dreams.[9]

i. Some oracles are not so easily consulted as others. For instance, at Lebadeia there is an oracle of Trophonius, son of Erginus the Argonaut, where the suppliant must purify himself several days beforehand, and lodge in a building dedicated to Good Fortune and a certain Good Genius, bathing only in the river Hercyna and sacrificing to Trophonius, to his nurse Demeter Europe, and to other deities. There he feeds on sacred flesh, especially that of a ram which has been sacrificed to the shade of Agamedes, the brother of Trophonius, who helped him to build Apollo's temple at Delphi.

j. When fit to consult the oracle, the suppliant is led down to the river by two boys, thirteen years of age, and there bathed and anointed. Next, he drinks from a spring called the Water of Lethe, which will help him to forget his past; and also from another, close by, called the

Water of Memory, which will help him to remember what he has seen
and heard. Dressed in country boots and a linen tunic, and wearing
fillets like a sacrificial victim, he then approaches the oracular chasm.
This resembles a huge bread-baking pot eight yards deep, and after
descending by a ladder, he finds a narrow opening at the bottom
through which he thrusts his legs, holding in either hand a barley-cake
mixed with honey. A sudden tug at his ankles, and he is pulled through
as if by the swirl of a swift river, and in the darkness a blow falls on his
skull, so that he seems to die, and an invisible speaker then reveals the
future to him, besides many mysterious secrets. As soon as the voice
has finished, he loses all sense and understanding, and is presently
returned, feet foremost, to the bottom of the chasm, but without the
honey-cakes; after which he is enthroned on the so-called Chair of
Memory and asked to repeat what he has heard. Finally, still in a dazed
condition, he returns to the house of the Good Genius, where he
regains his senses and the power to laugh.

k. The invisible speaker is one of the Good Genii, belonging to the
Golden Age of Cronus, who have descended from the moon to take
charge of oracles and initiatory rites, and act as chasteners, watchers,
and saviours everywhere; he consults the ghost of Trophonius who is
in serpent form and gives the required oracle as payment for the suppliant's honey-cake.[10]

1. Herodotus: ii. 55 and viii. 134; Dionysius of Halicarnassus: i. 15;
   Homer: *Odyssey* xiv. 328; Aeschylus: *Prometheus Bound* 832;
   Suidas *sub* Dodona; Sophocles: *Oedipus Tyrannus* 900.
2. Aeschylus: *Eumenides* 1–19; Pausanias: x. 5. 3–5.
3. Pausanias: ii. 24. 1; Plutarch: *Pyrrhus* 31; Herodotus, viii. 134
   and i. 78; Tacitus: *Annals* ii. 54.
4. Pausanias: vii. 21. 5 and 22. 2.
5. Strabo: viii. 6. 22; Pliny: *Natural History* xxviii. 41; Apollodorus:
   i. 9. 27.
6. Pausanias: vii. 25. 6.
7. *Ibid.*: ii. 27. 2.
8. *Ibid.*: i. 34. 2; Herodotus: viii. 134.
9. Plutarch: *Cleomenes* 7; Pausanias: iii. 26. 1.
10. Pausanias: ix. 39. 1–5; Plutarch: *On Socrates's Demon* xxii. and
    The Face on the Orb of the Moon xxx.

*

1. All oracles were originally delivered by the Earth-goddess, whose
authority was so great that patriarchal invaders made a practice of seizing
her shrines and either appointing priests or retaining the priestesses in

their own service. Thus Zeus at Dodona, and Ammon in the Oasis of Siwwa, took over the cult of the oracular oak, sacred to Dia or Dione (see 7. 1) – as the Hebrew Jehovah did that of Ishtar's oracular acacia (1 Chronicles xiv. 15) – and Apollo captured the shrines of Delphi and Argos. At Argos, the prophetess was allowed full freedom; at Delphi, a priest intervened between prophetess and votary, translating her incoherent utterances into hexameters; at Dodona, both the Dove-priestesses and Zeus's male prophets deliver oracles.

2. Mother Earth's shrine at Delphi was founded by the Cretans, who left their sacred music, ritual, dances, and calendar as a legacy to the Hellenes. Her Cretan sceptre, the labrys, or double-axe, named the priestly corporation at Delphi, the Labryadae, which was still extant in Classical times. The temple made from bees' wax and feathers refers to the goddess as Bee (see 7.3; 18.3 and 47.1) and as Dove (see 1. b and 62.a); the temple of fern recalls the magical properties attributed to fern-seed at the summer and winter solstices (Sir James Frazer devotes several pages to the subject in his Golden Bough); the shrine of laurel recalls the laurel-leaf chewed by the prophetess and her companions in their orgies – Daphnis is a shortened form of Daphoenissa ('the bloody one'), as Daphne is of Daphoene (see 21. 6 and 46. 2). The shrine of bronze engulfed by the earth may merely mark the fourth stage of a Delphic song that, like 'London Bridge is Broken Down', told of the various unsuitable materials with which the shrine was successively built; but it may also refer to an underground tholos, the tomb of a hero who was incarnate in the python. The tholos, a beehive-shaped ghost-house, appears to be of African origin, and introduced into Greece by way of Palestine. The Witch of Endor presided at a similar shrine, and the ghost of Adam gave oracles at Hebron. Philostratus refers to the golden birds in his Life of Apollonius of Tyana vi. 11 and describes them as siren-like wrynecks; but Pindar calls them nightingales (Fragment quoted by Athenaeus 290e). Whether the birds represented oracular nightingales, or wrynecks used as love-charms (see 152. a) and rain-inducers (Marinus on Proclus 28), is disputable.

3. Inspection of entrails seems to have been an Indo-European mantic device. Divination by the throw of four knucklebone dice was perhaps alphabetical in origin: since 'signs', not numbers, were said to be marked on the only four sides of each bone which could turn up. Twelve consonants and four vowels (as in the divinatory Irish Ogham called 'O'Sullivan's') are the simplest form to which the Greek alphabet can be reduced. But, in Classical times, numbers only were marked – 1, 3, 4, and 6 on each knucklebone – and the meanings of all their possible combinations had been codified. Prophecy from dreams is a universal practice.

4. Apollo's priests exacted virginity from the Pythian priestesses at

Delphi, who were regarded as Apollo's brides; but when one of them was scandalously seduced by a votary, they had thereafter to be at least fifty years old on installation, though still dressing as brides. Bull's blood was thought to be highly poisonous, because of its magical potency (see 155. a): the blood of sacred bulls, sometimes used to consecrate a whole tribe, as in *Exodus* xxiv. 8, was mixed with great quantities of water before being sprinkled on the fields as a fertilizer. The priestess of Earth, however, could drink whatever Mother Earth herself drank.

5. Hera, Pasiphaë, and Ino were all titles of the Triple-goddess, the interdependence of whose persons was symbolized by the tripod on which her priestess sat.

6. The procedure at the oracle of Trophonius – which Pausanias himself visited – recalls Aeneas's descent, mistletoe in hand, to Avernus, where he consulted his father Anchises, and Odysseus's earlier consultation of Teiresias; it also shows the relevance of these myths to a common form of initiation rite in which the novice suffers a mock-death, receives mystical instruction from a pretending ghost, and is then reborn into a new clan, or secret society. Plutarch remarks that the Trophoniads – the mystagogues in the dark den – belong to the pre-Olympian age of Cronus, and correctly couples them with the Idaean Dactyls who performed the Samothracian Mysteries.

7. Black poplar was sacred to the Death-goddess at Pagae, and Persephone had a black poplar grove in the Far West (Pausanias: x. 30. 3 and see 170. *l*).

8. Amphilochus and Mopsus had killed each other, but their ghosts agreed to found a joint oracle (see 169. *e*).

52

THE ALPHABET

THE Three Fates or, some say, Io the sister of Phoroneus, invented the five vowels of the first alphabet, and the consonants B and T; Palamedes, son of Nauplius, invented the remaining eleven consonants; and Hermes reduced these sounds to characters, using wedge shapes because cranes fly in wedge formation, and carried the system from Greece to Egypt. This was the Pelasgian alphabet, which Cadmus later brought back to Boeotia, and which Evander of Arcadia, a Pelasgian, introduced into Italy, where his mother Carmenta formed the familiar fifteen characters of the Latin alphabet.

b. Other consonants have since been added to the Greek alphabet by Simonides of Samos, and Epicharmus of Sicily; and two vowels, long O and short E, by the priests of Apollo, so that his sacred lyre now has one vowel for each of its seven strings.

c. Alpha was the first of the eighteen letters, because *alphe* means honour, and *alphainein* is to invent, and because the Alpheius is the most notable of rivers; moreover, Cadmus, though he changed the order of the letters, kept alpha in this place, because *aleph*, in the Phoenician tongue, means an ox, and because Boeotia is the land of oxen.[1]

> 1. Hyginus: *Fabula* 277; Isidore of Seville: *Origins* viii. 2. 84; Philostratus: *Heroica* x. 3; Pliny: *Natural History* vii. 57; Scholiast on Homer's *Iliad* xix. 593; Plutarch: *Symposiacs* ix. 3.

*

1. The Greek alphabet was a simplification of the Cretan hieroglyphs. Scholars are now generally agreed that the first written alphabet developed in Egypt during the eighteenth century B.C. under Cretan influence; which corresponds with Aristides's tradition, reported by Pliny, that an Egyptian called Menos ('moon') invented it 'fifteen years before the reign of Phoroneus, King of Argos'.

2. There is evidence, however, that before the introduction of the modified Phoenician alphabet into Greece an alphabet had existed there as a religious secret held by the priestesses of the Moon – Io, or the Three Fates: that it was closely linked with the calendar, and that its letters were represented not by written characters, but by twigs cut from different trees typical of the year's sequent months.

3. The ancient Irish alphabet, like that used by the Gallic druids of whom Caesar wrote, might not at first be written down, and all its letters were named after trees. It was called the *Beth-luis-nion* ('birch-rowan-ash') after its first three consonants; and its canon, which suggests a Phrygian provenience, corresponded with the Pelasgian and the Latin alphabets, namely thirteen consonants and five vowels. The original order was, A, B, L, N, O, F, S, H, U, D, T, C, E, M, G, Ng or Gn, R, I, which is likely also to have been the order used by Hermes. Irish ollaves made it into a deaf-and-dumb language, using finger-joints to represent the different letters, or one of verbal cyphers. Each consonant represented a twenty-eight-day month of a series of thirteen, beginning two days after the winter solstice; namely:

1	Dec. 24	B	birch, or wild olive
2	Jan. 21	L	rowan
3	Feb. 18	N	ash
4	March 18	F	alder, or cornel

5	April 15	S	willow; SS (Z), blackthorn
6	May 13	H	hawthorn, or wild pear
7	June 10	D	oak, or terebinth
8	July 8	T	holly, or prickly oak
9	Aug. 5	C	nut; CC (Q), apple, sorb or quince
10	Sept. 2	M	vine
11	Sept. 30	G	ivy
12	Oct. 28	Ng or Gn	reed, or guelder rose
13	Nov. 25	R	elder, or myrtle

4. About 400 B.C., as the result of a religious revolution, the order was changed as follows to correspond with a new calendar system: B, L, F, S, N, H, D, T, C, Q, M, G, Ng, Z, R. This is the alphabet associated with Heracles Ogmius, or 'Ogma Sunface', as the earlier is with Phoroneus (see 132. 3).

5. Each vowel represented a quarterly station of the year: O (gorse) the Spring Equinox; U (heather) the Summer Solstice; E (poplar) the Autumn Equinox. A (fir, or palm) the birth-tree, and I (yew) the death-tree, shared the Winter Solstice between them. This order of trees is implicit in Greek and Latin myth and the sacral tradition of all Europe and, *mutatis mutandis*, Syria and Asia Minor. The goddess Carmenta (see 86. 2 and 132. 6) invented B and T as well as the vowels, because each of these calendar-consonants introduced one half of her year, as divided between the sacred king and his tanist.

6. Cranes were sacred to Hermes (see 17. 3 and 36. 2), protector of poets before Apollo usurped his power; and the earliest alphabetic characters were wedge-shaped. Palamedes ('ancient intelligence'), with his sacred crane (Martial: *Epigrams* xiii. 75) was the Carian counterpart of the Egyptian god Thoth, inventor of letters, with his crane-like ibis; and Hermes was Thoth's early Hellenic counterpart (see 162. 5). That Simonides and Epicharmus added new letters to the alphabet is history, not myth; though exactly why they did so remains doubtful. Two of the additions, *xi* and *psi*, were unnecessary, and the removal of the aspirate (H) and *digamma* (F) impoverished the canon.

7. It can be shown that the names of the letters preserved in the Irish *Beth-luis-nion*, which are traditionally reported to have come from Greece and reached Ireland by way of Spain (see 132. 5), formed an archaic Greek charm in honour of the Arcadian White Goddess Alphito who, by Classical times, had degenerated into a mere nursery bogey. The Cadmean order of letters, perpetuated in the familiar ABC, seems to be a deliberate mis-arrangement by Phoenician merchants; they used the secret alphabet for trade purposes but feared to offend the goddess by revealing its true order.

This complicated and important subject is discussed at length in *The White Goddess* (Chapters 1–15 and 21).

8. The vowels added by the priests of Apollo to his lyre were probably those mentioned by Demetrius, an Alexandrian philosopher of the first century B.C., when he writes in his dissertation *On Style*:

In Egypt the priests sing hymns to the Gods by uttering the seven vowels in succession, the sound of which produces as strong a musical impression on their hearers as if the flute and lyre were used ... but perhaps I had better not enlarge on this theme.

This suggests that the vowels were used in therapeutic lyre music at Apollo's shrines.

53

THE DACTYLS

SOME say that while Rhea was bearing Zeus, she pressed her fingers into the soil to ease her pangs and up sprang the Dactyls: five females from her left hand, and five males from her right. But it is generally held that they were living on Phrygian Mount Ida long before the birth of Zeus, and some say that the nymph Anchiale bore them in the Dictaean Cave near Oaxus. The male Dactyls were smiths and first discovered iron in near-by Mount Berecynthus; and their sisters, who settled in Samothrace, excited great wonder there by casting magic spells, and taught Orpheus the Goddess's mysteries: their names are a well-guarded secret.[1]

b. Others say that the males were the Curetes who protected Zeus's cradle in Crete, and that they afterwards came to Elis and raised a temple to propitiate Cronus. Their names were Heracles, Paeonius, Epimedes, Iasius, and Acesidas. Heracles, having brought wild-olive from the Hyperboreans to Olympia, set his younger brothers to run a race there, and thus the Olympic Games originated. It is also said that he crowned Paeonius, the victor, with a spray of wild-olive; and that, afterwards, they slept in beds made from its green leaves. But the truth is that wild-olive was not used for the victor's crown until the seventh Olympiad, when the Delphic Oracle had ordered Iphitus to substitute it for the apple-spray hitherto awarded as the prize of victory.[2]

c. Acmon, Damnameneus, and Celmis are titles of the three eldest

Dactyls; some say that Celmis was turned to iron as a punishment for insulting Rhea.³

1. Diodorus Siculus: v. 64; Sophocles: *The Deaf Satyrs*, quoted by Strabo: x. 3. 22; Apollonius Rhodius: 509 and 1130.
2. Pausanias: v. 7. 4; Phlegon of Tralles: *Fragmenta Historica Graeca* iii. 604.
3. Scholiast on Apollonius Rhodius: i. 1129; Ovid: *Metamorphoses* iv. 281.

*

1. The Dactyls personify the fingers, and Heracles's Olympic race is a childish fable illustrated by drumming one's fingers on a table, omitting the thumb – when the forefinger always wins the race. But Orphic secret lore was based on a calendar sequence of magical trees, each allotted a separate finger joint in the sign-language and a separate letter of the Orphic calendar-alphabet, which seems to have been Phrygian in origin (see 52. 3). Wild-olive belongs to the top-joint of the thumb, supposedly the seat of virility and therefore called Heracles. This Heracles was said to have had leaves growing from his body (Palaephatus: 37). The system is recalled in the popular Western finger-names: e.g. 'fool's finger', which corresponds with Epimedes, the middle finger, and the 'physic finger', which corresponds with Iasius, the fourth; and in the finger-names of palmistry: e.g. Saturn of Epimedes – Saturn having shown himself slow-witted in his struggle with Zeus; and Apollo, god of healing, for Iasius. The forefinger is given to Jupiter, or Zeus, who won the race. The little finger, Mercury or Hermes, is the magical one. Throughout primitive Europe, metallurgy was accompanied by incantations, and the smiths therefore claimed the fingers of the right hand as their Dactyls, leaving the left to the sorceresses.

2. The story of Acmon, Damnameneus, and Celmis, whose names refer to smithcraft, is another childish fable, illustrated by tapping the forefinger on the thumb, as a hammer on an anvil, and then slipping the tip of the middle finger between them, as though it were a piece of red-hot iron. Iron came to Crete through Phrygia from farther along the Southern Black Sea coast; and Celmis, being a personification of smelted iron, will have been obnoxious to the Great Goddess Rhea, patroness of smiths, whose religious decline began with the smelting of iron and the arrival of the iron-weaponed Dorians. She had recognized only gold, silver, copper, lead, and tin as terrestrial ores; though lumps of meteoric iron were highly prized because of their miraculous origin, and one may have fallen on Mount Berecynthus. An unworked lump was found in a neolithic deposit at Phaestus beside a squatting clay image of the goddess, sea-shells, and offering bowls. All early Egyptian iron is meteoric: it

contains a high proportion of nickel and is nearly rust-proof. Celmis's insult to Hera gave the middle finger its name: *digita impudica*.

3. The Olympic games originated in a foot race, run by girls, for the privilege of becoming the priestess of the Moon-goddess Hera (Pausanias: v. 16. 2); and since this event took place in the month Parthenios, 'of the maiden', it seems to have been annual. When Zeus married Hera – when, that is, a new form of sacred kingship had been introduced into Greece by the Achaeans (see 12. 7) – a second foot race was run by young men for the dangerous privilege of becoming the priestess's consort, Sun to her Moon, and thus King of Elis; just as Antaeus made his daughter's suitors race for her (Pindar: *Pythian Odes* ix), following the example of Icarius (see 160. *d*) and Danaus (see 60. *m*).

4. The Games were thereafter held every four years, instead of annually, the girls' foot race being run at a separate festival, either a fortnight before, or a fortnight after the Olympian Games proper; and the sacred kingship, conferred on the victor of the foot race at his marriage to the new priestess, is recalled in the divine honours that the victory continued to bestow in Classical times. Having been wreathed with Heracles's or Zeus's olive, saluted as 'King Heracles', and pelted with leaves like a Jack o' Green, he led the dance in a triumphal procession and ate sacrificial bull's flesh in the Council Hall.

5. The original prize, an apple, or an apple-spray, had been a promise of immortality when he was duly killed by his successor; for Plutarch (*Symposiac Questions* v. 2) mentions that though a foot race was the sole contest in the original Olympic Games, a single combat also took place, which ended only in the death of the vanquished. This combat is mythologically recorded in the story that the Olympic Games began with a wrestling match between Zeus and Cronus for the possession of Elis (Pausanias: v. 7), namely the midsummer combat between the king and his tanist; and the result was a foregone conclusion – the tanist came armed with a spear.

6. A scholiast on Pindar (*Olympian Odes* iii. 33), quoting Comarchus, shows that the Elian New Year was reckoned from the full moon nearest to the winter solstice, and that a second New Year began at midsummer. Presumably therefore the new Zeus-Heracles, that is to say, the winner of the foot race, killed the Old Year tanist, Cronus-Iphicles, at midwinter. Hence Heracles first instituted the Games and named the sepulchral Hill of Cronus 'at a season when the summit was wet with much snow' (Pindar: *Olympian Odes* x. 49).

7. In ancient times, Zeus-Heracles was pelted with oak-leaves and given the apple-spray at midsummer, just before being killed by his tanist; he had won the royal wild-olive branch at midwinter. The replacement of the apple by wild-olive, which is the tree that drives

away evil spirits, implied the abolition of this death-combat, and the conversion of the single year, divided into two halves, into a Great Year. This began at midwinter, when solar and lunar time coincided favourably for a Sun-and-Moon marriage, and was divided into two Olympiads of four years apiece; the king and his tanist reigning successively or concurrently. Though by Classical times the solar chariot race – for which the mythological authority is Pelops's contest with Oenomaus for Deidameia (see 109. 3) – had become the most important event in the Games, it was still thought somehow unlucky to be pelted with leaves after a victory in the foot race; and Pythagoras advised his friends to compete in this event but not to win it. The victory-ox, eaten at the Council Hall, was clearly a surrogate for the king, as at the Athenian Buphonia festival (see 21. 13).

8. Olympia is not a Mycenaean site and the pre-Achaean myths are therefore unlikely to have been borrowed from Crete; they seem to be Pelasgian.

54

THE TELCHINES

THE nine dog-headed, flipper-handed Telchines, Children of the Sea, originated in Rhodes, where they founded the cities of Cameirus, Ialysus, and Lindus; and migrating thence to Crete, became its first inhabitants. Rhea entrusted the infant Poseidon to their care, and they forged his trident but, long before this, had made for Cronus the toothed sickle with which he castrated his father Uranus; and were, moreover, the first to carve images of the gods.

b. Yet Zeus resolved to destroy them by a flood, because they had been interfering with the weather, raising magic mists and blighting crops by means of sulphur and Stygian water. Warned by Artemis, they all fled overseas: some to Boeotia, where they built the temple of Athene at Teumessus; some to Sicyon, some to Lycia, others to Orchomenus, where they were the hounds that tore Actaeon to pieces. But Zeus destroyed the Teumessian Telchines with a flood; Apollo, disguised as a wolf, destroyed the Lycian ones, though they had tried to placate him with a new temple; and they are no longer to be found at Orchomenus. Rumour has it that some are still living in Sicyon.[1]

1. Eustathius on Homer, p. 771–2; Ovid: *Metamorphoses* vii. 365–7; Diodorus Siculus: iii. 55. 2–3; Strabo: xiv. 2. 7; Callimachus: *Hymn to Delos* 31; Servius on Virgil's *Aeneid* iv. 377.

*

1. That the nine Telchines were Children of the Sea, acted as the hounds of Artemis, created magic mists, and founded the cities named after the three Danaids, Cameira, Ialysa, and Linda (see 60. *d*) suggests that they were originally emanations of the Moon-goddess Danaë: each of her three persons in triad (see 60. *2*). 'Telchin' was derived by the Greek grammarians from *thelgein*, 'to enchant'. But, since women, dog and fish were likewise combined in pictures of Scylla the Tyrrhenian – who was also at home in Crete (see 91. *2*) – and in the figure-heads of Tyrrhenian ships, the word may be a variant of 'Tyrrhen' or 'Tyrsen'; *l* and *r* having been confused by the Libyans, and the next consonant being something between an aspirate and a sibilant. They were, it seems, worshipped by an early matriarchal people of Greece, Crete, Lydia, and the Aegean Islands, whom the invading patriarchal Hellenes persecuted; absorbed or forced to emigrate westward. Their origin may have been East African.

2. Magic mists were raised by willow spells. Styx water (see 31. *4*) was supposedly so holy that the least drop of it caused death, unless drunk from a cup made of a horse's hoof, which proves it sacred to the Mare-headed goddess of Arcadia. Alexander the Great is said to have been poisoned by Styx water (Pausanias: viii. 18. 2). The Telchines' magical use of it suggests that their devotees held near-by Mount Nonacris ('nine peaks'), at one time the chief religious centre of Greece; even the Olympic gods swore their most solemn oath by the Styx.

55

THE EMPUSAE

THE filthy demons called Empusae, children of Hecate, are ass-haunched and wear brazen slippers – unless, as some declare, each has one ass's leg and one brazen leg. Their habit is to frighten travellers, but they may be routed by insulting words, at the sound of which they flee shrieking. Empusae disguise themselves in the forms of bitches, cows, or beautiful maidens and, in the latter shape, will lie with men by night, or at the time of midday sleep, sucking their vital forces until they die.[1]

1. Aristophanes: *Frogs* 288 ff.; *Parliament of Women* 1056 and 1094; *Papyri Magici Graeci* iv. 2334; Philostratus: *Life of Apollonius of Tyana* iv. 25; Suidas *sub* Empusae.

*

1. The Empusae ('forcers-in') are greedily seductive female demons, a concept probably brought to Greece from Palestine, where they went by the name of Lilim ('children of Lilith') and were thought to be ass-haunched, the ass symbolizing lechery and cruelty. Lilith ('scritch-owl') was a Canaanite Hecate, and the Jews made amulets to protect themselves against her as late as the Middle Ages. Hecate, the real ruler of Tartarus (see 31. *f*), wore a brazen sandal – the golden sandal was Aphrodite's – and her daughters, the Empusae, followed this example. They could change themselves into beautiful maidens or cows, as well as bitches, because the Bitch Hecate, being a member of the Moon-triad, was the same goddess as Aphrodite, or cow-eyed Hera.

56
IO

Io, daughter of the River-god Inachus, was a priestess of Argive Hera. Zeus, over whom Iynx, daughter of Pan and Echo, had cast a spell, fell in love with Io, and when Hera charged him with infidelity and turned Iynx into a wryneck as a punishment, lied: 'I have never touched Io.' He then turned her into a white cow, which Hera claimed as hers and handed over for safe keeping to Argus Panoptes, ordering him: 'Tether this beast secretly to an olive-tree at Nemea.' But Zeus sent Hermes to fetch her back, and himself led the way to Nemea – or, some say, to Mycenae – dressed in woodpecker disguise. Hermes, though the cleverest of thieves, knew that he could not steal Io without being detected by one of Argus's hundred eyes; he therefore charmed him asleep by playing the flute, crushed him with a boulder, cut off his head, and released Io. Hera, having placed Argus's eyes in the tail of a peacock, as a constant reminder of his foul murder, set a gadfly to sting Io and chase her all over the world.

b. Io first went to Dodona, and presently reached the sea called the Ionian after her, but there turned back and travelled north to Mount Haemus and then, by way of the Danube's delta, coursed sun-wise around the Black Sea, crossing the Crimean Bosphorus, and following the River Hybristes to its source in the Caucasus, where Prometheus still languished on his rock. She regained Europe by way of Colchis, the land of the Chalybes, and the Thracian Bosphorus; then away she galloped through Asia Minor to Tarsus and Joppa, thence to Media, Bactria, and India and, passing south-westward through Arabia, across the Indian Bosphorus [the Straits of Bab-el-Mandeb], reached Ethiopia. Thence she travelled down from the sources of the Nile, where the pygmies make perpetual war with the cranes, and found rest at last in Egypt. There Zeus restored her to human form and, having married Telegonus, she gave birth to Epaphus – her son by Zeus, who had *touched* her to some purpose – and founded the worship of Isis, as she called Demeter. Epaphus, who was rumoured to be the divine bull Apis, reigned over Egypt, and had a daughter, Libya, the mother by Poseidon of Agenor and Belus.[1]

c. But some believe that Io bore Epaphus in a Euboean cave called Boösaule, and afterwards died there from the sting of the gadfly; and that, as a cow, she changed her colour from white to violet-red, and from violet-red to black.[2]

d. Others have a quite different story to tell. They say that Inachus, a son of Iapetus, ruled over Argos, and founded the city of Iopolis – for Io is the name by which the moon was once worshipped at Argos – and called his daughter Io in honour of the moon. Zeus Picus, King of the West, sent his servants to carry off Io, and outraged her as soon as she reached his palace. After bearing him a daughter named Libya, Io fled to Egypt, but found that Hermes, son of Zeus, was reigning there; so continued her flight to Mount Silpium in Syria, where she died of grief and shame. Inachus then sent Io's brothers and kinsfolk in search of her, warning them not to return empty-handed. With Triptolemus for their guide, they knocked on every door in Syria, crying: 'May the spirit of Io find rest!'; until at last they reached Mount Silpium, where a phantasmal cow addressed them with: 'Here am I, Io.' They decided that Io must have been buried on that spot, and therefore founded a second Iopolis, now called Antioch. In honour of Io, the Iopolitans knock at one another's door in the same way every year, using the same cry; and the Argives mourn annually for her.[3]

1. Callimachus: *On Birds, Fragment* 100; Apollodorus: ii. 1. 3; Hyginus: *Fabula* 145; Suidas *sub* Io; Lucian: *Dialogues of the Gods* 3; Moschus: *Idyll* ii. 59; Herodotus: i. 1 and ii. 41; Homer: *Iliad* iii. 6; Aeschylus: *Prometheus Bound* 705 ff. and *Suppliants* 547 ff.; Euripides: *Iphigeneia Among the Taurians* 382; Tzetzes: *On Lycophron* 835 ff.

2. Strabo: x. 1. 3; Stephanus of Byzantium *sub* Argura; Suidas *sub* Isis.

3. John Malalas: *Chronicles* ii. p. 28, ed. Dindorff.

*

1. This myth consists of several strands. The Argives worshipped the moon as a cow, because the horned new moon was regarded as the source of all water, and therefore of cattle fodder. Her three colours: white for the new moon, red for the harvest moon, black for the moon when it waned, represented the three ages of the Moon-goddess – Maiden, Nymph, and Crone (see 90. 3). Io changed her colour, as the moon changes, but for 'red' the mythographer substitutes 'violet' because *ion* is Greek for the violet flower. Woodpeckers were thought to be knocking for rain when they tapped on oak-trunks; and Io was the Moon as rain-bringer. The herdsmen needed rain most pressingly in late summer, when gadflies attacked their cattle and sent them frantic; in Africa, cattle-owning Negro tribes still hurry from pasture to pasture when attacked by them. Io's Argive priestesses seem to have performed an annual heifer-dance in which they pretended to be driven mad by gadflies, while woodpecker-men, tapping on oak-doors and calling 'Io! Io!', invited the rain to fall and relieve their torments. This seems to be the origin of the myth of the Coan women who were turned into cows (see 137. s). Argive colonies founded in Euboea, the Bosphorus, the Black Sea, Syria, and Egypt, took their rain-making dance with them. The wryneck, the Moon-goddess's prime orgiastic bird, nests in willows, and was therefore concerned with water-magic (see 152. 2).

2. The legend invented to account for the eastward spread of this ritual, as well as the similarity between the worship of Io in Greece, Isis in Egypt, Astarte in Syria, and Kali in India, has been grafted on two unrelated stories: that of the holy moon-cow wandering around the heavens, guarded by the stars – there is a cognate Irish legend of the 'Green Stripper' – and that of the Moon-priestesses whom the leaders of the invading Hellenes, each calling himself Zeus, violated to the dismay of the local population. Hera, as Zeus's wife, is then made to express jealousy of Io, though Io was another name for 'cow-eyed' Hera. Demeter's mourning for Persephone is recalled in the Argive festival of mourning for Io, since Io has been equated in the myth with Demeter.

Moreover, every three years Demeter's Mysteries were celebrated at Celeae ('calling'), near Corinth, and said to have been founded by a brother of Celeus ('woodpecker'), King of Eleusis. Hermes is called the son of Zeus Picus ('woodpecker') – Aristophanes in his *Birds* (480) accuses Zeus of stealing the woodpecker's sceptre – as Pan is said to have been Hermes's son by the Nymph Dryope ('woodpecker'); and Faunus, the Latin Pan, was the son of Picus ('woodpecker') whom Circe turned into a woodpecker for spurning her love (Ovid: *Metamorphoses* xiv. 6). Faunus's Cretan tomb bore the epitaph: 'Here lies the woodpecker who was also Zeus' (Suidas *sub* Picos). All three are rain-making shepherd-gods. Libya's name denotes rain, and the winter rains came to Greece from the direction of Libya.

3. Zeus's fathering of Epaphus, who became the ancestor of Libya, Agenor, Belus, Aegyptus, and Danaus, implies that the Zeus-worshipping Achaeans claimed sovereignty over all the sea-peoples of the south-eastern Mediterranean.

4. The myth of pygmies and cranes seems to concern the tall cattle-breeding tribesmen who had broken into the upper Nile-valley from Somaliland and driven the native pygmies southward. They were called 'cranes' because, then as now, they would stand for long periods on one leg, holding the ankle of the other with the opposite hand, and leaning on a spear.

57

PHORONEUS

THE first man to found and people a market-town was Io's brother Phoroneus, son of the River-god Inachus and the Nymph Melia; later its name, Phoronicum, was changed to Argos. Phoroneus was also the first to discover the use of fire, after Prometheus had stolen it. He married the Nymph Cerdo, ruled the entire Peloponnese, and initiated the worship of Hera. When he died, his sons Pelasgus, Iasus, and Agenor divided the Peloponnese between them; but his son Car founded the city of Megara.[1]

1. Hyginus: *Fabulae* 143 and 274; Apollodorus: ii. 1. 1; Pausanias: i. 39. 4–6; ii. 15. 5 and iv. 40. 5.

*

1. Phoroneus's name, which the Greeks read as 'bringer of a price' in the sense that he invented markets, probably stands for Fearinus ('of the

dawn of the year', i.e. the Spring); variants are Bran, Barn, Bergn, Vron, Ephron, Gwern, Fearn, and Brennus. As the spirit of the alder-tree which presided over the fourth month in the sacred year (see 28. 1 and 5; 52. 3 and 170. 8), during which the Spring Fire Festival was celebrated, he was described as a son of Inachus, because alders grow by rivers. His mother is the ash-nymph Melia, because the ash, the preceding tree of the same series, is said to 'court the flash' – lightning-struck trees were primitive man's first source of fire. Being an oracular hero, he was also associated with the crow (see 50. 1). Phoroneus's discovery of the use of fire may be explained by the ancient smiths' and potters' preference for alder charcoal, which gives out more heat than any other. Cerdo ('gain' or 'art') is one of Demeter's titles; it was applied to her as weasel, or fox, both considered prophetic animals. 'Phoroneus' seems to have been a title of Cronus, with whom the crow and the alder are also associated (see 6. 2), and therefore the Titan of the Seventh Day. The division of Phoroneus's kingdom between his sons Pelasgus, Iasus, and Agenor recalls that of Cronus's kingdom between Zeus, Poseidon, and Hades; but perhaps describes a pre-Achaean partition of the Peloponnese.

2. Car is Q're, or Carius, or the Great God Ker, who seems to have derived his title from his Moon-mother Artemis Caria, or Caryatis.

58

EUROPE AND CADMUS

AGENOR, Libya's son by Poseidon and twin to Belus, left Egypt to settle in the Land of Canaan, where he married Telephassa, otherwise called Argiope, who bore him Cadmus, Phoenix, Cilix, Thasus, Phineus, and one daughter, Europe.[1]

b. Zeus, falling in love with Europe, sent Hermes to drive Agenor's cattle down to the seashore at Tyre, where she and her companions used to walk. He himself joined the herd, disguised as a snow-white bull with great dewlaps and small, gem-like horns, between which ran a single black streak. Europe was struck by his beauty and, on finding him gentle as a lamb, mastered her fear and began to play with him, putting flowers in his mouth and hanging garlands on his horns; in the end, she climbed upon his shoulders, and let him amble down with her to the edge of the sea. Suddenly he swam away, while she looked back in terror at the receding shore; one of her hands clung to his right horn, the other still held a flower-basket.[2]

c. Wading ashore near Cretan Gortyna, Zeus became an eagle and ravished Europe in a willow-thicket beside a spring; or, some say, under an evergreen plane-tree. She bore him three sons: Minos, Rhadamanthys, and Sarpedon.[3]

d. Agenor sent his sons in search of their sister, forbidding them to return without her. They set sail at once but, having no notion where the bull had gone, each steered a different course. Phoenix travelled westward, beyond Libya, to what is now Carthage, and there gave his name to the Punics; but, after Agenor's death, returned to Canaan, since renamed Phoenicia in his honour, and became the father of Adonis by Alphesiboea.[4] Cilix went to the Land of the Hypachaeans, which took his name, Cilicia;[5] and Phineus to Thynia, a peninsula separating the Sea of Marmara from the Black Sea, where he was later much distressed by harpies. Thasus and his followers, first making for Olympia, dedicated a bronze statue there to Tyrian Heracles, ten ells high, holding a club and a bow, but then set off to colonize the island of Thasos and work its rich gold mines. All this took place five generations before Heracles, son of Amphitryon, was born in Greece.[6]

e. Cadmus sailed with Telephassa to Rhodes, where he dedicated a brazen cauldron to Athene of Lindus, and built Poseidon's temple, leaving a herditary priesthood behind to care for it. They next touched at Thera, and built a similar temple, finally reaching the land of the Thracian Edonians, who received them hospitably. Here Telephassa died suddenly and, after her funeral, Cadmus and his companions proceeded on foot to the Delphic Oracle. When he asked where Europe might be found, the Pythoness advised him to give up his search and, instead, follow a cow and build a city wherever she should sink down for weariness.

f. Departing by the road that leads from Delphi to Phocis, Cadmus came upon some cowherds in the service of King Pelagon, who sold him a cow marked with a white full moon on each flank. This beast he drove eastward through Boeotia, never allowing her to pause until, at last, she sank down where the city of Thebes now stands, and here he erected an image of Athene, calling it by her Phoenician name of Onga.[7]

g. Cadmus, warning his companions that the cow must be sacrificed to Athene without delay, sent them to fetch lustral water from the

Spring of Ares, now called the Castalian Spring, but did not know that it was guarded by a great serpent. This serpent killed most of Cadmus's men, and he took vengeance by crushing its head with a rock. No sooner had he offered Athene the sacrifice, than she appeared, praising him for what he had done, and ordering him to sow the serpent's teeth in the soil. When he obeyed her, armed Sparti, or Sown Men, at once sprang up, clashing their weapons together. Cadmus tossed a stone among them and they began to brawl, each accusing the other of having thrown it, and fought so fiercely that, at last, only five survived: Echion, Udaeus, Chthonius, Hyperenor, and Pelorus, who unanimously offered Cadmus their services. But Ares demanded vengeance for the death of the serpent, and Cadmus was sentenced by a divine court to become his bondman for a Great Year.[8]

1. Apollodorus: iii. 1. 1; Hyginus: *Fabulae* 178 and 19; Pausanias: v. 25. 7; Apollonius Rhodius: ii. 178.
2. Ovid: *Metamorphoses* ii. 836 ff.; Moschus: *Idylls* ii. 37–62.
3. The Coins of Gortyna; Theophrastus: *History of Plants* i. 9. 5; Hyginus: *Fabula* 178.
4. Hyginus: *loc. cit.*; Apollodorus: iii. 1. 1 and 14. 4.
5. Herodotus: vii. 91.
6. Pausanias: v. 25. 7; Herodotus: iv. 47 and ii. 44.
7. Pausanias: ix. 12. 1–2.
8. Hyginus: *Fabula* 178; Apollodorus: iii. 4. 1–2.

*

1. There are numerous confusing variations of the genealogy given above: for instance, Thasus is alternatively described as the son of Poseidon, Cilix (Apollodorus: iii. 1. 1), or Tityus (Pindar: *Pythian Odes* iv. 46). Agenor is the Phoenician hero Chnas, who appears in *Genesis* as 'Canaan'; many Canaanite customs point to an East African provenience, and the Canaanites may have originally come to Lower Egypt from Uganda. The dispersal of Agenor's sons seems to record the westward flight of Canaanite tribes early in the second millennium B.C., under pressure from Aryan and Semitic invaders.

2. The story of Inachus's sons and their search for Io the moon-cow (see 56. *d*) has influenced that of Agenor's sons and their search for Europe. Phoenix is a masculine form of Phoenissa ('the red, or bloody one'), a title given to the moon as goddess of Death-in-Life. Europe means 'broad-face', a synonym for the full moon, and a title of the Moon-goddesses Demeter at Lebadia and Astarte at Sidon. If, however, the word is not *eur-ope* but *eu-rope* (on the analogy of *euboea*), it may also

mean 'good for willows' – that is, 'well-watered'. The willow rules the fifth month of the sacred year (see 52. 3), and is associated with witch-craft (see 28. 5) and with fertility rites throughout Europe, especially on May Eve, which falls in this month. Libya, Telephassa, Argiope, and Alphesiboea are all, similarly, titles of the Moon-goddess.

3. Zeus's rape of Europe, which records an early Hellenic occupation of Crete, has been deduced from pre-Hellenic pictures of the Moon-priestess triumphantly riding on the Sun-bull, her victim; the scene survives in eight moulded plaques of blue glass, found in the Mycenaean city of Midea. This seems to have been part of the fertility ritual during which Europe's May-garland was carried in procession (Athenaeus: p. 678 a–b). Zeus's seduction of Europe in eagle-disguise recalls his seduc-tion of Hera in cuckoo-disguise (see 12. a); since (according to Hesychius) Hella bore the title 'Europia'. Europe's Cretan and Corinthian name was Hellotis, which suggests Helice ('willow'); Helle (see 43. 1 and 70. 8) and Helen are the same divine character. Callimachus in his Epithalamion for Helen mentions that the plane-tree was also sacred to Helen. Its sanctity lay in its five-pointed leaves, representing the hand of the goddess (see 53. a), and its annual sloughing of bark; but Apollo borrowed it (see 160. 10), as the God Esmun did Tanit's (Neith's) open-hand emblem (see 21. 3).

4. It is possible that the story of Europe also commemorates a raid on Phoenicia by Hellenes from Crete. John Malalas will hardly have invented the 'Evil Evening' at Tyre when he writes: 'Taurus ("bull"), King of Crete, assaulted Tyre after a sea-battle during the absence of Agenor and his sons. They took the city that same evening and carried off many cap-tives, Europe among them; this event is still recalled in the annual "Evil Evening" observed at Tyre' (Chronicles ii. p. 30, ed. Dindorff). Hero-dotus (1. 2) agrees with Malalas (see 160. 1).

5. Tyrian Heracles, whom Theseus worshipped at Olympia, was the god Melkarth; and a small tribe, speaking a Semitic language, seems to have moved up from the Syrian plains to Cadmeia in Caria – Cadmus is a Semitic word meaning 'eastern' – whence they crossed over to Boeotia towards the end of the second millennium, seized Thebes, and became masters of the country. The myth of the Sown Men and Cad-mus's bondage to Ares suggest that the invading Cadmeans secured their hold on Boeotia by successfully intervening in a civil war among the Pelasgian tribes who claimed to be autochthonous; and that they accepted the local rule of an eight-year reign for the sacred king. Cadmus killed the serpent in the same sense as Apollo killed the Python at Delphi (see 21. 12). The names of the Sown Men – Echion ('viper'); Udaeus ('of the earth'); Chthonius ('of the soil'); Hyperenor ('man who comes up') and Pelorus ('serpent') – are characteristic of oracular heroes. But 'Pelorus' suggests that all Pelasgians, not merely the Thebans, claimed to be born

in this way; their common feast being the Peloria (see 1. 2). Jason's crop of dragon's teeth was probably sown at Iolcus or Corinth, not Colchis (see 152. 3).

6. Troy and Antioch were also said to have been founded on sites selected by sacred cows (see 158. h and 56. d). But it is less likely that this practice was literally carried out, than that the cow was turned loose in a restricted part of a selected site and the temple of the Moon-goddess founded where she lay down. A cow's strategic and commercial sensibilities are not highly developed.

59

CADMUS AND HARMONIA

WHEN Cadmus had served eight years in bondage to Ares, to expiate the murder of the Castalian serpent, Athene secured him the land of Boeotia. With the help of his Sown Men, he built the Theban acropolis, named 'The Cadmea' in his own honour and, after being initiated into the mysteries which Zeus had taught Iasion, married Harmonia, the daughter of Aphrodite and Ares; some say that Athene had given her to him when he visited Samothrace.[1]

b. This was the first mortal wedding ever attended by the Olympians. Twelve golden thrones were set up for them in Cadmus's house, which stood on the site of the present Theban market place; and they all brought gifts. Aphrodite presented Harmonia with the famous golden necklace made by Hephaestus – originally it had been Zeus's love-gift to Cadmus's sister Europe – which conferred irresistible beauty on its wearer.[2] Athene gave her a golden robe, which similarly conferred divine dignity on its wearer, also a set of flutes; and Hermes a lyre. Cadmus's own present to Harmonia was another rich robe; and Electra, Iasion's mother, taught her the rites of the Great Goddess; while Demeter assured her a prosperous barley harvest by lying with Iasion in a thrice-ploughed field during the celebrations. The Thebans still show the place where the Muses played the flute and sang on this occasion, and where Apollo performed on the lyre.[3]

c. In his old age, to placate Ares, who had not yet wholly forgiven him for killing the serpent, Cadmus resigned the Theban throne in favour of his grandson Pentheus, whom his daughter Agave had borne to Echion the Sown Man, and lived quietly in the city. But when Pentheus was done to death by his mother, Dionysus foretold that Cadmus and Harmonia, riding in a chariot drawn by heifers, would rule over barbarian hordes. These same barbarians, he said, would sack many Greek cities until, at last, they plundered a temple of Apollo, whereupon they would suffer just punishment; but Ares would rescue Cadmus and Harmonia, after turning them into serpents, and they would live happily for all time in the Islands of the Blessed.[4]

d. Cadmus and Harmonia therefore emigrated to the land of the Encheleans who, when attacked by the Illyrians, chose them as their rulers, in accordance with Dionysus's advice. Agave was now married to Lycotherses, King of Illyria, at whose court she had taken refuge after her murder of Pentheus; but on hearing that her parents commanded the Enchelean forces, she murdered Lycotherses too, and gave the kingdom to Cadmus.[5]

e. In their old age, when the prophecy had been wholly fulfilled, Cadmus and Harmonia duly became blue-spotted black serpents, and were sent by Zeus to the Islands of the Blessed. But some say that Ares changed them into lions. Their bodies were buried in Illyria, where Cadmus had built the city of Buthoë. He was succeeded by Illyrius, the son of his old age.[6]

1. Pausanias: ix. 5. 1; Diodorus Siculus: v. 48; Apollodorus: iii. 4. 2.
2. Diodorus Siculus: v. 49 and iv. 65. 5; Pindar: *Pythian Odes* iii. 94; Pausanias: ix. 12. 3; Pherecydes, quoted by Apollodorus: iii. 4. 2.
3. Diodorus Siculus: v. 49; Pausanias: ix. 12. 3
4. Hyginus: *Fabula* 6; Apollodorus: iii. 4. 2; Euripides: *Bacchae* 43 and 1350 ff.
5. Hyginus: *Fabulae* 184 and 240.
6. Ovid: *Metamorphoses* iv. 562–602; Apollodorus: iii. 5. 4; Ptolemy Hephaestionos; i; Apollonius Rhodius: iv. 517.

*

1. Cadmus's marriage to Harmonia, in the presence of the Twelve Olympian deities, is paralleled by Peleus's marriage to Thetis (see 81. *l*), and seems to record a general Hellenic recognition of the Cadmeian conquerors of Thebes, after they had been sponsored by the Athenians and decently initiated into the Samothracian Mysteries. His founding of Buthoë constitutes a claim by the Illyrians to rank as Greeks, and therefore to take part in the Olympic Games. Cadmus will have had an oracle in Illyria, if he was pictured there as a serpent; and the lions, into which he

and Harmonia are also said to have been transformed, were perhaps twin heraldic supporters of the Great Goddess's aniconic image – as on the famous Lion Gate at Mycenae. The mythographer suggests that he was allowed to emigrate with a colony at the close of his reign, instead of being put to death (see 117. 5).

60

BELUS AND THE DANAIDS

KING BELUS, who ruled at Chemmis in the Thebaid, was the son of Libya by Poseidon, and twin-brother of Agenor. His wife Anchinoë, daughter of Nilus, bore him the twins Aegyptus and Danaus, and a third son, Cepheus.[1]

b. Aegyptus was given Arabia as his kingdom; but also subdued the country of the Melampodes, and named it Egypt after himself. Fifty sons were born to him of various mothers: Libyans, Arabians, Phoenicians, and the like. Danaus, sent to rule Libya, had fifty daughters, called the Danaids, also born of various mothers: Naiads, Hamadryads, Egyptian princesses of Elephantis and Memphis, Ethiopians, and the like.

c. On Belus's death, the twins quarrelled over their inheritance, and as a conciliatory gesture Aegyptus proposed a mass-marriage between the fifty princes and the fifty princesses. Danaus, suspecting a plot, would not consent and, when an oracle confirmed his fears that Aegyptus had it in his mind to kill all the Danaids, prepared to flee from Libya.[2]

d. With Athene's assistance, he built a ship for himself and his daughters – the first two-prowed vessel that ever took to sea – and they sailed towards Greece together, by way of Rhodes. There Danaus dedicated an image to Athene in a temple raised for her by the Danaids, three of whom died during their stay in the island; the cities of Lindus, Ialysus, and Cameirus are called after them.[3]

e. From Rhodes they sailed to the Peloponnese and landed near Lerna, where Danaus announced that he was divinely chosen to become King of Argos. Though the Argive King, Gelanor, naturally laughed at this claim, his subjects assembled that evening to discuss it. Gelanor would doubtless have kept the throne, despite Danaus's declaration that Athene was supporting him, had not the Argives postponed their decision until dawn, when a wolf came boldly down from the hills, attacked a herd of cattle grazing near the city walls, and killed the leading bull. This they read as an omen that Danaus would take the throne by violence if he were opposed, and therefore persuaded Gelanor to resign it peacefully.

f. Danaus, convinced that the wolf had been Apollo in disguise, dedicated the famous shrine to Wolfish Apollo at Argos, and became so powerful a ruler that all the Pelasgians of Greece called themselves Danaans. He also built the citadel of Argos, and his daughters brought the Mysteries of Demeter, called Thesmophoria, from Egypt and taught these to the Pelasgian women. But, since the Dorian invasion, the Thesmophoria are no longer performed in the Peloponnese, except by the Arcadians.[4]

g. Danaus had found Argolis suffering from a prolonged drought, since Poseidon, vexed by Inachus's decision that the land was Hera's, had dried up all the rivers and streams. He sent his daughters in search of water, with orders to placate Poseidon by any means they knew. One of them, by name Amymone, while chasing a deer in the forest, happened to disturb a sleeping satyr. He sprang up and tried to ravish her; but Poseidon, whom she invoked, hurled his trident at the satyr. The fleeing satyr dodged, the trident stuck quivering in a rock, and Poseidon himself lay with Amymone, who was glad that she could carry out her father's instructions so pleasantly. On learning her errand, Poseidon pointed to his trident and told her to pull it from the rock. When she did so, three streams of water jetted up from the three tine-holes. This spring, now named Amymone, is the source of the river Lerna, which never fails, even at the height of summer.[5]

h. At Amymone the monstrous Hydra was born to Echidne under a plane-tree. It lived in the near-by Lernaean Lake, to which murderers come for purification – hence the proverb: 'A Lerna of evils.'[6]

i. Aegyptus now sent his sons to Argos, forbidding them to return until they had punished Danaus and his whole family. On their arrival, they begged Danaus to reverse his former decision and let them marry his daughters – intending, however, to murder them on the wedding night. When he still refused, they laid siege to Argos. Now, there are no springs on the Argive citadel, and though the Danaids afterwards invented the art of sinking wells, and supplied the city with several of

these, including four sacred ones, it was waterless at the time in question. Seeing that thirst would soon force him to capitulate. Danaus
promised to do what the sons of Aegyptus asked, as soon as they raised
the siege.[7]

j. A mass-marriage was arranged, and Danaus paired off the couples:
his choice being made in some cases because the bride and bridegroom
had mothers of equal rank, or because their names were similar – thus
Cleite, Sthenele, and Chrysippe married Cleitus, Sthenelus, and Chrysippus – but in most cases he drew lots from a helmet.[8]

k. During the wedding-feast Danaus secretly doled out sharp pins
which his daughters were to conceal in their hair; and at midnight each
stabbed her husband through the heart. There was only one survivor;
on Artemis's advice, Hypermnestra saved the life of Lynceus, because
he had spared her maidenhead; and helped him in his flight to the city
of Lyncea, sixty furlongs away. Hypermnestra begged him to light a
beacon as a signal that he had reached safety, undertaking to answer it
with another beacon from the citadel; and the Argives still light annual
beacon-fires in commemoration of this pact. At dawn, Danaus learned
of Hypermnestra's disobedience, and she was tried for her life; but
acquitted by the Argive judges. She therefore raised an image to Victorious Aphrodite in the shrine of Wolfish Apollo, and also dedicated
a sanctuary to Persuasive Artemis.[9]

l. The murdered men's heads were buried at Lerna, and their bodies
given full funeral honours below the walls of Argos; but, although
Athene and Hermes purified the Danaids in the Lernaean Lake with
Zeus's permission, the Judges of the Dead have condemned them to
the endless task of carrying water in jars perforated like sieves.[10]

m. Lynceus and Hypermnestra were reunited, and Danaus, deciding
to marry off the other daughters as fast as he could before noon on the
day of their purification, called for suitors. He proposed a marriage
race starting from the street now called Apheta: the winner to have
first choice of a wife, and the others the next choices, in their order of
finishing the race. Since he could not find enough men who would
risk their lives by marrying murderesses, only a few ran; but when the
wedding night passed without disaster to the new bridegrooms, more
suitors appeared, and another race was run on the following day. All
descendants of these marriages rank as Danaans; and the Argives still
celebrate the race in their so-called Hymenaean Contest. Lynceus later
killed Danaus, and reigned in his stead. He would willingly have killed

his sisters-in-law at the same time, to avenge his murdered brothers, had the Argives permitted this.[11]

n. Meanwhile, Aegyptus had come to Greece, but when he learned of his sons' fate, fled to Aroe, where he died, and was buried at Patrae, in a sanctuary of Serapis.[12]

o. Amymone's son by Poseidon, Nauplius, a famous navigator, discovered the art of steering by the Great Bear, and founded the city of Nauplius, where he settled the Egyptian crew that had sailed with his grandfather. He was the ancestor of Nauplius the Wrecker, who used to lure hostile ships to their death by lighting false beacons.[13]

1. Herodotus: ii. 91; Euripides, quoted by Apollodorus: ii. 1. 4.
2. Apollodorus: ii. 1. 5; Hyginus: *Fabula* 168; Eustathius on Homer, p. 37.
3. Hyginus: *loc. cit.*; Apollodorus: ii. 1. 4; Herodotus: ii. 234; Diodorus Siculus: v. 58. 1; Strabo: xiv. 2. 8.
4. Pausanias: ii. 38. 4 and 19. 3; Euripides, quoted by Strabo: viii. 6. 9; Strabo: *loc. cit.*; Herodotus: ii. 171; Plutarch: *On the Malice of Herodotus* 13.
5. Hyginus: *Fabula* 169; Apollodorus: ii. 1. 4.
6. Pausanias: ii. 37. 1 and 4; Strabo: viii. 6. 8.
7. Hyginus: *Fabula* 168; Apollodorus: ii. 1. 5; Strabo: viii. 6. 9.
8. Apollodorus: *loc. cit.*; Hyginus: *Fabula* 170.
9. Apollodorus: *loc. cit.*; Pausanias: ii. 25. 4; 19. 6 and 21. 1.
10. Apollodorus: *loc. cit.*; Lucian: *Marine Dialogues* vi; Hyginus: *Fabula* 168; Ovid: *Heroides* xiv; Horace: *Odes* iii. 11. 30.
11. Pindar: *Pythian Odes* ix. 117 ff.; Pausanias: iii. 12. 2; Hyginus: *Fabula* 170; Servius on Virgil's *Aeneid* x. 497.
12. Pausanias: vii. 21. 6.
13. Apollonius Rhodius: i. 136–8; Theon on Aratus's *Phenomena* 27; Pausanias: iv. 35. 2.

*

1. This myth records the early arrival in Greece of Helladic colonists from Palestine, by way of Rhodes, and their introduction of agriculture into the Peloponnese. It is claimed that they included emigrants from Libya and Ethiopia, which seems probable (see 6. *1* and 8. *2*). Belus is the Baal of the Old Testament, and the Bel of the Apocrypha; he had taken his name from the Sumerian Moon-goddess Belili, whom he ousted.

2. The three Danaids, also known as the Telchines, or 'enchanters', who named the three chief cities of Rhodes, were the Triple Moon-goddess Danaë (see 54. *1* and 73. *4*). The names Linda, Cameira, and Ialysa seem to be worn-down forms of *linodeousa* ('binder with linen thread'), *catamerizousa* ('sharer out'), and *ialemistria* ('wailing woman') – they are, in fact, the familiar Three Fates, or Moerae, otherwise known as Clotho, Lachesis, and Atropos (see 10. 1) because they exercised these very functions. The classical theory of the linen-thread was that the goddess tied the human being to the end of a carefully measured thread, which she paid out yearly, until the time came for her to cut it and thereby relinquish his soul to death. But originally she bound the wailing infant with a linen swaddling band on which his clan and family marks were embroidered and thus assigned him his destined place in society.

3. Danaë's Sumerian name was Dam-kina. The Hebrews called her Dinah (*Genesis* xxxiv), also masculinized as Dan. Fifty Moon-priestesses were the regular complement of a college, and their duty was to keep the land watered by rain-making charms, irrigation, and well-digging; hence the Danaids' name has been connected with the Greek word *dānos*, 'parched', and with *danos*, 'a gift', the first *a* of which is sometimes long, sometimes short. The twinship of Agenor and Belus, like that of Danaus and Aegyptus, points to a regal system at Argos, in which each co-king married a Chief-priestess and reigned for fifty lunar months, or half a Great Year. Chief-priestesses were chosen by a foot race (the origin of the Olympic Games), run at the end of the fifty months, or of forty-nine in alternate years (see 53. 4). And the Near Year foot race at Olympia (see 53. 3), Sparta (see 160. d), Jerusalem (Hooke: *Origin of Early Semitic Ritual*, 1935, p. 53), and Babylon (Langdon: *Epic of Creation*, lines 57 and 58), was run for the sacred kingship, as at Argos. A Sun-king must be swift.

4. The Hydra (see 34. 3 and 60. h), destroyed by Heracles, seems to have personified this college of water-providing priestesses (see 124. 2–4), and the myth of the Danaids apparently records two Hellenic attempts to seize their sanctuary, the first of which failed signally. After the second, successful attempt, the Hellenic leader married the Chief-priestess, and distributed the water-priestesses as wives among his chieftains. 'The street called Apheta' will have been the starting-point in the girls' race for the office of Chief-priestess; but also used in the men's foot race for the sacred kingship (see 53. 3 and 160. d). Lynceus, a royal title in Messene too (see 74. 1), means 'of the lynx' – the caracal, a sort of lion, famous for its sharp sight.

5. 'Aegyptus' and 'Danaus' seem to have been early titles of Theban co-kings; and since it was a widespread custom to bury the sacred king's head at the approaches of a city, and thus protect it against invasion (see 146. 2), the supposed heads of Aegyptus's sons buried at Lerna were probably those of successive sacred kings. The Egyptians were called Melampodes ('black feet') because they paddled about in the black Nile mud during the sowing season.

6. A later, monogamous, society represented the Danaids with their

leaking water-pots as undergoing eternal punishment for matricide. But in the icon from which this story derived, they were performing a necessary charm: sprinkling water on the ground to produce rain showers by sympathetic magic (see 41. 5 and 68. 1). It seems that the sieve, or leaking pot, remained a distinguishing mark of the wise woman many centuries after the abolition of the Danaid colleges: Philostratus writes (*Life of Apollonius of Tyana* vi. 11) of 'women with sieves in their hands who go about pretending to heal cattle for simple cowherds.'

7. Hypermnestra's and Lynceus's beacon-fires will have been those lighted at the Argive Spring Festival to celebrate the triumph of the Sun. It may be that at Argos the sacred king was put to death with a long needle thrust through his heart: a comparatively merciful end.

8. The Thesmophoria ('due offerings') were agricultural orgies celebrated at Athens (see 48. *b*), in the course of which the severed genitals of the sacred king, or his surrogate, were carried in a basket; these were replaced in more civilized times by phallus-shaped loaves and live serpents. Apollo Lycius may mean 'Apollo of the Light', rather than 'Wolfish Apollo', but the two concepts were connected by the wolves' habit of howling at the full moon.

61

LAMIA

BELUS had a beautiful daughter, Lamia, who ruled in Libya, and on whom Zeus, in acknowledgement of her favours, bestowed the singular power of plucking out and replacing her eyes at will. She bore him several children, but all of them except Scylla were killed by Hera in a fit of jealousy. Lamia took her revenge by destroying the children of others, and behaved so cruelly that her face turned into a nightmareish mask.

b. Later, she joined the company of the Empusae, lying with young men and sucking their blood while they slept.[1]

1. Diodorus Siculus: xx. 41; Suidas *sub* Lamia; Plutarch: *On Curiosity* 2; Scholiast on Aristophanes's *Peace* 757; Strabo: i. 11. 8; Eustathius on Homer p. 1714; Aristotle: *Ethics* vii. 5.

*

1. Lamia was the Libyan Neith, the Love-and-Battle goddess, also named Anatha and Athene (see 8. *1* and 25. *2*), whose worship the

Achaeans suppressed; like Alphito of Arcadia, she ended as a nursery
bogey (see 52. 7). Her name, Lamia, seems to be akin to *lamyros* ('glut-
tonous'), from *laimos* ('gullet') – thus, of a woman: 'lecherous' – and
her ugly face is the prophylactic Gorgon mask worn by her priestesses
during their Mysteries (see 33. 3), of which infanticide was an integral
part. Lamia's removable eyes are perhaps deduced from a picture of the
goddess about to bestow mystic sight on a hero by proffering him an eye
(see 73. 8). The Empusae were incubae (see 55. 1).

62

LEDA

SOME say that when Zeus fell in love with Nemesis, she fled from him
into the water and became a fish; he pursued her as a beaver [?],
ploughing up the waves. She leaped ashore, and transformed herself
into this wild beast or that, but could not shake Zeus off, because he
borrowed the form of even fiercer and swifter beasts. At last she took
to the air as a wild goose; he became a swan, and trod her triumphantly
at Rhamnus in Attica. Nemesis shook her feathers resignedly, and came
to Sparta, where Leda, wife of King Tyndareus, presently found a
hyacinth-coloured egg lying in a marsh, which she brought home and
hid in a chest: from it Helen of Troy was hatched.[1] But some say that
this egg dropped from the moon, like the egg that, in ancient times,
plunged into the river Euphrates and, being towed ashore by fishes
and hatched by doves, broke open to reveal the Syrian Goddess of
Love.[2]

b. Others say that Zeus, pretending to be a swan pursued by an eagle,
took refuge in Nemesis's bosom, where he ravished her and that, in due
process of time, she laid an egg, which Hermes threw between Leda's
thighs, as she sat on a stool with her legs apart. Thus Leda gave birth to
Helen, and Zeus placed the images of Swan and Eagle in the Heavens,
to commemorate this ruse.[3]

c. The most usual account, however, is that it was Leda herself with
whom Zeus companied in the form of a swan beside the river Eurotas;
that she laid an egg from which were hatched Helen, Castor, and
Polydeuces; and that she was consequently deified as the goddess

Nemesis.⁴ Now, Leda's husband Tyndareus had also lain with her the same night and, though some hold that all these three were Zeus's children – and Clytaemnestra too, who had been hatched, with Helen, from a second egg – others record that Helen alone was a daughter of Zeus, and that Castor and Polydeuces were Tyndareus's sons;⁵ others again, that Castor and Clytaemnestra were children of Tyndareus, while Helen and Polydeuces were children of Zeus.⁶

1. Athenaeus, quoting Homer's *Cypria* p. 334b; Apollodorus: iii. 10. 7; Sappho: *Fragment* 105; Pausanias: i. 33. 7; Eratosthenes: *Catasterismoi* 25.
2. Athenaeus: 57 f.; Plutarch: *Symposiacs* ii. 3. 3; Hyginus: *Fabula* 197.
3. Hyginus: *Poetic Astronomy* ii. 8.
4. Lactantius: i. 21; Hyginus: *Fabula* 77; First Vatican Mythographer: 78 and 204.
5. Homer: *Odyssey* xi. 299; *Iliad* iii. 426; Euripides: *Helena* 254, 1497 and 1680.
6. Pindar: *Nemean Odes* x. 80; Apollodorus: iii. 10. 6–7.

*

1. Nemesis was the Moon-goddess as Nymph (see 32. 2) and, in the earliest form of the love-chase myth, she pursued the sacred king through his seasonal changes of hare, fish, bee, and mouse – or hare, fish, bird, and grain of wheat – and finally devoured him. With the victory of the patriarchal system, the chase was reversed: the goddess now fled from Zeus, as in the English ballad of the Coal-black Smith (see 89. 2). She had changed into an otter or beaver to pursue the fish, and Castor's name ('beaver') is clearly a survival of this myth, whereas that of Polydeuces ('much sweet wine') records the character of the festivities during which the chase took place.

2. *Lada* is said to be the Lycian (i.e. Cretan) word for 'woman', and Leda was the goddess Latona, or Leto, or Lat, who bore Apollo and Artemis at Delos (see 14. 2). The hyacinth-coloured egg recalls the blood-red Easter egg of the Druids, called the *glain*, for which they searched every year by the seashore; in Celtic myth it was laid by the goddess as sea-serpent. The story of its being thrown between Leda's thighs may have been deduced from a picture of the goddess seated on the birth-stool, with Apollo's head protruding from her womb.

3. Helen[a] and Helle, or Selene, are local variants of the Moon-goddess (see 43. 1; 70. 8; and 159. 1), whose identity with Lucian's Syrian goddess is emphasized by Hyginus. But Hyginus's account is confused: it was the goddess herself who laid the world-egg after coupling with the serpent

Ophion, and who hatched it on the waters, adopting the form of a dove.
She herself rose from the Void (see 1. *a*). Helen had two temples near
Sparta: one at Therapnae, built on a Mycenaean site; another at Dendra,
connected with a tree cult, as her Rhodian shrine also was (see 88. *10*).
Pollux (x. 191) mentions a Spartan festival called the Helenephoria,
closely resembling Athene's Thesmophoria at Athens (see 48. *b*), during
which certain unmentionable objects were carried in a special basket
called a *helene*; such a basket Helen herself carries in reliefs showing her
accompanied by the Dioscuri. The objects may have been phallic emblems; she was an orgiastic goddess.

4. Zeus tricked Nemesis, the goddess of the Peloponnesian swan cult,
by appealing to her pity, exactly as he had tricked Hera of the Cretan
cuckoo cult (see 12. *a*). This myth refers, it seems, to the arrival at Cretan
or Pelasgian cities of Hellenic warriors who, to begin with, paid homage
to the Great Goddess and provided her priestesses with obedient consorts,
but eventually wrested the supreme sovereignty from her.

63

IXION

IXION, a son of Phlegyas, the Lapith king, agreed to marry Dia,
daughter of Eioneus, promising rich bridal gifts and inviting Eioneus
to a banquet; but had laid a pitfall in front of the palace, with a great
charcoal fire underneath, into which the unsuspecting Eioneus fell and
was burned.

b. Though the lesser gods thought this a heinous deed, and refused to
purify Ixion, Zeus, having behaved equally ill himself when in love, not
only purified him but brought him to eat at his table.

c. Ixion was ungrateful, and planned to seduce Hera who, he guessed,
would be glad of a chance to revenge herself on Zeus for his frequent
unfaithfulness. Zeus, however, reading Ixion's intentions, shaped a
cloud into a false Hera with whom Ixion, being too far gone in drink
to notice the deception, duly took his pleasure. He was surprised in the
act by Zeus, who ordered Hermes to scourge him mercilessly until he
repeated the words: 'Benefactors deserve honour', and then bind him
to a fiery wheel which rolled without cease through the sky.

d. The false Hera, afterwards called Nephele, bore Ixion the outcast child Centaurus who, when he grew to manhood, is said to have sired horse-centaurs on Magnesian mares, of whom the most celebrated was the learned Cheiron.[1]

1. Scholiast on Apollonius Rhodius: iii. 62; Hyginus: *Fabulae* 33 and 62; Pindar: *Pythian Odes* ii. 33–89, with scholiast; Lucian: *Dialogues of the Gods* 6; Scholiast on Euripides's *Phoenician Women* 1185.

*

1. Ixion's name, formed from *ischys* ('strength') and *io* ('moon') (see 52. 2), also suggests *ixias* ('mistletoe'). As an oak-king with mistletoe genitals (see 50. 2), representing the thunder-god, he ritually married the rain-making Moon-goddess; and was then scourged, so that his blood and sperm would fructify the earth (see 116. 4), beheaded with an axe, emasculated, spread-eagled to a tree, and roasted; after which his kinsmen ate him sacramentally. *Eion* is the Homeric epithet for a river; but Dia's father is called Deioneus, meaning 'ravager', as well as Eioneus.

2. The Moon-goddess of the oak-cult was known as Dia ('of the sky'), a title of the Dodonan Oak-goddess (see 51. 1) and therefore of Zeus's wife Hera. That old-fashioned kings called themselves Zeus (see 45. 2; 68. 1; and 156. 4) and married Dia of the Rain Clouds, naturally displeased the Olympian priests, who misinterpreted the ritual picture of the spread-eagled Lapith king as recording his punishment for impiety, and invented the anecdote of the cloud. On an Etruscan mirror, Ixion is shown spread-eagled to a fire-wheel, with mushroom tinder at his feet; elsewhere, he is bound in the same 'fivefold bond' with which the Irish hero Curoi tied Cuchulain – bent backwards into a hoop (Philostratus: *Life of Apollonius of Tyana* vii. 12), with his ankles, wrists, and neck tied together, like Osiris in the *Book of the Dead*. This attitude recalls the burning wheels rolled downhill at European midsummer festivities, as a sign that the sun has reached its zenith and must now decline again until the winter solstice. Ixion's pitfall is unmetaphorical: surrogate victims were needed for the sacred king, such as prisoners taken in battle or, failing these, travellers caught in traps. The myth seems to record a treaty made by Zeus's Hellenes with the Lapiths, Phlegyans, and Centaurs, which was broken by the ritual murder of Hellenic travellers and the seizure of their womenfolk; the Hellenes demanded, and were given, an official apology.

3. Horses were sacred to the moon, and hobby-horse dances, designed to make rain fall, have apparently given rise to the legend that the Centaurs were half horse, half man. The earliest Greek representation of Centaurs – two men joined at the waist to horses' bodies – is found on a Mycenaean gem from the Heraeum at Argos; they face each other and

are dancing. A similar pair appear on a Cretan bead-seal; but, since there was no native horse cult in Crete, the motif has evidently been imported from the mainland. In archaic art, the satyrs were also pictured as hobby-horse men, but later goats. Centaurus will have been an oracular hero with a serpent's tail, and the story of Boreas's mating with mares is therefore attached to him (see 48. e).

64

ENDYMION

ENDYMION was the handsome son of Zeus and the Nymph Calyce, an Aeolian by race though Carian by origin, and ousted Clymenus from the kingdom of Elis. His wife, known by many different names, such as Iphianassa, Hyperippe, Chromia, and Neis, bore him four sons; he also fathered fifty daughters on Selene, who had fallen desperately in love with him.[1]

b. Endymion was lying asleep in a cave on Carian Mount Latmus one still night when Selene first saw him, lay down by his side, and gently kissed his closed eyes. Afterwards, some say, he returned to the same cave and fell into a dreamless sleep. This sleep, from which he has never yet awakened, came upon him either at his own request, because he hated the approach of old age; or because Zeus suspected him of an intrigue with Hera; or because Selene found that she preferred gently kissing him to being the object of his too fertile passion. In any case, he has never grown a day older, and preserves the bloom of youth on his cheeks. But others say that he lies buried at Olympia, where his four sons ran a race for the vacant throne, which Epeius won.[2]

c. One of his defeated sons, Aetolus, later competed in a chariot-race at the funeral games of Azan, son of Arcas, the first ever celebrated in Greece. Since the spectators were unaware that they should keep off the course, Aetolus's chariot accidentally ran over Apis, son of Phoroneus, and fatally injured him. Salmoneus, who was present, banished Aetolus across the Gulf of Corinth, where he killed Dorus and his brothers and conquered the land now called Aetolia after him.[3]

1. Apollodorus: i. 7. 5–6; Pausanias: v. 8. 1 and 1. 2.
2. Apollodorus: i. 7. 6; Scholiast on Theocritus's *Idylls* iii. 49; Cicero; *Tuscan Debates* i. 38; Pausanias: v. 1. 3.

3. Pausanias: viii. 4. 2–3 and v. 1. 6; Apollodorus: i. 7. 6; Strabo: viii. 3. 33.

*

1. This myth records how an Aeolian chief invaded Elis, and accepted the consequences of marrying the Pelasgian Moon-goddess Hera's representative – the names of Endymion's wives are all moon-titles – head of a college of fifty water-priestesses (see 60. 3). When his reign ended he was duly sacrificed and awarded a hero shrine at Olympia. Pisa, the city to which Olympia belonged, is said to have meant in the Lydian (or Cretan) language 'private resting-place': namely, of the Moon (Servius on Virgil x. 179).

2. The name Endymion, from *enduein* (Latin: *inducere*), refers to the Moon's seduction of the king, as though she were one of the Empusae (see 55. *a*); but the ancients explain it as referring to *somnum ei inductum*, 'the sleep put upon him'.

3. Aetolus, like Pelops, will have driven his chariot around the Olympian stadium in impersonation of the sun (see 69. *1*); and his accidental killing of Apis, which is made to account for the Elean colonization of Aetolia, seems to be deduced from a picture of the annual chariot crash, in which the king's surrogate died (see 71. *1* and 109. *4*). But the foot race won by Epeius ('successor') was the earlier event (see 53. *3*). The existence of an Endymion sanctuary on Mount Latmus in Caria suggests that an Aeolian colony from Elis settled there. His ritual marriage with Hera, like Ixion's, will have offended the priests of Zeus (see 63. *2*).

4. Apis is the noun formed from *apios*, a Homeric adjective usually meaning 'far off' but, when applied to the Peloponnese (Aeschylus: *Suppliants* 262), 'of the pear-tree' (see 74. *6*).

65

PYGMALION AND GALATEA

PYGMALION, son of Belus, fell in love with Aphrodite and, because she would not lie with him, made an ivory image of her and laid it in his bed, praying to her for pity. Entering into this image, Aphrodite brought it to life as Galatea, who bore him Paphus and Metharme. Paphus, Pygmalion's successor, was the father of Cinyras, who founded the Cyprian city of Paphos and built a famous temple to Aphrodite there.[1]

1. Apollodorus: iii. 14. 3; Ovid: *Metamorphoses* x. 243 ff.; Arnobius: *Against the Nations* vi. 22.

*

1. Pygmalion, married to Aphrodite's priestess at Paphos, seems to have kept the goddess's white cult-image (cf. 1 *Samuel* xix. 13) in his bed as a means of retaining the Cyprian throne. If Pygmalion was, in fact, succeeded by a son whom this priestess bore him, he will have been the first king to impose the patrilinear system on the Cypriots. But it is more likely that, like his grandson Cinyras (see 18. *5*), he refused to give up the goddess's image at the end of his eight-year reign; and that he prolonged this by marriage with another of Aphrodite's priestesses – technically his daughter, since she was heiress to the throne – who is called Metharme ('change'), to mark the innovation.

66

AEACUS

THE River-god Asopus – whom some call the son of Oceanus and Tethys; some, of Poseidon and Pero; others, of Zeus and Eurynome – married Metòpe, daughter of the river Ladon, by whom he had two sons and either twelve or twenty daughters.[1]

b. Several of these had been carried off and ravished on various occasions by Zeus, Poseidon, or Apollo, and when the youngest, Aegina, twin sister of Thebe, one of Zeus's victims, also disappeared, Asopus set out in search of her. At Corinth he learned that Zeus was once again the culprit, went vengefully in pursuit, and found him embracing Aegina in a wood. Zeus, who was unarmed, fled ignominiously through the thickets and, when out of sight, transformed himself into a rock until Asopus had gone by; whereupon he stole back to Olympus and from the safety of its ramparts pelted him with thunderbolts. Asopus still moves slowly from the wounds he then received, and lumps of burned coal are often fetched from his river bed.[2]

c. Having thus disposed of Aegina's father, Zeus conveyed her secretly to the island then called Oenone, or Oenopia, where he lay with her in the form of an eagle, or of a flame, and cupids hovered over their couch, administering the gifts of love.[3] In course of time Hera discovered that Aegina had borne Zeus a son named Aeacus, and angrily resolved to destroy every inhabitant of Oenone, where he was now king. She introduced a serpent into one of its streams, which befouled the water and hatched out thousands of eggs; so that swarms of serpents went wriggling over the fields into all the other streams and rivers. Thick darkness and a drowsy heat spread across the island, which Aeacus had renamed Aegina, and the pestilential South Wind blew for no less than four months. Crops and pastures dried up, and famine ensued; but the islanders were chiefly plagued with thirst and, when their wine was exhausted, would crawl to the nearest stream, where they died as they drank its poisonous water.

d. Appeals to Zeus were in vain: the emaciated suppliants and their sacrificial beasts fell dead before his very altars, until hardly a single warm-blooded creature remained alive.[4]

e. One day, Aeacus's prayers were answered with thunder and lightning. Encouraged by this favourable omen, he begged Zeus to replenish the empty land, giving him as many subjects as there were ants carrying grains of corn up a near-by oak. The tree, sprung from a Dodonian acorn, was sacred to Zeus; at Aeacus's prayer, therefore, it trembled, and a rustling came from its widespread boughs, not caused by any wind. Aeacus, though terrified, did not flee, but repeatedly kissed the tree-trunk and the earth beneath it. That night, in a dream, he saw a shower of ants falling to the ground from the sacred oak, and springing up as men. When he awoke, he dismissed this as deceitful fantasy; but suddenly his son Telamon called him outside to watch a host of men approaching, and he recognized their faces from his dream. The plague of serpents had vanished, and rain was falling in a steady stream.

f. Aeacus, with grateful thanks to Zeus, divided the deserted city and lands among his new people, whom he called Myrmidons, that is 'ants', and whose descendants still display an ant-like thrift, patience, and tenacity. Later, these Myrmidons followed Peleus into exile from Aegina, and fought beside Achilles and Patroclus at Troy.[5]

g. But some say that Achilles's allies, the Myrmidons, were so named in honour of King Myrmidon, whose daughter Eurymedusa was seduced by Zeus in the form of an ant – which is why ants are sacred in Thessaly. And others tell of a nymph named Myrmex who, when her companion Athene invented the plough, boasted that she had made the discovery herself, and was turned into an ant as a punishment.[6]

h. Aeacus, who married Endeis of Megara, was widely renowned for his piety, and held in such honour that men longed to feast their eyes upon him. All the noblest heroes of Sparta and Athens clamoured to fight under his command, though he had made Aegina the most difficult of the Aegean islands to approach, surrounding it with sunken rocks and dangerous reefs, as a protection against pirates.[7] When all Greece was afflicted with a drought caused by Pelops's murder of the Arcadian king Stymphalus or, some say, by the Athenians' murder of Androgeus, the Delphic Oracle advised the Greeks: 'Ask Aeacus to pray for your delivery!' Thereupon every city sent a herald to Aeacus, who ascended Mount Panhellenius, the highest peak in his island, robed as a priest of Zeus. There he sacrificed to the gods, and prayed for an end to the drought. His prayer was answered by a loud thunder clap, clouds obscured the sky, and furious showers of rain soaked the whole land of Greece. He then dedicated a sanctuary to Zeus on Panhellenius, and a cloud settling on the mountain summit has ever since been an unfailing portent of rain.[8]

i. Apollo and Poseidon took Aeacus with them when they built the walls of Troy, knowing that unless a mortal joined in this work, the city would be impregnable and its inhabitants capable of defying the gods. Scarcely had they finished their task when three grey-eyed serpents tried to scale the walls. Two chose the part just completed by the gods, but tumbled down and died; the third, with a cry, rushed at Aeacus's part and forced his way in. Apollo then prophesied that Troy would fall more than once, and that Aeacus's sons would be among its captors, both in the first and fourth generations; as indeed came to pass in the persons of Telamon and Ajax.[9]

j. Aeacus, Minos, and Rhadamanthys were the three of Zeus's sons whom he would have most liked to spare the burden of old age. The Fates, however, would not permit this, and Zeus, by graciously accepting their ban, provided the other Olympians with a good example.[10]

k. When Aeacus died, he became one of the three Judges in Tartarus, where he gives laws to the shades, and is even called upon to arbitrate quarrels that may arise between the gods. Some add that he keeps the keys of Tartarus, imposes a toll and checks the ghosts brought down by Hermes against Atropos's invoice.[11]

1. Apollodorus: iii. 12. 6; Diodorus Siculus: iv. 72.

2. Diodorus Siculus: *loc. cit.*; Pindar: *Isthmian Odes* viii. 17 ff.; Callimachus: *Hymn to Delos* 78; Apollodorus: *loc. cit.*; Lactantius
   on Statius's *Thebaid* vii. 215.

3. Apollodorus: iii. 12. 6; Pindar: *loc. cit.*; Scholiast on Homer's
   Iliad i. 7; Pindar: *Nemean Odes* viii. 6; Ovid: *Metamorphoses* vi.
   113.

4. Hyginus: *Fabula* 52; Ovid: *Metamorphoses* vii. 520 ff.

5. Ovid: *Metamorphoses* vii. 614 ff.; Hyginus: *loc cit.*; Apollodorus:
   loc. cit.; Pausanias: ii. 29. 2; Strabo: viii. 6. 19 and ix. 5. 9.

6. Servius on Virgil's *Aeneid* ii. 7 and iv. 402; Clement of Alexandria: *Address to the Gentiles* ii. 39. 6.

7. Apollodorus: iii. 12. 6; Pindar: *Nemean Odes* viii. 8 ff.; Pausanias:
   ii. 29. 5.

8. Diodorus Siculus: iv. 61. 1; Clement of Alexandria: *Stromateis*
   vi. 3. 28; Pausanias: ii. 30. 4; Theophrastus: *Weather Signs* i. 24.

9. Pindar: *Olympian Odes* viii. 30 ff., with scholiast.

10. Ovid: *Metamorphoses* ix. 426 ff.

11. *Ibid.*: xiii. 25; Pindar: *Isthmian Odes* viii. 24; Apollodorus: iii. 12.
    6; Lucian: *Dialogues of the Dead* xx. 1; *Charon* 2; and *Voyage
    Below* iv.

*

1. Asopus's daughters ravished by Apollo and Poseidon will have been
colleges of Moon-priestesses in the Asopus valley of the North-eastern
Peloponnese, whose fertile lands were seized by the Aeolians. Aegina's
rape seems to record a subsequent Achaean conquest of Phlius, a city at
the headwaters of the Asopus; and an unsuccessful appeal made by their
neighbours for military aid from Corinth. Eurynome and Tethys (see
1. *a* and *d*), the names of Asopus's mother, were ancient titles of the
Moon-goddess, and 'Pero' points to *pera*, a leather bag (see 36. 1), and
thus to Athene's goat-skin aegis – as 'Aegina' also does.

2. The Aeacus myth concerns the conquest of Aegina by Phthiotian
Myrmidons, whose tribal emblem was an ant. Previously, the island
was, it seems, held by goat-cult Pelasgians, and their hostility towards the
invaders is recorded in Hera's poisoning of the streams. According to
Strabo, who always looked for reasonable explanations of myths, but
seldom looked far enough, the soil of Aegina was covered by a layer of
stones, and the Aeginetans called themselves Myrmidons because, like
ants, they had to excavate before they could till their fields, and because
they were troglodytes (Strabo: viii. 6. 16). But the Thessalian legend of
Myrmex is a simple myth of origin: the Phthiotian Myrmidons claimed
to be autochthonous, as ants are, and showed such loyalty to the laws of
their priestess, the Queen Ant, that Zeus's Hellenic representative who
married her had to become an honorary ant himself. If Myrmex was, in

fact, a title of the Mother-goddess of Northern Greece, she might well claim to have invented the plough, because agriculture had been established by immigrants from Asia Minor before the Hellenes reached Athens.

3. The Phthiotian colonists of Aegina later merged their myths with those of Achaean invaders from Phlius on the river Asopus; and, since these Phlians had retained their allegiance to the oak-oracle of Dodona (see 51. *a*), the ants are described as falling from a tree, instead of emerging from the ground.

4. In the original myth, Aeacus will have induced the rain-storm not by an appeal to Zeus, but by some such magic as Salmoneus used (see 68. *1*). His law-giving in Tartarus, like that of Minos and Rhadamanthys, suggests that an Aeginetan legal code was adopted in other parts of Greece. It probably applied to commercial, rather than criminal law, judging from the general acceptance, in Classical times, of the Aeginetan talent as the standard weight of precious metal. It was of Cretan origin and turned the scales at 100 lb. *avoirdupois*.

67

SISYPHUS

SISYPHUS, son of Aeolus, married Atlas's daughter Merope, the Pleiad, who bore him Glaucus, Ornytion, and Sinon, and owned a fine herd of cattle on the Isthmus of Corinth.[1]

b. Near him lived Autolycus, son of Chione, whose twin-brother Philammon was begotten by Apollo, though Autolycus himself claimed Hermes as his father.[2]

c. Now, Autolycus was a past master in theft, Hermes having given him the power of metamorphosing whatever beasts he stole, from horned to unhorned, or from black to white, and contrariwise. Thus, although Sisyphus noticed that his own herds grew steadily smaller, while those of Autolycus increased, he was unable at first to convict him of theft; and therefore, one day, engraved the inside of all his cattle's hooves with the monogram SS or, some say, with the words 'Stolen by Autolycus'. That night Autolycus helped himself as usual, and at dawn hoof-prints along the road provided Sisyphus with sufficient evidence to summon neighbours in witness of the theft. He visited Autolycus's stable, recognized his stolen beasts by their marked hooves and, leaving his witnesses to remonstrate with the thief, hurried around the house, entered by the portal, and while the argument was in progress outside seduced Autolycus's daughter Anticleia, wife to Laertes the Argive. She bore him Odysseus, the manner of whose conception is enough to account for the cunning he habitually showed, and for his nickname 'Hypsipylon'.[3]

d. Sisyphus founded Ephyra, afterwards known as Corinth, and peopled it with men sprung from mushrooms, unless it be true that Medea gave him the kingdom as a present. His contemporaries knew him as the worst knave on earth, granting only that he promoted Corinthian commerce and navigation.[4]

e. When, on the death of Aeolus, Salmoneus usurped the Thessalian throne, Sisyphus, who was the rightful heir, consulted the Delphic Oracle and was told: 'Sire children on your niece; they will avenge you!' He therefore seduced Tyro, Salmoneus's daughter, who, happening to discover that his motive was not love for her, but hatred of her father, killed the two sons she had borne him. Sisyphus entered then the market place of Larissa [? produced the dead bodies, falsely accused Salmoneus of incest and murder] and had him expelled from Thessaly.[5]

f. After Zeus's abduction of Aegina, her father the River-god Asopus came to Corinth in search of her. Sisyphus knew well what had happened to Aegina but would not reveal anything unless Asopus undertook to supply the citadel of Corinth with a perennial spring. Asopus accordingly made the spring Peirene rise behind Aphrodite's temple, where there are now images of the goddess, armed; of the Sun; and of Eros the Archer. Then Sisyphus told him all he knew.[6]

g. Zeus, who had narrowly escaped Asopus's vengeance, ordered his brother Hades to fetch Sisyphus down to Tartarus and punish him everlastingly for his betrayal of divine secrets. Yet Sisyphus would not be daunted: he cunningly put Hades himself in handcuffs by persuading him to demonstrate their use, and then quickly locking them. Thus Hades was kept a prisoner in Sisyphus's house for some days – an impossible situation, because nobody could die, even men who had been beheaded or cut in pieces; until at last Ares, whose interests were threatened, came hurrying up, set him free, and delivered Sisyphus into his clutches.

h. Sisyphus, however, kept another trick in reserve. Before descending to Tartarus, he instructed his wife Merope not to bury him; and, on reaching the Palace of Hades went straight to Persephone, and told her that, as an unburied person, he had no right to be there but should have been left on the far side of the river Styx. 'Let me return to the upper world,' he pleaded, 'arrange for my burial, and avenge the neglect shown me. My presence here is most irregular. I will be back within three days.' Persephone was deceived and granted his request; but as soon as Sisyphus found himself once again under the light of the sun, he repudiated his promise to Persephone. Finally, Hermes was called upon to hale him back by force.[7]

i. It may have been because he had injured Salmoneus, or because he had betrayed Zeus's secret, or because he had always lived by robbery and often murdered unsuspecting travellers – some say that it was Theseus who put an end to Sisyphus's career, though this is not generally mentioned among Theseus's feats – at any rate, Sisyphus was given an exemplary punishment.[8] The Judges of the Dead showed him a huge block of stone – identical in size with that into which Zeus had turned himself when fleeing from Asopus – and ordered him to roll it up the brow of a hill and topple it down the farther slope. He has never yet succeeded in doing so. As soon as he has almost reached the summit, he is forced back by the weight of the shameless stone, which bounces to the very bottom once more; where he wearily retrieves it and must begin all over again, though sweat bathes his limbs, and a cloud of dust rises above his head.[9]

j. Merope, ashamed to find herself the only Pleiad with a husband in the Underworld – and a criminal too – deserted her six starry sisters in the night sky and has never been seen since. And as the whereabouts of Neleus's tomb on the Corinthian Isthmus was a secret which Sisyphus refused to divulge even to Nestor, so the Corinthians are now equally reticent when asked for the whereabouts of Sisyphus's own burial place.[10]

1. Apollodorus: i. 9. 3; Pausanias: ii. 4. 3; Servius on Virgil's *Aeneid* ii. 79.
2. Hyginus: *Fabula* 200.
3. Polyaenus: vi. 52; Hyginus: *Fabula* 201; Suidas *sub* Sisyphus; Sophocles: *Ajax* 190; Scholiast on Sophocles's *Philoctetes* 417.
4. Apollodorus: i. 9. 3; Ovid: *Metamorphoses* vii. 393; Eumelus, quoted by Pausanias: ii. 3. 8; Homer: *Iliad* vi. 153; Scholiast on Aristophanes's *Acarnanians* 390; Scholiast on Sophocles's *Ajax* 190; Tzetzes: *On Lycophron* 980; Ovid: *Heroides* xii. 203; Horace: *Satires* ii. 17. 12.

5. Hyginus: *Fabula* 60.

6. Pausanias: ii. 5. 1.

7. Theognis: 712 ff.; Eustathius on Homer's *Iliad* pp. 487, 631, and 1702.

8. Servius on Virgil's *Aeneid* vi. 616; Scholiast on Statius's *Thebaid* ii. 380; Hyginus: *Fabula* 38.

9. Scholiast on Homer's *Iliad* i. 180; Pausanias: x. 31. 3; Ovid: *Metamorphoses* iv. 459; Homer: *Odyssey* xi. 593–600.

10. Ovid: *Fasti* i. 175–6; Eumelus, quoted by Pausanias: ii. 2. 2.

*

1. 'Sisyphus', though the Greeks understood it to mean 'very wise', is spelt *Sesephus* by Hesychius, and is thought to be a Greek variant of Tesup, the Hittite Sun-god, identical with Atabyrius the Sun-god of Rhodes (see 42. 4 and 93. 1), whose sacred animal was a bull. Bronze statuettes and reliefs of this bull, dating from the fourteenth century B.C., have been found, marked with a sceptre and two disks on the flank, and with a trefoil on the haunch. Raids on the Sun-god's marked cattle are a commonplace in Greek myth: Odysseus's companions made them (see 170. *u*), so also did Alcyoneus, and his contemporary, Heracles (see 132. *d* and *w*). But Autolycus's use of magic in his theft from Sisyphus recalls the story of Jacob and Laban (*Genesis* xxix and xxx). Jacob, like Autolycus, had the gift of turning cattle to whatever colour he wanted, and thus diminished Laban's flocks. The cultural connexion between Corinth and Canaan, which is shown in the myths of Nisus (see 91. 1), Oedipus (see 105. 1 and 7), Alcathous (see 110. 2), and Melicertes (see 70. 2), may be Hittite. Alcyoneus also came from Corinth.

2. Sisyphus's 'shameless stone' was originally a sun-disk, and the hill up which he rolled it is the vault of Heaven; this made a familiar enough icon. The existence of a Corinthian Sun cult is well established: Helius and Aphrodite are said to have held the acropolis in succession, and shared a temple there (Pausanias: ii. 4. 7). Moreover, Sisyphus is invariably placed next to Ixion in Tartarus, and Ixion's fire-wheel is a symbol of the sun. This explains why the people of Ephyra sprang from mushrooms, mushrooms were the ritual tinder of Ixion's fire-wheel (see 63. 2), and the Sun-god demanded human burnt sacrifices to inaugurate his year. Anticleia's seduction has been deduced perhaps from a picture showing Helius's marriage to Aphrodite; and the mythographer's hostility towards Sisyphus voices Hellenic disgust at the strategic planting of non-Hellenic settlements on the narrow isthmus separating the Peloponnese from Attica. His outwitting of Hades probably refers to a sacred king's refusal to abdicate at the end of his reign (see 170. 1). To judge from the sun-bull's markings, he contrived to rule for two Great Years, represented by the sceptre and the sun-disks, and obtained the Triple-goddess's

assent, represented by the trefoil. Hypsipylon, Odysseus's nickname, is the masculine form of Hypsipyle: a title, probably, of the Moon-goddess (see 106. 3).

3. Sisyphus and Neleus were probably buried at strategic points on the Isthmus as a charm against invasion (see 101. 3 and 146. 2). A lacuna occurs in Hyginus's account of Sisyphus's revenge on Salmoneus; I have supplied a passage (*para. e, above*) which makes sense of the story.

4. Peirene, the spring on the citadel of Corinth where Bellerophon took Pegasus to drink (see 75. c), had no efflux and never failed (Pausanias: ii. 5. 1; Strabo: vii. 6. 21). Peirene was also the name of a fountain outside the city gate, on the way from the market-place to Lechaeum, where Peirene ('of the osiers') – whom the mythographers describe as the daughter of Achelous, or of Oebalus (Pausanias: *loc. cit.*); or of Asopus and Metope (Diodorus Siculus: iv. 72) – was said to have been turned into a spring when she wept for her son Cenchrias ('spotted serpent'), whom Artemis had unwittingly killed. 'Corinthian bronze' took its characteristic colour from being plunged red-hot into this spring (Pausanias: ii. 3. 3).

5. One of the seven Pleiads disappeared in early Classical times, and her absence had to be explained (see 41. 6).

6. A question remains: was the double-S really the monogram of Sisyphus? The icon illustrating the myth probably showed him examining the tracks of the stolen sheep and cattle which, since they 'parted the hoof', were formalized as CƆ. This sign stood for SS in the earliest Greek script, and could also be read as the conjoined halves of the lunar month and all that these implied – waxing and waning, increase and decline, blessing and cursing. Animals which 'parted the hoof' were self-dedicated to the Moon – they are the sacrifices ordained at the New Moon Festivals in *Leviticus* – and the SS will therefore have referred to Selene the Moon, *alias* Aphrodite, rather than to Sisyphus, who as Sun-king merely held her sacred herd in trust (see 42. 1). The figure CƆ, representing the full moon (as distinguished from O, representing the simple sun-disk) was marked on each flank of the sacred cow which directed Cadmus to the site of Thebes (see 58. f).

68

SALMONEUS AND TYRO

SALMONEUS, a son, or grandson, of Aeolus and Enarete, reigned for a time in Thessaly before leading an Aeolian colony to the eastern confines of Elis, where he built the city of Salmonia near the source of the river Enipeus, a tributary of the Alpheius.[1] Salmoneus was hated by his subjects, and went so far in his royal insolence as to transfer Zeus's sacrifices to his own altars, and announce that he was Zeus. He even drove through the streets of Salmonia, dragging brazen cauldrons, bound with hide, behind his chariot to simulate Zeus's thunder, and hurling oaken torches into the air; some of these, as they fell, scorched his unfortunate subjects, who were expected to mistake them for lightning. One fine day Zeus punished Salmoneus by hurling a real thunderbolt, which not only destroyed him, chariot and all, but burned down the entire city.[2]

b. Alcidice, Salmoneus's wife, had died many years before, in giving birth to a beautiful daughter named Tyro. Tyro was under the charge of her stepmother Sidero, and treated with great cruelty as the cause of the family's expulsion from Thessaly; having killed the two sons she bore to her evil uncle Sisyphus. She now fell in love with the river Enipeus, and haunted its banks day after day, weeping for loneliness. But the River-god, although amused and even flattered by her passion, would not show her the least encouragement.

c. Poseidon decided to take advantage of this ridiculous situation. Disguising himself as the River-god, he invited Tyro to join him at the confluence of the Enipeus and the Alpheius; and there threw her into a magic sleep, while a dark wave rose up like a mountain and curled its crest to screen his knavery. When Tyro awoke, and found herself ravished, she was aghast at the deception; but Poseidon laughed as he told her to be off home and keep quiet about what had happened. Her reward, he said, would be fine twins, sons of a better father than a mere river-god.[3]

d. Tyro contrived to keep her secret until she bore the promised twins, but then, unable to face Sidero's anger, exposed them on a mountain. A passing horse-herd took them home with him, but not before his brood-mare had kicked the elder in the face. The horse-herd's wife reared the boys, giving the bruised one to the mare for suckling and calling him Pelias; the other, whom she called Neleus, took his savage nature from the bitch which served as his foster-mother. But some say that the twins were found floating down the Enipeus in a wooden ark. As soon as Pelias and Neleus discovered their mother's name and learned how unkindly she had been treated, they set out to avenge her. Sidero took refuge in the temple of Hera; but Pelias struck her down as she clung to the horns of the altar. This was the first of many insults that he offered the goddess.[4]

e. Tyro later married her uncle Cretheus, founder of Iolcus, to whom she bore Aeson, father of Jason the Argonaut; he also adopted Pelias and Neleus as his sons.[5]

f. After Cretheus's death, the twins came to blows: Pelias seized the throne of Iolcus, exiled Neleus, and kept Aeson a prisoner in the palace. Neleus led Cretheus's grandsons Melampus and Bias with a mixed company of Achaeans, Phthiotians, and Aeolians to the land of Messene, where he drove the Lelegans out of Pylus, and raised the city to such a height of fame that he is now acclaimed as its founder. He married Chloris; but all their twelve children, except Nestor, were eventually killed by Heracles.[6]

1. Apollodorus: i. 7. 3; Hyginus: *Poetic Astronomy* ii. 20; Strabo: viii. 3. 32.
2. Diodorus Siculus: iv. 68. 1; Apollodorus: i. 9. 7; Hyginus: *Fabula* 61.
3. Apollodorus: i. 9. 8; Homer: *Odyssey* xi. 235 ff.; Lucian: *Marine Dialogues* 13.
4. Apollodorus: *loc. cit.*; Eustathius on Homer's *Odyssey* xi. 253; Sophocles: *Tyro*, quoted by Aristotle: *Poetics* xvi. 1454.
5. Pausanias: iv. 2. 3; Apollodorus: i. 9. 11; Hyginus: *Fabula* 12.
6. Hesiod: *Theogony* 996; Scholiast on Euripides's *Alcestis* 255; Diodorus Siculus: iv. 68. 6; Pausanias: iv. 2. 3; 36. 1 and x. 29. 3; Homer: *Iliad* xi. 682.

*

1. Antigonus of Carystus (*Account of Marvellous Things* 15) records that a rain-bringing bronze wagon was kept at Crannon: which in time of drought the people drove over rough ground to shake it and make it clang – and also (as Crannonian coins show) to splash about the water from the jars which it contained. Rain always came, acccording to Antigonus. Thus Salmoneus's charm for inducing thunderstorms will have been common religious practice: like rattling pebbles in a dry gourd, tapping on oak doors, rolling stones about in a chest, dancing, beating shields, or swinging bull-roarers. He was pictured as a criminal only when the impersonation of Zeus had been forbidden by the Achaean central authority (see 45. 2). To judge from the Danaids' sieves (see 60. 6), and the Argive cow dance (see 56. 1), rain-making was originally a female prerogative – as it remains among certain primitive African tribes, such as the Hereros and the Damaras – but passed into the sacred king's hands when the Queen permitted him to act as her deputy (see 136. 4).

2. Tyro was the Goddess-mother of the Tyrians and Tyrrhenians, or Tyrsenians, and perhaps also of the Tirynthians; hers is probably a pre-Hellenic name, but supplied Greek with the word *tyrsis* ('walled city'), and so with the concept of 'tyranny'. Her ill-treatment by Sidero recalls that of Antiope by Dirce, a myth which it closely resembles (see 76. *a*); and may originally have recorded an oppression of the Tyrians by their neighbours, the Sidonians. River water was held to impregnate brides who bathed in it – bathing was also a purifying ritual after menstruation, or child-birth – and it is likely that Tyro's Enipeus, like the Scamander (see 137. *3*), was invoked to take away virginity. The anecdote of Tyro's seduction by Poseidon purports to explain why Salmoneus's descendants were sometimes called 'Sons of Enipeus', which was their original home, and sometimes 'Sons of Poseidon', because of their naval fame. Her previous seduction by Sisyphus suggests that the Corinthian Sun cult had been planted at Salmonia; Antiope was also connected by marriage with Sisyphus (see 76. *b*).

3. Tyro's ark, in which she sent the twins floating down the Enipeus, will have been of alder-wood, like that in which Rhea Silvia sent Romulus and Remus floating down the Tiber. The quarrel of Pelias and Neleus, with that of Eteocles and Polyneices, Acrisius and Proetus, Atreus and Thyestes, and similar pairs of kings, seems to record the breakdown of the system by which king and tanist ruled alternately for forty-nine or fifty months in the same kingdom (see 69. *1*; 73. *a* and 106. *b*).

4. The horns of the altar to which Sidero clung were those habitually fixed to the cult-image of the Cow-goddess Hera, Astarte, Io, Isis, or Hathor; and Pelias seems to have been an Achaean conqueror who forcibly reorganized the Aeolian Goddess cult of Southern Thessaly. In Palestine horned altars, like that to which Joab clung (1 *Kings* ii. 28, etc.), survived the dethronement of the Moon-cow and her golden Calf.

69

ALCESTIS

ALCESTIS, the most beautiful of Pelias's daughters, was asked in marriage by many kings and princes. Not wishing to endanger his political position by refusing any of them, and yet clearly unable to satisfy more than one, Pelias let it be known that he would marry Alcestis to the man who could yoke a wild boar and a lion to his chariot and drive them around the race-course. At this, Admetus King of Pherae summoned

Apollo, whom Zeus had bound to him for one year as a herdsman, and asked: 'Have I treated you with the respect due to your godhead?' 'You have indeed,' Apollo assented, 'and I have shown my gratitude by making all your ewes drop twins.' 'As a final favour, then,' pleaded Admetus, 'pray help me to win Alcestis, by enabling me to fulfil Pelias's conditions.' 'I shall be pleased to do so,' replied Apollo. Heracles lent him a hand with the taming of the wild beasts and presently Admetus was driving his chariot around the race-course at Iolcus, drawn by this savage team.[1]

b. It is not known why Admetus omitted the customary sacrifice to Artemis before marrying Alcestis, but the goddess was quick enough to punish him. When, flushed with wine, anointed with essences and garlanded with flowers, he entered the bridal chamber that night, he recoiled in horror. No lovely naked bride awaited him on the marriage couch, but a tangled knot of hissing serpents. Admetus ran shouting for Apollo, who kindly intervened with Artemis on his behalf. The neglected sacrifice having been offered at once, all was well, Apollo even obtaining Artemis's promise that, when the day of Admetus's death came, he should be spared on condition that a member of his family died voluntarily for love of him.

c. This fatal day came sooner than Admetus expected. Hermes flew into the palace one morning and summoned him to Tartarus. General consternation prevailed; but Apollo gained a little time for Admetus by making the Three Fates drunk, and thus delayed the fatal scission of his life's thread. Admetus ran in haste to his old parents, clasped their knees, and begged each of them in turn to surrender him the butt-end of existence. Both roundly refused, saying that they still derived much enjoyment from life, and that he should be content with his appointed lot, like everyone else.

d. Then, for love of Admetus, Alcestis took poison and her ghost descended to Tartarus; but Persephone considered it an evil thing that a wife should die instead of a husband. 'Back with you to the upper air!' she cried.[2]

e. Some tell the tale differently. They say that Hades came in person to fetch Admetus and that, when he fled, Alcestis volunteered to take his place; but Heracles arrived unexpectedly with a new wild-olive club, and rescued her.[3]

1. Hyginus: *Fabula* 50; Apollodorus: iii. 10. 4; Callimachus: *Hymn*

to Apollo 47–54; Scholiast on Euripides's *Alcestis* 2; Fulgentius: i. 27.

2. Apollodorus: i. 9. 15.
3. Euripides: *Alcestis*.

*

1. The yoking of a lion and a wild boar to the same chariot is the theme of a Theban myth (see 106. *a*), where the original meaning has been equally obscured. Lion and boar were the animal symbols given to the first and second halves of the Sacred Year, respectively – they constantly occur, in opposition, on Etruscan vases – and the oracle seems to have proposed a peaceful settlement of the traditional rivalry between the sacred king and his tanist. This was that the kingdom should be divided in halves, and that they should reign concurrently, as Proetus and Acrisius eventually did at Argos (see 73. *a*), rather than keep it entire, and rule alternately – as Polyneices and Eteocles did at Thebes (see 106. *b*). A circuit of the race-course in a chariot was a proof of royalty (see 64. *3*).

2. Artemis was hostile to monogamic marriage because she belonged to the pre-Hellenic cult in which women mated promiscuously outside their own clans; so the Hellenes propitiated her with wedding sacrifices, carrying torches of the chaste hawthorn in her honour. The patriarchal practice of suttee, attested here and in the myths of Evadne (see 106. *l*) and Polyxena (see 168. *k*), grew from the Indo-European custom which forbade widows to remarry; once this ban was relaxed, suttee became less attractive (see 74. *a*).

3. In the first version of this myth, Persephone refused Alcestis's sacrifice – Persephone represents the matriarchal point of view. In the second version, Heracles forbade it, and was chosen as the instrument of Zeus's will, that is to say of patriarchal ethics, on the ground that he once harrowed Hell and rescued Theseus (see 103. *d*). Wild-olive served in Greece to expel evil influences (see 119. *2*); as the birch did in Italy and northern Europe (see 52. *3*).

70

ATHAMAS

ATHAMAS the Aeolian, brother of Sisyphus and Salmoneus, ruled over Boeotia. At Hera's command, he married Nephele, a phantom whom Zeus created in her likeness when he wished to deceive Ixion the

Lapith, and who was now wandering disconsolately about the halls of Olympus. She bore Athamas two sons: Phrixus and Leucon, and a daughter, Helle. But Athamas resented the disdain in which Nephele held him and, falling in love with Ino, daughter of Cadmus, brought her secretly to his palace at the foot of Mount Laphystium, where he begot Learchus and Melicertes on her.

b. Learning about her rival from the palace servants, Nephele returned in a fury to Olympus, complaining to Hera that she had been insulted. Hera took her part, and vowed: 'My eternal vengeance shall fall upon Athamas and his House!'

c. Nephele thereupon went back to Mount Laphystium, where she publicly reported Hera's vow, and demanded that Athamas should die. But the men of Boeotia, who feared Athamas more than Hera, would not listen to Nephele; and the women of Boeotia were devoted to Ino, who now persuaded them to parch the seed-corn, without their husbands' knowledge, so that the harvest would fail. Ino foresaw that when the grain was due to sprout, but no blade appeared, Athamas would send to ask the Delphic Oracle what was amiss. She had already bribed Athamas's messengers to bring back a false reply: namely, that the land would regain its fertility only if Nephele's son Phrixus were sacrificed to Zeus on Mount Laphystium.

d. This Phrixus was a handsome young man, with whom his aunt Biadice, Cretheus's wife, had fallen in love, and whom, when he rebuffed her advances, she accused of trying to ravish her. The men of Boeotia, believing Biadice's story, applauded Apollo's wise choice of a sin-offering and demanded that Phrixus should die; whereupon Athamas, loudly weeping, led Phrixus to the mountain top. He was on the point of cutting his throat when Heracles, who happened to be in the neighbourhood, came running up and wrested the sacrificial flint from his hand. 'My father Zeus,' Heracles exclaimed, 'loathes human sacrifices!' Nevertheless, Phrixus would have perished despite this plea, had not a winged golden ram, supplied by Hermes at Hera's order – or, some say, by Zeus himself – suddenly flown down to the rescue from Olympus.

'Climb on my back!' cried the ram, and Phrixus obeyed.

'Take me too!' pleaded Helle. 'Do not leave me to the mercy of my father.'

e. So Phrixus pulled her up behind him, and the ram flew eastwards, making for the land of Colchis, where Helius stables his horses. Before long, Helle felt giddy and lost her hold; she fell into the straits between Europe and Asia, now called the Hellespont in her honour; but Phrixus reached Colchis safely, and there sacrificed the ram to Zeus the Deliverer. Its golden fleece became famous a generation later when the Argonauts came in search of it.

f. Overawed by the miracle of Mount Laphystium, Athamas's messengers confessed that they had been bribed by Ino to bring back a false reply from Delphi; and presently all her wiles, and Biadice's, came to light. Nephele thereupon again demanded that Athamas should die, and the sacrificial fillet, which Phrixus had worn, was placed on his head; only Heracles's renewed intervention saved him from death.

g. But Hera was incensed with Athamas and drove him mad, not only on Nephele's account, but because he had connived at Ino's harbouring of the infant Dionysus, Zeus's bastard by her sister Semele, who was living in the palace disguised as a girl. Seizing his bow, Athamas suddenly yelled: 'Look, a white stag! Stand back while I shoot!' So saying, he transfixed Learchus with an arrow, and proceeded to tear his still-quivering body into pieces.

h. Ino snatched up Melicertes, her younger son, and fled; but would hardly have escaped Athamas's vengeance, had not the infant Dionysus temporarily blinded him, so that he began to flog a she-goat in mistake for her. Ino ran to the Molurian Rock, where she leaped into the sea and was drowned – this rock afterwards became a place of ill repute, because the savage Sciron used to hurl strangers from it. But Zeus, remembering Ino's kindness to Dionysus, would not send her ghost down to Tartarus and deified her instead as the Goddess Leucothea. He also deified her son Melicertes as the God Palaemon, and sent him to the Isthmus of Corinth riding on dolphin-back; the Isthmian Games, founded in his honour by Sisyphus, are still celebrated there every fourth year.

i. Athamas, now banished from Boeotia, and childless because his remaining son, Leucon, had sickened and died, enquired from the Delphic Oracle where he should settle, and was told: 'Wherever wild beasts entertain you to dinner.' Wandering aimlessly northward, without food or drink, he came on a wolf-pack devouring a flock of sheep in a desolate Thessalian plain. The wolves fled at his approach, and he and his starving companions ate what mutton had been left. Then he recalled the oracle and, having adopted Haliartus and Conorea, his Corinthian grand-nephews, founded a city which he called Alos, from his wanderings, or from his serving-maid Alos; and the country was called Athamania; afterwards he married Themisto and raised a new family.[1]

j. Others tell the tale differently. Omitting Athamas's marriage to Nephele, they say that one day, after the birth of Learchus and Melicertes, his wife Ino went out hunting and did not return. Bloodstains on a torn tunic convinced him that she had been killed by wild beasts; but the truth was that a sudden Bacchic frenzy had seized her when she was attacked by a lynx. She had strangled it, flayed it with her teeth and nails, and gone off, dressed only in the pelt, for a prolonged revel on Mount Parnassus. After an interval of mourning, Athamas married Themisto who, a year later, bore him twin sons. Then, to his dismay, he learned that Ino was still alive. He sent for her at once, installed her in the palace nursery, and told Themisto: 'We have a likely-looking nurse-maid, a captive taken in the recent raid on Mount Cithaeron.' Themisto, whom her maids soon undeceived, visited the nursery, pretending not to know who Ino was. She told her: 'Pray, nurse, get ready a set of white woollen garments for my two sons, and a set of mourning garments for those of my unfortunate predecessor Ino. They are to be worn tomorrow.'

k. The following day, Themisto ordered her guards to break into the royal nursery and kill the twins who were dressed in mourning, but spare the other two. Ino, however, guessing what was in Themisto's mind, had provided white garments for her own sons, and mourning garments for her rival's. Thus Themisto's twins were murdered, and the news sent Athamas mad; he shot Learchus dead, mistaking him for a stag, but Ino escaped with Melicertes, sprang into the sea, and became immortal.

l. Others, again, say that Phrixus and Helle were Nephele's children by Ixion. One day, as they wandered in a wood, their mother came upon them in a Bacchic frenzy, leading a golden ram by the horns. 'Look,' she babbled, 'here is a son of your cousin Theophane. She had too many suitors, so Poseidon changed her into a ewe and himself into a ram, and tupped her on the Island of Crumissa.'

'What happened to the suitors, mother?' asked little Helle.

'They became wolves,' Ino answered, 'and howl for Theophane all night long. Now ask me no more questions, but climb on this ram's back, both of you, and ride away to the kingdom of Colchis, where Helius's son Aeëtes reigns. As soon as you arrive, sacrifice it to Ares.'

m. Phrixus carried out his mother's strange instructions, and hung up the golden fleece in a temple of Ares at Colchis, where it was guarded by a dragon; and, many years later his son Presbon, or Cytisorus, coming to Orchomenus from Colchis, rescued Athamas as he was being sacrificed for a sin-offering.[2]

1. Pausanias: i. 44. 11; ix. 34. 4–5 and 23. 3; Apollodorus: i. 7. 3 and iii. 4. 3; Hyginus: *Fabulae* 2 and 4; *Poetic Astronomy* ii. 20; Fragments of Sophocles's *Athamas;* Nonnus: *Dionysiaca* x. 1 ff.; Scholiast on Homer's *Iliad* vii. 86; Eustathius on the same; Ovid: *Metamorphoses* iv. 480–541; *Etymologicum Magnum* 70. 8; Stephanus of Byzantium *sub* Athamania.
2. Hyginus: *Fabulae* 1, 3, 5 and 88; Fragments of Euripides's *Ino;* Herodotus: vii. 197; Pausanias: ix. 34. 5.

*

1. Athamas's name is connected in the myth with Athamania, the city which he is said to have founded in the Thessalian wilderness; but seems formed, rather, from *Ath* ('high'), and *amaein* ('to reap') – meaning 'the king dedicated to the Reaper on High', namely the Goddess of the Harvest Moon. The conflict between his rival wives Ino and Nephele was probably one between early Ionian settlers in Boeotia, who had adopted the worship of the Corn-goddess Ino, and the pastoral Aeolian invaders. An attempt to make over the agricultural rites of the Ionian goddess Ino to the Aeolian thunder-god and his wife Nephele, the rain-cloud, seems to have been foiled by the priestesses' parching of the seed-corn.

2. The myth of Athamas and Phrixus records the annual mountain sacrifice of the king, or of the king's surrogate – first a boy dressed in a ram's fleece, and later a ram – during the New Year rain-inducing festival which shepherds celebrated at the Spring Equinox. Zeus's ram-sacrifice on the summit of Mount Pelion, not far from Laphystium, took place in April when, according to the Zodiac, the Ram was in the ascendant; the chief men of the district used to struggle up, wearing white sheep-skins (Dicearchus: ii. 8), and the rite still survives there today in the mock-sacrifice and resurrection of an old man who wears a black sheep's mask (see 148. *10*). The mourning garments, ordered for the children sentenced to death, suggest that a black fleece was worn by the victim, and white ones by the priest and the spectators. Biadice's love for Phrixus recalls Potiphar's wife's love for Joseph, a companion myth from Canaan: much the same story is also told of Anteia and Bellerophon (see 75. *a*), Cretheis and Peleus (see 81. *g*), Phaedra and Hippolytus (see 101. *a–g*), Phylonome and Tenes (see 161. *g*).

3. That Nephele ('cloud') was Hera's gift to Athamas and created

in her own image, suggests that in the original version Athamas the Aeolian king himself represented the thunder-god, like his predecessor Ixion (see 63. 1), and his brother Salmoneus (see 68. 1); and that, when he married Themisto (who, in Euripides's version of the myth, is Ino's rival), she took the part of the thunder-god's wife.

4. Ino was Leucothea, 'the White Goddess', and proved her identity with the Triple Muse by revelling on Mount Parnassus. Her name ('she who makes sinewy') suggests ithyphallic orgies, and the sturdy growth of corn; boys will have been bloodily sacrificed to her before every winter sowing. Zeus is himself credited with having defied Ino in gratitude for her kindness to Dionysus, and Athamas bears an agricultural name in her honour; in other words, the Ionian farmers settled their religious differences with the Aeolian shepherds to their own advantage.

5. The myth, however, is a medley of early cult elements. The sacramental Zagreus cult, which became that of Dionysus the Kid (see 30. 3), is suggested when Athamas takes Ino for a she-goat; the sacramental Actaeon cult is suggested when he takes Learchus for a stag, shoots him, and tears him in pieces (see 22. 1). Ino's younger son Melicertes is the Canaanite Heracles Melkarth ('protector of the city'), alias Moloch who, as the new-born solar king, comes riding on dolphin-back towards the isthmus; and whose death, at the close of his four years' reign, was celebrated at the Isthmian Funeral Games. Infants were sacrificed to Melicertes on the Island of Tenedos, and probably also at Corinth (see 156.2), as they were to Moloch at Jerusalem (Leviticus xviii. 21 and 1 Kings xi. 7).

6. Only when Zeus became god of the clear sky and usurped the goddess's solar attributes did the fleece become golden – thus the First Vatican Mythographer says that it was 'the fleece in which Zeus ascended the sky' – but while he was inducer of the thunderstorm it had been purple-black (Simonides: Fragment 21).

7. In one version of the myth (Hippias: Fragment 12), Ino is called Gorgopis ('grim-faced'), a title of Athene's; and savage Sciron who hurled travellers over the cliff, took his name from the white parasol – more properly a paralune – carried in Athene's processions. The Molurian Rock was evidently the cliff from which the sacred king, or his surrogates, were thrown into the sea in honour of the Moon-goddess Athene, or Ino, the parasol being apparently used to break the fall (see 89. 6; 92. 3; 96. 3 and 98. 7).

8. Helle's drowning parallels Ino's. Both are Moon-goddesses, and the myth is ambivalent: it represents the nightly setting of the Moon and, at the same time, the abandonment of Helle's lunar cult in favour of Zeus's solar one. Both are equally Sea-goddesses: Helle gave her name to the junction of two seas, Ino-Leucothea appeared to Odysseus in the guise of a seamew and rescued him from drowning (see 170. y).

9. Athamas's tribe is more likely to have migrated from Boeotian Mount Laphystium and Athamania to Thessalian Mount Laphystius and Athamania, than contrariwise; he had a strong connexion with Corinth, the kingdom of his brother Sisyphus, and is said to have founded the city of Acraephia to the east of Lake Copais, where there was a 'Field of Athamas' (Stephanus of Byzantium *sub* Acraephia; Pausanias: ix. 24. 1). Several of his sons are also credited with the foundation of Boeotian cities. He is indeed plausibly described as a son of Minyas, and King of Orchomenus, which would have given him power over the Copaic Plain and Mount Laphystium (Scholiast on Apollonius Rhodius: i. 230; Hellanicus on Apollonius Rhodius: iii. 265) and allied him with Corinth against the intervening states of Athens and Thebes. The probable reason for the Athamanians' northward wanderings into Thessaly was the disastrous war fought between Orchomenus and Thebes, recorded in the Heracles cycle (see 121. *d*). Nephele's ragings on the mountain recall the daughters of Minyas who are said to have been overtaken by a Bacchic frenzy on Mount Laphystium (Scholiast on Lycophron's *Alexandra* 1237): the alleged origin of the Agrionia festival at Orchomenus.

71

THE MARES OF GLAUCUS

GLAUCUS, son of Sisyphus and Merope, and father of Bellerophon, lived at Potniae near Thebes where, scorning the power of Aphrodite, he refused to let his mares breed. He hoped by this means to make them more spirited than other contestants in the chariot races which were his chief interest. But Aphrodite was vexed; and complained to Zeus that he had gone so far as to feed the mares on human flesh. When Zeus permitted her to take what action she pleased against Glaucus, she led the mares out by night to drink from a well sacred to herself, and graze on a herb called hippomanes which grew at its lip. This she did just before Jason celebrated the funeral games of Pelias on the seashore at Iolcus; and no sooner had Glaucus yoked the mares to his chariot pole than they bolted, overthrew the chariot, dragged him along the ground entangled in the reins, for the whole length of the stadium, and then ate him alive.[1] But some say that this took place at Potniae, not Iolcus; and others, that Glaucus leaped into the sea in grief for Melicertes son of Athamas; or that Glaucus was the name given to Melicertes after his death.[2]

b. Glaucus's ghost, called the Taraxippus, or Horse-scarer, still haunts the Isthmus of Corinth, where his father Sisyphus first taught him the charioteer's art, and delights in scaring the horses at the Isthmian Games, thus causing many deaths. Another horse-scarer is the ghost of Myrtilus whom Pelops killed. He haunts the stadium at Olympia, where charioteers offer him sacrifices in the hope of avoiding destruction.[3]

1. Homer: *Iliad* vi. 154; Apollodorus: ii. 3. 1; Pausanias: vi. 20. 9; Hyginus: *Fabulae* 250 and 273; Ovid: *Ibis* 557; Scholiast on Euripides's *Orestes* 318 and *Phoenician Women* 1131; Aelian: *Nature of Animals* xv. 25.
2. Strabo: ix. 2. 24; Athenaeus: vii. pp. 296–7.
3. Pausanias: vi. 20. 8.

*

1. The myths of Lycurgus (see 27. e) and Diomedes (see 130. b) suggest that the pre-Hellenic sacred king was torn in pieces at the close of his reign by women disguised as mares. In Hellenic times, this ritual was altered to death by being dragged at the tail of a four-horse chariot, as in the myths of Hippolytus (see 101. g), Laius (see 105. d), Oenomaus (see 109. j), Abderus (see 130. 1), Hector (see 163. 4), and others. At the Babylonian New Year festivities, when the Sun-god Marduk, incarnate in the King, was believed to be in Hell fighting the sea-monster Tiamat (see 73. 7), a chariot drawn by four masterless horses was let loose in the streets, to symbolize the chaotic state of the world during the demise of the crown; presumably with a puppet charioteer entangled in the reins. If the Babylonian ritual was of common origin with the Greek, a boy *interrex* will have succeeded to the King's throne and bed during his demise of a single day and, at dawn next morning, been dragged at the chariot's tail – as in the myths of Phaëthon (see 42. 2) and Hippolytus (see 101. g). The King was then reinstalled on his throne.

2. The myth of Glaucus is unusual: he is not only involved in a chariot-wreck, but eaten by the mares. That he despised Aphrodite and would not let his mares breed, suggests a patriarchal attempt to suppress Theban erotic festivities in honour of the Potniae, 'powerful ones', namely the Moon triad.

3. The Taraxippus seems to have been an archaic royal statue, marking the first turn of the race-course; horses new to the stadium were distracted by it at the moment when their charioteer was trying to cut in and take the inner berth; but this was also the place where the chariot-crash was staged for the old king, or his *interrex*, by the removal of his linch-pins (see 109. j).

4. Glaucus ('grey-green') is likely to have been in one sense the Minoan representative who visited the Isthmus (see 90. 7) with the annual edicts; and in another Melicertes (Melkarth 'guardian of the city'), a Phoenician title of the King of Corinth, who theoretically arrived every year, new-born, on dolphin-back (see 70. 5 and 87. 2), and was flung into the sea when his reign ended (see 96. 3).

72

MELAMPUS

MELAMPUS the Minyan, Cretheus's grandson, who lived at Pylus in Messene, was the first mortal to be granted prophetic powers, the first to practise as a physician, the first to build temples to Dionysus in Greece, and the first to temper wine with water.[1]

b. His brother Bias, to whom he was deeply attached, fell in love with their cousin Pero; but so many suitors came for her hand that she was promised by her father Neleus to the man who could drive off King Phylacus's cattle from Phylace. Phylacus prized these cattle above everything in the world, except his only son Iphiclus, and guarded them in person with the help of an unsleeping and unapproachable dog.

c. Now, Melampus could understand the language of birds, his ears having been licked clean by a grateful brood of young serpents: he had rescued these from death at the hands of his attendants and piously buried their parents' dead bodies. Moreover, Apollo, whom he met one day by the banks of the river Alpheius, had taught him to prophesy from the entrails of sacrificial victims.[2] It thus came to his knowledge that whoever tried to steal the cattle would be made a present of them, though only after being imprisoned for exactly one year. Since Bias was in despair, Melampus decided to visit Phylacus's byre by dead of night; but as soon as he laid his hand on a cow, the dog bit his leg, and Phylacus, springing up from the straw, led him away to prison. This was, of course, no more than Melampus expected.

d. On the evening before his year of imprisonment ended Melampus heard two woodworms talking at the end of a beam which was socketed into the wall above his head. One asked with a sigh of fatigue: 'How many days yet of gnawing, brother?'

The other worm, his mouth full of wood-dust, replied: 'We are making good progress. The beam will collapse tomorrow at dawn, if we waste no time in idle conversation.'

Melampus at once shouted: 'Phylacus, Phylacus, pray transfer me to another cell!' Phylacus, though laughing at Melampus's reasons for this request, did not deny him. When the beam duly collapsed and killed one of the women who was helping to carry out the bed, Phylacus was astounded at Melampus's prescience. 'I will grant you both your freedom and the cattle,' he said , 'if only you would cure my son Iphiclus of impotency.'

e. Melampus agreed. He began the task by sacrificing two bulls to Apollo, and after he had burned the thigh-bones with the fat, left their carcasses lying by the altar. Presently two vultures flew down, and one remarked to the other: 'It must be several years since we were last here – that time when Phylacus was gelding rams and we collected our perquisites.'

'I well remember it,' said the other vulture. 'Iphiclus, who was then still a child, saw his father coming towards him with a blood-stained knife, and took fright. He apparently feared to be gelded himself, because he screamed at the top of his voice. Phylacus drove the knife into the sacred pear-tree over there, for safe-keeping, while he ran to comfort Iphiclus. That fright accounts for the impotency. Look, Phylacus forgot to recover the knife! There it still is, sticking in the tree, but bark has grown over its blade, and only the end of its handle shows.'

'In that case,' remarked the first vulture, 'the remedy for Iphiclus's impotency would be to draw out the knife, scrape off the rust left by the ram's blood and administer it to him, mixed in water, every day for ten days.'

'I concur,' said the other vulture. 'But who, less intelligent than ourselves, would have the sense to prescribe such a medicine?'

f. Thus Melampus was able to cure Iphiclus, who soon begot a son named Podarces; and, having claimed first the cattle and then Pero, he presented her, still a virgin, to his grateful brother Bias.[3]

g. Now, Proetus, son of Abas, joint-king of Argolis with Acrisius, had married Stheneboea, who bore him three daughters named Lysippe, Iphinoë, and Iphianassa – but some call the two younger ones Hipponoë and Cyrianassa. Whether it was because they had offended Dionysus, or because they had offended Hera by their over-indulgence in love-affairs, or by stealing gold from her image at Tiryns, their father's capital, all three were divinely afflicted by madness and went raging on the mountains, like cows stung by the gadfly, behaving in a most disorderly fashion and assaulting travellers.[4]

h. Melampus, when he heard the news, came to Tiryns and offered to cure them, on condition that Proetus paid him with a third share of his kingdom.

'The price is far too high,' said Proetus brusquely; and Melampus retired.

The madness then spread to the Argive women, a great many of whom killed their children, deserted their homes, and went raving off to join Proetus's three daughters, so that no roads were safe, and sheep and cattle suffered heavy losses because the wild women tore them in pieces and devoured them raw. At this Proetus sent hastily for Melampus, to say that he accepted his terms.

'No, no.' said Melampus, 'as the disease has increased, so has my fee! Give me one third of your kingdom, and another third to my brother Bias, and I undertake to save you from this calamity. If you refuse, there will not be one Argive woman left in her home.'

When Proetus agreed, Melampus advised him: 'Vow twenty red oxen to Helius – I will tell you what to say – and all will be well.'

i. Proetus accordingly vowed the oxen to Helius, on condition that his daughters and their followers were cured; and Helius, who sees everything, at once promised Artemis the names of certain kings who had omitted their sacrifices to her, on condition that she persuaded Hera to remove the curse from the Argive women. Now, Artemis had recently hunted the Nymph Callisto to death for Hera's sake, so found no difficulty in carrying out her side of the bargain. This is the way that business is done in Heaven as on earth: hand washes hand.

j. Then Melampus, helped by Bias and a chosen company of sturdy young men, drove the disorderly crowd of women down from the mountains to Sicyon, where their madness left them, and then purified them by immersion in a holy well. Not finding Proetus's daughters among this rabble, Melampus and Bias went off again and chased all three of them to Lusi in Arcadia, where they took refuge in a cave overlooking the river Styx. There Lysippe and Iphianassa regained their sanity and were purified; but Iphinoë had died on the way.

k. Melampus then married Lysippe, Bias (whose wife Pero had recently died) married Iphianassa, and Proetus rewarded them both

according to his promise. But some say that Proetus's true name was
Anaxagoras.[5]

1. Apollodorus: ii. 2. 2; Athenaeus: ii. p. 45.
2. Apollodorus: i. 9. 11.
3. Homer *Odyssey* xi. 281–97, with scholiasts; Apollodorus: i. 9. 12.
4. Hesiod: *Catalogue of Women*; Apollodorus: ii. 4. 1; Diodorus
   Siculus: iv. 68; Servius on Virgil's *Eclogues* vi. 48.
5. Apollodorus: ii. 2. 1–2; Bacchylides: *Epinicia* x. 40–112; Herodotus: ix. 34; Diodorus Siculus: iv. 68; Pausanias: ii. 18. 4; iv. 36.
   3; v. 5. 5 and viii. 18. 3; Scholiast on Pindar's *Nemean Odes* ix. 13.

*

1. It was a common claim of wizards that their ears had been licked by
serpents, which were held to be incarnate spirits of oracular heroes ('The
Language of Animals' by J. R. Frazer, *Archaeological Review* i, 1888),
and that they were thus enabled to understand the language of birds and
insects (see 105. *g* and 158. *p*). Apollo's priests appear to have been more
than usually astute in claiming prophesy by this means.

2. Iphiclus's disability is factual rather than mythical: the rust of the
gelding-knife would be an appropriate psychological cure for impotence
caused by a sudden fright, and in accordance with the principles of sympathetic magic. Apollodorus describes the tree into which the knife was
thrust as an oak, but it is more likely to have been the wild pear-tree
sacred to the White Goddess of the Peloponnese (see 74. *6*), which fruits
in May, the month of enforced chastity; Phylacus had insulted the goddess by wounding her tree. The wizard's claim to have been told of
the treatment by vultures – important birds in augury (see 119. *i*) –
would strengthen the belief in its efficacy. Pero's name has been interpreted as meaning 'maimed or deficient', a reference to Iphiclus's disability, which is the main point of the story, rather than as meaning
'leather bag', a reference to her control of the winds (see 36. *1*).

3. It appears that 'Melampus', a leader of Aeolians from Pylus, seized
part of Argolis from the Canaanite settlers who called themselves Sons
of Abas (the Semitic word for 'father'), namely the god Melkarth (see
70. *5*), and instituted a double kingdom. His winning of the cattle from
Phylacus ('guardian'), who has an unsleeping dog, recalls Heracles's
Tenth Labour, and the myth is similarly based on the Hellenic custom of
buying a bride with the proceeds of a cattle raid (see 132. *1*).

4. 'Proetus' seems to be another name for Ophion, the Demiurge
(see 1. *a*). The mother of his daughters was Stheneboea, the Moon-goddess as cow – namely Io, who was maddened in much the same way (see
56. *a*) – and their names are titles of the same goddess in her destructive
capacity as Lamia (see 61. *1*), and as Hippolyte, whose wild mares tore

the sacred king to pieces at the end of his reign (see 71. *a*). But the orgy for which the Moon-priestesses dressed as mares should be distinguished from the rain-making gadfly dance for which they dressed as heifers (see 56. *1*); and from the autumn goat-cult revel, when they tore children and animals to pieces under the toxic influence of mead, wine, or ivy-beer (see 27. *2*). The Aeolians' capture of the goddess's shrine at Lusi, recorded here in mythic form, will have put an end to the wild-mare orgies; Demeter's rape by Poseidon (see 16. *5*) records the same event. Libations poured to the Serpent-goddess in an Arcadian shrine between Sicyon and Lusi may account for the story of Iphinoë's death.

5. The official recognition at Delphi, Corinth, Sparta, and Athens of Dionysus's ecstatic wine cult, given many centuries later, was aimed at the discouragement of all earlier, more primitive, rites; and seems to have put an end to cannibalism and ritual murder, except in the wilder parts of Greece. At Patrae in Achaea, for instance, Artemis Tridaria ('threefold assigner of lots') had required the annual sacrifice of boys and girls, their heads wreathed with ivy and corn, at her harvest orgies. This custom, said to atone for the desecration of the sanctuary by two lovers, Melanippus and Comaetho priestess of Artemis, was ended by the arrival of a chest containing an image of Dionysus, brought by Eurypylus (see 160. *x*) from Troy (Pausanias: vii. 19. 1–3).

6. *Melampodes* ('black feet'), is a common Classical name for the Egyptians (see 60. *5*); and these stories of how Melampus understood what birds or insects were saying are likely to be of African, not Aeolian, origin.

73

PERSEUS

ABAS, King of Argolis and grandson of Danaus, was so renowned a warrior that, after he died, rebels against the royal House could be put to flight merely by displaying his shield. He married Aglaia, to whose twin sons, Proetus and Acrisius, he bequeathed his kingdom, bidding them rule alternately. Their quarrel, which began in the womb, became more bitter than ever when Proetus lay with Acrisius's daughter Danaë, and barely escaped alive.[1] Since Acrisius now refused to give up the throne at the end of his term, Proetus fled to the court of Iobates, King of Lycia, whose daughter Stheneboea, or Anteia, he married;

returning presently at the head of a Lycian army to support his claims to the succession. A bloody battle was fought, but since neither side gained the advantage, Proetus and Acrisius reluctantly agreed to divide the kingdom between them. Acrisius's share was to be Argos and its environs; Proetus's was to be Tiryns, the Heraeum (now part of Mycenae), Midea, and the coast of Argolis.[2]

b. Seven gigantic Cyclopes, called Gasterocheires, because they earned their living as masons, accompanied Proetus from Lycia, and fortified Tiryns with massive walls, using blocks of stone so large that a mule team could not have stirred the least of them.[3]

c. Acrisius, who was married to Aganippe, had no sons, but only this one daughter Danaë whom Proteus had seduced; and, when he asked an oracle how to procure a male heir, was told: 'You will have no sons, and your grandson must kill you.' To forestall this fate, Acrisius imprisoned Danaë in a dungeon with brazen doors, guarded by savage dogs; but, despite these precautions, Zeus came upon her in a shower of gold, and she bore him a son named Perseus. When Acrisius learned of Danaë's condition, he would not believe that Zeus was the father, and suspected his brother Proetus of having renewed his intimacy with her; but, not daring to kill his own daughter, locked her and the infant Perseus in a wooden ark, which he cast into the sea. This ark was washed towards the island of Seriphos, where a fisherman named Dictys netted it, hauled it ashore, broke it open and found both Danaë and Perseus still alive. He took them at once to his brother, King Polydectes, who reared Perseus in his own house.[4]

d. Some years passed and Perseus, grown to manhood, defended Danaë against Polydectes who, with his subjects' support, had tried to force marriage upon her. Polydectes then assembled his friends and, pretending that he was about to sue for the hand of Hippodameia, daughter of Pelops, asked them to contribute one horse apiece as his love-gift. 'Seriphos is only a small island,' he said, 'but I do not wish to cut a poor figure beside the wealthy suitors from the mainland. Will you be able to help me, noble Perseus?'

'Alas,' answered Perseus, 'I possess no horse, nor any gold to buy one. But if you intend to marry Hippodameia, and not my mother, I will contrive to win whatever gift you name.' He added rashly: 'Even the Gorgon Medusa's head, if need be.'

e. 'That would indeed please me more than any horse in the world,' replied Polydectes at once.[5] Now, the Gorgon Medusa had serpents for hair, huge teeth, protruding tongue, and altogether so ugly a face that all who gazed at it were petrified with fright.

f. Athene overheard the conversation at Seriphos and, being a sworn enemy of Medusa's, for whose frightful appearance she had herself been responsible, accompanied Perseus on his adventure. First she led him to the city of Deicterion in Samos, where images of all the three Gorgons are displayed, thus enabling him to distinguish Medusa from her immortal sisters Stheno and Euryale; then she warned him never to look at Medusa directly, but only at her reflection, and presented him with a brightly-polished shield.

g. Hermes also helped Perseus, giving him an adamantine sickle with which to cut off Medusa's head. But Perseus still needed a pair of winged sandals, a magic wallet to contain the decapitated head, and the dark helmet of invisibility which belonged to Hades. All these things were in the care of the Stygian Nymphs, from whom Perseus had to fetch them; but their whereabouts were known only to the Gorgons' sisters, the three swan-like Graeae, who had a single eye and tooth among the three of them. Perseus accordingly sought out the Graeae on their thrones at the foot of Mount Atlas. Creeping up behind them, he snatched the eye and tooth, as they were being passed from one sister to another, and would not return either until he had been told where the Stygian Nymphs lived.[6]

h. Perseus then collected the sandals, wallet, and helmet from the nymphs, and flew westwards to the Land of the Hyperboreans, where he found the Gorgons asleep, among rain-worn shapes of men and wild beasts pertrified by Medusa. He fixed his eyes on the reflection in the shield, Athene guided his hand, and he cut off Medusa's head with one stroke of the sickle; whereupon, to his surprise, the winged horse Pegasus, and the warrior Chrysaor grasping a golden falchion, sprang fully-grown from her dead body. Perseus was unaware that these had been begotten on Medusa by Poseidon in one of Athene's temples, but decided not to antagonize them further. Hurriedly thrusting the head into his wallet, he took flight; and though Stheno and Euryale, awakened by their new nephews, rose to pursue him, the helmet made Perseus invisible, and he escaped safely southward.[7]

i. At sunset, Perseus alighted near the palace of the Titan Atlas to whom, as a punishment for his inhospitality, he showed the Gorgon's head and thus transformed him into a mountain; and on the following day turned eastward and flew across the Libyan desert, Hermes helping him to carry the weighty head. By the way he dropped the Graeae's eye and tooth into Lake Triton; and some drops of Gorgon blood fell on the desert sand, where they bred a swarm of venomous serpents, one of which later killed Mopsus the Argonaut.[8]

j. Perseus paused for refreshment at Chemmis in Egypt, where he is still worshipped, and then flew on. As he rounded the coast of Philistia to the north, he caught sight of a naked woman chained to a sea-cliff, and instantly fell in love with her. This was Andromeda, daughter of Cepheus, the Ethiopian King of Joppa, and Cassiopeia.[9] Cassiopeia had boasted that both she and her daughter were more beautiful than the Nereids, who complained of this insult to their protector Poseidon. Poseidon sent a flood and a female sea-monster to devastate Philistia; and when Cepheus consulted the Oracle of Ammon, he was told that his only hope of deliverance lay in sacrificing Andromeda to the monster. His subjects had therefore obliged him to chain her to a rock, naked except for certain jewels, and leave her to be devoured.

k. As Perseus flew towards Andromeda, he saw Cepheus and Cassiopeia watching anxiously from the shore near by, and alighted beside them for a hurried consultation. On condition that, if he rescued her, she should be his wife and return to Greece with him, Perseus took to the air again, grasped his sickle and, diving murderously from above, beheaded the approaching monster, which was deceived by his shadow on the sea. He had drawn the Gorgon's head from the wallet, lest the monster might look up, and now laid it face downwards on a bed of leaves and sea-weed (which instantly turned to coral), while he cleansed his hands of blood, raised three altars and sacrificed a calf, a cow, and a bull to Hermes, Athene, and Zeus respectively.[10]

l. Cepheus and Cassiopeia grudgingly welcomed him as their son-in-law and, on Andromeda's insistence, the wedding took place at once; but the festivities were rudely interrupted when Agenor, King Belus's twin brother, entered at the head of an armed party, claiming Andromeda for himself. He was doubtless summoned by Cassiopeia, since she and Cepheus at once broke faith with Perseus, pleading that the promise of Andromeda's hand had been forced from them by circumstances, and that Agenor's claim was the prior one.

'Perseus must die!' cried Cassiopeia fiercely.

m. In the ensuing fight, Perseus struck down many of his opponents but, being greatly outnumbered, was forced to snatch the Gorgon's head from its bed of coral and turn the remaining two hundred of them to stone.[11]

n. Poseidon set the images of Cepheus and Cassiopeia among the stars – the latter, as a punishment for her treachery, is tied in a market-basket which, at some seasons of the year, turns upside-down, so that she looks ridiculous. But Athene afterwards placed Andromeda's image in a more honourable constellation, because she had insisted on marrying Perseus, despite her parents' ill faith. The marks left by her chains are still pointed out on a cliff near Joppa; and the monster's petrified bones were exhibited in the city itself until Marcus Aemilius Scaurus had them taken to Rome during his aedileship.[12]

o. Perseus returned hurriedly to Seriphos, taking Andromeda with him, and found that Danaë and Dictys, threatened by the violence of Polydectes who, of course, never intended to marry Hippodameia, had taken refuge in a temple. He therefore went straight to the palace where Polydectes was banqueting with his companions, and announced that he had brought the promised love-gift. Greeted by a storm of insults, he displayed the Gorgon's head, averting his own gaze as he did so, and turned them all to stone; the circle of boulders is still shown in Seriphos. He then gave the head to Athene, who fixed it on her aegis; and Hermes returned the sandals, wallet, and helmet to the guardianship of the Stygian nymphs.[13]

p. After raising Dictys to the throne of Seriphos, Perseus set sail for Argos, accompanied by his mother, his wife, and a party of Cyclopes. Acrisius, hearing of their approach, fled to Pelasgian Larissa; but Perseus happened to be invited there for the funeral games which King Teutamides was holding in honour of his dead father, and competed in the fivefold contest. When it came to the discus-throw, his discus, carried out of its path by the wind and the will of the Gods, struck Acrisius's foot and killed him.[14]

q. Greatly grieved, Perseus buried his grandfather in the temple of Athene which crowns the local acropolis and then, being ashamed to reign in Argos, went to Tiryns, where Proetus had been succeeded by his son Megapenthes, and arranged to exchange kingdoms with him. So Megapenthes moved to Argos, while Perseus reigned in Tiryns and presently won back the other two parts of Proetus's original kingdom.

r. Perseus fortified Midea, and founded Mycenae, so called because, when he was thirsty, a mushroom [*mycos*] sprang up, and provided him with a stream of water. The Cyclopes built the walls of both cities.[15]

*

s. Others give a very different account of the matter. They say that Polydectes succeeded in marrying Danaë, and reared Perseus in the temple of Athene. Some years later, Acrisius heard of their survival and sailed to Seriphos, resolving this time to kill Perseus with his own hand. Polydectes intervened and made each of them solemnly swear never to attempt the other's life. However, a storm arose and, while Acrisius's ship was still hauled up on the beach, weather-bound, Polydectes died. During his funeral games, Perseus threw a discus which accidentally struck Acrisius on the head and killed him. Perseus then sailed to Argos and claimed the throne, but found that Proetus had usurped it, and therefore turned him into stone; thus he now reigned over the whole of Argolis, until Megapenthes avenged his father's death by murdering him.[16]

t. As for the Gorgon Medusa, they say that she was a beautiful daughter of Phorcys, who had offended Athene, and led the Libyans of Lake Tritonis in battle. Perseus, coming from Argos with an army, was helped by Athene to assassinate Medusa. He cut off her head by night, and buried it under a mound of earth in the market place at Argos. This mound lies close to the grave of Perseus's daughter Gorgophone, notorious as the first widow ever to remarry.[17]

1. Servius on Virgil's *Aeneid* iii. 286; Scholiast on Euripides's *Orestes* 965; Apollodorus: ii. 2. 1 and 4. 7.
2. Homer: *Iliad* vi. 160; Apollodorus: ii. 2. 1; Pausanias: ii. 16. 2.
3. Pausanias: ii. 25. 7; Strabo: viii. 6. 11.
4. Hyginus: *Fabula* 63; Apollodorus: ii. 4. 1; Horace: *Odes* iii. 16. 1.
5. Apollodorus: ii. 4. 2.
6. Apollodorus: *loc. cit.*; Hyginus: *Poetic Astronomy* ii. 12.
7. Pindar: *Pythian Odes* x. 31; Ovid: *Metamorphoses* iv. 780; Apollodorus: ii. 4. 3.
8. Euripides: *Electra* 459–63; Hyginus: *Poetic Astronomy* ii. 12; Apollonius Rhodius: iv. 1513 ff.
9. Herodotus: ii. 91; Tzetzes: *On Lycophron* 836; Strabo: i. 2. 35; Pliny: *Natural History* vi. 35.
10 Apollodorus: ii. 4. 3; Hyginus: *Fabula* 64; Ovid: *Metamorphoses* iv. 740 ff.
11. Hyginus: *loc. cit.*; Ovid: *Metamorphoses* v. 1–235; Apollodorus: *loc. cit.*

12. Hyginus: *Poetic Astronomy* ii. 9–10 and 12; Josephus: *Jewish Wars* iii. 9. 2; Pliny: *Natural History* ix. 4.
13. Strabo: x. 5. 10; Apollodorus: ii. 4. 3.
14. Scholiast on Euripides's *Orestes* 953; Apollodorus: ii. 4. 4.
15. Clement of Alexandria: *Address to the Greeks* iii. 45; Apollodorus: ii. 4. 4–5.
16. Ovid: *Metamorphoses* v. 236–41; Hyginus: *Fabulae* 63 and 244.
17. Pausanias: ii. 21. 6–8.

*

1. The myth of Acrisius and Proetus records the foundation of an Argive double-kingdom: instead of the king's dying every midsummer, and being succeeded by his tanist for the rest of the year, each reigned in turn for forty-nine or fifty months – namely half a Great Year (see 106. 1). This kingdom was later, it seems, divided in halves, with co-kings ruling concurrently for an entire Great Year. The earlier theory, that the bright spirit of the Waxing Year, and his tanist twin, the dark spirit of the Waning Year, stand in endless rivalry pervades Celtic and Palestinian myth, as well as the Greek and Latin.

2. Two such pairs of twins occur in *Genesis*: Esau and Jacob (*Genesis* xxiv. 24–6), Pharez (see 159. 4) and Zarah (*Genesis* xxxviii. 27–30), both of whom quarrel for precedence in the womb, like Acrisius and Proetus. In the simpler Palestinian myth of Mot and Aleyn, the twins quarrel about a woman, as do Acrisius and Proetus; and as their counterparts do in Celtic myth – for instance, Gwyn and Gwythur, in the *Mabinogion*, duel every May Eve until the end of the world for the hand of Creiddylad, daughter of Llyr (Cordelia, daughter of King Lear). This woman is, in each case, a Moon-priestess, marriage to whom confers kingship.

3. The building of Argos and Tiryns by the seven Gasterocheires ('bellies with hands'), and the death of Acrisius, are apparently deduced from a picture of a walled city: seven sun-disks, each with three limbs but no head (see 23. 2), are placed above it, and the sacred king is being killed by an eighth sun-disk, with wings, which strikes his sacred heel. This would mean that seven yearly surrogates die for the king, who is then himself sacrificed at the priestess's orders; his successor, Perseus, stands by.

4. The myth of Danaë, Perseus, and the ark seems related to that of Isis, Osiris, Set, and the Child Horus. In the earliest version, Proetus is Perseus's father, the Argive Osiris; Danaë is his sister-wife, Isis; Perseus, the Child Horus; and Acrisius, the jealous Set who killed his twin Osiris and was taken vengeance on by Horus. The ark is the acacia-wood boat in which Isis and Horus searched the Delta for Osiris's body. A similar story occurs in one version of the Semele myth (see 27. 6), and in that of Rhoeo (see 160. 7). But Danaë, imprisoned in the brazen dungeon, where she bears a child, is the subject of a familiar New Year icon (see 43.2); Zeus's impregnation of Danaë with a shower of gold must refer to

the ritual marriage of the Sun and the Moon, from which the New Year king was born. It can also be read as pastoral allegory: 'water is gold' for the Greek shepherd, and Zeus sends thunder-showers on the earth – Danaë. The name 'Deicterion' means that the Gorgon's head was shown there to Perseus.

5. Dynastic disputes at Argos were complicated by the existence of an Argive colony in Caria – as appears both in this myth and in that of Bellerophon (see 75. *b*); when Cnossus fell about 1400 B.C., the Carian navy was, for a while, one of the strongest in the Mediterranean. The myths of Perseus and Bellerophon are closely related. Perseus killed the monstrous Medusa with the help of winged sandals; Bellerophon used a winged horse, born from the decapitated body of Medusa, to kill the monstrous Chimaera. Both feats record the usurpation by Hellenic invaders of the Moon-goddess's powers, and are unified in an archaic Boeotian vase-painting of a Gorgon-headed mare. This mare is the Moon-goddess, whose calendar-symbol was the Chimaera (see 75. *2*); and the Gorgon-head is a prophylactic mask, worn by her priestesses to scare away the uninitiated (see 33. *3*), which the Hellenes stripped from them.

6. In the second and simpler version of the myth, Perseus fights a Libyan queen, decapitates her, and buries her head in the market place of Argos. This must record an Argive conquest of Libya, the suppression there of the matriarchal system, and the violation of the goddess Neith's mysteries (see 8. *1*). The burial of the head in the market place suggests that sacred relics were locked in a chest there, with a prophylactic mask placed above them, to discourage municipal diggers from disturbing the magic. Perhaps the relics were a pair of little pigs, like those said in the *Mabinogion* to have been buried by King Lud in a stone chest at Carfax, Oxford, as a protective charm for the whole Kingdom of Britain; though pigs, in that context, may be a euphemism for children.

7. Andromeda's story has probably been deduced from a Palestinian icon of the Sun-god Marduk, or his predecessor Bel, mounted on his white horse and killing the sea-monster Tiamat. This myth also formed part of Hebrew mythology: Isaiah mentions that Jehovah (Marduk) hacked Rahab in pieces with a sword (*Isaiah* li. 9); and according to *Job* x. 13 and xxvi. 12, Rahab was the Sea. In the same icon, the jewelled, naked Andromeda, standing chained to a rock, is Aphrodite, or Ishtar, or Astarte, the lecherous Sea-goddess, 'ruler of men'. But she is not waiting to be rescued; Marduk has bound her there himself, after killing her emanation, Tiamat the sea-serpent, to prevent further mischief. In the Babylonian Creation Epic, it was she who sent the Flood. Astarte, as Sea-goddess, had temples all along the Palestinian coast, and at Troy she was Hesione, 'Queen of Asia', whom Heracles is said to have rescued from another sea-monster (see 137. *2*).

8. A Greek colony planted at Chemmis apparently towards the end of the second millennium B.C., identified Perseus with the god Chem, whose hieroglyph was a winged bird and a solar disk; and Herodotus emphasizes the connexion between Danaë, Perseus's mother, and the Libyan invasion of Argos by the Danaans. The myth of Perseus and the mushroom is perhaps told to account for an icon showing a hero studying a mushroom. Fire, mistaken for water, is spouting from it under a blazing sun. Here is tinder for his fire-wheel (see 63. 2).

9. The second, simpler version of the myth suggests that Perseus's visit to the Graeae, his acquisition of the eye, tooth, wallet, sickle, and helmet of darkness, and his pursuit by the other Gorgons after the decapitation of Medusa are extraneous to his quarrel with Acrisius. In the *White Goddess* (Chapter 13), I postulate that these fairy-tale elements are misreadings of a wholly different icon: which show Hermes, wearing his familiar winged sandals and helmet, being given a magic eye by the Three Fates (see 61. 1). This eye symbolizes the gift of perception: Hermes is enabled to master the tree-alphabet, which they have invented. They also give him a divinatory tooth, like the one used by Fionn in the Irish legend; a sickle, to cut alphabetic twigs from the grove; a crane-skin bag, in which to stow these safely; and a Gorgon-mask, to scare away the curious. Hermes is flying through the sky to Tartessus, where the Gorgons had a sacred grove (see 132. 3), escorted, not pursued, by a triad of goddesses wearing Gorgon-masks. On the earth below, the goddess is shown again, holding up a mirror which reflects a Gorgon's face, to emphasize the secrecy of his lesson (see 52. 7). Hermes's association with the Graeae, the Stygian Nymphs, and the helmet of invisibility proves that he is the subject of this picture; the confusion between him and Perseus may have arisen because Hermes, as the messenger of Death, had also earned the title of *Pterseus*, 'the destroyer'.

74

THE RIVAL TWINS

WHEN the male line of Polycaon's House had died out after five generations, the Messenians invited Perieres, the son of Aeolus, to be their king, and he married Perseus's daughter Gorgophone. She survived him and was the first widow to remarry, her new husband being Oebalus the Spartan.[1] Hitherto it had been customary for women to commit suicide on the death of their husbands: as did Meleager's daughter Polydora, whose husband Protesilaus was the first to leap ashore when the Greek fleet reached the coast of Troy; Marpessa; Cleopatra; and Evadne, daughter of Phylacus, who threw herself on the funeral pyre when her husband perished at Thebes.[2]

b. Aphareus and Leucippus were Gorgophone's sons by Perieres, whereas Tyndareus and Icarius were her sons by Oebalus.[3] Tyndareus succeeded his father on the throne of Sparta, Icarius acting as his co-king; but Hippocoön and his twelve sons expelled both of them – though some, indeed, say that Icarius (later to become Odysseus's father-in-law) took Hippocoön's side. Taking refuge with King Thestius in Aetolia, Tyndareus married his daughter Leda, who bore him Castor and Clytaemnestra, at the same time bearing Helen and Polydeuces to Zeus.[4] Later, having adopted Polydeuces, Tyndareus regained the Spartan throne, and was one of those whom Asclepius raised from the dead. His tomb is still shown at Sparta.[5]

c. Meanwhile, his half-brother Aphareus had succeeded Perieres on the throne of Messene, where Leucippus – from whom, the Messenians say, the city of Leuctra took its name – acted as his co-king and enjoyed the lesser powers. Aphareus took to wife his half-sister Arene, who bore him Idas and Lynceus; though Idas was, in truth, Poseidon's son.[6] Now, Leucippus's daughters, the Leucippides, namely Phoebe, a priestess of Athene, and Hilaeira, a priestess of Artemis, were betrothed to their cousins, Idas and Lynceus; but Castor and Polydeuces, who are commonly known as the Dioscuri, carried them off, and had sons by them; which occasioned a bitter rivalry between the two sets of twins.[7]

d. The Dioscuri, who were never separated from one another in any adventure, became the pride of Sparta. Castor was famous as a soldier and tamer of horses, Polydeuces as the best boxer of his day; both won prizes at the Olympic Games. Their cousins and rivals were no less devoted to each other; Idas had greater strength than Lynceus, but Lynceus had such sharp eyes that he could see in the dark or divine the whereabouts of buried treasure.[8]

e. Now, Evenus, a son of Ares, had married Alcippe, by whom he became the father of Marpessa. In an attempt to keep her a virgin, he invited each of her suitors in turn to run a chariot race with him; the victor would win Marpessa, the vanquished would forfeit his head. Soon many heads were nailed to the walls of Evenus's house and Apollo, falling in love with Marpessa, expressed his disgust of so barbarous a custom; and said that he would soon end it by challenging

Evenus to a race. But Idas had also set his heart on Marpessa, and begged a winged chariot from his father Poseidon.⁹ Before Apollo could act, he had driven to Aetolia, and carried Marpessa away from the midst of a band of dancers. Evenus gave chase, but could not overtake Idas, and felt such mortification that, after killing his horses, he drowned himself in the river Lycormas, ever since called the Evenus.¹⁰

f. When Idas reached Messene, Apollo tried to take Marpessa from him. They fought a duel, but Zeus parted them, and ruled that Marpessa herself should decide whom she preferred to marry. Fearing that Apollo would cast her off when she grew old, as he had done with many another of his loves, she chose Idas for her husband.¹¹

g. Idas and Lynceus were among the Calydonian hunters, and sailed in the *Argo* to Colchis. One day, after the death of Aphareus, they and the Dioscuri patched up their quarrel sufficiently to join forces in a cattle-raid on Arcadia. The raid proved successful, and Idas was chosen by lot to divide the booty among the four of them. He therefore quartered a cow, and ruled that half the spoil should go to the man who ate his share first, the remainder to the next quickest. Almost before the others had settled themselves to begin the contest, Idas bolted his own share and then helped Lynceus to bolt his; soon down went the last gobbet, and he and Lynceus drove the cattle away towards Messene. The Dioscuri remained, until Polydeuces, the slower of the two, had finished eating; whereupon they marched against Messene, and protested to the citizens that Lynceus had forfeited his share by accepting help from Idas, and that Idas had forfeited his by not waiting until all the contestants were ready. Idas and Lynceus happened to be away on Mount Taygetus, sacrificing to Poseidon; so the Dioscuri seized the disputed cattle, and other plunder as well, and then hid inside a hollow oak to await their rivals' return. But Lynceus had caught sight of them from the summit of Taygetus; and Idas, hurrying down the mountain slope, hurled his spear at the tree and transfixed Castor. When Polydeuces rushed out to avenge his brother, Idas tore the carved headstone from Aphareus's tomb, and threw it at him. Although badly crushed, Polydeuces contrived to kill Lynceus with his spear; and at this point Zeus intervened on behalf of his son, striking Idas dead with a thunderbolt.¹²

h. But the Messenians say that Castor killed Lynceus, and that Idas, distracted by grief, broke off the fight and began to bury him. Castor then approached and insolently demolished the monument which Idas had just raised, denying that Lynceus was worthy of it. 'Your brother put up no better fight than a woman would have done!' he cried tauntingly. Idas turned, and plunged his sword into Castor's belly; but Polydeuces took instant vengeance on him.[13]

i. Others say that it was Lynceus who mortally wounded Castor in a battle fought at Aphidna; others again, that Castor was killed when Idas and Lynceus attacked Sparta; and still others, that both Dioscuri survived the fight, Castor being killed later by Meleager and Polyneices.[14]

j. It is generally agreed, at least, that Polydeuces was the last survivor of the two sets of twins and that, after setting up a trophy beside the Spartan race-course to celebrate his victory over Lynceus, he prayed to Zeus: 'Father, let me not outlive my dear brother!' Since, however, it was fated that only one of Leda's sons should die, and since Castor's father Tyndareus had been a mortal, Polydeuces, as the son of Zeus, was duly carried up to Heaven. Yet he refused immortality unless Castor might share it, and Zeus therefore allowed them both to spend their days alternately in the upper air, and under the earth at Therapne. In further reward of their brotherly love, he set their images among the stars as the Twins.[15]

k. After the Dioscuri had been deified, Tyndareus summoned Menelaus to Sparta, where he resigned the kingdom to him; and since the House of Aphareus was now also left without an heir, Nestor succeeded to the throne of all Messenia, except for the part ruled over by the sons of Asclepius.[16]

l. The Spartans still show the house where the Dioscuri lived. It was afterwards owned by one Phormio, whom they visited one night, pretending to be strangers from Cyrene. They asked him for lodging, and begged leave to sleep in their old room. Phormio replied that they were welcome to any other part of the house but that, regrettably, his daughter was now occupying the room of which they spoke. Next morning, the girl and all her possessions had vanished, and the room was empty, except for images of the Dioscuri and some herb-benjamin laid upon a table.[17]

m. Poseidon made Castor and Polydeuces the saviours of shipwrecked sailors, and granted them power to send favourable winds; in response to a sacrifice of white lambs offered on the prow of any ship, they will come hastening through the sky, followed by a train of sparrows.[18]

n. The Dioscuri fought with the Spartan fleet at Aegospotamoi, and the victors afterwards hung up two golden stars in their honour at Delphi; but these fell down and disappeared shortly before the fatal battles of Leuctra.[19]

o. During the second Messenian War, a couple of Messenians aroused the Dioscuri's anger by impersonating them. It happened that the Spartan army was celebrating a feast of the demi-gods, when twin spearmen rode into the camp at full gallop, dressed in white tunics, purple cloaks, and egg-shell caps. The Spartans fell down to worship them, and the pretended Dioscuri, two Messenian youths named Gonippus and Panormus, killed many of them. After the battle of the Boar's Grave, therefore, the Dioscuri sat on a wild pear-tree, and spirited away the shield belonging to the victorious Messenian commander Aristomenes, which prevented him from pressing on the Spartan retreat, and thus saved many lives; again, when Aristomenes attempted to assault Sparta by night, the phantoms of the Dioscuri and of their sister Helen turned him back. Later, Castor and Polydeuces forgave the Messenians, who sacrificed to them when Epaminondas founded the new city of Messene.[20]

p. They preside at the Spartan Games, and because they invented the war-dance and war-like music are the patrons of all bards who sing of ancient battles. In Hilaeira and Phoebe's sanctuary at Sparta, the two priestesses are still called Leucippides, and the egg from which Leda's twins were hatched is suspended from the roof.[21] The Spartans represent the Dioscuri by two parallel wooden beams, joined by two transverse ones. Their co-kings always take these into battle and when, for the first time, a Spartan army was led by one king alone, it was decreed that one beam should also remain at Sparta. According to those who have seen the Dioscuri, the only noticeable difference between them is that Polydeuces's face bears the scars of boxing. They dress alike: each has his half egg-shell surmounted by a star, each his spear and white horse. Some say that Poseidon gave them their horses; others, that Polydeuces's Thessalian charger was a gift from Hermes.[22]

1. Pausanias: iv. 2. 2 and iii. 1. 4; Apollodorus: i. 9. 5.
2. *Cypria*, quoted by Pausanias: iv. 2. 5; Pausanias: iii. 1. 4.
3. Apollodorus: i. 9. 5; Pausanias: *loc. cit.*
4. Pausanias: *loc. cit.*; Apollodorus: iii. 10. 5–7.
5. Panyasis, quoted by Apollodorus: iii. 10. 3; Pausanias: iii. 17. 4.
6. Pausanias: iii. 26. 3 and iv. 2. 3; Apollodorus: iii. 10. 3.

7. Apollodorus: iii. 11. 2; Hyginus: *Fabula* 80.
8. Apollodorus: *loc. cit.* and iii. 10. 3; Homer: *Odyssey* xi. 300; Pausanias: iv. 2. 4; Hyginus: *Fabula* 14; Palaephatus: *Incredible Stories* x.
9. Hyginus: *Fabula* 242; Apollodorus: i. 7. 8; Plutarch: *Parallel Stories* 40; Scholiast and Eustathius on Homer's *Iliad* ix. 557.
10. Plutarch: *loc. cit.*; Apollodorus: *loc. cit.*
11. Apollodorus: i. 7. 9.
12. Apollodorus: i. 8. 2; i. 9. 16 and iii. 11. 2; Theocritus: *Idylls* xxii. 137 ff.; Pindar: *Nemean Odes* x. 55 ff.
13. Hyginus: *Fabula* 80.
14. Ovid: *Fasti* v. 699 ff.; Hyginus: *Poetic Astronomy* ii. 22; Theocritus: *loc. cit.*; Scholiast on Homer's *Odyssey* xi. 300.
15. Pausanias: iii. 14. 7; Apollodorus: iii. 11. 2; Pindar: *Nemean Odes* x. 55 ff.; Lucian: *Dialogues of the Gods* 26; Hyginus: *loc. cit.*
16. Apollodorus: *loc. cit.*; Pausanias: iv. 3. 1.
17. Pausanias: iii. 16. 3.
18. Hyginus: *Poetic Astronomy* ii. 22; Euripides: *Helen* 1503; *Homeric Hymn to the Dioscuri* 7 ff.
19. Cicero: *On Divination* i. 34. 75 and ii. 32. 68.
20. Pausanias: iv. 27. 1; iv. 16. 2 and v. 27. 3.
21. Pindar: *Nemean Odes* x. 49; Cicero: *On Oratory* ii. 8. 86; Theocritus: *Idylls* xxii. 215–20; Pausanias: iii. 16. 1–2.
22. Plutarch: *On Brotherly Love* i; Herodotus: v. 75; Lucian: *Dialogues of the Gods* 26; Hyginus: *Poetic Astronomy* ii. 22; Ptolemy Hephaestionos: viii. quoted by Photius: p. 409.

*

1. In order to allow the sacred king precedence over his tanist, he was usually described as the son of a god, by a mother on whom her husband subsequently fathered a mortal twin. Thus Heracles is Zeus's son by Alcmene, but his twin Iphicles is the son of her husband Amphitryon: a similar story is told about the Dioscuri of Laconia, and about their rivals, Idas and Lynceus of Messenia. The perfect harmony existing between the twins themselves marks a new stage in the development of kingship, when the tanist acts as vizier and chief-of-staff (see 94. *1*), being nominally less powerful than the sacred king. Castor therefore, not Polydeuces, is the authority on war – he even instructs Heracles in military arts, thus identifying himself with Iphicles – and Lynceus, not Idas, is gifted with acute vision. But until the double-kingdom system had been evolved, the tanist was not regarded as immortal, nor granted the same posthumous status as his twin.

2. The Spartans were frequently at war with the Messenians and, in Classical times, had sufficient military power, and influence over the Delphic Oracle, to impose their twin heroes on the rest of Greece, as enjoying greater favour with Father Zeus than any other pair; and the Spartan kingdom did indeed outlast all its rivals. Had this not been so, the constellation of the Twins might have commemorated Heracles and Iphicles, or Idas and Lynceus, or Acrisius and Proetus − instead of merely Castor and Polydeuces, who were not even the only heroes privileged to ride white horses: every hero worthy of a hero-feast was a horseman. It is these sunset feasts, at which a whole ox was eaten by the hero's descendants, that account for the gluttony attributed to Lepreus (see 138. *h*) and Heracles (see 143. *a*); and here to Idas, Lynceus and their rivals.

3. Marriage to the Leucippides enroyalled the Spartan co-kings. They were described as priestesses of Athene and Artemis, and given moonnames, being, in fact, the Moon-goddess's representatives; thus, in vasepaintings, the chariot of Selene is frequently attended by the Dioscuri. As the Spirit of the Waxing Year, the sacred king would naturally mate with Artemis, a Moon-goddess of spring and summer; and his tanist, as Spirit of the Waning Year, with Athene, who had become a Moongoddess of autumn and winter. The mythographer is suggesting that the Spartans defeated the Messenians, and that their leaders forcibly married the heiresses of Arene, a principal city of Messenia, where the Mareheaded Mother was worshipped; thus establishing a claim to the surrounding region.

4. Similarly with Marpessa: apparently the Messenians made a raid on the Aetolians in the Evenus valley, where the Sow-mother was worshipped, and carried off the heiress, Marpessa ('snatcher' or 'gobbler'). They were opposed by the Spartans, worshippers of Apollo, who grudged them their success; the dispute was then referred to the central authority at Mycenae, which supported the Messenians. But Evenus's chariot-race with Idas recalls the Pelops-Oenomaus (see 109. *j*) and the Heracles-Cycnus (see 143. *e–g*) myths. In each case the skulls of the king's rivals are mentioned. The icon from which all these stories are deduced must have shown the old king heading for his destined chariot crash (see 71. *1*) after having offered seven annual surrogates to the goddess (see 42. *2*). His horses are sacrificed as a preliminary to the installation of the new king (see 29. *1* and 81. *4*). The drowning of Evenus is probably misread: it shows Idas being purified before marriage and then riding off triumphantly in the Queen's chariot. Yet these Pelasgian marriage rites have been combined in the story with the Hellenic custom of marriage by capture. The fatal cattle-raid may record a historical incident: a quarrel between the Messenians and Spartans about the sharing of spoil in a joint expedition against Arcadia (see 17. *1*).

5. Castor and Polydeuces's visit to Phormio's house is disingenuously described: the author is relating another trick played on the stupid Spartans by an impersonation of their national heroes. Cyrene, where the

Dioscuri were worshipped, supplied herb-benjamin, a kind of asafoetida, the strong smell and taste of which made it valued as a condiment. The two Cyrenian merchants were obviously what they professed themselves to be, and when they went off with Phormio's daughter, left their wares behind in payment: Phormio decided to call it a miracle.

6. Wild pear-trees were sacred to the Moon because of their white blossom, and the most ancient image of the Death-goddess Hera, in the Heraeum at Mycenae, was made of pear-wood. Plutarch (*Greek Questions* 51) and Aelian (*Varia Historia* iii. 39) mention the pear as a fruit peculiarly venerated at Argos and Tiryns; hence the Peloponnese was called Apia, 'of the pear-tree' (see 64. 4). Athene, also a Death-goddess, had the surname Oncë ('pear-tree') at her pear-sanctuary in Boeotia. The Dioscuri chose this tree for their perch in order to show that they were genuine heroes; moreover, the pear-tree forms fruit towards the end of May (see 72. 2), when the sun is in the house of the Twins; and when the sailing season begins in the Eastern Mediterranean. Sparrows that follow the Dioscuri, when they appear in answer to sailors' prayers, belong to the Sea-goddess Aphrodite; Xuthus ('sparrow'), the father of Aeolus (see 43. 1), was an ancestor of the Dioscuri, who worshipped her.

7. In the *Homeric Hymn to the Dioscuri* (7 ff.), it is not made clear whether Castor and Polydeuces are followed by sparrows or whether they come darting on 'sparrowy wings' through the upper air, to help distressed sailors; but on Etruscan mirrors they are sometimes pictured as winged. Their symbol at Sparta, the *docana*, represented the two supporting pillars of a shrine; another symbol consisted of two amphoras, each entwined by a serpent – the serpents being the incarnate Dioscuri who came to eat food placed in the amphoras.

8. Gorgophone defied the Indo-European convention of suttee by marrying again (see 69. 2; 74. *a* and 106. *l*).

75

BELLEROPHON

BELLEROPHON, son of Glaucus and grandson of Sisyphus, left Corinth under a cloud, having first killed one Bellerus – which earned him his nickname Bellerophontes, shortened to Bellerophon – and then his own brother, whose name is usually given as Deliades.[1] He fled as a suppliant to Proetus, King of Tiryns; but (so ill luck would have it) Anteia, Proetus's wife whom some call Stheneboea, fell in love with him at sight. When he rejected her advances, she accused him of having tried to seduce her, and Proetus, who believed the story, grew incensed. Yet he dared not risk the Furies' vengeance by the direct murder of a suppliant, and therefore sent him to Anteia's father Iobates, King of Lycia, carrying a sealed letter, which read: 'Pray remove the bearer from this world; he has tried to violate my wife, your daughter.'

b. Iobates, equally loth to ill-treat a royal guest, asked Bellerophon to do him the service of destroying the Chimaera, a fire-breathing she-monster with lion's head, goat's body, and serpent's tail. 'She is', he explained, 'a daughter of Echidne, whom my enemy, the King of Caria, has made a household pet.' Before setting about this task, Bellerophon consulted the seer Polyeidus, and was advised to catch and tame the winged horse Pegasus, beloved by the Muses of Mount Helicon, for whom he had created the well Hippocrene by stamping his moon-shaped hoof.[2]

c. Pegasus was absent from Helicon, but Bellerophon found him drinking at Peirene, on the Acropolis of Corinth, another of his wells; and threw over his head a golden bridle, Athene's timely present. But some say that Athene gave Pegasus already bridled to Bellerophon; and others, that Poseidon, who was really Bellerophon's father, did so. Be that as it may, Bellerophon overcame the Chimaera by flying above her on Pegasus's back, riddling her with arrows, and then thrusting between her jaws a lump of lead which he had fixed to the point of his spear. The Chimaera's fiery breath melted the lead, which trickled down her throat, searing her vitals.[3]

d. Iobates, however, far from rewarding Bellerophon for this daring feat, sent him at once against the warlike Solymians and their allies, the Amazons; both of whom he conquered by soaring above them, well out of bowshot, and dropping large boulders on their heads. Next, in the Lycian Plain of Xanthus, he beat off a band of Carian pirates led by one Cheimarrhus, a fiery and boastful warrior, who sailed in a ship adorned with a lion figurehead and a serpent stern. When Iobates showed no gratitude even then but, on the contrary, sent the palace guards to ambush him on his return, Bellerophon dismounted and prayed that, while he advanced on foot, Poseidon would flood the Xanthian Plain behind him. Poseidon heard his prayer, and sent great waves rolling slowly forward as Bellerophon approached Iobates's palace; and, because no man could persuade him to retire, the Xanthian women hoisted their skirts to the waist and came rushing towards him full butt, offering themselves to him one and all, if only he would relent. Bellerophon's modesty was such that he turned tail and ran; and the waves retreated with him.

e. Convinced now that Proetus must have been mistaken about the attempt on Anteia's virtue, Iobates produced the letter, and demanded an exact account of the affair. On learning the truth, he implored Bellerophon's forgiveness, gave him his daughter Philonoë in marriage, and made him heir to the Lycian throne. He also praised the Xanthian women for their resourcefulness and ordered that, in future, all Xanthians should reckon descent from the mother, not the father.

f. Bellerophon, at the height of his fortune, presumptuously undertook a flight to Olympus, as though he were an immortal; but Zeus sent a gadfly, which stung Pegasus under the tail, making him rear and fling Bellerophon ingloriously to earth. Pegasus completed the flight to Olympus, where Zeus now uses him as a pack-beast for thunderbolts; and Bellerophon, who had fallen into a thorn-bush, wandered about the earth, lame, blind, lonely and accursed, always avoiding the paths of men, until death overtook him.[4]

1. Apollodorus: i. 9. 3; Homer: *Iliad* vi. 155.
2. Homer: *Iliad* vi. 160; Eustathius *on the same text*; Apollodorus: ii. 3. 1; Antoninus Liberalis: 9; Homer: *Iliad* xvi. 328 ff.
3. Hesiod *Theogony* 319 ff.; Apollodorus: ii. 3. 2; Pindar: *Olympian Odes* xiii. 63 ff.; Pausanias: ii. 4. 1; Hyginus: *Fabula* 157; Scholiast on Homer's *Iliad* vi. 155; Tzetzes: *On Lycophron* 17.
4. Pindar: *Olympian Odes* xiii. 87–90; *Isthmian Odes* vii. 44; Apollodorus: *loc. cit.*; Plutarch: *On the Virtues of Women* 9; Homer: *Iliad* vi. 155–203 and xvi. 328; Ovid: *Metamorphoses* ix. 646; Tzetzes: *On Lycophron* 838.

*

1. Anteia's attempted seduction of Bellerophon has several Greek parallels (see 70. 2), besides a Palestinian parallel in the story of Joseph and Potiphar's wife, and an Egyptian parallel in *The Tale of the Two Brothers*. The provenience of the myth is uncertain.

2. Echnide's daughter, the Chimaera, who is depicted on a Hittite building at Carchemish, was a symbol of the Great Goddess's tripartite Sacred Year – lion for spring, goat for summer, serpent for winter. A damaged glass plaque found at Dendra near Mycenae shows a hero tussling with a lion, from the back of which emerges what appears to be a goat's head; the tail is long and serpentine. Since the plaque dates from a period when the goddess was still supreme, this icon – paralleled in an

Etruscan fresco at Tarquinia, though the hero here is mounted, like Bellerophon – must be read as a king's coronation combat against men in beast disguise (see 81. 2 and 123. 1) who represent the different seasons of the year. After the Achaean religious revolution which subordinated the goddess Hera to Zeus, the icon became ambivalent: it could also be read as recording the suppression by Hellenic invaders, of the ancient Carian calendar.

3. Bellerophon's taming of Pegasus, the Moon-horse used in rain-making, with a bridle provided by Athene, suggests that the candidate for the sacred kingship was charged by the Triple Muse ('mountain goddess'), or her representative, with the capture of a wild horse; thus Heracles later rode Arion ('moon-creature on high') when he took possession of Elis (see 138. g). To judge from primitive Danish and Irish practice, the flesh of this horse was sacramentally eaten by the king after his symbolic rebirth from the Mare-headed Mountain-goddess. But this part of the myth is equally ambivalent: it can also be read as recording the seizure by Hellenic invaders of the Mountain-goddess's shrines at Ascra on Mount Helicon, and Corinth. A similar event is recorded in Poseidon's violation of the Mare-headed Arcadian Demeter (see 16. f), on whom he begot this same Moon-horse Arion; and of Medusa, on whom he begot Pegasus (see 73. h); which explains Poseidon's intrusion into the story of Bellerophon. How Zeus humbled Bellerophon is a moral anecdote told to discourage revolt against the Olympian faith; Bellerophon, the dart-bearer, flying across the sky, is the same character as his grandfather Sisyphus, or Tesup (see 67. 1), a solar hero whose cult was replaced by that of solar Zeus; he is therefore given a similarly luckless end, which recalls that of Helius's son Phaëthon (see 42. 2).

4. Bellerophon's enemies, the Solymians, were Children of Salma. Since all cities and capes beginning with the syllable *salm* have an easterly situation, she was probably the Goddess of the Spring Equinox; but she soon became masculinized as the Sun-god Solyma, or Selin, Solomon, or Ab-Salom, who gave his name to Jerusalem. The Amazons were the Moon-goddess's fighting priestesses (see 100. 1).

5. Bellerophon's retreat from the Xanthian women may have been deduced from an icon which showed the Wild Women maddened with *hippomanes* – either a herb, or the slimy vaginal issue of a mare in heat, or the black membrane cut from the forehead of a new-born foal – closing in on the sacred king by the seashore at the end of his reign. Their skirts were hoisted, as in the erotic worship of Egyptian Apis (Diodorus Siculus: i. 85), so that when they dismembered him, his spurting blood would quicken their wombs. Since Xanthus ('yellow') is the name of one of Achilles's horses, and of one belonging to Hector, and of one given to Peleus by Poseidon, these women perhaps wore ritual horse-masks

with moon-yellow manes, like those of palominos; for wild mares had
eaten Bellerophon's father Glaucus by the seashore of Corinth (see 71. 1).
Yet this reformed myth retains a primitive element: the approach of
naked women from the chieftain's own clan, with whom intercourse
was forbidden, would force him to retreat and hide his face, and in Irish
legend this same ruse was employed against Cuchulain, when his fury
could not otherwise be checked. The account of the Xanthian matrilineal
reckoning of descent has been turned inside out: it was the Hellenes who,
on the contrary, managed to enforce patrilineal reckoning on all Carians,
except the conservative Xanthians.

6. Cheimarrhus's name is derived from *chimaros*, or *chimaera* ('goat');
both his fiery nature and his ship with the lion figurehead and serpent
stern have been introduced into Bellerophon's story by some euhemerist
to explain away the fire-breathing Chimaera. Mount Chimaera ('goat-
mountain') was also the name of an active volcano near Phaselis in Lycia
(Pliny: *Natural History* ii. 106 and v. 27), which accounts for the fiery
breath.

76

ANTIOPE

SOME say that when Zeus seduced Antiope, daughter of Nycteus the
Theban, she fled to the King of Sicyon, who agreed to marry her, and
thus occasioned a war in which Nycteus was killed. Antiope's uncle
Lycus presently defeated the Sicyonians in a bloody battle and brought
her back, a widow, to Thebes. After giving birth in a wayside thicket
to the twins Amphion and Zethus, whom Lycus at once exposed on
Mount Cithaeron, she was cruelly ill-treated for many years by her
aunt Dirce. At last, she contrived to escape from the prison in which she
was immured, and fled to the hut where Amphion and Zethus, whom
a passing cattleman had rescued, were now living. But they mistook
Antiope for a runaway slave, and refused to shelter her. Dirce then
came rushing up in a Bacchic frenzy, seized hold of Antiope, and
dragged her away.

'My lads,' cried the cattleman, 'you had better beware of the Furies!'
'Why the Furies?' they asked.
'Because you have refused to protect your mother, who is now
being carried off for execution by that savage aunt of hers.'
The twins at once went in pursuit, rescued Antiope, and tied Dirce

by the hair to the horns of a wild bull, which made short work of her.[1]

b. Others say that the river Asopus was Antiope's father, and that one night the King of Sicyon impersonated Lycus, to whom she was married, and seduced her. Lycus divorced Antiope in consequence and married Dirce, thus leaving Zeus free to court the lonely Antiope, and get her with child. Dirce, suspecting that this was Lycus's doing, confined Antiope in a dark dungeon; from which, however, she was freed by Zeus just in time to bring forth Amphion and Zethus on Mount Cithaeron. The twins grew up among the cattlemen with whom Antiope had taken refuge and, when they were old enough to understand how unkindly their mother had been treated, she persuaded them to avenge her. They met Dirce roaming the slopes of Mount Cithaeron in a Bacchic frenzy, tied her by the hair to the horns of a wild bull and, when she was dead, flung her body on the ground; where a spring welled up, afterwards called the Dircaean Stream. But Dionysus avenged this murder of his votary: he sent Antiope raging madly all over Greece until at last Phocus, a grandson of Sisyphus, cured and married her in Phocis.

c. Amphion and Zethus visited Thebes, where they expelled King Laius and built the lower city, Cadmus having already built the upper. Now Zethus had often taunted Amphion for his devotion to the lyre given him by Hermes. 'It distracts you', he would say, 'from useful work.' Yet when they became masons, Amphion's stones moved to the sound of his lyre and gently slid into place, while Zethus was obliged to use main force, lagging far behind his brother. The twins ruled jointly in Thebes, where Zethus married Thebe, after whom the city – previously known as Cadmeia – is now named; and Amphion married Niobe. But all her children except two were shot dead by Apollo and Artemis, whose mother Leto she had insulted. Amphion was himself killed by Apollo for trying to take vengeance on the Delphic priests, and further punished in Tartarus.[2] Amphion and Zethus are buried in one grave at Thebes, which is guarded carefully when the sun is in Taurus; for then the people of Phocian Tithorea try to steal earth from the mound and place it on the grave of Phocus and Antiope. An oracle once said that this act would increase the fertility of all Phocis at the expense of Thebes.[3]

1. Hyginus: *Fabula* 8; Apollodorus: iii. 5. 5; Pausanias: ii. 6. 2; Euripides: *Antiope*, Fragments; Apollonius Rhodius: iv. 1090, with scholiast.

2. Homer: *Odyssey* xi. 260; Hyginus: *Fabula* 7; Pausanias: vi. 20. 8;
ix. 5. 3 and 17. 4; Horace: *Epistles* i. 18. 41; Apollonius Rhodius:
i. 735–41.

3. Pausanias: ix. 17. 3.

*

1. These two versions of the Dirce myth show how free the mythographers felt to make their narrative fit the main elements of a literary
tradition which, in this case, seems to have been deduced from a series
of sacred icons. Antiope, emerging joyfully out of her dungeon and
followed by the scowling Dirce, recalls Core's annual reappearance in
Hecate's company (see 24. *k*). She is called Antiope ('confronting') in this
context, because her face is upturned to the sky, not bent towards the
Underworld, and 'Daughter of Night' – Nycteis, not Nycteus – because
she emerges from the darkness. The 'raging on the mountain' by Dirce
and Antiope has been misinterpreted as a Bacchic orgy; theirs was clearly
an erotic gadfly dance, for which they behaved like Moon-heifers in heat
(see 56. *1*). Dirce's name ('double') stands for the horned moon, and the
icon from which the myth is taken will have shown her not being tied to
the bull in punishment, but ritually marrying the bull-king (see 88. *7*).
A secondary meaning may be concealed in *dirce*: namely 'cleft', that is,
'in an erotic condition'. The Dircaean spring, like Hippocrene, will have
been moon-shaped. Antiope's sons are the familiar royal twins borne by
the Moon-goddess: her sacred king and his tanist.

2. Amphion's three-stringed lyre, with which he raised the walls of
Lower Thebes – since Hermes was his employer, it can have had only
three strings – was constructed to celebrate the Triple-goddess, who
reigned in the air, on earth, and in the Underworld, and will have been
played during the building to safeguard the city's foundations, gates, and
towers. The name 'Amphion' ('native of two lands') records his citizen-
ship of Sicyon and Thebes.

77

NIOBE

NIOBE, sister of Pelops, had married Amphion King of Thebes and
borne him seven sons and seven daughters, of whom she was so
inordinately proud that, one day, she disparaged Leto herself for having
only two children: Apollo and Artemis. Mante, the prophetic daughter
of Teiresias, overhearing this rash remark, advised the Theban women

to placate Leto and her children at once: burning frankincense and wreathing their hair with laurel branches. When the scent of incense was already floating in the air, Niobe appeared, followed by a throng of attendants and dressed in a splendid Phrygian robe, her long hair flowing loose. She interrupted the sacrifice and furiously asked why Leto, a woman of obscure parentage, with a mannish daughter and a womanish son, should be preferred to her, Niobe, grandchild of Zeus and Atlas, the dread of the Phrygians, and a queen of Cadmus's royal house? Though fate or ill-luck might carry off two or three of her children, would she not still remain the richer?

b. Abandoning the sacrifice, the terrified Theban women tried to placate Leto with murmured prayers, but it was too late. She had already sent Apollo and Artemis, armed with bows, to punish Niobe's presumption. Apollo found the boys hunting on Mount Cithaeron and shot them down one by one, sparing only Amyclas, who had wisely offered a propitiatory prayer to Leto. Artemis found the girls spinning in the palace and, with a quiverful of arrows, despatched all of them, except Meliboëa, who had followed Amyclas's example. These two survivors hastened to build Leto a temple, though Meliboëa had turned so pale with fear that she was still nicknamed Chloris when she married Neleus some years later. But some say that none of Niobe's children survived, and that her husband Amphion was also killed by Apollo.

c. For nine days and nine nights Niobe bewailed her dead, and found no one to bury them, because Zeus, taking Leto's part, had turned all the Thebans into stone. On the tenth day, the Olympians themselves deigned to conduct the funeral. Niobe fled overseas to Mount Sipylus, the home of her father Tantalus, where Zeus, moved by pity, turned her into a statue which can still be seen weeping copiously in the early summer.[1]

d. All men mourned for Amphion, deploring the extinction of his race, but none mourned for Niobe, except her equally proud brother Pelops.[2]

1. Hyginus: *Fabulae* 9 and 10; Apollodorus: iii. 5. 6; Homer: *Iliad* xxiv. 612 ff.; Ovid: *Metamorphoses* vi. 146–312; Pausanias: v. 16. 3; viii. 2. 5 and i. 21. 5; Sophocles: *Electra* 150–52.
2. Ovid: *Metamorphoses* vi. 401–4.

*

1. The number of Niobe's children is given by Homer as twelve and (according to various scholiasts) by Hesiod as twenty, by Herodotus as

four, and by Sappho as eighteen; but the account followed by Euripides
and Apollodorus, which makes the best sense, is that she had seven sons
and seven daughters. Since Niobe, in the Theban version of the myth,
was a grand-daughter of the Titan Atlas, and, in the Argive version, was
daughter or mother of Phoroneus (see 57. *a*), also described as a Titan
(Apollodorus: ii. 1. 1 and Scholiast on Euripides's *Orestes* 932), and of
Pelasgus; and could claim to be the first mortal woman violated by Zeus
(Diodorus Siculus: iv. 9. 14; Apollodorus: *loc. cit.*; Pausanias: ii. 22. 6),
the myth may concern the defeat of the seven Titans and Titanesses by
the Olympians. If so, it records the supersession of the calendar system
prevailing in Pelasgian Greece, Palestine, Syria, and North-western
Europe; which was based on a month divided into four weeks of seven
days, each ruled by one of the seven planetary bodies (see 1. *3* and 43. *4*).
Amphion and his twelve children, in Homer's version of the myth
(*Iliad* xxiv. 603–17), perhaps stand for the thirteen months of this calendar.
Mount Sipylus may have been the last home in Asia Minor of the Titan
cult, as Thebes was in Greece. The statue of Niobe is a crag of roughly
human shape, which seems to weep when the sun's arrows strike its
winter cap of snow, and the likeness is reinforced by a Hittite Goddess-
mother carved in rock on the same mountain and dating from perhaps
the late fifteenth century B.C. 'Niobe' probably means snowy – the *b*
representing the *v* in the Latin *nivis*, or the *ph* in the Greek *nipha*. One of
her daughters is called Chiade by Hyginus: a word which makes no sense
in Greek, unless it be a worn-down form of *chionos niphades*, 'snow
flakes'.

2. Parthenius (*Love Stories* 33) gives a different account of Niobe's
punishment: by Leto's contrivance, Niobe's father fell incestuously in
love with her and, when she repulsed him, burned her children to death;
her husband was then mangled by a wild boar, and she threw herself
from a rock. This story, confirmed by the scholiast on Euripides's
Phoenician Women (159), is influenced by the myths of Cinyras, Smyrna
and Adonis (see 18. *h*), and by the custom of burning children to the god
Moloch (see 70. 5 and 156. 2).

78

CAENIS AND CAENEUS

POSEIDON once lay with the Nymph Caenis, daughter of Elatus the
Magnesian or, some say, of Coronus the Lapith, and asked her to name
a love-gift.

'Transform me', she said, 'into an invulnerable fighter. I am weary of being a woman.'

Poseidon obligingly changed her sex, and she became Caeneus, waging war with such success that the Lapiths soon elected her their king; and she even begot a son, Coronus, whom Heracles killed many years later while fighting for Aegimius the Dorian. Exalted by this new condition, Caeneus set up a spear in the middle of the market-place, where the people congregated, and made them sacrifice to it as if to a god, and honour no other deity whatsoever.

b. Zeus, hearing of Caeneus's presumption, instigated the Centaurs to an act of murder. During the wedding of Peirithous they made a sudden attack on her, but she had no difficulty in killing five or six of them, without incurring the slightest wound, because their weapons rebounded harmlessly from her charmed skin. However, the remaining Centaurs beat her on the head with fir logs, until they had driven her under the earth, and then piled a mound of logs above. So Caeneus smothered and died. Presently out flew a sandy-winged bird, which the seer Mopsus, who was present, recognized as her soul; and when they came to bury her, the corpse was again a woman's.[1]

1. Apollodorus: i. 9. 16; ii. 7. 7 and *Epitome* i. 22; Apollonius Rhodius: i. 57–64, with scholiast; Hyginus: *Fabula* 14; *Oxyrhynchus Papyri* xiii. p. 133 ff.; Servius on Virgil's *Aeneid* vi. 448; Ovid: *Metamorphoses* xii. 458–531; Scholiast on Homer's *Iliad* i. 264.

*

1. This myth has three distinct strands. First, a custom which still prevails in Albania, of girls joining a war-band and dressing in men's clothes, so that when they are killed in battle the enemy is surprised to discover their sex. Second, a refusal of the Lapiths to accept Hellenic overlordship; the spear set up for worship is likely to have been a maypole in honour of the New Moon-goddess Caenis, or Elate ('fir-tree'), to whom the fir was sacred. The Lapiths were then defeated by the Aeolians of Iolcus who, with the help of their allies the Centaurs, subjected them to their god Poseidon, but did not interfere with tribal law. Only, as at Argos, the clan chieftainess will have been obliged to assume an artificial beard to assert her right to act as magistrate and commander: thus Caenis became Caeneus, and Elate became Elatus. A similar change of sex is still announced by the Queen of the South, a joint ruler of the Lozi Kingdom in the Zambesi basin, when she enters the council chamber: 'I am transformed to a man!' – but this is because one of her ancestresses usurped a patriarchal throne. Third, the ritual recorded on a black-figured oil jar (see 9. 1), in

which naked men, armed with mallets, beat an effigy of Mother Earth on the head, apparently to release Core, the Spirit of the New Year: 'Caenis' means 'new'.

2. The variety of sandy-winged bird released from the effigy will depend on the season at which the rite was performed. If spring, it may have been a cuckoo (see 12. 1).

79

ERIGONE

ALTHOUGH Oeneus was the first mortal to be given a vine plant by Dionysus, Icarius anticipated him in the making of wine. He offered a sample from his trial jarful to a party of shepherds in the Marathonian woods beneath Mount Pentelicus, who, failing to mix it with water, as Oenopion later advised, grew so drunk that they saw everything double, believed themselves bewitched, and killed Icarius. His hound Maera watched while they buried him under a pine-tree and, afterwards, led his daughter Erigone to the grave by catching at her robe, and then dug up the corpse. In despair, Erigone hanged herself from the pine, praying that the daughters of Athens should suffer the same fate as hers while Icarius remained unavenged. Only the gods heard her, and the shepherds fled overseas, but many Athenian maidens were found hanging from the pine one after another, until the Delphic Oracle explained that it was Erigone who demanded their lives. The guilty shepherds were sought out at once and hanged, and the present Vintage Festival instituted, during which libations are poured to Icarius and Erigone, while girls swing on ropes from the branches of the tree, their feet resting on small platforms; this is how swings were invented. Masks are also hung from the branches, which twist around with the wind.

b. The image of Maera the hound was set in the sky, and became the Lesser Dog-star; some, therefore, identify Icarius with Boötes and Erigone with the constellation of the Virgin.[1]

1. Scholiast on Homer's *Iliad* xxii. 29; Nonnus: *Dionysiaca* xlvii. 34–245; Hyginus: *Fabula* 130 and *Poetic Astronomy* ii. 4; Apollodorus: i. 8. 1 and iii. 14. 7; Athenaeus: xiv. 10; Festus *sub* Oscil-

lantes; Statius: *Thebaid* xi. 644–7; Servius on Virgil's *Georgics* ii. 388–9.

*

1. Maera was the name given to Priam's wife Hecabe, or Hecuba, after her transformation into a dog (see 168. *1*), and since Hecuba was really the three-headed Death-goddess Hecate (see 31. *7*), the libations poured to Erigone and Icarius were probably meant for her. The valley in which this ceremony took place is now called 'Dionysus'. Erigone's pine will have been the tree under which Attis the Phrygian was castrated and bled to death (Ovid: *Fasti* iv. 221 ff.; Servius on Virgil's *Aeneid* ix. 116), and the explanation of the myth seems to be that when the Lesser Dog-star was in the ascendant, the shepherds of Marathon sacrificed one of their number as an annual victim to the goddess called Erigone.

2. Icarius means 'from the Icarian Sea', i.e. from the Cyclades, whence the Attis cult came to Attica. Later, the Dionysus cult was superimposed on it; and the story of the Athenian girls' suicide may have been told to account for the masks of Dionysus, hung from a pine-tree in the middle of a vineyard, which turned with the wind and were supposed to fructify the vines wherever they looked. Dionysus was usually portrayed as a long-haired, effeminate youth, and his masks would have suggested hanged women. But it is likely that dolls representing the fertility goddess Ariadne or Helen were previously hung from fruit-trees (see 88. *10* and 98. *5*). The girls' swinging at the vintage festival will have been magical in its original intention: perhaps the semi-circular flight of the swing represented the rising and setting of the new moon. This custom may have been brought to Attica from Crete, since a terracotta group found at Hagia Triada shows a girl swinging between two pillars, on each of which a bird is perched.

3. The name Erigone is explained by the mythographer as 'child of strife', because of the trouble she occasioned; but its obvious meaning is 'plentiful offspring', a reference to the plentiful crop induced by the dolls.

80

THE CALYDONIAN BOAR

OENEUS, King of Calydon in Aetolia, married Althaea. She first bore him Toxeus, whom Oeneus killed with his own hands for rudely leaping over the fosse which had been dug in defence of the city; and then Meleager, said to have been, in reality, her son by Ares. When

Meleager was seven days old, the Fates came to Althaea's bedroom and announced that he could live only so long as a certain brand on the hearth remained unburned. She at once snatched the brand from the fire, extinguishing it with a pitcherful of water, and then hid it in a chest.

b. Meleager grew up to be a bold and invulnerable fighter, and the best javelin-thrower in Greece, as he proved at Acastus's funeral games. He might still be alive but for an indiscretion committed by Oeneus who, one summer, forgot to include Artemis in his yearly sacrifices to the twelve gods of Olympus. Artemis, when informed of this neglect by Helius, sent a huge boar to kill Oeneus's cattle and labourers, and to ravage his crops; but Oeneus despatched heralds, inviting all the bravest fighters of Greece to hunt the boar, and promising that whoever killed it should have its pelt and tusks.

c. Many answered the call, among them Castor and Polydeuces from Sparta; Idas and Lynceus from Messene; Theseus from Athens and Peirithous from Larissa; Jason from Iolcus and Admetus from Pherae; Nestor from Pylus; Peleus and Eurytion from Phthia; Iphicles from Thebes; Amphiaraus from Argos; Telamon from Salamis; Caeneus from Magnesia; and finally Ancaeus and Cepheus from Arcadia, followed by their compatriot, the chaste, swift-footed Atalanta, only daughter of Iasus and Clymene.[1] Iasus had wished for a male heir and Atalanta's birth disappointed him so cruelly that he exposed her on the Parthenian Hill near Calydon, where she was suckled by a bear which Artemis sent to her aid. Atalanta grew to womanhood among a clan of hunters who found and reared her, but remained a virgin, and always carried arms. On one occasion she came fainting for thirst to Cyphanta and there, calling on Artemis, and striking a rock with the point of her spear, made a spring of water gush out. But she was not yet reconciled to her father.[2]

d. Oeneus entertained the huntsmen royally for nine days; and though Ancaeus and Cepheus at first refused to hunt in company with a woman, Meleager declared, on Oeneus's behalf, that unless they withdrew their objection he would cancel the chase altogether. The truth was that Meleager had married Idas's daughter Cleopatra, but now felt a sudden love for Atalanta and wished to ingratiate himself with her. His uncles, Althaea's brothers, took an immediate dislike to the girl, convinced that her presence could lead only to mischief, because he kept sighing deeply and exclaiming: 'Ah, how happy the man whom she marries!' Thus the chase began under bad auspices; Artemis herself had seen to this.

e. Amphiaraus and Atalanta were armed with bows and arrows; others with boar-spears, javelins, or axes, each being so anxious to win the pelt for himself that hunt discipline was neglected. At Meleager's suggestion, the company advanced in a half-moon, at some paces' interval, through the forest where the boar had its lair.

f. The first blood shed was human. When Atalanta posted herself on the extreme right flank at some distance from her fellow-hunters, two Centaurs, Hylaeus and Rhaecus, who had joined the chase, decided to ravish her, each in turn assisting the other. But as soon as they ran towards her, she shot them both down and went to hunt at Meleager's side.

g. Presently the boar was flushed from a water-course overgrown with willows. It came bounding out, killed two of the hunters, hamstrung another, and drove young Nestor, who afterwards fought at Troy, up a tree. Jason and several others flung ill-aimed javelins at the boar, Iphicles alone contriving to graze its shoulder. Then Telamon and Peleus went in boldly with boar-spears; but Telamon tripped over a tree root and, while Peleus was pulling him to his feet, the boar saw them and charged. Atalanta let fly a timely arrow, which sank in behind the ear, and sent it scurrying off. Ancaeus sneered: 'That is no way to hunt! Watch me!' He swung his battle-axe at the boar as it charged, but was not quick enough; the next instant he lay castrated and disembowelled. In his excitement, Peleus killed Eurytion with a javelin aimed at the boar, which Amphiaraus had succeeded in blinding with an arrow. Next, it rushed at Theseus, whose javelin flew wide; but Meleager also flung and transfixed its right flank, and then, as the boar whirled around in pain, trying to dislodge the missile, drove his hunting-spear deep under its left shoulder-blade to the heart.

The boar fell dead at last.

At once, Meleager flayed it, and presented the pelt to Atalanta, saying: 'You drew first blood, and had we left the beast alone, it would soon have succumbed to your arrow.'

h. His uncles were deeply offended. The eldest, Plexippus, argued that Meleager had won the pelt himself and that, on his refusal, it should have gone to the most honourable person present – namely himself, as Oeneus's brother-in-law. Plexippus's younger brother supported him with the contention that Iphicles, not Atalanta, had drawn first blood. Meleager, in a lover's rage, killed them both.

i. Althaea, as she watched the dead bodies being carried home, set a curse upon Mcleager; which prevented him from defending Calydon when his two surviving uncles declared war on the city and killed many of its defenders. At last his wife Cleopatra persuaded him to take up arms, and he killed both these uncles, despite their support by Apollo; whereupon the Furies instructed Althaea to take the unburned brand from the chest and cast it on the fire. Meleager felt a sudden scorching of his inwards, and the enemy overcame him with ease. Althaea and Cleopatra hanged themselvess, and Artemis turned all but two of Meleager's shrieking sisters into guinea-hens, which she brought to her island of Leros, the home of evil-livers.[3]

j. Delighted by Atalanta's success, Iasus recognized her at last as his daughter; but when she arrived at the palace his first words were: 'My child, prepare to take a husband!' – a disagreeable announcement, since the Delphic Oracle had warned her against marriage. She answered: 'Father, I consent on one condition. Any suitor for my hand must either beat me in a foot race, or else let me kill him.' 'So be it,' said Iasus.

k. Many unfortunate princes lost their lives in consequence, because she was the swiftest mortal alive; but Melanion, a son of Amphidamas the Arcadian, invoked Aphrodite's assistance. She gave him three golden apples, saying: 'Delay Atalanta by letting these fall, one after the other, in the course of the race.' The stratagem was successful. Atalanta stopped to pick up each apple in turn and reached the winning-post just behind Melanion.

l. The marriage took place, but the Oracle's warning was justified because, one day, as they passed by a precinct of Zeus, Melanion persuaded Atalanta to come inside and lie with him there. Vexed that his precinct had been defiled, Zeus changed them both into lions; for lions do not mate with lions, but only with leopards, and they were thus prevented from ever again enjoying each other. This was Aphrodite's punishment first for Atalanta's obstinacy in remaining a virgin, and then for her lack of gratitude in the matter of the golden apples.[4] But some say that before this Atalanta had been untrue to Melanion and borne Meleager a child called Parthenopaeus, whom she exposed on the same hill where the she-bear had suckled her. He too survived and afterwards defeated Idas in Ionia and marched with the Seven Champions against Thebes. According to others, Ares, not Meleager, was Parthenopaeus's father;[5] Atalanta's husband was not Melanion but Hippomenes; and she was the daughter of Schoeneus, who ruled

Boeotian Onchestus. It is added that she and he profaned a sanctuary not of Zeus but of Cybele, who turned them into lions and yoked them to her chariot.[6]

1. Aelian: *Varia Historia* xiii. 1; Callimachus: *Hymn to Artemis* 216.
2. Apollodorus: iii. 9. 2.
3. Homer: *Iliad* ix. 527–600; Apollodorus: i. 8. 2–3; Hyginus: *Fabulae* 171, 174, and 273; Ovid: *Metamorphoses* viii. 270–545; Diodorus Siculus: iv. 48; Pausanias: iv. 2. 5; viii. 4. 7; and x. 31. 2; Callimachus: *Hymn to Artemis* 220–24; Antoninus Liberalis: 2; Athenaeus: xiv. 71.
4. Apollodorus: iii. 9. 2; Hyginus: *Fabula* 185; Servius on Virgil's *Aeneid* iii. 113; First Vatican Mythographer: 39.
5. Hyginus: *Fabulae* 70, 99, and 270; First Vatican Mythographer: 174.
6. Apollodorus: iii. 9. 2, quoting Euripides's *Meleager*; Ovid: *Metamorphoses* x. 565 ff.; Tzetzes: *Chiliades* xiii. 453; Lactantius on Statius's *Thebaid* vi. 563; Hyginus: *Fabula* 185.

*

1. Greek physicians credited the marshmallow (*althaia*, from *althainein*, 'to cure') with healing virtue and, being the first spring flower from which bees suck honey, it had much the same mythic importance as ivy-blossom, the last. The Calydonian hunt is heroic saga, based perhaps on a famous boar hunt, and on an Aetolian clan feud occasioned by it. But the sacred king's death at the onset of a boar – whose curved tusks dedicated it to the moon – is ancient myth (see 18. *3*), and explains the introduction into the theory of heroes from several different Greek states who had suffered this fate. The boar was peculiarly the emblem of Calydon (see 106. *c*), and sacred to Ares, Meleager's reputed father.

2. Toxeus's leap over the fosse is paralleled by Remus's leap over Romulus's wall; it suggests the widespread custom of sacrificing a royal prince at the foundation of a city (1 *Kings* xvi. 34). Meleager's brand recalls several Celtic myths: a hero's death taking place when some external object – a fruit, a tree, or an animal – is destroyed.

3. Artemis was worshipped as a *meleagris*, or guinea-hen, in the island of Leros, and on the Athenian Acropolis; the cult is of East African origin, to judge from this particular variety of guinea-fowl – which had a blue wattle, as opposed to the red-wattled Italian bird introduced from Numidia – and its queer cluckings were taken to be sounds of mourning. Devotees of neither Artemis nor Isis might eat guinea-fowl. The Lerians' reputation for evil-living may have been due to their religious conservatism, like the Cretan's reputation for lying (see 45. *2*).

4. She-bears were sacred to Artemis (see 22. *4*), and Atalanta's race

against Melanion is probably deduced from an icon wich showed the doomed king, with the golden apples in his hand (see 32. *1* and 53. *5*), being chased to death by the goddess. A companion icon will have shown an image of Artemis supported by two lions, as on the gate at Mycenae, and on several Mycenaean and Cretan seals. The second version of the myth seems to be the older, if only because Schoeneus, Atalanta's father, stands for Schoenis, a title of Aphrodite's; and because Zeus does not figure in it.

5. Why the lovers were punished – here the mythographers mistakenly refer to Pliny, though Pliny says, on the contrary, that lions vigorously punish lionesses for mating with leopards (*Natural History* viii. 17) – is a problem of greater interest than Sir James Frazer in his notes on Apollodorus allows. It seems to record an old exogamic ruling, according to which members of the same totem clan could not marry one another, nor could lion clansmen marry into the leopard clan, which belonged to the same sub-phratry; as the lamb and goat clans could not intermarry at Athens (see 97. *3*).

6. Oeneus was not the only Hellenic king who withheld a sacrifice from Artemis (see 69. *b* and 72. *i*). Her demands were much more severe than those of other Olympian deities, and even in Classical times included holocausts of living animals. These Oeneus will hardly have denied her; but the Arcadian and Boeotian practice was to sacrifice the king himself, or a surrogate, as the Actaeon stag (see 22. *1*); and Oeneus may well have refused to be torn in pieces.

81

TELAMON AND PELEUS

The mother of Aeacus's two elder sons, namely Telamon and Peleus, was Endeis, Sciron's daughter. Phocus, the youngest, was a son of the Nereid Psamathe, who had turned herself into a seal while unsuccessfully trying to escape from Aeacus's embraces. They all lived together in the island of Aegina.[1]

b. Phocus was Aeacus's favourite, and his excellence at athletic games drove Telamon and Peleus wild with jealousy. For the sake of peace, therefore, he led a party of Aeginetan emigrants to Phocis – where another Phocus, a son of Ornytion the Corinthian, had already colonized the neighbourhood of Tithorea and Delphi – and in the course of time his sons extended the state of Phocis to its present limits.

One day Aeacus sent for Phocus, perhaps intending to bequeath him the island kingdom; but, encouraged by their mother, Telamon and Peleus plotted to kill him on his return. They challenged Phocus to a fivefold athletic contest, and whether it was Telamon who felled him, as if accidentally, by throwing a stone discus at his head, and Peleus who then despatched him with an axe, or whether it was the other way about, has been much disputed ever since. In either case, Telamon and Peleus were equally guilty of fratricide, and together hid the body in a wood, where Aeacus found it. Phocus lies buried close to the Aeaceum.[2]

c. Telamon took refuge in the island of Salamis, where Cychreus was king, and sent back a messenger, denying any part in the murder. Aeacus, in reply, forbade him ever again to set foot in Aegina, though permitting him to plead his case from the sea. Rather than stand and shout on the rocking deck of his ship anchored behind the breakers, Telamon sailed one night into what is now called the Secret Harbour, and sent masons ashore to build a mole, which would serve him as rostrum; they finished this task before dawn, and it is still to be seen. Aeacus, however, rejected his eloquent plea that Phocus's death was accidental, and Telamon returned to Salamis, where he married the king's daughter Glauce, and succeeded to Cychreus's throne.[3]

d. This Cychreus, a son of Poseidon and Salamis, daughter of the river Asopus, had been chosen King of Salamis when he killed a serpent to end its widespread ravages. But he kept a young serpent of the same breed which behaved in the same destructive way until expelled by Eurylochus, a companion of Odysseus; Demeter then welcomed it at Eleusis as one of her attendants. But some explain that Cychreus himself, called 'Serpent' because of his cruelty, was banished by Eurylochus and took refuge at Eleusis, where he was appointed to a minor office in Demeter's sanctuary. He became, at all events, one of the guardian heroes of Salamis, the Serpent Isle; there he was buried, his face turned to the west, and appeared in serpent form among the Greek ships at the famous victory of Salamis. Sacrifices were offered at his tomb, and when the Athenians disputed the possession of the island with the Megarians, Solon the famous law-giver sailed across by night and propitiated him.[4]

e. On the death of his wife Glauce, Telamon married Periboea of Athens, a grand-daughter of Pelops, who bore him Great Ajax; and later the captive Hesione, daughter of Laomedon, who bore him the equally well-known Teucer.[5]

f. Peleus fled to the court of Actor, King of Phthia, by whose adopted son Eurytion he was purified. Actor then gave him his daughter Polymela in marriage, and a third part of the kingdom. One day Eurytion, who ruled over another third part, took Peleus to hunt the Calydonian boar, but Peleus speared him accidentally and fled to Iolcus, where he was once more purified, this time by Acastus, son of Pelias.[6]

g. Acastus's wife, Cretheis, tried to seduce Peleus and, when he rebuffed her advances, lyingly told Polymela: 'He intends to desert you and marry my daughter Sterope.' Polymela believed Cretheis's mischievous tale, and hanged herself. Not content with the harm she had done, Cretheis went weeping to Acastus, and accused Peleus of having attempted her virtue.

h. Loth to kill the man whom he had purified, Acastus challenged him to a hunting contest on Mount Pelion. Now, in reward for his chastity, the gods had given Peleus a magic sword, forged by Daedalus, which had the property of making its owner victorious in battle and equally successful in the chase. Thus he soon piled up a great heap of stags, bears, and boars; but when he went off to kill even more, Acastus's companions claimed the prey as their master's and jeered at his want of skill. 'Let the dead beasts decide this matter with their own mouths!' cried Peleus, who had cut out their tongues, and now produced them from a bag to prove that he had easily won the contest.[7]

i. After a festive supper, in the course of which he outdid all others as a trencherman, Peleus fell fast asleep. Acastus then robbed him of his magic sword, hid it under a pile of cow-dung, and stole away with his followers. Peleus awoke to find himself deserted, disarmed, and surrounded by wild Centaurs, who were on the point of murdering him; however, their king Cheiron not only intervened to save his life, but divined where the sword lay hidden and restored it to him.[8]

j. Meanwhile, on the advice of Themis, Zeus chose Peleus to be the husband of the Nereid Thetis, whom he would have married himself, had he not been discouraged by the Fates' prophecy that any son born to Thetis would become far more powerful than his father. He was also vexed that Thetis had rejected his advances, for her foster-mother Hera's sake, and therefore vowed that she should never marry an immortal. Hera, however, gratefully decided to match her with the noblest of mortals, and summoned all Olympians to the wedding when the moon should next be full, at the same time sending her messenger

Iris to King Cheiron's cave with an order for Peleus to make ready.[9]

k. Now, Cheiron foresaw that Thetis, being immortal, would at first resent the marriage; and, acting on his instructions, Peleus concealed himself behind a bush of parti-coloured myrtle-berries on the shores of a Thessalian islet, where Thetis often came, riding naked on a harnessed dolphin, to enjoy her midday sleep in the cave which this bush half screened. No sooner had she entered the cave and fallen asleep than Peleus seized hold of her. The struggle was silent and fierce. Thetis turned successively into fire, water, a lion, and a serpent;[10] but Peleus had been warned what to expect, and clung to her resolutely, even when she became an enormous slippery cuttle-fish and squirted ink at him – a change which accounts for the name of Cape Sepias, the near-by promontory, now sacred to the Nereids. Though burned, drenched, mauled, stung, and covered with sticky sepia ink, Peleus would not let her go and, in the end, she yielded and they lay locked in a passionate embrace.[11]

l. Their wedding was celebrated outside Cheiron's cave on Mount Pelion. The Olympians attended, seated on twelve thrones. Hera herself raised the bridal torch, and Zeus, now reconciled to his defeat, gave Thetis away. The Fates and the Muses sang; Ganymedes poured nectar; and the fifty Nereids performed a spiral dance on the white sands. Crowds of Centaurs attended the ceremony, wearing chaplets of grass, brandishing darts of fir, and prophesying good fortune.[12]

m. Cheiron gave Peleus a spear; Athene had polished its shaft, which was cut from an ash on the summit of Pelion; and Hephaestus had forged its blade. The Gods' joint gift was a magnificent suit of golden armour, to which Poseidon added the two immortal horses Balius and Xanthus – by the West Wind out of the Harpy Podarge.[13]

n. But the goddess Eris, who had not been invited, was determined to put the divine guests at loggerheads, and while Hera, Athene, and Aphrodite were chatting amicably together, arm in arm, she rolled a golden apple at their feet. Peleus picked it up, and stood embarrassed by its inscription: 'To the Fairest!', not knowing which of the three might be intended. This apple was the protocatarctical cause of the Trojan War.[14]

o. Some describe Peleus's wife Thetis as Cheiron's daughter, and a mere mortal; and say that Cheiron, wishing to honour Peleus, spread the rumour that he had married the goddess, her mistress.[15]

p. Meanwhile Peleus, whose fortunes the kindly Cheiron had restored, and who now also acquired large herds of cattle as a dowry, sent some of these to Phthia as an indemnity for his accidental killing of Eurytion; but, when the payment was refused by the Phthians, left them to roam at will about the countryside. This proved to have been a fortunate decision, because a fierce wolf which Psamathe had sent after them, to avenge the death of her son Phocus, so glutted its hunger on these masterless cattle that it could hardly crawl. When Peleus and Thetis came face to face with the wolf, it made as if to spring at Peleus's throat, but Thetis glowered balefully, with protruded tongue and turned it into a stone, which is still pointed out on the road between Locris and Phocis.[16]

q. Later, Peleus returned to Iolcus, where Zeus supplied him with an army of ants transformed into warriors; and thus he became known as King of the Myrmidons. He captured the city single-handed, killed first Acastus, then the cowering Cretheis; and led his Myrmidons into the city between the pieces of her dismembered body.[17]

r. Thetis successively burned away the mortal parts of her six sons by Peleus, in order to make them immortal like herself, and sent each of them in turn up to Olympus. But Peleus contrived to snatch the seventh from her when she had already made all his body, except the ankle-bone, immortal by laying it on the fire and afterwards rubbing it with ambrosia; the half-charred ankle-bone had escaped this final treatment. Enraged by his interference, Thetis said farewell to Peleus, and returned to her home in the sea, naming her son 'Achilles', because he had as yet placed *no lips* to her breast. Peleus provided Achilles with a new ankle-bone, taken from the skeleton of the swift giant Damysus, but this was fated to prove his undoing.[18]

s. Too old to fight at Troy himself, Peleus later gave Achilles the golden armour, the ashen spear, and the two horses which had been his wedding presents. He was eventually expelled from Phthia by Acastus's sons, who no longer feared him when they heard of Achilles's death; but Thetis instructed him to visit the cave by the myrtle-bush, where he had first mastered her, and wait there until she took him away to live with her for ever in the depths of the sea. Peleus went to the cave, and eagerly watched the passing ships, hoping that one of them might be bringing his grandson Neoptolemus back from Troy.[19]

t. Neoptolemus, meanwhile, was refitting his shattered fleet in Molossia and, when he heard of Peleus's banishment, disguised himself as a Trojan captive and took ship for Iolcus, there contriving to kill

Acastus's sons and seize the city. But Peleus, growing impatient, had
chartered a vessel for a voyage to Molossia; rough weather drove her
to the island of Icos, near Euboea, where he died and was buried, thus
forfeiting the immortality which Thetis had promised him.[20]

1. Apollodorus: iii. 12. 6; Pindar: *Nemean Odes* v. 13.
2. Plutarch: *Parallel Stories* 25; Pausanias: x. 1. 1 and ii. 29. 7;
   Apollodorus: *loc. cit.*; *The Alcmaeonis*, quoted by scholiast on
   Euripides's *Andromache* 687; Tzetzes: *On Lycophron* 175; Diodorus Siculus: iv. 72.
3. Apollodorus: iii. 12. 7; Pausanias: ii. 29. 7; Diodorus Siculus: *loc. cit.*
4. Apollodorus: *loc. cit.*; Hesiod, quoted by Strabo: ix. 1. 9; Stephanus of Byzantium *sub* Kychreios Pagos; Eustathius on Dionysius's
   Description of the Earth 507; Plutarch: *Solon* 9; Lycophron: *Cassandra* 110; Pausanias: i. 36. 1.
5. Apollodorus: *loc. cit.*
6. *Ibid.*: iii. 13. 1–2; Diodorus Siculus: *loc. cit.*; Tzetzes: *On Lycophron* 175; Eustathius on Homer's *Iliad* ii. 648.
7. Pindar: *Nemean Odes* v. 26 ff. and iv. 59; Scholiast on Pindar's
   Nemean Odes iv. 54 and 59; Zenobius: *Proverbs* v. 20; Apollodorus: *loc. cit.*
8. Apollodorus: iii. 13. 3; Hesiod, quoted by Scholiast on Pindar's
   Nemean Odes iv. 59.
9. Apollonius Rhodius: iv. 790 ff.; Pindar: *Isthmian Odes* viii. 41ff.
10. Ovid: *Metamorphoses* xi. 221 ff.; Sophocles: *Troilus*, quoted by
    scholiast on Pindar's *Nemean Odes* iii. 35; Apollodorus: iii. 13. 5;
    Pindar: *Nemean Odes* iv. 62; Pausanias: v. 18. 1.
11. Tzetzes: *On Lycophron* 175 and 178; Scholiast on Apollonius
    Rhodius i. 582; Herodotus: vii. 191; Philostratus: *Heroica* xix. 1.
12. Euripides: *Iphigeneia in Aulis* 703 ff. and 1036 ff.; Apollonius
    Rhodius: iv. 790; Catullus: xliv. 305 ff.
13. Apollodorus: iii. 13. 5; Homer: *Iliad* xvi. 144; xviii. 84 and xvi.
    149; *Cypria* quoted by scholiast on Homer's *Iliad* xvi. 140.
14. Hyginus: *Fabula* 92; Fulgentius: iii. 7.
15. Apollonius Rhodius: i. 558; Scholiast on Apollonius Rhodius iv.
    816.
16. Antoninus Liberalis: *Transformations* 38; Tzetzes: *On Lycophron*
    175 and 901.
17. Tzetzes: *On Lycophron* 175; Homer: *Iliad* xxiv. 536; Pindar: *Ne-
    mean Odes* iii. 34; Apollodorus: iii. 13. 7; Scholiast on Apollonius
    Rhodius: i. 224.
18. Ptolemy Hephaestionos: iv, quoted by Photius: p. 487; Apollo-
    dorus: iii. 13. 6; Lycophron: *Cassandra* 178 ff.; Scholiast on
    Homer's *Iliad* xvi. 37.
19. Homer: *Iliad* xviii. 434 and xvi. 149; Euripides: *Trojan Women*
    1128, with scholiast; *Andromache* 1253 ff.

20. Dictys Cretensis: vi. 7–9; Stephanus of Byzantium *sub* Icos; *Palatine Anthology* vii. 2. 9 ff.

*

1. The myth of Aeacus, Psamathe ('sandy shore'), and Phocus ('seal') occurs in the folklore of almost every European country. Usually the hero sees a flock of seals swimming towards a deserted shore under a full moon, and then stepping out of their skins to reveal themselves as young women. He hides behind a rock, while they dance naked on the sand, then seizes one of the seal skins, thus winning power over its owner, whom he gets with child. Eventually they quarrel; she regains her skin and swims away. The dance of the fifty Nereids at Thetis's wedding, and her return to the sea after the birth of Achilles, appear to be fragments of the same myth – the origin of which seems to have been a ritual dance of fifty seal-priestesses, dedicated to the Moon, which formed a proem to the Chief-priestess's choice of a sacred king. Here the scene is set in Aegina but, to judge from the story of Peleus's struggle near Cape Sepias, a similar ritual was performed in Magnesia by a college of cuttle-fish priestesses – the cuttle-fish appears prominently in Cretan works of art, including the standard weight from the Royal Treasury at Cnossus, and also on megalithic monuments at Carnac and elsewhere in Brittany. It has eight tentacles, as the sacred anemone of Pelion has eight petals: eight being the number of fertility in Mediterranean myth. Peleus ('muddy') may have become the sacred king's title after he had been anointed with sepia, since he is described as the son of Endeis, 'the entangler', a synonym for the cuttle-fish.

2. Acastus's hunting party, the subsequent banquet, and the loss of Peleus's magic sword seem to be mistakenly deduced from an icon which showed the preliminaries to a coronation ceremony: coronation implying marriage to the tribal heiress. The scene apparently included the king's ritual combat with men dressed as beasts, and the drawing of a regal sword from a cleft rock (misinterpreted by the mythographer as a heap of cow dung) – as in the myths of Theseus (see 95. *e*) and King Arthur of Lyonesse. But the ashen spear cut by Cheiron from Mount Pelion is an earlier symbol of sovereignty than the sword.

3. Thetis's transformations suggest a display of the goddess's seasonal powers presented in a sequence of dances (see 9. *d* and 32. *b*). The myrtle behind which Peleus first met her, emblemized the last month of his predecessor's reign (see 52. *3* and 109. *4*); and therefore served as their rendezvous when his own reign ended.

This myth seems to record a treaty-marriage, attended by representatives of twelve confederate tribes or clans, between a Phthian prince and the Moon-priestess of Iolcus in Thessaly.

4. It may well be that the author of the old English *Seege or Battayle of Troy* drew on a lost Classical source when he made Peleus 'half man, half horse': that is to say, Peleus was adopted into an Aeacid horse-cult clan. Such an adoption will have implied a sacrificial horse-feast (see 75. 3): which explains the wedding gift of Balius and Xanthus without a chariot for them to draw. The Centaurs of Magnesia and the Thessalians of Iolcus seem to have been bound by an exogamic alliance: hence the statement by the scholiast on Apollonius Rhodius that Peleus's wife was, in reality, Cheiron's daughter.

5. Peleus's embarrassment when he looked at the apple thrown down by Eris suggests a picture of the Moon-goddess, in triad, presenting the apple of immortality to the sacred king (see 32. 4; 53. 5; and 159. 3). Acastus's murder, and Peleus's march into the city between the dismembered pieces of Cretheis's body, may be a misinterpretation of an icon which showed a new king about to ride through the streets of his capital after having ritually hacked his predecessor in pieces with an axe.

6. The frequent murders, accidental or intentional, which caused princes to leave home and be purified by foreign kings, whose daughters they then married, are an invention of later mythographers. There is no reason to suppose that Peleus left Aegina, or Phthia, under a cloud; at a time when kingship went by matrilineal succession, candidates for the throne always came from abroad, and the new king was reborn into the royal house after ritually murdering his predecessor. He then changed his name and tribe, which was expected to throw the vengeful ghost of the murdered man off his scent. Similarly, Telamon of Aegina went to Salamis, was chosen as the new king, killed the old king – who became an oracular hero – and married the chief-priestess of an owl college. It was found convenient, in more civilized times, when much the same ritual was used to purify ordinary criminals, to forget that kingship implied murder, and to suggest that Peleus, Telamon, and the rest had been involved in crimes or scandals unconnected with their accession to the throne. The scandal is frequently a false accusation of having attempted a queen's virtue (see 75. *a* and 101. *e*). Cychreus's connexion with the Eleusinian Mysteries and Telamon's marriage to an Athenian princess became important when, in 620 B.C., Athens and Megara disputed the possession of Salamis. The Spartans judged the case, and the Athenian ambassadors successfully based their claim on Telamon's connexion with Attica (Plutarch: *Solon* 8 and 9).

7. Phocus's death by the discus, like that of Acrisius (see 72. *p*), seems to be a misinterpretation of an icon which showed the end of the seal-king's reign – the flying discus being a sun-disk; as the myth makes plain, the sacrificial weapon was an axe. Several heroes besides Achilles were

killed by a heel wound, and not only in Greek but in Egyptian, Celtic, Lydian, Indian, and Norse mythology (see 90. 8 and 92. 10).

8. The burning of Thetis's sons was common practice: the yearly sacrifice of boy surrogates for the sacred king (see 24. 10 and 156. 2). At the close of the eighth year the king himself died (see 91. 4 and 109. 3). A parallel in the Indian *Mahabharata* is the drowning by the Ganges-goddess of her seven sons by the God Krishna. He saves the last, Bhishma; then she deserts him. Actor's division of his kingdom into three parts is paralleled in the myth of Proetus (see 72. h): the sacred king, instead of letting himself be sacrificed when his reign was due to end, retained one part of his kingdom, and bequeathed the remainder to his successors. Subsequent kings insisted on a lifetime tenure of sovereignty.

9. Peleus's death at Cos suggests that his name was a royal title there as well as at Phthia, Iolcus, and Salamis. He became king of the Myrmidons because the Phthians worshipped their goddess as Myrmex ('ant' – see 66. 2). Antoninus Liberalis's story of Thetis and the wolf seems to have been deduced from an icon which showed a priestess of Wolfish Aphrodite (Pausanias: ii. 31. 6) wearing a Gorgon mask as she sacrifices cattle.

82

ARISTAEUS

HYPSEUS, a high-king of the Lapiths, whom the Naiad Creusa bore to the River-god Peneius, married Chlidanope, another Naiad, and had by her a daughter, Cyrene. Cyrene despised spinning, weaving, and similar household tasks; instead, she would hunt wild beasts on Mount Pelion all day and half the night, explaining that her father's flocks and herds needed protection. Apollo once watched her wrestling with a powerful lion; he summoned King Cheiron the Centaur to witness the combat (from which Cyrene, as usual, emerged triumphant), asking her name, and whether she would make him a suitable bride. Cheiron laughed. He was aware that Apollo not only knew her name, but had already made up his mind to carry her off, either when he saw her guarding Hypseus's flocks by the river Peneius, or when she received two hunting dogs from his hands as a prize for winning the foot race at Pelias's funeral games.[1]

b. Cheiron further prophesied that Apollo would convey Cyrene overseas to the richest garden of Zeus, and make her the queen of a great city, having first gathered an island people about a hill rising from a plain. Welcomed by Libya to a golden palace, she would win a queendom equally beneficent to hunters and farmers, and there bear him a son. Hermes would act as man-midwife and carry the child, called Aristeus, or Aristaeus, to the enthroned Hours and Mother Earth, bidding them feed him on nectar and ambrosia. When Aristaeus grew to manhood, he would win the titles of 'Immortal Zeus', 'Pure Apollo', and 'Guardian of the Flocks'.[2]

c. Apollo duly took Cyrene away in his golden chariot, to the site of what is now the city of Cyrene; Aphrodite was waiting to greet their arrival, and bedded them without delay in Libya's golden chamber. That evening Apollo promised Cyrene a long life in which to indulge her passion for hunting and reign to over a fertile country. He then left her to the care of certain Myrtle-nymphs, children of Hermes, on the near by-hills, where she bore Aristaeus and, after a second visit from Apollo, Idmon the seer. But she also lay with Ares one night, and bore him the Thracian Diomedes, owner of the man-eating mares.[3]

d. The Myrtle-nymphs, nicknaming Aristaeus 'Agreus' and 'Nomius', taught him how to curdle milk for cheese, build bee-hives, and make the oleaster yield the cultivated olive. These useful arts he passed on to others, who gratefully paid him divine honours. From Libya he sailed to Boeotia, after which Apollo led him to Cheiron's cave for instruction in certain Mysteries.

e. When Aristaeus had grown to manhood, the Muses married him to Autonoë, by whom he became the father of the ill-fated Actaeon, and of Macris, nurse to Dionysus. They also taught him the art of healing and prophecy, and set him to watch over their sheep which grazed across the Athamantian Plain of Phthia, and about Mount Othrys, and in the valley of the river Apidanus. It was here that Aristaeus perfected the art of hunting, taught him by Cyrene.[4]

f. One day he went to consult the Delphic Oracle, and was told to visit the island of Ceos, where he would be greatly honoured. Setting sail at once, Aristaeus found that the scorching Dog-star had caused a plague among the islanders, in vengeance of Icarius whose secret murderers were sheltering among them. Aristaeus summoned the people, raised a great altar in the mountains, and offered sacrifices on it to Zeus, at the same time propitiating the Dog-star by putting the murderers to death. Zeus was gratified and ordered the Etesian Winds, in future, to cool all Greece and its adjacent islands for forty days from the Dog-star's rising. Thus the plague ceased, and the Ceans not only showered

Aristaeus with gratitude, but still continue to propitiate the Dog-star every year before its appearance.[5]

g. He then visited Arcadia and, later, settled at Tempe. But there all his bees died and, greatly distressed, he went to a deep pool in the river Peneius where he knew that Cyrene would be staying with her Naiad sisters. His aunt, Arethusa, heard an imploring voice through the water, put out her head, recognized Aristaeus, and invited him down to the wonderful palace of the Naiads. These washed him with water drawn from a perpetual spring and, after a sacrificial feast, he was advised by Cyrene: 'Bind my cousin Proteus, and force him to explain why your bees sickened.'

h. Proteus was taking his midday rest in a cave on the island of Pharos, sheltering from the heat of the Dog-star, and Aristaeus, having overcome him, despite his changes, learned that the bees' sickness was his punishment for having caused Eurydice's death; and it was true that, when he had made love to her on the river-bank near Tempe, she had fled from him and been bitten by a serpent.

i. Aristaeus now returned to the Naiads' palace, where Cyrene instructed him to raise four altars in the woods to the Dryads, Eurydice's companions, and sacrifice four young bulls and four heifers; then to pour a libation of blood, leaving the carcasses where they lay; and finally to return in the morning, nine days later, bringing poppies of forgetfulness, a fatted calf, and a black ewe to propitiate the ghost of Orpheus, who had now joined Eurydice below. Aristaeus obeyed and, on the ninth morning, a swarm of bees rose from the rotting carcasses, and settled on a tree. He captured the swarm, which he put into a hive; and the Arcadians now honour him as Zeus for having taught them this method of raising new swarms of bees.[6]

j. Later, distressed by the death of his son Actaeon, which roused in him a hatred of Boeotia, he sailed with his followers to Libya, where he asked Cyrene for a fleet in which to emigrate. She gladly complied, and soon he was at sea again, making north-westward. Enchanted by the savage beauty of Sardinia, his first landfall, he began to cultivate it and, having begotten two sons there, was presently joined by Daedalus; but is said to have founded no city there.[7]

k. Aristaeus visited other distant lands, and spent some years in Sicily, where he received divine honours, especially from the olive-growers. Finally he went to Thrace, and supplemented his education by taking part in the Mysteries of Dionysus. After living for a while

near Mount Haemus, and founding the city of Aristaeum, he disappeared without trace, and is now worshipped as a god both by the
Thracian barbarians and by civilized Greeks.[8]

1. Pindar: *Pythian Odes* ix. 5 ff.; Apollonius Rhodius: ii. 500 ff.;
   Callimachus: *Hymn to Artemis* 206.
2. Pindar: *loc. cit.*
3. Diodorus Siculus: iv. 81; Pindar: *loc. cit.*; Apollonius Rhodius:
   loc. cit.; Hyginus: *Fabula* 14; Apollodorus: ii. 5. 8.
4. Diodorus Siculus: *loc cit.*; Apollodorus: iii. 4. 4; Apollonius
   Rhodius: iv. 1131 and ii. 500 ff.; Pindar: *loc. cit.*
5. Apollonius Rhodius: ii. 500 ff.; Diodorus Siculus: iv. 82;
   Hyginus: *Poetic Astronomy* ii. 4.
6. Virgil: *Georgics* iv. 317–558; Pindar, quoted by Servius on Virgil's
   Georgics i. 14.
7. Servius: *loc. cit.*
8. Diodorus Siculus: *loc cit.*; Pausanias: x. 17. 3.

*

1. Aristaeus's origins have been embroidered upon by Pindar, to
flatter a descendant of Battus who, in 691 B.C., led a colony from Thera
to Libya, where he founded Cyrene, and was the first king of a long
dynasty. The Cyreneans claimed their ancestor Aristaeus – according to
Justin (xiii. 7), Battus ('tongue-tied') was only his nickname – as the son
of Apollo, because Apollo had been worshipped in Thera; and the port of
Cyrene was consequently called Apollonia. But Cyrene was a mythological figure long before Battus's time. Her association with the Centaurs
shows that she was goddess of a Magnesian horse cult imported to Thera;
for Cheiron's name also appears in early Theran rock inscriptions. The
myth of Idmon's birth from Cyrene and Ares refers to this earlier goddess.

2. Myrtle is originally a death-tree (see 109. *4*), and the Myrtle-nymphs
were therefore prophetesses capable of instructing young Aristaeus; but
it became symbolic of colonization, because emigrants took myrtle-
boughs with them to demonstrate that they had ended an epoch.

3. Aristaeus was a cult-title of Arcadian and Cean Zeus; and elsewhere
of Apollo and Hermes. According to Servius (on Virgil's *Georgics* i. 14)
Hesiod called Aristaeus 'a pastoral Apollo'. At Tanagra in Boeotia (Pausanias: ix. 22. 1) Hermes was known as 'Ram-bearer', and fish were
sacred to him at Pharae in Achaea (Pausanias: vii. 22. 2). Thus a tomb-
painting at Cyrene shows 'Aristaeus' surrounded by sheep and fish and
carrying a ram. His wanderings are offered in explanation of the cult-
title Aristaeus, which occurs in Sicily, Sardinia, Ceos, Boeotia, Thessaly,
Macedonia, and Arcadia. The Dog-star is the Egyptian god Thoth,
identified with Hermes, who was known as Aristaeus by the Ceans.

4. His raising of bees from the carcasses of cattle has been mistold by

Virgil. They will have swarmed, rather, from the lion which Cyrene killed, or which was killed in her honour. This myth, like that of Samson's bees which swarmed from a lion's carcass, seems to be deduced from a primitive icon showing a naked woman tussling amorously with a lion, while a bee hovers above the carcass of another lion. The naked woman is the Lion-goddess Cyrene, or Hepatu the Hittite, or Anatha of Syria, or Hera the Lion-goddess of Mycenae, and her partner is the sacred king, who is due to die under the midsummer sign of Leo, emblemized by a knife in the Egyptian Zodiac. Like Theseus or Heracles, he wears a lion mask and skin, and is animated by the spirit of the dead lion, his predecessor, which appears as a bee (see 90. *3*). This is spring-time, when bees first swarm, but afterwards, as the Midsummer Bee-goddess, she will sting him to death, and emasculate him (see 18. *3*). The lion which the sacred king himself killed – as did both Heracles and his friend Phylius (see 153. *e–f*) in the Peloponnese; or Cyzicus on Mount Dindymum in the Sea of Marmara (see 149. *h*); or Samson in Philistia (*Judges* xiv. 6); or David at Bethlehem (1 *Samuel* xvii. 34) – was one of the beasts which challenged him to a ritual combat at his coronation.

5. Virgil's account of Aristaeus's visit to the river Peneius illustrates the irresponsible use of myth: Proteus, who lived at Pharos off the Nile Delta, has been dragged into the story by the heels – there was a famous Oracle of Apollo at Tempe, which Aristaeus, his son, would naturally have consulted; Arethusa, a Peloponnesian stream, had no business in the Peneius; and Aristaeus is shown different chambers in the Naiads' palace where the sources of the Tiber, the Po, the Anio, the Phasis, and other widely separated rivers are kept – a mythologically absurd conception.

6. Exports of oil to Sicily will have been more profitable to the Cretans than that of olive-grafts; but once Hellenic colonies had been founded on the southern coast in late Mycenaean times, olive-culture was established there. The Aristaeus who visited Sicily may be identified with Zeus Morius, who was responsible for distributing grafts of the sacred olive-trees descended from the one planted by Athene on the Athenian Acropolis (see 16. *c*). He may also have introduced the science of bee-keeping which came to Athens from Minoan Crete, where professional bee-keepers had a bee and a glove as their trade device, and used terracotta hives. The Greek word for bee-bread, *cerinthos*, is Cretan; and so must all the related words be, such as *cērion*, 'honey-bomb', *cērinos*, 'waxen', and *cēraphis*, 'bee-moth' – a kind of locust. Cer, in fact, whose name (also spelt *Car* or *Q're*) came generally to mean 'fate', 'doom', or 'destiny' – multiplied into *ceres*, 'spites, plagues, or unseen ills' – must have been the Cretan Bee-goddess, a goddess of Death in Life. Thus the Sphinx-goddess of Thebes is called by Aeschylus (*Seven Against Thebes* 777) 'the man-snatching Cer'.

MIDAS

MIDAS, son of the Great Goddess of Ida, by a satyr whose name is not remembered, was a pleasure-loving King of Macedonian Bromium, where he ruled over the Brigians (also called Moschians) and planted his celebrated rose gardens.[1] In his infancy, a procession of ants was observed carrying grains of wheat up the side of his cradle and placing them between his lips as he slept – a prodigy which the soothsayers read as an omen of the great wealth that would accrue to him; and when he grew older, Orpheus tutored him.[2]

b. One day, the debauched old satyr Silenus, Dionysus's former pedagogue, happened to straggle from the main body of the riotous Dionysian army as it marched out of Thrace into Boeotia, and was found sleeping off his drunken fit in the rose gardens. The gardeners bound him with garlands of flowers and led him before Midas, to whom he told wonderful tales of an immense continent lying beyond the Oceans stream – altogether separate from the conjoined mass of Europe, Asia, or Africa – where splendid cities abound, peopled by gigantic, happy, and long-lived inhabitants, and enjoying a remarkable legal system. A great expedition – at least ten million strong – once set out thence across the Ocean in ships to visit the Hyperboreans; but on learning that theirs was the best land that the old world had to offer, retired in disgust. Among other wonders, Silenus mentioned a frightful whirlpool beyond which no traveller may pass. Two streams flow close by, and trees growing on the banks of the first bear fruit that causes those who eat it to weep and groan and pine away. But fruit growing by the other stream renews the youth even of the very aged: in fact, after passing backwards through middle age, young manhood, and adolescence, they become children again, then infants – and finally disappear! Midas, enchanted by Silenus's fictions, entertained him for five days and nights, and then ordered a guide to escort him to Dionysus's headquarters.[3]

c. Dionysus, who had been anxious on Silenus's account, sent to ask how Midas wished to be rewarded. He replied without hesitation: 'Pray grant that all I touch be turned into gold.' However, not only stones, flowers, and the furnishings of his house turned to gold but, when he sat down to table, so did the food he ate and the water he drank. Midas soon begged to be released from his wish, because he was fast dying of hunger and thirst; whereupon Dionysus, highly entertained, told him to visit the source of the river Pactolus, near Mount Tmolus, and there wash himself. He obeyed, and was at once freed from the golden touch, but the sands of the river Pactolus are bright with gold to this day.[4]

d. Midas, having thus entered Asia with his train of Brigians, was adopted by the childless Phrygian King Gordius. While only a poor peasant, Gordius had been surprised one day to see a royal eagle perch on the pole of his ox-cart. Since it seemed prepared to settle there all day, he drove the team towards Phrygian Telmissus, now a part of Galatia, where there was a reliable oracle; but at the gate of the city he met a young prophetess who, when she saw the eagle still perched on the pole, insisted on his offering immediate sacrifices to Zeus the King. 'Let me come with you, peasant,' she said, 'to make sure that you choose the correct victims.' 'By all means,' replied Gordius. 'You appear to be a wise and considerate young woman. Are you prepared to marry me?' 'As soon as the sacrifices have been offered,' she answered.

e. Meanwhile, the King of Phrygia had died suddenly, without issue, and an oracle announced: 'Phrygians, your new king is approaching with his bride, seated in an ox-cart!'

When the ox-cart entered the market place of Telmissus, the eagle at once attracted popular attention, and Gordius was unanimously acclaimed king. In gratitude, he dedicated the cart to Zeus, together with its yoke, which he had knotted to the pole in a peculiar manner. An oracle then declared that whoever discovered how to untie the knot would become the lord of all Asia. Yoke and pole were consequently laid up in the Acropolis at Gordium, a city which Gordius had founded, where the priests of Zeus guarded them jealously for centuries – until Alexander the Macedonian petulantly cut the knot with his sword.[5]

f. After Gordius's death, Midas succeeded to the throne, promoted the worship of Dionysus, and founded the city of Ancyra. The Brigians who had come with him became known as Phrygians, and the kings of Phrygia are alternately named Midas and Gordius to this day; so that the first Midas is now mistakenly described as a son of Gordius.[6]

g. Midas attended the famous musical contest between Apollo and Marsyas, umpired by the River-god Tmolus. Tmolus awarded the prize to Apollo who, when Midas dissented from the verdict, punished him with a pair of ass's ears. For a long time, Midas managed to conceal these under a Phrygian cap; but his barber, made aware of the deformity, found it impossible to keep the shameful secret close, as Midas had enjoined him to do on pain of death. He therefore dug a hole in the river-bank and, first making sure that nobody was about, whispered into it: 'King Midas has ass's ears!' Then he filled up the hole, and went away, at peace with himself until a reed sprouted from the bank and whispered the secret to all who passed. When Midas learned that his disgrace had become public knowledge, he condemned the barber to death, drank bull's blood, and perished miserably.[7]

1. Hyginus: *Fabula* 274; Philostratus: *Life of Apollonius of Tyana* vi. 27; Herodotus: i. 14 and viii. 138.
2. Cicero: *On Divination* i. 36; Valerius Maximus: i. 6. 3; Ovid: *Metamorphoses* xi. 92–3.
3. Aelian: *Varia Historia* iii. 18.
4. Plutarch: *Minos* 5; Ovid: *Metamorphoses* xi. 90 ff.; Hyginus: *Fabula* 191; Virgil; *Eclogues* vi. 13 ff.
5. Arrian: *Anabasis of Alexander* ii. 3.
6. Justin: xi. 7; Pausanias: i. 4. 5; Aelian: *Varia Historia* iv. 17.
7. Ovid: *Metamorphoses* xi. 146 ff.; Persius: *Satires* i. 121; Strabo: i. 3. 21.

*

1. Midas has been plausibly identified with Mita, King of the Moschians ('calf-men'), or Mushki, a people of Pontic origin who, in the middle of the second millennium B.C., occupied the western part of Thrace, afterwards known as Macedonia; they crossed the Hellespont about the year 1200 B.C., broke the power of the Hittites in Asia Minor, and captured Pteria, their capital. 'Moschians' refers perhaps to a cult of the bull-calf as the spirit of the sacred year. Midas's rose gardens and the account of his birth suggest an orgiastic cult of Aphrodite, to whom the rose was sacred. The story of the golden touch has been invented to account for the riches of the Mita dynasty, and for the presence of gold in the Pactolus river; and it is often said that the ass's ears were suggested by Midas's representation as a satyr, with hideously lengthened ears, in Athenian comic drama.

2. But since asses were sacred to his benefactor Dionysus, who set a pair of them among the stars (Hyginus: *Poetic Astronomy* ii. 23), it is likely that the original Midas gloried in his ass disguise. A pair of ass's ears at the tip of a reed sceptre was the token of royalty carried by all Egyptian dynastic gods, in memory of the time when ass-eared Set (see 35. 4) ruled their pantheon. Set had greatly declined in power until his temporary

revival by the Hyksos kings of the early second millennium B.C.; but because the Hittites formed part of the great horde of northern conquerors led by the Hyksos, ass-eared Midas may well have claimed sovereignty over the Hittite Empire in Set's name. In pre-dynastic times, Set had ruled the second half of the year, and annually murdered his brother Osiris, the spirit of the first half, whose emblem was a bull: they were, in fact, the familiar rival twins perpetually contending for the favours of their sister, the Moon-goddess Isis.

3. It is likely that the icon from which the story of Midas's barber derives showed the death of the ass-king. His sun-ray hair, the seat of royal power, is shorn off, like Samson's (see 91. 1); his decapitated head is buried in a hole to guard the city of Ancyra from invasion. The reed is an ambivalent symbol: as the 'tree' of the twelfth month (see 52. 3), it gives him an oracular warning of imminent death; it also enroyals his successor. Because of the great magical potency of bull's blood, only priestesses of the Earth-mother could drink it without harm (see 51. 4 and 155. a), and being the blood of Osiris, it would be peculiarly poisonous to an ass-king.

4. The secret of the Gordian knot seems to have been a religious one, probably the ineffable name of Dionysus, a knot-cypher tied in the rawhide thong. Gordium was the key to Asia (Asia Minor) because its citadel commanded the only practicable trade route from Troy to Antioch; and the local priestess or priest will have communicated the secret to the King of Phrygia alone, as the High-priest alone was entrusted with the ineffable name of Jehovah at Jerusalem. Alexander's brutal cutting of the knot, when he marshalled his army at Gordium for the invasion of Greater Asia, ended an ancient dispensation by placing the power of the sword above that of religious mystery. Gordius (from *gruzein*, 'to grunt' or 'grumble') was perhaps so named from the muttering at his oracular shrine.

5. Why the story of the Atlantic Continent should have been attributed to the drunken Silenus may be divined from three incidents reported by Plutarch (*Life of Solon* 25–9). The first is that Solon travelled extensively in Asia Minor and Egypt; the second, that he believed the story of Atlantis (see 39. b) and turned it into an epic poem; the third, that he quarrelled with Thespis the dramatist who, in his plays about Dionysus, put ludicrous speeches, apparently full of topical allusions, into the mouths of satyrs. Solon asked: 'Are you not alarmed, Thespis, to tell so many lies to so large an audience?' When Thespis answered: 'What does it matter when the whole play is a joke?', Solon struck the ground violently with his staff: 'Encourage such jokes in our theatre, and they will soon creep into our contracts and treaties!' Aelian, who quotes Theopompus as his authority, seems to have had access at second or third

hand to a comedy by Thespis, or his pupil Pratinas, ridiculing Solon for
the Utopian lies told in the epic poem, and presenting him as Silenus,
wandering footloose about Egypt and Asia Minor (see 27. *b*). Silenus and
Solon are not dissimilar names and as Silenus was tutor to Dionysus, so
Solon was tutor to Peisistratus who – perhaps on his advice – founded
the Dionysian rites at Athens (see 27. *5*).

6. It is possible that Solon during his travels had picked up scraps of
Atlantian lore which he incorporated in his epic, and which lent themselves to theatrical parody: such as the Gaelic legend of a Land of Youth
beyond the Ocean – where Niamh of the Golden Hair took Oisin, and
whence he returned centuries later on a visit to Ireland. Oisin, it will be
recalled, was disgusted with the degeneracy of his own people compared
with Niamh's, and bitterly regretted having come back. The unnavigable
whirlpool is the famous one, assumed by ancient physicists, where the
Ocean spills over the edge of the world into nothingness. Solon seems
also to have heard geographers discussing the possible existence of an
Atlantic Continent: Erathosthenes, Mela, Cicero, and Strabo speculated
on it and Seneca foretold its discovery in the second act of his *Medea* – a
passage which is said to have made a deep impression on the young
Columbus.

84

CLEOBIS AND BITON

CLEOBIS and Biton, two young Argives, were the sons of Hera's
priestess at Argos. When the time came for her to perform the rites of
the goddess, and the white oxen which were to draw her sacred chariot
had not yet arrived from the pasture, Cleobis and Biton, harnessing
themselves to the chariot, dragged it to the temple, a distance of nearly
five miles. Pleased with their filial devotion, the priestess prayed that
the goddess would grant them the best gift she could bestow on mortals; and when she had performed her rites, they went to sleep in the
temple, never to wake again.[1]

b. A similar gift was granted to Agamedes and Trophonius, sons of
Erginus. These twins had built a stone threshold upon foundations laid
by Apollo himself for his temple at Delphi. His oracle told them: 'Live
merrily and indulge yourselves in every pleasure for six days; on the
seventh, your heart's desire shall be granted.' On the seventh day both

were found dead in their beds. Hence it is said: 'Those whom the gods love die young.²

c. Trophonius was later awarded an oracle of his own at Lebadeia in Boeotia.³

1. Herodotus: i. 31; Pausanias: ii. 20. 2.
2. Pindar, quoted by Plutarch: *Consolation to Apollonius* 14; *Homeric Hymn to Apollo* 294–99; Menander: *Fragments of Greek Comedy* iv. 105, ed. Meinecke.
3. Herodotus: i. 46; Euripides: *Ion* 300.

*

1. The myth of Cleobis and Biton apparently refers to the human sacrifices offered when a new temple was dedicated to the Moon-goddess: at Argos, twin brothers were chosen as surrogates for the co-kings, and harnessed to a moon-chariot in place of the white bulls, the usual sacrifice. They will have been buried under the temple threshold to keep away hostile influences (see 169. *h*); perhaps this was why the twins Castor and Polydeuces (see 62. *c*) were sometimes called Oebalides, which may mean 'sons of the temple threshold' rather than 'of the speckled sheep-skin'. The priests of Apollo evidently adopted this practice at Delphi, although they denied the Moon-goddess, to whom the sacrifice should have been made, any foothold in the temple.

2. The seventh day, which was sacred to the Titan Cronus (and to Cronian Jehovah at Jerusalem) had 'repose' as its planetary function; but 'repose' signified death in the goddess's honour – hence the hero-oracle awarded to Trophonius (see 51. *1*).

85

NARCISSUS

NARCISSUS was a Thespian, the son of the blue Nymph Leiriope, whom the River-god Cephisus had once encircled with the windings of his streams, and ravished. The seer Teiresias told Leiriope, the first person ever to consult him: 'Narcissus will live to a ripe old age, provided that he never knows himself.' Anyone might excusably have fallen in love with Narcissus, even as a child, and when he reached the age of sixteen, his path was strewn with heartlessly rejected lovers of both sexes; for he had a stubborn pride in his own beauty.

b. Among these lovers was the nymph Echo, who could no longer use her voice, except in foolish repetition of another's shout: a punishment for having kept Hera entertained with long stories while Zeus's concubines, the mountain nymphs, evaded her jealous eye and made good their escape. One day when Narcissus went out to net stags, Echo stealthily followed him through the pathless forest, longing to address him, but unable to speak first. At last Narcissus, finding that he had strayed from his companions, shouted: 'Is anyone here?'

'Here!' Echo answered, which surprised Narcissus, since no one was in sight.

'Come!'

'Come!'

'Why do you avoid me?'

'Why do you avoid me?'

'Let us come together here!'

'Let us come together here!' repeated Echo, and joyfully rushed from her hiding place to embrace Narcissus. Yet he shook her off roughly, and ran away. 'I will die before you ever lie with me!' he cried.

'Lie with me!' Echo pleaded.

But Narcissus had gone, and she spent the rest of her life in lonely glens, pining away for love and mortification, until only her voice remained.[1]

c. One day, Narcissus sent a sword to Ameinius, his most insistent suitor, after whom the river Ameinius is named; it is a tributary of the river Helisson, which flows into the Alpheius. Ameinius killed himself on Narcissus's threshold, calling on the gods to avenge his death.

d. Artemis heard the plea, and made Narcissus fall in love, though denying him love's consummation. At Donacon in Thespia he came upon a spring, clear as silver, and never yet disturbed by cattle, birds, wild beasts, or even by branches dropping off the trees that shaded it; and as he cast himself down, exhausted, on the grassy verge to slake his thirst, he fell in love with his reflection. At first he tried to embrace and kiss the beautiful boy who confronted him, but presently recognized himself, and lay gazing enraptured into the pool, hour after hour. How could he endure both to possess and yet not to possess? Grief was destroying him, yet he rejoiced in his torments; knowing at least that his other self would remain true to him, whatever happened.

e. Echo, although she had not forgiven Narcissus, grieved with him;

she sympathetically echoed 'Alas! Alas!' as he plunged a dagger in his
breast, and also the final 'Ah, youth, beloved in vain, farewell!' as he
expired. His blood soaked the earth, and up sprang the white narcissus
flower with its red corollary, from which an unguent balm is now dis-
tilled at Chaeronea. This is recommended for affections of the ears
(though apt to give headaches), and as a vulnerary, and for the cure of
frost-bite.[2]

1. Ovid: *Metamorphoses* iii. 341–401.
2. Pausanias: viii. 29. 4 and ix. 31. 6; Ovid: *Metamorphoses* 402–510;
   Conon: *Narrations* 24; Pliny: *Natural History* xxi. 75.

*

1. The 'narcissus' used in the ancient wreath of Demeter and Persephone (Sophocles: *Oedipus at Colonus* 682–4), and also called *leirion* was
the three-petalled blue fleur-de-lys or iris: sacred to the Triple-goddess,
and worn as a chaplet when the Three Solemn Ones (see 115. c), or
Erinnyes, were being placated. It flowers in late autumn, shortly before
the 'poet's narcissus', which is perhaps why Leiriope has been described
as Narcissus's mother. This fanciful moral tale – incidentally accounting
for the medicinal properties of narcissus-oil, a well-known *narcotic*, as
the first syllable of 'Narcissus' implies – may be deduced from an icon
which showed the despairing Alcmaeon (see 107. e), or Orestes (see
114. a), lying crowned with lilies, beside a pool in which he has vainly
tried to purify himself after murdering his mother; the Erinnyes having
refused to be placated. Echo, in this icon, would represent the mocking
ghost of his mother, and Ameinius his murdered father.
2. But *-issus*, like *-inthus*, is a Cretan termination, and both Narcissus
and Hyacinthus seem to have been names for the Cretan springflower-
hero whose death the goddess bewails on the gold ring from the Mycenaean Acropolis; elsewhere he is called Antheus (see 159. 4), a surname of
Dionysus. Moreover, the lily was the royal emblem of the Cnossian king.
In a painted relief found among the Palace ruins, he walks, sceptre in hand,
through a lily-meadow, wearing a crown and necklace of fleur-de-lys.

86

PHYLLIS AND CARYA

PHYLLIS, a Thracian princess, was in love with Acamas a son of
Theseus, who had gone to fight at Troy. When Troy fell, and the

Athenian fleet returned, Phyllis paid frequent visits to the shore, hoping to sight his ship; but this had been delayed by a leak, and she died of grief after her ninth fruitless visit, at a place called Enneodos. She was metamorphosed by Athene into an almond-tree, and Acamas, arriving on the following day, embraced only her rough bark. In response to his caresses the branches burst into flower instead of leaf, which has been a peculiarity of almond-trees ever since. Every year, the Athenians dance in her honour, and in his.[1]

b. And Carya, daughter of a Laconian king, was beloved of Dionysus, but died suddenly at Caryae, and was metamorphosed by him into a walnut-tree. Artemis brought the news to the Laconians, who thereupon built a temple to Artemis Caryatis, from which Caryatids – female statues used as columns – take their name. At Caryae too, the Laconian women dance annually in the goddess's honour, having been instructed by the Dioscuri.[2]

1. Lucian: *On the Dance* 40; Hyginus: *Fabula* 59; Servius on Virgil's *Eclogues* v. 10; First Vatican Mythographer 159.
2. Pausanias: iii. 10. 8 and iv. 16. 5; Servius on Virgil's *Eclogues* viii. 29.

*

1. Both these myths are told to account for the festal use of almond or walnut, in honour of Car, or Carya (see 57. 2), otherwise known as Metis (see 1. d and 9. d), the Titaness of Wisdom; and are apparently deduced from an icon which showed a young poet worshipping a nut-tree in the goddess's presence, while nine young women performed a round dance. Enneodos, which occurs also in the legend of the Thracian Phyllis who drove Demophon mad (see 169. i), means 'nine journeys', and the number nine was connected with nuts by the Irish bards, and nuts with poetic inspiration; and in their tree-alphabet (see 52. 3) the letter *coll* ('C'), meaning 'hazel', also expressed the number nine. According to the Irish *Dinnschenchas*, the fountain of inspiration in the river Boyne was overhung by the nine hazels of poetic art, and inhabited by spotted fish which sang. Another Caryae ('walnut-trees') in Arcadia, stood close to a stream reported by Pausanias to contain the same peculiar kind of fish (Pausanias: vii. 14. 1–3 and 21. 1; Athenaeus: viii. p. 331).

2. The goddess Car, who gave her name to Caria, became the Italian divinatory goddess Carmenta, 'Car the Wise' (see 52. 5; 82. 6; 95. 5 and 132. o), and the Caryatids are her nut-nymphs – as the Meliae are ash-nymphs; the Mēliae, apple-nymphs; and the Dryads, oak-nymphs. Pliny has preserved the tradition that Car invented augury (*Natural History*

viii. 57). Phyllis ('leafy') may be a humble Greek version of the Palestinian and Mesopotamian Great Goddess Belili; in the Demophon myth she is associated with Rhea (see 169. j).

87

ARION

ARION of Lesbos, a son of Poseidon and the Nymph Oneaea, was a master of the lyre, and invented the dithyramb in Dionysus's honour. One day his patron Periander, tyrant of Corinth, reluctantly gave him permission to visit Taenarus in Sicily, where he had been invited to compete in a musical festival. Arion won the prize, and his admirers showered on him so many rich gifts that these excited the greed of the sailors engaged to bring him back to Corinth.

'We much regret, Arion, that you will have to die,' remarked the captain of the ship.

'What crime have I committed?' asked Arion.

'You are too rich,' replied the captain.

'Spare my life, and I will give you all my prizes,' Arion pleaded.

'You would only retract your promise on reaching Corinth,' said the captain, 'and so would I, in your place. A forced gift is no gift.'

'Very well,' cried Arion resignedly. 'But pray allow me to sing a last song.'

When the captain gave his permission, Arion, dressed in his finest robe, mounted on the prow, where he invoked the gods with impassioned strains, and then leaped overboard. The ship sailed on.

b. However, his song had attracted a school of music-loving dolphins, one of which took Arion on his back, and that evening he overtook the ship and reached the port of Corinth several days before it cast anchor there. Periander was overjoyed at his miraculous escape, and the dolphin, loth to part from Arion, insisted on accompanying him to court, where it soon succumbed to a life of luxury. Arion gave it a splendid funeral.

When the ship docked, Periander sent for the captain and crew, whom he asked with pretended anxiety for news of Arion.

'He has been delayed at Taenarus,' the captain answered, 'by the lavish hospitality of the inhabitants.'

Periander made them all swear at the dolphin's tomb that this was the truth, and then suddenly confronted them with Arion. Unable to deny their guilt, they were executed on the spot. Apollo later set the images of Arion and his lyre among the stars.[1]

c. Nor was Arion the first man to have been saved by a dolphin. A dolphin rescued Enalus when he leaped overboard to join his sweetheart Phineis who, in accordance with an oracle, had been chosen by lot and thrown into the sea to appease Amphitrite – for this was the expedition which the sons of Penthilus were leading to Lesbos as the island's first colonists – and the dolphin's mate rescued Phineis. Another dolphin saved Phalanthus from drowning in the Crisaean Sea on his way to Italy. Likewise Icadius, the Cretan brother of Iapys, when shipwrecked on a voyage to Italy, was guided by a dolphin to Delphi and gave the place its name; for the dolphin was Apollo in disguise.[2]

1. Herodotus: i. 24; Scholiast on Pindar's *Olympian Odes* xiii. 25; Hyginus: *Fabula* 194; Pausanias: iii. 25. 5.
2. Plutarch: *Banquet of the Seven Wise Men* 20; Pausanias: x. 13. 5; Servius on Virgil's *Aeneid* iii. 332.

*

1. Both Arion and Periander are historical characters of the seventh century B.C., and a fragment of Arion's *Hymn to Poseidon* survives. The story is perhaps based partly on a tradition that Arion's songs attracted a school of dolphins and thus dissuaded some sailors from murdering him for his money – dolphins and seals are notoriously susceptible to music – partly on a misinterpretation of a statue which showed the god Palaemon, lyre in hand, arriving at Corinth on dolphin-back (see 70. 5). Mythic colour is lent to the story by making Arion a son of Poseidon, as was his namesake, the wild horse Arion (see 16. *f*), and by giving his name to the Lyre constellation. Pausanias, a level-headed and truthful writer, doubts Herodotus's hearsay story about Arion; but reports that he has seen with his own eyes the dolphin at Poroselene, which was mauled by fishermen, but had its wounds dressed by a boy, coming in answer to the boy's call and gratefully allowing him to ride on its back (iii. 25. 5). This suggests that the ritual advent of the New Year Child was dramatically presented at Corinth with the aid of a tame dolphin trained by the Sun-priests.

2. The myth of Enalus and Phineis is probably deduced from an icon which showed Amphitrite and Triton riding on dolphins. Enalus is also associated by Plutarch with an octopus cult, and his name recalls that of

Oedipus the Corinthian New Year Child (see 105. *1*), whose counterpart he will have been at Mytilene, as Phalanthus was in Italy. Taras, a son of Poseidon by Minos's daughter Satyraea ('of the satyrs'), was the dolphin-riding New Year Child of Tarentum, which he is said to have founded, and where he had a hero shrine (Pausanias: x. 10. 4 and 13. 5; Strabo: vi. 3. 2); Phalanthus, the founder of Dorian Tarentum in 708 B.C., took over the dolphin cult from the Cretanized Sicels whom he found there.

3. Icadius's name, which means 'twentieth', is connected perhaps with the date of the month on which his advent was celebrated.

88

MINOS AND HIS BROTHERS

WHEN Zeus left Europe, after having fathered Minos, Rhadamanthys, and Sarpedon on her in Crete, she married Asterius, the reigning king, whose father Tectamus son of Dorus had brought a mixed colony of Aeolian and Pelasgian settlers to the island and there married a daughter of Cretheus the Aeolian.[1]

b. This marriage proving childless, Asterius adopted Minos, Rhadamanthys, and Sarpedon, and made them his heirs. But when the brothers grew to manhood, they quarrelled for the love of a beautiful boy named Miletus, begotten by Apollo on the Nymph Areia, whom some call Deione, and others, Theia.[2] Miletus having decided that he liked Sarpedon best, was driven from Crete by Minos, and sailed with a large fleet to Caria in Asia Minor, where he founded the city and kingdom of Miletus. For the previous two generations, this country, then called Anactoria, had been ruled by the giant Anax, a son of Uranus and Mother Earth, and by his equally gigantic son Asterius. The skeleton of Asterius, whom Miletus killed and afterwards buried on an islet lying off Lade, has lately been disinterred; it is at least ten cubits long. Some, however, say that Minos suspected Miletus of plotting to overthrow him and seize the kingdom; but that he feared Apollo, and therefore refrained from doing more than warn Miletus, who fled to Caria of his own accord.[3] Others say that the boy who occasioned the quarrel was not Miletus but one Atymnius, a son of Zeus and Cassiopeia, or of Phoenix.[4]

c. After Asterius's death, Minos claimed the Cretan throne and, in proof of his right to reign, boasted that the gods would answer whatever prayer he offered them. First dedicating an altar to Poseidon, and making all preparations for a sacrifice, he then prayed that a bull might emerge from the sea. At once, a dazzlingly white bull swam ashore, but Minos was so struck by its beauty that he sent it to join his own herds, and slaughtered another instead. Minos's claim to the throne was accepted by every Cretan, except Sarpedon who, still grieving for Miletus, declared that it had been Asterius's intention to divide the kingdom equally between his three heirs; and, indeed, Minos himself had already divided the island into three parts, and chosen a capital for each.[5]

d. Expelled from Crete by Minos, Sarpedon fled to Cilicia in Asia Minor, where he allied himself with Cilix against the Milyans, conquered them, and became their king. Zeus granted him the privilege of living for three generations; and when he finally died, the Milyan kingdom was called Lycia, after his successor Lycus, who had taken refuge with him upon being banished from Athens by Aegeus.[6]

e. Meanwhile, Minos had married Pasiphaë, a daughter of Helius and the nymph Crete, otherwise known as Perseis. But Poseidon, to avenge the affront offered him by Minos, made Pasiphaë fall in love with the white bull which had been withheld from sacrifice. She confided her unnatural passion to Daedalus, the famous Athenian craftsman, who now lived in exile at Cnossus, delighting Minos and his family with the animated wooden dolls he carved for them. Daedalus promised to help her, and built a hollow wooden cow, which he upholstered with a cow's hide, set on wheels concealed in its hooves, and pushed into the meadow near Gortys, where Poseidon's bull was grazing under the oaks among Minos's cows. Then, having shown Pasiphaë how to open the folding doors in the cow's back, and slip inside with her legs thrust down into its hindquarters, he discreetly retired. Soon the white bull ambled up and mounted the cow, so that Pasiphaë had all her desire, and later gave birth to the Minotaur, a monster with a bull's head and a human body.[7]

f. But some say that Minos, having annually sacrificed to Poseidon the best bull in his possession, withheld his gift one year, and sacrificed merely the next best; hence Poseidon's wrath; others say that it was Zeus whom he offended; others again, that Pasiphaë had failed for several years to propitiate Aphrodite, who now punished her with this monstrous lust. Afterwards, the bull grew savage and devastated the whole of Crete, until Heracles captured and brought it to Greece where it was eventually killed by Theseus.[8]

g. Minos consulted an oracle to know how he might best avoid scandal and conceal Pasiphaë's disgrace. The response was: 'Instruct Daedalus to build you a retreat at Cnossus!' This Daedalus did, and Minos spent the remainder of his life in the inextricable maze called the Labyrinth, at the very heart of which he concealed Pasiphaë and the Minotaur.[9]

h. Rhadamanthys, wiser than Sarpedon, remained in Crete; he lived at peace with Minos, and was awarded a third part of Asterius's dominions. Renowned as a just and upright law-giver, inexorable in his punishment of evildoers, he legislated both for the Cretans and for the islanders of Asia Minor, many of whom voluntarily adopted his judicial code. Every ninth year, he would visit Zeus's cave and bring back a new set of laws, a custom afterwards followed by his brother Minos.[10] But some deny that Rhadamanthys was Minos's brother, and call him a son of Hephaestus; as others deny that Minos was Zeus's son, making him the son of Lycastus and the nymph of Ida. He bequeathed land in Crete to his son Gortys, after whom the Cretan city is named, although the Tegeans insist that Gortys was an Arcadian, the son of Tegeates.[11] Rhadamanthys also bequeathed land in Asia Minor to his son Erythrus; and the island of Chios to Oenopion, the son of Ariadne, whom Dionysus first taught how to make wine; and Lemnos to Thoas, another of Ariadne's sons: and Cournos to Enyues; and Peparethos to Staphylus; and Maroneia to Euanthes; and Paros to Alcaeus; and Delos to Anius; and Andros to Andrus.[12]

i. Rhadamanthys eventually fled to Boeotia because he had killed a kinsman, and lived there in exile at Ocaleae, where he married Alcmene, Heracles's mother, after the death of Amphitryon. His tomb, and that of Alcmene, are shown at Haliartus, close to a plantation of the tough canes brought from Crete, from which javelins and flutes are cut. But some say that Alcmene was married to Rhadamanthys in the Elysian Fields, after her death.[13] For Zeus had appointed him one of the three Judges of the Dead; his colleagues were Minos and Aeacus, and he resided in the Elysian Fields.[14]

1. Diodorus Siculus: iv. 60 and v. 80.
2. Diodorus Siculus: iv. 60; Apollodorus: iii. 1. 2; Ovid: *Metamorphoses* ix. 442; Antoninus Liberalis: *Transformations* 30.
3. Pausanias: vii. 2. 3 and i. 35. 5; Ovid: *Metamorphoses* ix. 436 ff.

4. Apollodorus: *loc. cit.*; Scholiast on Apollonius Rhodius: ii. 178.
5. Strabo: x. 4. 8.
6. Apollodorus: *loc. cit.*; Herodotus: i. 173.
7. Diodorus Siculus: *loc. cit.*; Pausanias: vii. 4. 5; Virgil: *Eclogues* vi.
   5 ff.; Apollodorus: *loc. cit.* and iii. 1. 3–4.
8. Diodorus Siculus: iv. 77. 2 and 13. 4; First Vatican Mythographer:
   47; Hyginus: *Fabula* 40 [*but the text is corrupt*].
9. Ovid: *Metamorphoses* viii. 155 ff.; Apollodorus: iii. 1. 4.
10. Diodorus Siculus: iv. 60 and v. 79; Apollodorus: iii. 1. 2; Strabo:
    loc. cit.
11. Cinaethon, quoted by Pausanias: viii. 53. 2; Diodorus Siculus: iv.
    60; Pausanias: viii. 53. 2.
12. Scholiast on Apollonius Rhodius: iii. 997; Diodorus Siculus: v.
    79. 1–2.
13. Tzetzes: *On Lycophron* 50; Apollodorus: ii. 4. 11; Plutarch:
    Lysander 28; Strabo: ix. 11. 30; Pherecydes, quoted by Antoninus
    Liberalis: *Transformations* 33.
14. Diodorus Siculus: v. 79; Homer: *Odyssey* iv. 564.

*

1. Sir Arthur Evans's classification of successive periods of pre-Classical Cretan Culture as Minoan I, II, and III suggests that the ruler of Crete was already called Minos in the early third millennium B.C.; but this is misleading. Minos seems to have been the royal title of an Hellenic dynasty which ruled Crete early in the second millennium, each king ritually marrying the Moon-priestess of Cnossus and taking his title of 'Moon-being' from her. Minos is anachronistically made the successor of Asterius the grandson of Dorus, whereas the Dorians did not invade Crete until the close of the second millennium. It is more likely that the Aeolians and Pelasgians (perhaps including 'Ionians from Attica') brought in by Tectamus ('craftsman') – a name which identifies him with Daedalus, and with Hephaestus, Rhadamanthys's alleged father – were Minos's original companions; and that Asterius ('starry') is a masculinization of Asterië, the goddess as Queen of Heaven and creatrix of the planetary powers (see 1. *d*). *Crete* itself is a Greek word, a form of *crateia*, 'strong, or ruling, goddess' – hence Creteus, and Cretheus. Messrs M. Ventris and J. Chadwick's recent researches into the hitherto undeciphered Linear Script B, examples of which have been found at Pylus, Thebes, and Mycenae, as well as among the ruins of the Cnossian palace sacked in 1400 B.C., show that the official language at Cnossus in the middle of the second millennium was an early form of Aeolic Greek. The script seems to have been originally invented for use with a non-Aryan language and adapted to Greek with some difficulty. (Whether inscriptions in Linear Script A are written in Greek or Cretan has not yet been established.) A great number of names from Greek mythology occur in both Cretan and mainland tablets, among them: Achilles, Idomeneus, Theseus, Cretheus, Nestor, Ephialtes, Xuthus, Ajax, Glaucus, and Aeolus – which suggests that many of these myths date back beyond the Fall of Troy.

2. Since Miletus is a masculine name, the familiar myth of two brothers who quarrel for the favours of a woman was given a homosexual turn. The truth seems to be that, during a period of disorder following the Achaean sack of Cnossus in about 1400 B.C., numerous Greek-speaking Cretan aristocrats of Aeolo-Pelasgian or Ionian stock, for whom the Moon-goddess was the supreme deity, migrated with their native dependants to Asia Minor, especially to Caria, Lycia, and Lydia; for, disregarding the tradition of Sarpedon's dynasty in Lycia, Herodotus records that the Lycians of his time still reckoned by matrilinear descent (Herodotus: i. 173; Strabo: xii. 8. 5), like the Carians (see 75. 5). *Miletos* may be a native Cretan word, or a transliteration of *milteios*, 'the colour of red ochre, or red lead'; and therefore a synonym for Erythrus, or Phoenix, both of which mean 'red'. Cretan complexions were redder than Hellenic ones, and the Lycians and Carians came of partly Cretan stock; as did the Puresati (Philistines), whose name also means 'red men' (see 38. *3*).

3. The gigantic rulers of Anactoria recall the Anakim of *Genesis*, giants (*Joshua* xiv. 13) ousted by Caleb from the oracular shrine which had once belonged to Ephron the son of Heth (Tethys?). Ephron gave his name to Hebron (*Genesis* xxiii. 16), and may be identified with Phoroneus. These Anakim seem to have come from Greece, as members of the Sea-people's confederation which caused the Egyptians so much trouble in the fourteenth century B.C. Lade, the burial place of Anax's son Asterius, was probably so called in honour of the goddess Lat, Leto, or Latona (see 14. *2*), and that this Asterius bears the same name as Minos's father suggests that the Milesians brought it with them from the Cretan Miletus (see 25. *6*). According to a plausible tradition in the Irish *Book of Invasions*, the Irish Milesians originated in Crete, fled to Syria by way of Asia Minor, and thence sailed west in the thirteenth century B.C. to Gaetulia in North Africa, and finally reached Ireland by way of Brigantium (Compostela, in North-western Spain).

4. Miletus's claim to be Apollo's son suggests that the Milesian kings were given solar attributes, like those of Corinth (see 67. *2*).

5. The triumph of Minos, son of Zeus, over his brothers refers to the Dorian's eventual mastery of Crete, but it was Poseidon to whom Minos sacrificed the bull, which again suggests that the earlier holders of the title 'Minos' were Aeolians. Crete had for centuries been a very rich country and, in the late eighth century B.C., was shared between the Achaeans, Dorians, Pelasgians, Cydonians (Aeolians), and in the far west of the island, 'true Cretans' (*Odyssey* xix. 171–5). Diodorus Siculus tries to distinguish Minos son of Zeus from his grandson, Minos son of

Lycastus; but two or three Minos dynasties may have successively reigned in Cnossus.

6. Sarpedon's name ('rejoicing in a wooden ark') suggests that he brought with him to Lycia (see 162. *n*) the ritual of the Sun-hero who, at New Year, makes his annual reappearance as a child floating in an ark – like Moses, Perseus (see 73. *c*), Anius (see 160. *t*), and others. A Cretan connexion with the Perseus myth is provided by Pasiphaë's mother Perseis. Zeus's concession to Sarpedon, that he should live for three generations, means perhaps that instead of the usual eight years – a Great Year – which was the length of Minos's reign, he was allowed to keep his throne until the nineteenth year, when a closer synchronization of solar and lunar time occurred than at the end of eight; and thus broke into the third Great Year (see 67. 2).

7. Since 'Pasiphaë', according to Pausanias (iii. 26. 1), is a title of the Moon; and 'Itone', her other name, a title of Athene as rain-maker (Pausanias: ix. 34. 1), the myth of Pasiphaë and the bull points to a ritual marriage under an oak between the Moon-priestess, wearing cow's horns, and the Minos-king, wearing a bull's mask (see 76. 1). According to Hesychius (*sub* Carten), 'Gortys' stands for *Carten*, the Cretan word for a cow; and the marriage seems to have been understood as one between Sun and Moon, since there was a herd of cattle sacred to the Sun in Gortys (Servius on Virgil's *Eclogues* vi. 60). Daedalus's discreet retirement from the meadow suggests that this was not consummated publicly in the Pictish or Moesynoechian style. Many later Greeks disliked the Pasiphaë myth, and preferred to believe that she had an affair not with a bull, but with a man called Taurus (Plutarch: *Theseus* 19; Palaephatus: *On Incredible Stories* ii). White bulls, which were peculiarly sacred to the Moon (see 84. 1), figured in the annual sacrifice on the Alban mount at Rome, in the cult of Thracian Dionysus, in the mistletoe-and-oak ritual of the Gallic Druids (see 50. 2) and, according to the *Book of the Dun Cow*, in the divinatory rites which preceded an ancient Irish coronation.

8. Minos's palace at Cnossus was a complex of rooms, ante-rooms, halls, and corridors in which a country visitor might easily lose his way. Sir Arthur Evans suggests that this was the Labyrinth, so called from the *labrys*, or double-headed axe; a familiar emblem of Cretan sovereignty – shaped like a waxing and a waning moon joined together back to back, and symbolizing the creative as well as the destructive power of the goddess. But the maze at Cnossus had a separate existence from the palace; it was a true maze, in the Hampton Court sense, and seems to have been marked out in mosaic on a pavement as a ritual dancing pattern – a pattern which occurs in places as far apart as Wales and North-eastern Russia, for use in the Easter maze-dance. This dance was performed in Italy (Pliny: *Natural History* xxxvi. 85), and in Troy (Scholiast on Euripides's

Andromache 1139), and seems to have been introduced into Britain, towards the end of the third millennium B.C., by neolithic immigrants from North Africa. Homer describes the Cnossus maze (*Iliad* xviii. 592):

> Daedalus in Cnossus once contrived
> A dancing-floor for fair-haired Ariadne

and Lucian refers to popular dances in Crete connected with Ariadne and the Labyrinth (*On the Dance* 49).

9. The cult of Rhadamanthys may have been brought from Boeotia to Crete, and not contrariwise. Haliartus, where he had a hero-shrine, was apparently sacred to the 'White Goddess of Bread', namely Demeter; for *Halia*, 'of the sea', was a title of the Moon as Leucothea, 'the White Goddess' (Diodorus Siculus: v. 55), and *artos* means 'bread'. Alcmene ('strong in wrath') is another Moon-title. Though said to be a Cretan word, Rhadamanthys may stand for *Rhabdomantis*, 'divining with a wand', a name taken from the reed-bed at Haliartus, where his spirit stirred the tops oracularly (see 83. 3). If so, the tradition of his having legislated for all Crete and the islands of Asia Minor will mean that a similar oracle in Crete was consulted at the beginning of each new reign, and that its pronouncements carried authority wherever Cretan weights, measures, and trading conventions were accepted. He is called a son of Zeus, rather than of Hephaestus, doubtless because the Rhadamanthine oracles came from the Dictaean Cave, sacred to Zeus (see 7. b).

10. At Petsofa in Crete a hoard of human heads and limbs, of clay, have been found, each with a hole through which a string could be passed. If once fixed to wooden trunks they may have formed part of Daedalus's jointed dolls, and represented the Fertility-goddess. Their use was perhaps to hang from a fruit-tree, with their limbs moving about in the wind, to ensure good crops. Such a doll is shown hanging from a fruit-tree in the famous gold ring from the Acropolis Treasure at Mycenae. Tree worship is the subject of several Minoan works of art, and Ariadne, the Cretan goddess, is said to have hanged herself (*Contest of Homer and Hesiod* 14), as the Attic Erigone did (see 79. a). Artemis the Hanged One, who had a sanctuary at Condyleia in Arcadia (Pausanias: viii. 23. 6), and Helen of the Trees, who had a sanctuary at Rhodes and is said to have been hanged by Polyxo (Pausanias: iii. 19. 10), may be variants of the same goddess.

89

THE LOVES OF MINOS

MINOS lay with the nymph Paria, whose sons colonized Paros and were later killed by Heracles; also with Androgeneia, the mother of the lesser Asterius,[1] as well as many others; but especially he pursued Britomartis of Gortyna, a daughter of Leto. She invented hunting-nets and was a close companion to Artemis, whose hounds she kept on a leash.[2]

b. Britomartis hid from Minos under thick-leaved oak-saplings in the water meadows, and then for nine months he pursued her over craggy mountains and level plains until, in desperation, she threw herself into the sea, and was hauled to safety by fishermen. Artemis deified Britomartis under the name of Dictynna; but on Aegina she is worshipped as Aphaea, because she vanished; at Sparta as Artemis, surnamed 'the Lady of the Lake'; and on Cephallonia as Laphria; the Samians, however, use her true name in their invocations.[3]

c. Minos's many infidelities so enraged Pasiphaë that she put a spell upon him: whenever he lay with another woman he discharged, not seeds, but a swarm of noxious serpents, scorpions, and millepedes, which preyed on her vitals.[4] One day, Procris, daughter of the Athenian King Erechtheus, whom her husband Cephalus had deserted, visited Crete. Cephalus was provoked to this by Eos, who fell in love with him. When he politely refused her advances, on the ground that he could not deceive Procris, with whom he had exchanged vows of perpetual faithfulness, Eos protested that Procris, whom she knew better than he did, would readily forswear herself for gold. Since Cephalus indignantly denied this, Eos metamorphosed him into the likeness of one Pteleon, and advised him to tempt Procris to his bed by offering her a golden crown. He did so, and, finding that Procris was easily seduced, felt no compunction about lying with Eos, of whom she was painfully jealous.

d. Eos bore Cephalus a son named Phaëthon; but Aphrodite stole him while still a child, to be the night-watchman of her most sacred shrines; and the Cretans call him Adymnus, by which they mean the morning and the evening star.[5]

e. Meanwhile, Procris could not bear to stay in Athens, her desertion being the subject of general gossip, and therefore came to Crete, where Minos found her no more difficult to seduce than had the supposed Pteleon. He bribed her with a hound that never failed to catch his quarry, and a dart that never missed its mark, both of which had been given him by Artemis.[6] Procris, being an ardent huntress, gladly accepted these, but insisted that Minos should take a prophylactic draught – a decoction of magical roots invented by the witch Circe –

to prevent him from filling her with reptiles and insects. This draught
had the desired effect, but Procris feared that Pasiphaë might bewitch
her, and therefore returned hurriedly to Athens, disguised as a handsome boy, having first changed her name to Pterelas. She never saw
Minos again.

f. Cephalus, whom she now joined on a hunting expedition, did not
recognize her and coveted Laelaps, her hound, and the unerring dart so
much that he offered to buy them, naming a huge sum of silver. But
Procris refused to part with either, except for love, and when he agreed
to take her to his bed, tearfully revealed herself as his wife. Thus they
were reconciled at last, and Cephalus enjoyed great sport with the dog
and the dart. But Artemis was vexed that her valuable gifts should thus
be bandied from hand to hand by these mercenary adulterers, and
plotted revenge. She put it into Procris's head to suspect that Cephalus
was still visiting Eos when he rose two hours after midnight and went
off to hunt.

g. One night Procris, wearing a dark tunic, crept out after him in
the half light. Presently he heard a rustle in a thicket behind him,
Laelaps growled and stiffened, Cephalus let fly with the unerring dart
and transfixed Procris. In due course the Areiopagus sentenced him to
perpetual banishment for murder.[7]

h. Cephalus retired to Thebes, where King Amphitryon, the supposed father of Heracles, borrowed Laelaps to hunt the Teumessian
vixen which was ravaging Cadmeia. This vixen, divinely fated never
to be caught, could be appeased only by the monthly sacrifice of a child.
But, since Laelaps was divinely fated to catch whatever he pursued,
doubt arose in Heaven as to how this contradiction should be resolved:
in the end, Zeus angrily settled it by turning both Laelaps and the
vixen into stone.[8]

i. Cephalus next assisted Amphitryon in a successful war against the
Teleboans and Taphians. Before it began, Amphitryon made all his
allies swear by Athene and Ares not to hide any of the spoils; only one,
Panopeus, broke this oath and was punished by begetting a coward, the
notorious Epeius.[9] The Teleboan king was Pterelaus, on whose head
Poseidon, his grandfather, had planted a golden lock of immortality.
His daughter Comaetho fell in love with Amphitryon and, wishing to
gain his affections, plucked out the golden lock, so that Pterelaus died
and Amphitryon swiftly conquered the Teleboans with the help of
Cephalus; but he sentenced Comaetho to death for parricide.

j. Cephalus's share of the Teleboan dominions was the island of Cephallenia, which still bears his name. He never pardoned Minos for having seduced Procris and given her the fatal dart; nor yet could he acquit himself of responsibility. After all, he had been the first to forswear himself, because Procris's affair with the supposed Pteleon could not be reckoned as a breach of faith; 'No, no,' he grieved, 'I should never have bedded with Eos!' Though purified of his guilt, he was haunted by Procris's ghost and, fearing to bring misfortune on his companions, went one day to Cape Leucas, where he had built a temple to Apollo of the White Rock, and plunged into the sea from the cliff top. As he fell he called aloud on the name of Pterelas; for it was under this name that Procris had been most dear to him.[10]

1. Apollodorus: ii. 5. 9 and iii. 1. 2; Nonnus: *Dionysiaca* xiii. 222 and xl. 284.
2. Solinus: xi. 8; Callimachus: *Hymn to Artemis* 189; Euripides: *Iphigeneia Among the Taurians* 126; Diodorus Siculus: v. 76; Aristophanes: *Frogs* 1359.
3. Pausanias: ii. 30.3 and iii. 14. 2; Antoninus Liberalis: *Transformations* 40; Herodotus: iii. 59.
4. Antoninus Liberalis: *Transformations* 41.
5. Hesiod: *Theogony* 986; Solinus: xi. 9; Nonnus: *Dionysiaca* xi. 131 and xii. 217.
6. Apollodorus: ii. 4. 7; Ovid: *Metamorphoses* vii. 771; Hyginus: *Fabula* 189.
7. Apollodorus: *loc. cit.* and iii. 15. 1; Antoninus Liberalis: *loc. cit.*; Hyginus: *Fabulae* 125 and 189; Scholiast on Callimachus's *Hymn to Artemis* 209.
8. Pausanias: i. 37. 6 and ix. 19. 1.
9. Tzetzes: *On Lycophron* 933.
10. Apollodorus: ii. 4. 7; Strabo: x. 2. 9 and 14.

*

1. Minos's seduction of nymphs in the style of Zeus doubtless records the Cnossian king's ritual marriage to Moon-priestesses of various city states in his empire.

2. The Moon-goddess was called Britomartis in Eastern Crete. Hence the Greeks identified her with Artemis (Diodorus Siculus: v. 76; Euripides: *Hippolytus* 145 and *Iphigeneia Among the Taurians* 127; Hesychius *sub* Britomartis), and with Hecate (Euripides: *Hippolytus* 141, with scholiast). In Western Crete she was Dictynna, as Virgil knew: 'They called the Moon Dictynna after your name' (Virgil: *Ciris* 305). Dictynna is connected in the myth with *dictyon*, which means a net, of the sort used for hunting or fishing; and *Dicte* is apparently a worn-down form of

dictynnaeon – 'Dictynna's place'. After the introduction of the patriarchal system a murderous chase of the sacred king by the goddess armed with a net was converted into a love chase of the goddess by the sacred king (see 9. *1* and 32. *b*). Both chases occur frequently in European folklore (see 62. *1*). Minos's pursuit of Britomartis, which is paralleled in Philistia by Moxus's, or Mopsus's, chase of Derceto, begins when the oaks are in full leaf – probably in the Dog Days, which was when Set pursued Isis and the Child Horus in the water meadows of the Nile Delta – and ends nine months later, on May Eve. Zeus's seduction of Europe was also a May Eve event (see 58. *3*).

3. To judge from the ritual of the Celtic North, where the goddess is called Goda ('the Good') – Neanthes translates the syllable *brito* as 'good' (*Greek Historical Fragments* iii, ed. Müller) – she originally rode on a goat, naked except for a net, with an apple in one hand, and accompanied by a hare and a raven, to her annual love-feast. The carved *miserere* seat in Coventry Cathedral, where she was thus portrayed, recorded the pre-Christian May Eve ceremonies at Southam and Coventry, from which the legend of Lady Godiva has been piously evolved. In Celtic Germany, Scandinavia, and probably England too, Goda had ritual connexion with the goat, or with a man dressed in goat-skins – the sacred king who later became the Devil of the witch cult. Her apple is a token of the king's approaching death; the hare symbolizes the chase, during which she turns herself into a greyhound; her net will catch him when he becomes a fish; the raven will give oracles from his tomb.

4. It seems that, in Crete, the goat-cult preceded the bull-cult, and that Pasiphaë originally married a goat-king. Laphria ('she who wins booty'), Dictynna's title in Aegina, was also a title of the goat-goddess Athene, who is said to have been assaulted by the goatish Pallas, whose skin she flayed and converted into her aegis (see 9. *a*). 'Laphria' suggests that the goddess was the pursuer, not the pursued. Inscriptions from Aegina show that the great temple of Artemis belonged to Artemis Aphaea ('not dark', to distinguish her from Hecate); in the myth, Aphaea is taken to mean *aphanes*, 'disappearing'.

5. The story of Minos and Procris has passed from myth into anecdote, and from anecdote into street-corner romance, recalling some of the tales in the *Golden Ass*. Being linked with Minos's war against Athens, and the eventual downfall of Cnossus, it records, perhaps, the Cretan king's demand for a ritual marriage with the High-priestess of Athens, which the Athenians resented. Pteleon ('elm-grove'), the name of Procris's seducer, may refer to the vine-cult which spread from Crete in the time of Minos (see 88. *h*), since vines were trained on elms; but it may also be derived from *ptelos*, 'wild boar'. In that case, Cephalus and Pteleon will have originally been the sacred king and his tanist, disguised

as a wild boar (see 18. 7). Pasiphaë's witchcrafts are characteristics of an angry Moon-goddess; and Procris counters them with the witchcrafts of Circe, another title of the same goddess.

6. Cephalus's leap from the white rock at Cape Leucas rightly reminds Strabo (x. 2. 9) that the Leucadians used every year to fling a man, provided with wings to break his fall, and even with live birds corded to his body, over the cliff into the sea. The victim, a *pharmacos*, or scapegoat, whose removal freed the island from guilt, seems also to have carried a white sunshade as a parachute (see 70. 7). Boats were waiting to pick him up if he survived, and convey him to some other island (see 96. 3).

7. The myth of Comaetho and Pterelaus refers to the cutting of the solar king's hair before his death (see 83. 3; 91. 1 and 95. 5); but the name Pterelaus suggests that the winged *pharmacos* flung to his death was originally the king. The syllable *elāos*, or *elaios*, stands for the wild olive which, like the birch in Italy and North-western Europe, was used for the expulsion of evil spirits (see 52. 3); and in the Rhodian dialect *elaios* meant simply *pharmacos*. But the fates of Pterelaus and Cephalus are mythically linked by Procris's adoption of the name Pterelas, and this suggests that she was really the priestess of Athene, who launched the feathered Cephalus to his death.

8. The fox was the emblem of Messene (Apollodorus: ii. 8. 5 – see 49. 2 and 146. 6); probably because the Aeolians worshipped the Moongoddess as a vixen; and the myth of the Teumessian vixen may record Aeolian raids on Cadmeia in search of child sacrifices, to which Zeusworshipping Achaeans put an end.

9. Phaëthon and Adymnus (from *a-dyomenos*, 'he who does not set') are both allegorical names for the planet Venus. But Phaëthon, son of Eos and Cephalus, has been confused by Nonnus with Phaëthon, son of Helius, who drove the sun-chariot and was drowned (see 42. *d*); and with Atymnius (from *atos* and *hymnos*, 'insatiate of heroic praise'), a sun-hero worshipped by the Milesians (see 88. *b*).

10. Epeius, who built the wooden horse (see 167. *a*), appears in early legends as an outstandingly courageous warrior; but his name was ironically applied to boasters, until it became synonymous with cowardice (Hesychius *sub* Epeius).

90

THE CHILDREN OF PASIPHAË

AMONG Pasiphaë's children by Minos were Acacallis, Ariadne, Androgeus, Catreus, Glaucus, and Phaedra.[1] She also bore Cydon to Hermes, and Libyan Ammon to Zeus.[2]

b. Ariadne, beloved first by Theseus, and then by Dionysus, bore many famous children. Catreus, who succeeded Minos on the throne, was killed in Rhodes by his own son. Phaedra married Theseus and won notoriety for her unfortunate love-affair with Hippolytus, her stepson. Acacallis was Apollo's first love; when he and his sister Artemis came for purification to Tarrha, from Aegialae on the mainland, he found Acacallis at the house of Carmanor, a maternal relative, and seduced her. Minos was vexed, and banished Acacallis to Libya where, some say, she became the mother of Garamas, though others claim that he was the first man ever to be born.[3]

c. Glaucus, while still a child, was playing ball one day in the palace at Cnossus or, perhaps, chasing a mouse, when he suddenly disappeared. Minos and Pasiphaë searched high and low but, being unable to find him, had recourse to the Delphic Oracle. They were informed that whoever could give the best simile for a recent portentous birth in Crete would find what was lost. Minos made enquiries and learned that a heifer-calf had been born among his herds which changed its colour thrice a day – from white to red, and from red to black. He summoned his soothsayers to the palace, but none could think of a simile until Polyeidus the Argive, a descendant of Melampus, said: 'This calf resembles nothing so much as a ripening blackberry [or mulberry].' Minos at once commanded him to go in search of Glaucus.[4]

d. Polyeidus wandered through the labyrinthine palace, until he came upon an owl sitting at the entrance to a cellar, frightening away a swarm of bees, and took this for an omen. Below in the cellar he found a great jar used for the storing of honey, and Glaucus drowned in it, head downwards. Minos, when this discovery was reported to him, consulted with the Curetes, and followed their advice by telling Polyeidus: 'Now that you have found my son's body, you must restore him to life!' Polyeidus protested that, not being Asclepius, he was incapable of raising the dead. 'Ah, I know better,' replied Minos. 'You will be locked in a tomb with Glaucus's body and a sword, and there you will remain until my orders have been obeyed!'

e. When Polyeidus grew accustomed to the darkness of the tomb he saw a serpent approaching the boy's corpse and, seizing his sword, killed it. Presently another serpent, gliding up, and finding that its mate was dead, retired, but came back shortly with a magic herb in its mouth, which it laid on the dead body. Slowly the serpent came to life again.

f. Polyeidus was astounded, but had the presence of mind to apply the same herb to the body of Glaucus, and with the same happy result. He and Glaucus then shouted loudly for help, until a passer-by heard them and ran to summon Minos, who was overjoyed when he opened the tomb and found his son alive. He loaded Polyeidus with gifts, but would not let him return to Argos until he had taught Glaucus the art of divination. Polyeidus unwillingly obeyed, and when he was about to sail home, told Glaucus: 'Boy, spit into my open mouth!' Glaucus did so, and immediately forgot all that he had learned.[5]

g. Later, Glaucus led an expedition westward, and demanded a kingdom from the Italians; but they despised him for failing to be so great a man as his father; however, he introduced the Cretan military girdle and shield into Italy, and thus earned the name Labicus, which means 'girdled'.[6]

h. Androgeus visited Athens, and won every contest in the All-Athenian Games. But King Aegeus knew of his friendship for the fifty rebellious sons of Pallas and fearing that he might persuade his father Minos to support these in an open revolt, conspired with the Megareans to have him ambushed at Oenoë on the way to Thebes, where he was about to compete in certain funeral games. Androgeus defended himself with courage, and a fierce battle ensued in which he was killed.[7]

i. News of Androgeus's death reached Minos while he was sacrificing to the Graces on the island of Paros. He threw down the garlands and commanded the flute-players to cease, but completed the ceremony; to this day they sacrifice to the Graces of Paros without either music or flowers.[8]

j. Glaucus son of Minos has sometimes been confused with Anthedonian Glaucus, son of Anthedon, or of Poseidon, who once observed the restorative property of a certain grass, sown by Cronus in the Golden Age, when a dead fish (or, some say, a hare) was laid upon it and came to life again. He tasted the herb and, becoming immortal, leaped into the sea, where he is now a marine god, famous for his amorous adventures. His underwater home lies off the coast of Delos, and every year he visits all the ports and islands of Greece, issuing oracles much prized by sailors and fishermen – Apollo himself is described as Glaucus's pupil.[9]

1. Pausanias: viii. 53. 2; Diodorus Siculus: iv. 60; Apollodorus: iii. 1. 2.
2. Pausanias: *loc. cit.*; Plutarch: *Agis* 9.

3. Plutarch: *Theseus* 20; Apollodorus: iii. 2. 1–2; Euripides: *Hippolytus*; Pausanias: ii. 7. 7; Apollonius Rhodius: iv. 1493 ff.

4. Hyginus: *Fabula* 136; Apollodorus: iii. 3. 1; Pausanias: i. 43. 5.

5. Apollodorus: *loc. cit.*; Hyginus: *loc. cit.*

6. Servius on Virgil's *Aeneid* vii. 796.

7. Diodorus Siculus: iv. 60. 4; Apollodorus: iii. 15. 7; Servius on Virgil's *Aeneid* vi. 14; Hyginus: *Fabula* 41.

8. Apollodorus: iii. 15. 7.

9. Athenaeus: vii. 48; Tzetzes: *On Lycophron* 754; Ovid: *Metamorphoses* xiii. 924 ff.; Pausanias: ix. 22. 6; Servius on Virgil's *Georgics* i. 437.

*

1. Pasiphaë as the Moon (see 51. *h*) has been credited with numerous sons: Cydon, the eponymous hero of Cydon near Tegea, and of the Cydonian colony on Crete; Glaucus, a Corinthian sea-hero (see 71. 4); Androgeus, in whose honour annual games were celebrated at Ceramicus, and whom the Athenians worshipped as 'Eurygyes' ('broad-circling'), to show that he was a spirit of the solar year (Hesychius *sub* Androgeus); Ammon, the oracular hero of the Ammon Oasis, later equated with Zeus; and Catreus, whose name seems to be a masculine form of Catarrhoa, the Moon as rain-maker. Her daughters Ariadne and Phaedra are reproductions of herself; Ariadne, though read as *ariagne*, 'most pure', appears to be a Sumerian name, *Ar-ri-an-de*, 'high fruitful mother of the barley', and Phaedra occurs in South Palestinian inscriptions as *Pdri*.

2. The myth of Acacallis ('unwalled') apparently records the capture, by invading Hellenes from Aegialae, of the West Cretan city of Tarrha which, like other Cretan cities, was unwalled (see 98. 1); and the flight of the leading inhabitants to Libya, where they became the rulers of the unwarlike Garamantians.

3. White, red, and black, the colours of Minos's heifer, were also those of Io the Moon-cow (see 56. 1); those of Augeias's sacred bulls (see 127.1); and on a Caeretan vase (*Monumenti Inediti* vi–vii. p. 77) those of the Minos bull which carried off Europe. Moreover, clay or plaster tripods sacred to the Cretan goddess found at Ninou Khani, and a similar tripod found at Mycenae, were painted in white, red, and black and according to Ctesias's *Indica*, these were the colours of the unicorn's horn – the unicorn, as a calendar symbol represented the Moon-goddess's dominion over the five seasons of the Osirian year, each of which contributed part of an animal to its composition. That Glaucus was chasing a mouse may point to a conflict between the Athenian worshippers of Athene, who had an owl (*glaux*) for her familiar, and the worshippers of Apollo Smintheus ('Mouse Apollo'); or the original story may have been that Minos gave him a mouse coated with honey to swallow – a desperate remedy prescribed for sick children in the ancient Eastern Mediterranean. His

manner of death may also refer to the use of honey as an embalming fluid – many jar-burials of children occur in Cretan houses – and the owl was a bird of death. The bees are perhaps explained by a misreading of certain cut gems (Weiseler: *Denkmale der Alten Kunst* ii. 252), which showed Hermes summoning the dead from burial jars, while their souls hovered above in the form of bees (see 39. *8* and 82. *4*).

4. Polyeidus is both the shape-shifting Zagreus (see 30. *a*) and the demi-god Asclepius, whose regenerative herb seems to have been mistle-toe (see 50. *2*), or its Eastern-European counterpart, the loranthus. The Babylonian legend of Gilgamesh provides a parallel to the serpent's revivification. His herb of eternal life is stolen from him by a serpent, which thereupon casts its slough and grows young again; Gilgamesh, unable to recover the herb, resigns himself to death. It is described as resembling buckthorn: a plant which the Greeks took as a purge before performing their Mysteries.

5. Glaucus's spitting into the open mouth of Polyeidus recalls a similar action of Apollo when Cassandra failed to pay him for the gift of pro-phecy; in Cassandra's case, however, the result was not that she lost the gift, but that no one believed her (see 158. *q*).

6. The goddesses to whom Minos sacrificed without the customary flutes or flowers, when he heard that his son had died, were the Pariae, or Ancient Ones (see 89. *a*), presumably the Three Fates, euphemistically called the 'Graces'. Myth has here broken down into street-corner anec-dote. Androgeus's death is a device used to account for the Cretan quarrel with Athens (see 98. *c*), based, perhaps, on some irrelevant tradition of a murder done at Oenoë.

7. Anthedonian Glaucus's oracular gifts, his name, and his love-affairs, one of which was with Scylla (see 170. *t*), suggest that he was a personifi-cation of Cretan sea-power. Both Minos (who received his oracles from Zeus) and Poseidon, patron of the Cretan confederacy (see 39. *7*), had enjoyed Scylla (see 91. *2*); and Anthedon ('rejoicing in flowers') was apparently a title of the Cretan Springflower hero incarnate in every Late Minoan king (see 85. *2*). The King of Cnossus seems to have been connected by sacred marriages with all member states of his confederacy (see 89. *1*); hence Glaucus's amatory reputation. It is probable that a representative from Cnossus made an annual progress around the Cretan overseas dependencies in the style of Talos (see 92. *7*), giving out the latest oracular edicts. Delos was a Cretan island and perhaps a distribution centre for oracles brought from the Dictaean Cave at Cnossus. But this Glaucus also resembles Proteus, the oracular sea-god of Cretan Pharos (see 169. *6*), and Melicertes the sea-god of Corinth, identified with another Glaucus (see 71. *4*). Cronus's grass of the Golden Age may have been the magical *herbe d'or* of the Druids.

8. A version of the Glaucus myth is quoted from the Lydian historian
Xanthus by Pliny (*Natural History* xxv. 14) and Nonnus (*Dionysiaca* xxv.
451–551), and commemorated on a series of coins from Sardis. When the
hero Tylon, or Tylus ('knot' or 'phallus'), was fatally bitten in the heel
by a poisonous serpent (see 117. 1), his sister Moera ('fate') appealed to
the giant Damasen (subduer'), who avenged him. Another serpent then
fetched 'the flower of Zeus' from the woods, and laid it on the lips of its
dead mate, which came to life again; Moera followed this example and
similarly restored Tylus.

91

SCYLLA AND NISUS

MINOS was the first king to control the Mediterranean Sea, which he
cleared of pirates, and in Crete ruled over ninety cities. When the
Athenians had murdered his son Androgeus, he decided to take vengeance on them, and sailed around the Aegean collecting ships and armed
levies. Some islanders agreed to help him, some refused. Siphnos was
yielded to him by the Princess Arne, whom he bribed with gold; but
the gods changed her into a jackdaw which loves gold and all things
that glitter. He made an alliance with the people of Anaphe, but was
rebuffed by King Aeacus of Aegina and departed, swearing revenge;
Aeacus then answered an appeal from Cephalus to join the Athenians
against Minos.[1]

b. Meanwhile, Minos was harrying the Isthmus of Corinth. He laid
siege to Nisa, ruled by Nisus the Egyptian, who had a daughter named
Scylla. A tower stood in the city, built by Apollo [and Poseidon?], and
at its foot lay a musical stone which, if pebbles were dropped upon it
from above, rang like a lyre – because Apollo had once rested his lyre
there while he was working as a mason. Scylla used to spend much time
at the top of the tower, playing tunes on the stone with a lapful of
pebbles; and here she climbed daily when the war began, to watch the
fighting.

c. The siege of Nisa was protracted, and Scylla soon came to know
the name of every Cretan warrior. Struck by the beauty of Minos, and
by his magnificent clothes and white charger, she fell perversely in love

with him. Some say that Aphrodite willed it so; others blame Hera.[2]

d. One night Scylla crept into her father's chamber, and cut off the famous bright lock on which his life and throne depended; then, taking from him the keys of the city gate, she opened it, and stole out. She made straight for Minos's tent, and offered him the lock of hair in exchange for his love. 'It is a bargain!' cried Minos; and that same night, having entered the city and sacked it, he duly lay with Scylla; but would not take her to Crete, because he loathed the crime of parricide. Scylla, however, swam after his ship, and clung to the stern until her father Nisus's soul in the form of a sea-eagle swooped down upon her with talons and hooked beak. The terrified Scylla let go and was drowned; her soul flew off as a ciris-bird, which is well known for its purple breast and red legs.[3] But some say that Minos gave orders for Scylla to be drowned; and others that her soul became the fish ciris, not the bird of that name.[4]

e. Nisa was afterwards called Megara, in honour of Megareus, a son of Oenope by Hippomenes; he had been Nisus's ally and married his daughter Iphinoë, and is said to have succeeded him on the throne.[5]

f. This war dragged on until Minos, finding that he could not subdue Athens, prayed Zeus to avenge Androgeus's death; and the whole of Greece was consequently afflicted with earthquakes and famine. The kings of the various city states assembled at Delphi to consult the Oracle, and were instructed to make Aeacus offer up prayers on their behalf. When this had been done, the earthquakes everywhere ceased, except in Attica.

g. The Athenians thereupon sought to redeem themselves from the curse by sacrificing to Persephone the daughters of Hyacinthus, namely Antheis, Aegleis, Lyctaea, and Orthaea, on the grave of the Cyclops Geraestus. These girls had come to Athens from Sparta. Yet the earthquakes continued and, when the Athenians again consulted the Delphic Oracle, they were told to give Minos whatever satisfaction he might ask; which proved to be a tribute of seven youths and seven maidens, sent every nine years to Crete as a prey for the Minotaur.[6]

h. Minos then returned to Cnossus, where he sacrificed a hecatomb of bulls in gratitude for his success; but his end came in the ninth year.[7]

1. Strabo: x. 4. 8 and 15; Ovid: *Metamorphoses* vii. 480–viii. 6.
2. Hyginus: *Fabula* 198; Virgil: *Ciris*.
3. Apollodorus: iii. 15. 8; Hyginus: *loc. cit.*; Ovid: *Metamorphoses* viii. 6–151; Virgil: *loc. cit.*; Pausanias: ii. 34. 7.

4. Apollodorus: *loc. cit.*; Pausanias: *loc. cit.*
5. Pausanias: i. 39. 4–5.
6. Diodorus Siculus: iv. 61.
7. Ovid: *Metamorphoses* viii. 152 ff.; Homer: *Odyssey* xix. 178.

*

1. The historical setting of the Scylla myth is apparently a dispute between the Athenians and their Cretan overlords not long before the sack of Cnossus in 1400 B.C. The myth itself, almost exactly repeated in the Taphian story of Pterelaus and Comaetho, recalls those of Samson and Delilah in Philistia; Curoi, Blathnat, and Cuchulain in Ireland; Llew Llaw, Blodeuwedd, and Gronw in Wales: all variations on a single pattern. It concerns the rivalry between the sacred king and his tanist for the favour of the Moon-goddess who, at midsummer, cuts off the king's hair and betrays him. The king's strength resides in his hair, because he represents the Sun; and his long yellow locks are compared to its rays. Delilah shears Samson's hair before calling in the Philistines; Blathnat ties Curoi's to a bed-post before summoning her lover Cuchulain to kill him; Blodeuwedd ties Llew Llaw's to a tree before summoning her lover Gronw. Llew Llaw's soul takes the form of an eagle, and Blodeuwedd ('fair flower aspect'), a woman magically made of nine different flowers, is metamorphosed into an owl – as Scylla perhaps also was in the original Greek legend. A collation of these five myths shows that Scylla-Comaetho-Blodeuwedd-Blathnat-Delilah is the Moon-goddess in her spring and summer aspect as Aphrodite Comaetho ('bright-haired'); in the autumn she turns into an owl, or a *ciris*, and becomes the Death-goddess Athene – who had many bird-epiphanies, including the owl (see 97. 4) – or Hera, or Hecate. Her name Scylla indicates that the king was torn to pieces after his head had been shaven. As in the myth of Llew Llaw, the punishment subsequently inflicted on the traitress is a late moral addition.

2. Ovid (*Art of Love* i. 331) identifies this Scylla with a namesake whom Aphrodite turned into a dog-monster because Poseidon had seduced her (see 16. 2), and says that she harboured wild dogs in her womb and loins as a punishment for cutting off Nisus's lock. Ovid is rarely mistaken in his mythology, and he may here be recording a legend that Pasiphaë's curse upon Minos made him fill Scylla's womb with puppies, rather than with serpents, scorpions, and millepedes. Pasiphaë and Amphritrite are the same Moon-and-Sea-goddess, and Minos, as the ruler of the Mediterranean, became identified with Poseidon.

3. The sacrifice of the daughters of Hyacinthus on Geraestus's tomb may refer to the 'gardens of Adonis' planted in honour of the doomed king – being cut flowers, they withered in a few hours. But Geraestus was a pre-Achaean Cyclops (see 3. *b*), and according to the *Etymologicum*

Magnum (*sub* Geraestides), his daughters nursed the infant Zeus at Gortyna; moreover, Geraestion was a city in Arcadia where Rhea swaddled Zeus. The Hyacinthides, then, were probably the nurses, not the daughters, of Hyacinthus: priestesses of Artemis who, at Cnidus, bore the title 'Hyacinthotrophos' ('nurse of Hyacinthus'), and identifiable with the Geraestides, since the annually dying Cretan Zeus (see 7. 1) was indistinguishable from Hyacinthus. Perhaps, therefore, the myth concerns four dolls hung from a blossoming fruit-tree, to face the cardinal points of the compass, in a fructifying ceremony of the 'Hanged Artemis' (see 79. 2 and 88. 10).

4. The seven Athenian youths dedicated to the Minotaur were probably surrogates sacrificed annually in place of the Cnossian king. It will have been found convenient to use foreign victims, rather than native Cretans; as happened with the Canaanite ritual of Crucifixion for which, in the end, captives and criminals sufficed as Tammuz's surrogates. 'Every ninth year' means 'at the end of every Great Year of one hundred lunations'. After seven boys had been sacrificed for the sacred king, he himself died (see 81. 8). The seven Athenian maidens were not sacrificed; perhaps they became attendants on the Moon-priestess, and performed acrobatic feats at bull-fights, such as are shown in Cretan works of art: a dangerous but not necessarily fatal sport.

5. A set of musical stones may have existed at Megara on the model of a xylophone; it would not have been difficult to construct. But perhaps there is a recollection here of Memmon's singing statue in Egypt: hollow, with an orifice at the back of the open mouth, through which the hot air forced itself at dawn when the sun warmed the stone (see 164. 2).

92

DAEDALUS AND TALOS

THE parentage of Daedalus is disputed. His mother is named Alcippe by some; by others, Merope; by still others, Iphinoë; and all give him a different father, though it is generally agreed that he belonged to the royal house of Athens, which claimed descent from Erechtheus. He was a wonderful smith, having been instructed in his art by Athene herself.[1]

b. One of his apprentices, Talos the son of his sister Polycaste, or Perdix, had already surpassed him in craftsmanship while only twelve years old. Talos happened one day to pick up the jawbone of a serpent or, some say, a fish's spine; and, finding that he could use it to cut a stick in half, copied it in iron and thereby invented the saw. This, and other inventions of his – such as the potter's wheel, and the compass for marking out circles – secured him a great reputation at Athens, and Daedalus, who himself claimed to have forged the first saw, soon grew unbearably jealous.[2] Leading Talos up to the roof of Athene's temple on the Acropolis, he pointed out certain distant sights, and suddenly toppled him over the edge. Yet, for all his jealousy, he would have done Talos no harm had he not suspected him of incestuous relations with his mother Polycaste. Daedalus then hurried down to the foot of the Acropolis, and thrust Talos's corpse into a bag, proposing to bury it secretly. When challenged by passers-by, he explained that he had piously taken up a dead serpent, as the law required – which was not altogether untrue, Talos being an Erechtheid – but there were bloodstains on the bag, and his crime did not escape detection, whereupon the Areiopagus banished him for murder. According to another account he fled before the trial could take place.[3]

c. Now, the soul of Talos – whom some call Calus, Circinus, or Tantalus – flew off in the form of a partridge, but his body was buried where it had fallen. Polycaste hanged herself when she heard of his death, and the Athenians built a sanctuary in her honour beside the Acropolis.[4]

d. Daedalus took refuge in one of the Attic demes, whose people are named Daedalids after him; and then in Cretan Cnossus, where King Minos delighted to welcome so skilled a craftsman. He lived there for some time, at peace and in high favour, until Minos, learning that he had helped Pasiphaë to couple with Poseidon's white bull, locked him up for a while in the Labyrinth, together with his son Icarus, whose mother, Naucrate, was one of Minos's slaves; but Pasiphaë freed them both.[5]

e. It was not easy, however, to escape from Crete, since Minos kept all his ships under military guard, and now offered a large reward for his apprehension. But Daedalus made a pair of wings for himself, and another for Icarus, the quill feathers of which were threaded together, but the smaller ones held in place by wax. Having tied on Icarus's pair for him, he said with tears in his eyes: 'My son, be warned! Neither soar too high, lest the sun melt the wax; nor swoop too low, lest the feathers be wetted by the sea.' Then he slipped his arms into his own pair of wings and they flew off. 'Follow me closely,' he cried, 'do not set your own course!'

As they sped away from the island in a north-easterly direction, flapping their wings, the fishermen, shepherds, and ploughmen who gazed upwards mistook them for gods.

f. They had left Naxos, Delos, and Paros behind them on the left hand, and were leaving Lebynthos and Calymne behind on the right, when Icarus disobeyed his father's instructions and began soaring towards the sun, rejoiced by the lift of his great sweeping wings. Presently, when Daedalus looked over his shoulder, he could no longer see Icarus; but scattered feathers floated on the waves below. The heat of the sun had melted the wax, and Icarus had fallen into the sea and drowned. Daedalus circled around, until the corpse rose to the surface, and then carried it to the near-by island now called Icaria, where he buried it. A partridge sat perched on a holm-oak and watched him, chattering for delight – the soul of his sister Polycaste, at last avenged. This island has now given its name to the surrounding sea.[6]

g. But some, disbelieving the story, say that Daedalus fled from Crete in a boat provided by Pasiphaë; and that, on their way to Sicily, they were about to disembark at a small island, when Icarus fell into the sea and drowned. They add that it was Heracles who buried Icarus; in gratitude for which, Daedalus made so lifelike a statue of him at Pisa that Heracles mistook it for a rival and felled it with a stone. Others say that Daedalus invented sails, not wings, as a means of outstripping Minos's galleys; and that Icarus, steering carelessly, was drowned when their boat capsized.[7]

h. Daedalus flew westward until, alighting at Cumae near Naples, he dedicated his wings to Apollo there, and built him a golden-roofed temple. Afterwards, he visited Camicus in Sicily, where he was hospitably received by King Cocalus, and lived among the Sicilians, enjoying great fame and erecting many fine buildings.[8]

i. Meanwhile, Minos had raised a considerable fleet, and set out in search of Daedalus. He brought with him a Triton shell, and wherever he went promised to reward anyone who could pass a linen thread through it: a problem which, he knew, Daedalus alone would be able to solve. Arrived at Camicus, he offered the shell to Cocalus, who undertook to have it threaded; and, sure enough, Daedalus found out how to do this. Fastening a gossamer thread to an ant, he bored a hole at the point of the shell and lured the ant up the spirals by smearing honey on the edges of the hole. Then he tied the linen thread to the other end of the gossamer and drew that through as well. Cocalus returned the threaded shell, claiming the reward, and Minos, assured that he had at last found Daedalus's hiding-place, demanded his surrender. But Cocalus's daughters were loth to lose Daedalus, who made them such beautiful toys, and with his help they concocted a plot. Daedalus led a pipe through the roof of the bathroom, down which they poured boiling water or, some say, pitch upon Minos, while he luxuriated in a warm bath. Cocalus, who may well have been implicated in the plot, returned the corpse to the Cretans, saying that Minos had stumbled over a rug and fallen into a cauldron of boiling water.[9]

j. Minos's followers buried him with great pomp, and Zeus made him a judge of the dead in Tartarus, with his brother Rhadamanthys and his enemy Aeacus as colleagues. Since Minos's tomb occupied the centre of Aphrodite's temple at Camicus, he was honoured there for many generations by great crowds of Sicilians who came to worship Aphrodite. In the end, his bones were returned to Crete by Theron, the tyrant of Acragas.

k. After Minos's death the Cretans fell into complete disorder, because their main fleet was burned by the Sicilians. Of the crews who were forced to remain overseas, some built the city of Minoa, close to the beach where they had landed; others, the city of Hyria in Messapia; still others, marching into the centre of Sicily, fortified a hill which became the city of Enguos, so called from a spring which flows *close by*. There they built a temple of the Mothers, whom they continued to honour greatly, as in their native Crete.[10]

l. But Daedalus left Sicily to join Iolaus, the nephew and charioteer of Tirynthian Heracles, who led a body of Athenians and Thespians to Sardinia. Many of his works survive to this day in Sardinia; they are called Daedaleia.[11]

m. Now, Talos was also the name of Minos's bull-headed bronze servant, given him by Zeus to guard Crete. Some say that he was a survivor of the brazen race who sprang from the ash-trees; others, that he was forged by Hephaestus in Sardinia, and that he had a single vein which ran from his neck down to his ankles, where it was stoppered by a bronze pin. It was his task to run thrice daily around the island of Crete and throw rocks at any foreign ship; and also to go thrice yearly, at a more leisurely pace, through the villages of Crete, displaying Minos's laws inscribed on brazen tablets. When the Sardinians tried to

invade the island, Talos made himself red-hot in a fire and destroyed
them all with his burning embrace, grinning fiercely; hence the expression 'a Sardonic grin'. In the end, Medea killed Talos by pulling out the
pin and letting his life-blood escape; though some say that Poeas the
Argonaut wounded him in the ankle with a poisoned arrow.[12]

1. Apollodorus: iii. 15. 8; Plutarch: *Theseus* 19; Pherecydes, quoted
   by Scholiast on Sophocles's *Oedipus at Colonus* 472; Hyginus:
   Fabula 39.
2. Apollodorus: *loc. cit.*; Ovid: *Metamorphoses* viii. 236–59; Hyginus:
   Fabula 274; Pliny: *Natural History* vii. 57.
3. Fulgentius: *Myths* iii. 2; First Vatican Mythographer: 232; Second
   Vatican Mythographer: 130; Diodorus Siculus: iv. 76. 6; Hyginus: *Fabula* 39; Pausanias: vii. 4. 5.
4. Pausanias: i. 21. 6; Servius on Virgil's *Aeneid* vi. 14; Hellanicus,
   quoted by Scholiast on Euripides's *Orestes* 1650; Ovid: *loc. cit.*;
   Suidas and Photius *sub* Sanctuary of Perdix.
5. Diodorus Siculus: *loc. cit.*; Apollodorus: *Epitome* i. 12.
6. Isidore of Seville: *Origins* xiv. 6; Hyginus: *Fabula* 40; Ovid:
   Metamorphoses viii. 182–235.
7. Diodorus Siculus: iv. 77; Apollodorus: ii. 6. 3; Pausanias: ix.
   11. 2–3.
8. Virgil: *Aeneid* vi. 14 ff.; Pausanias: vii. 4. 5; Diodorus Siculus:
   iv. 78.
9. Pausanias: *loc. cit.*; Apollodorus: *Epitome* i. 14–15; Zenobius:
   Proverbs iv. 92; Diodorus Siculus: iv. 79.
10. Diodorus Siculus: *loc. cit.*; Herodotus: vii. 170.
11. Pausanias: vii. 2. 2; Diodorus Siculus: iv. 30.
12. Suidas *sub* Risus Sardonicus; Apollonius Rhodius: *Argonautica*
    1639 ff.; Apollodorus: i. 9. 26; Plato: *Minos* 320c.

*

1. Hephaestus is sometimes described as Hera's son by Talos (see 12. *c*),
and Talos as Daedalus's young nephew; but Daedalus was a junior member of the House of Erechtheus, which was founded long after the birth
of Hephaestus. Such chronological discrepancies are the rule in mythology. Daedalus ('bright' or 'cunningly wrought'), Talos ('sufferer'),
and Hephaestus ('he who shines by day'), are shown by the similarity of
their attributes to be merely different titles of the same mythical character; Icarus (from *io-carios*, 'dedicated to the Moon-goddess Car') may
be yet another of his titles. For Hephaestus the smith-god married
Aphrodite, to whom the partridge was sacred; the sister of Daedalus the
smith was called Perdix ('partridge'); the soul of Talos the smith flew
off as a partridge; a partridge appeared at the burial of Daedalus's son
Icarus. Besides, Hephaestus was flung from Olympus; Talos was flung

from the Acropolis. Hephaestus hobbled when he walked; one of Talos's names was Tantalus ('hobbling, or lurching'); a cock-partridge hobbles in his love-dance, holding one heel ready to strike at rivals. Moreover, the Latin god Vulcan hobbled. His cult had been introduced from Crete, where he was called Velchanus and had a cock for his emblem, because the cock crows at dawn and was therefore appropriate to a Sun-hero. But the cock did not reach Crete until the sixth century B.C., and is likely to have displaced the partridge as Velchanus's bird.

2. It seems that in the spring an erotic partridge dance was performed in honour of the Moon-goddess, and that the male dancers hobbled and wore wings. In Palestine this ceremony, called the *Pesach* ('the hobbling') was, according to Jerome, still performed at Beth-Hoglah ('the Shrine of the Hobbler'), where the devotees danced in a spiral. Beth-Hoglah is identified with 'the threshing-floor of Atad', on which mourning was made for the lame King Jacob, whose name may mean *Jah Aceb* ('the heel-god'). Jeremiah warns the Jews not to take part in these orgiastic Canaanite rites, quoting: 'The partridge gathereth young that she hath not brought forth.' Anaphe, an island to the north of Crete, with which Minos made a treaty (see 91. *a*), was famous in antiquity as a resting-place for migrant partridges.

3. The myth of Daedalus and Talos, like its variant, the myth of Daedalus and Icarus, seems to combine the ritual of burning the solar king's surrogate, who had put on eagle's wings (see 29. *1*), in the spring bonfire – when the Palestinian New Year began – with the rituals of flinging the partridge-winged *pharmacos*, a similar surrogate, over a cliff into the sea (see 96. *3*), and of pricking the king in the heel with a poisoned arrow (see *10 below*). But the fisherman's and peasant's admiration of the flying Daedalus is probably borrowed from an icon of the winged Perseus or Marduk (see 73. *7*).

4. In one sense the labyrinth from which Daedalus and Icarus escaped was the mosaic floor with the maze pattern, which they had to follow in the ritual partridge dance (see 98. *2*); but Daedalus's escape to Sicily, Cumae, and Sardinia refers perhaps to the flight of the native bronze-workers from Crete as the result of successive Hellenic invasions. The ruse of the Triton shell, and Minos's burial in a shrine of Aphrodite to whom this shell was sacred (see 11. *3*), suggest that Minos was also, in this context, regarded as Hephaestus, the Sea-goddess's lover. His death in a bath is an incident that has apparently become detached from the myth of Nisus and Scylla (see 91. *b–d*); Nisus's Celtic counterpart, Llew Llaw, was killed in a bath by a trick; and so was another sacred King, Agamemnon of Mycenae (see 112. *1*).

5. The name Naucrate ('sea-power') records the historical conse-quences of Minos's defeat in Sicily – the passing of sea-power from

Cretan into Greek hands. That she was one of Minos's slaves suggests a palace revolution of Hellenic mercenaries at Cnossus.

6. If Polycaste, the other name of Talos's mother Perdix, means *polycassitere*, 'much tin', it belongs to the myth of the bronze man, Talos's namesake. Cretan supremacy depended largely on plentiful supplies of tin, to mix with Cyprian copper; according to Professor Christopher Hawkes, the nearest source was the island of Majorca.

7. Talos is said by Hesychius to be a name for the Sun; originally, therefore, Talos will have coursed only once a day around Crete. Perhaps, however, the harbours of Crete were guarded against pirates by three watches which sent out patrols. And since Talos the Sun was also called Taurus ('the bull' – Bekker: *Anecdotae* i. 344. 10 ff.; Apollodorus: i. 9. 26), his thrice-yearly visit to the villages was probably a royal progress of the Sun-king, wearing his ritual bull-mask – the Cretan year being divided into three seasons (see 75. 2). Talos's red-hot embrace may record the human burnt sacrifices offered to Moloch, *alias* Melkarth, who was worshipped at Corinth as Melicertes (see 70. 5), and probably also known in Crete. Since this Talos came from Sardinia, where Daedalus was said to have fled when pursued by Minos, and was at the same time Zeus's present to Minos, the mythographers have simplified the story by giving Hephaestus, rather than Daedalus, credit for its construction; Hephaestus and Daedalus being the same character. The *sardonicus risus*, or *rictus*, a twisting of the facial muscles, symptomatic of lock-jaw, was perhaps so called because the stag-man of early Sardinian bronzes wears the same mirthless, gaping grin.

8. Talos's single vein belongs to the mystery of early bronze casting by the *cire-perdue* method. First, the smith made a beeswax image which he coated with a layer of clay, and laid in an oven. As soon as the clay had been well baked he pierced the spot between heel and ankle, so that the hot wax ran out and left a mould, into which molten bronze could be poured. When he had filled this, and the metal inside had cooled, he broke the clay, leaving a bronze image of the same shape as the original wax one. The Cretans brought the *cire-perdue* method to Sardinia, together with the Daedalus cult. Since Daedalus learned his craft from Athene, who was known as Medea at Corinth, the story of Talos's death may have been a misreading of an icon which showed Athene demonstrating the *cire-perdue* method. The tradition that melted wax caused Icarus's death seems to belong, rather, to the myth of his cousin Talos; because Talos the bronze man is closely connected with his namesake, the worker in bronze and the reputed inventor of compasses.

9. Compasses are part of the bronze-worker's mystery, essential for the accurate drawing of concentric circles when bowls, helmets, or masks have to be beaten out. Hence Talos was known as Circinus, 'the circular',

a title which referred both to the course of the sun and to the use of the compass (see 3. 2). His invention of the saw has been rightly emphasized: the Cretans had minute double-toothed turning-saws for fine work, which they used with marvellous dexterity. Talos is the son of an ash-tree nymph, because ash-charcoal yields a very high heat for smelting. This myth sheds light also on Prometheus's creation of man from clay; in Hebrew legend Prometheus's part was played by the Archangel Michael, who worked under the eye of Jehovah.

10. Poeas's shooting of Talos recalls Paris's shooting of Achilles, also in the heel, and the deaths of the Centaurs Pholus and Cheiron (see 126. 3). These myths are closely related. Pholus and Cheiron died from Heracles's poisoned arrows. Poeas was the father of Philoctetes and, when Heracles had been poisoned by another Centaur, ordered him to kindle the pyre; as a result, Philoctetes obtained the same arrows (see 145. f), one of which poisoned him (see 161. l). Paris then borrowed Thessalian Apollo's deadly arrows to kill Achilles, Cheiron's foster-son (see 164. j); and finally, when Philoctetes avenged Achilles by shooting Paris, he used another from Heracles's quiver (see 166. e). The Thessalian sacred king was, it seems, killed by an arrow smeared with viper venom, which the tanist drove between his heel and ankle.

11. In Celtic myth the labyrinth came to mean the royal tomb (*White Goddess* p. 105); and that it also did so among the early Greeks is suggested by its definition in the *Etymologicum Magnum* as 'a mountain cave', and by Eustathius (On Homer's *Odyssey* xi. p. 1688) as 'a subterranean cave'. Lars Porsena the Etruscan made a labyrinth for his own tomb (Varro, quoted by Pliny: *Natural History* xxxvi. 91–3), and there were labyrinths in the 'Cyclopean', i.e. pre-Hellenic, caves near Nauplia (Strabo: viii. 6. 2); on Samos (Pliny: *Natural History* xxxiv. 83); and on Lemnos (Pliny: *Natural History* xxxvi. 90). To escape from the labyrinth, therefore, is to be reincarnate.

12. Although Daedalus ranks as an Athenian, because of the Attic *deme* named in his honour, the Daedalic crafts were introduced into Attica from Crete, not contrariwise. The toys that he made for the daughters of Cocalus are likely to have been dolls with movable limbs, like those which pleased Pasiphaë and her daughter Ariadne (see 88. e), and which seem to have been used in the Attic tree cult of Erigone. At any rate, Polycaste, Daedalus's sister, hanged herself, as did two Erigones and Ariadne herself (see 79. 2 and 88. 10).

13. The Messapians of Hyria, later Uria, now Oria, were known in Classical times for their Cretan customs – kiss-curl, flower-embroidered robes, double-axe, and so on; and pottery found there can be dated to 1400 B.C., which bears out the story.

93

CATREUS AND ALTHAEMENES

CATREUS, Minos's eldest surviving son, had three daughters: Aerope, Clymene, and Apemosyne; and a son, Althaemenes. When an oracle predicted that Catreus would be killed by one of his own children, Althaemenes and the swift-footed Apemosyne piously left Crete, with a large following, in the hope of escaping the curse. They landed on the island of Rhodes, and founded the city of Cretinia, naming it in honour of their native island.[1] Althaemenes afterwards settled at Cameirus, where he was held in great honour by the inhabitants, and raised an altar to Zeus on the near-by Mount Atabyrius, from the summit of which, on clear days, he could gain a distant view of his beloved Crete. Around this altar he set brazen bulls, which roared aloud whenever danger threatened Rhodes.[2]

b. One day Hermes fell in love with Apemosyne, who rejected his advances and fled from him. That evening he surprised her near a spring. Again she turned to flee, but he had spread slippery hides on the one path of escape, so that she fell flat on her face and he succeeded in ravishing her. When Apemosyne returned to the palace, and ruefully told Althaemenes of this misadventure, he cried out 'Liar and harlot!' and kicked her to death.

c. Meanwhile Catreus, mistrusting Aerope and Clymene, the other two, banished them from Crete, of which he was now king. Aerope, after having been seduced by Thyestes the Pelopid, married Pleisthenes and became by him the mother of Agamemnon and Menelaus; and Clymene married Nauplius, the celebrated navigator. At last, in lonely old age and, so far as he knew, without an heir to his throne, Catreus went in search of Althaemenes, whom he loved dearly. Landing one night on Rhodes, he and his companions were mistaken for pirates, and attacked by the Cameiran cowherds. Catreus tried to explain who he was and why he had come, but the barking of dogs drowned his voice. Althaemenes rushed from the palace to beat off the supposed raid and, not recognizing his father, killed him with a spear. When he learned that the oracle had been fulfilled after all, despite his long, self-imposed exile, he prayed to be swallowed up by the earth. A chasm accordingly opened, and he disappeared, but is paid heroic honours to this day.[3]

1. Apollodorus: iii. 2. 1.
2. Diodorus Siculus: v. 78; Apollodorus: *loc. cit.*; Strabo: xiv. 2. 2;
   Scholiast on Pindar's *Olympian Odes* vii. 159.
3. Apollodorus: iii. 2. 1–2; Diodorus Siculus: *loc. cit.*

*

1. This artificial myth, which records a Mycenaeo-Minoan occupation
of Rhodes in the fifteenth century B.C., is intended also to account for
libations poured down a chasm to a Rhodian hero, as well as for erotic
sports in the course of which women danced on the newly-flayed hides
of sacrificial beasts. The termination *byrios*, or *buriash*, occurs in the royal
title of the Third Babylonian Dynasty, founded in 1750 B.C.; and the
deity of Atabyrius in Crete, like that of Atabyrium (Mount Tabor) in
Palestine, famous for its golden calf worship, was the Hittite Tesup, a
cattle-owning Sun-god (see 67. 1). Rhodes first belonged to the Sumerian
Moon-goddess Dam-Kina, or Danaë (see 60. 3), but passed into the
possession of Tesup (see 42. 4); and, on the breakdown of the Hittite
Empire, was colonized by Greek-speaking Cretans who retained the bull-
cult, but made Atabyrius a son of Proteus ('first man') and Eurynome
the Creatrix (see 1. *a*). In Dorian times Zeus Atabyrius usurped Tesup's
Rhodian cult. The roar of bulls will have been produced by the whirling
of *rhomboi*, or bull-roarers (see 30. 1), used to frighten away evil spirits. ·

2. Apemosyne's death at Cameira may refer to a brutal repression, by
the Hittite rather than the Cretan invaders, of a college of Oracular
priestesses at Cameirus. The three daughters of Catreus, like the Danaids,
are the familiar Moon-triad: Apemosyne being the third person, Cameira's counterpart. Catreus accidentally murdered by Althaemenes, like
Laius accidently murdered by his son Oedipus (see 105. *d*), and Odysseus
by his son Telegonus (see 170. *k*), will have been a predecessor in the
sacred kingship rather than a father; but the story has been mistold —
the son, not the father, should land from the sea and hurl the sting-ray
spear.

94

THE SONS OF PANDION

WHEN Erechtheus, King of Athens, was killed by Poseidon, his sons
Cecrops, Pandorus, Metion, and Orneus quarrelled over the succession;
and Xuthus, by whose verdict Cecrops, the eldest, became king, had to
leave Attica in haste.[1]

b. Cecrops, whom Metion and Orneus threatened to kill, fled first to Megara and then to Euboea, where Pandorus joined him and founded a colony. The throne of Athens fell to Cecrops's son Pandion, whose mother was Metiadusa, daughter of Eupalamus.[2] But he did not long enjoy his power, for though Metion died, his sons by Alcippe, of Iphinoë, proved to be as jealous as himself. These sons were named Daedalus, whom some, however, call his grandson; Eupalamus, whom others call his father; and Sicyon. Sicyon is also variously called the son of Erechtheus, Pelops, or Marathon, these genealogies being in great confusion.[3]

c. When the sons of Metion expelled Pandion from Athens he fled to the court of Pylas, Pylus, or Pylon, a Lelegian king of Megara,[4] whose daughter Pylia he married. Later, Pylas killed his uncle Bias and, leaving Pandion to rule Megara, took refuge in Messenia, where he founded the city of Pylus. Driven thence by Neleus and the Pelasgians of Iolcus, he entered Elis, and there founded a second Pylus. Pylia bore Pandion four sons at Megara: Aegeus, Pallas, Nisus, and Lycus, though Aegeus's jealous brothers spread the rumour that he was the bastard son of one Scyrius.[5] Pandion never returned to Athens. He enjoys a hero shrine in Megara, where his tomb is still shown on the Bluff of Athene the Diver-bird, in proof that this territory once belonged to Athens; it was disguised as this bird that Athene hid his father Cecrops under her wings, and carried him in safety to Megara.[6]

d. After Pandion's death his sons marched against Athens, drove out the sons of Metion, and divided Attica into four parts, as their father had instructed them to do. Aegeus, being the eldest, was awarded the sovereignty of Athens, while his brothers drew lots for the remainder of the kingdom: Nisus won Megara and the surrounding country as far west as Corinth; Lycus won Euboea; and Pallas Southern Attica, where he bred a rugged race of giants.[7]

e. Pylas's son Sciron, who married one of Pandion's daughters, disputed Nisus's claim to Megara, and Aeacus, called in to judge the dispute, awarded the kingship to Nisus and his descendants, but the command of its armies to Sciron. In those days Megara was called Nisa, and Nisus also gave his name to the port of Nisaea, which he founded. When Minos killed Nisus he was buried in Athens, where his tomb is still shown behind the Lyceum. The Megareans, however, who do not admit that their city was ever captured by the Cretans, claim that Megareus married Nisus's daughter Iphinoë and succeeded him.[8]

f. Aegeus, like Cecrops and Pandion, found his life constantly threatened by the plots of his kinsmen, among them Lycus, whom he is said to have exiled from Euboea. Lycus took refuge with Sarpedon, and gave his name to Lycia, after first visiting Aphareus at Arene, and initiating the royal household into the Mysteries the Great Goddesses Demeter and Persephone, and also into those of Atthis, at the ancient Messenian capital of Andania. This Atthis, who gave Attica its name, was one of the three daughters of Cranaus, the autochthonous king of Athens reigning at the time of the Deucalonian Flood. The oak-coppice at Andania, where Lycus purified the initiates, still bears his name.⁹ He had been granted the power of prophecy, and it was his oracle which later declared that if the Messenians kept a certain secret thing safely they would one day recover their partrimony, but if not, they would forfeit it for ever. Lycus was referring to an account of the Mysteries of the Great Goddess engraved on a sheet of tin, which the Messenians thereupon buried in a brazen urn between a yew and a myrtle, on the summit of Mount Ithone; Epaminondas the Theban eventually disinterred it when he restored the Messenians to their former glory.¹⁰

g. The Athenian Lyceum is also named in honour of Lycus; from the very earliest times it has been sacred to Apollo who there first received the surname 'Lycaean', and expelled wolves from Athens by the smell of his sacrifices.¹¹

1. Apollodorus: iii. 15. 1 and 5; Plutarch: *Theseus* 32; Pausanias: vii. 1. 2.
2. *Ibid.*: i. 5. 3; Eustathius on Homer p. 281; Apollodorus: iii. 15. 5.
3. Pherecydes, quoted by Scholiast on Sophocles's *Oedipus at Colonus* 472; Apollodorus: iii. 15. 8; Diodorus Siculus: iv. 76. 1; Pausanias: ii. 6. 3.
4. Apollodorus: iii. 15. 5; Pausanias: iv. 36. 1 and i. 29. 5.
5. Apollodorus: *loc. cit.*; Pausanias: iv. 36. 1.
6. Pausanias: i. 41. 6; i. 5. 3; and i. 39. 4; Hesychius *sub* Aethyia.
7. Apollodorus: iii. 15. 6; Sophocles, quoted by Strabo: i. 6; Pausanias: i. 5. 4 and i. 39. 4.
8. Pausanias: i. 39. 4–5 and 19. 5; Strabo: ix. 1. 6.
9. Herodotus: i. 173; Pausanias: i. 2. 5 and iv. 1. 4–5.
10. Pausanias: x. 12. 5; iv. 20. 2 and 26. 6.
11. *Ibid.*: i. 19. 4; Scholiast on Demosthenes: xxiv. 114.

*

1. Mythical genealogies such as these were quoted whenever the sovereignty of states or hereditary privileges came into dispute. The division of Megara between the sacred king, who performed necessary sacrifices, and his tanist, who commanded the army, is paralleled at Sparta (see 74. 1). Aegeus's name records the goat cult in Athens (see 8. 1), and Lycus's the wolf cult; any Athenian who killed a wolf was obliged to bury it by public subscription (Scholiast on Apollonius Rhodius: ii. 124). The diver-bird was sacred to Athene as protectress of ships and, since the Bluff of Athene overhung the sea, this may have been another of the cliffs from which her priestess launched the feathered *pharmacos* (see 70. 7; 89. 6; etc.). Atthis (*actes thea*, 'goddess of the rugged coast') seems to have been a title of the Attic Triple-goddess; her sisters were named Cranaë ('stony') and Cranaechme ('rocky point – Apollodorus: iii. 14. 5); and, since Procne and Philomela, when turned into birds, were jointly called Atthis (Martial: i. 54. 9 and v. 67. 2), she is likely to have been connected with the same cliff-top ritual. Atthis, as Athene, has several other bird epiphanies in Homer (see 97. 4). The Mysteries of the Great Goddesses, which concerned resurrection, had been buried between yew and myrtle because these stood, respectively, for the last vowel and the last consonant of the tree alphabet (see 52. 3), and were sacred to the Death-goddess.

95

THE BIRTH OF THESEUS

AEGEUS's first wife was Melite, daughter of Hoples: and his second, Chalciope, daughter of Rhexenor; but neither bore him any children. Ascribing this, and the misfortunes of his sisters Procne and Philomela, to Aphrodite's anger, he introduced her worship into Athens, and then went to consult the Delphic Oracle. The Oracle warned him not to untie the mouth of his bulging wine-skin until he reached the highest point of Athens, lest he die one day of grief, a response which Aegeus could not interpret.[1]

b. On his way home he called at Corinth; and here Medea made him swear a solemn oath that he would shelter her from all enemies if she ever sought refuge at Athens, and undertook in return to procure him a son by magic. Next, he visited Troezen, where his old comrades Pittheus and Troezen, sons of Pelops, had recently come from Pisa to share a kingdom with King Aetius. Aetius was the successor of his father Anthas, son of Poseidon and Alcyone who, having founded the cities Anthaea and Hyperea, had lately sailed off to found Halicarnassus in Caria. But Aetius seems to have enjoyed little power, because Pittheus, after Troezen's death, united Anthaea and Hyperea into a single city, which he dedicated jointly to Athene and Poseidon, calling it Troezen.[2]

c. Pittheus was the most learned man of his age, and one of his moral apothegms, on friendship, is often quoted: 'Blast not the hope that friendship hath conceived; but fill its measure high!' He founded a sanctuary of Oracular Apollo at Troezen, which is the oldest surviving shrine in Greece; and also dedicated an altar to the Triple-goddess Themis. Three white marble thrones, now placed above his tomb behind the temple of Artemis the Saviour, used to serve him and two others as judgement seats. He also taught the art of oratory in the Muses' sanctuary at Troezen – which was founded by Hephaestus's son Ardalus, the reputed inventor of the flute – and a treatise on rhetoric by his hand is extant.[3]

d. Now, while Pittheus was still living at Pisa, Bellerophon had asked to marry his daughter Aethra, but had been sent away to Caria in disgrace before the marriage could be celebrated; though still contracted to Bellerophon, she had little hope of his return. Pittheus, therefore, grieving at her enforced virginity, and influenced by the spell which Medea was casting on all of them from afar, made Aegeus drunk, and sent him to bed with Aethra. Later in the same night, Poseidon also enjoyed her. For, in obedience to a dream sent by Athene, she left the drunken Aegeus, and waded across to the island of Sphaeria, which lies close to the mainland of Troezen, carrying libations to pour at the tomb of Sphaerus, Pelops's charioteer. There, with Athene's connivance, Poseidon overpowered her, and Aethra subsequently changed the name of the island from Sphaeria to Hiera, and founded on it a temple of Apaturian Athene, establishing a rule that every Troezenian girl should henceforth dedicate her girdle to the goddess before marriage. Poseidon, however, generously conceded to Aegeus the paternity of any child born to Aethra in the course of the next four months.[4]

e. Aegeus, when he awoke and found himself in Aethra's bed, told her that if a son were born to them he must not be exposed or sent away, but secretly reared in Troezen. Then he sailed back to Athens, to celebrate the All-Athenian Festival, after hiding his sword and his sandals under a hollow rock, known as the Altar of Strong Zeus, which stood on the road from Troezen to Hermium. If, when the boy grew up, he could move this rock and recover the tokens, he was to be sent with them to Athens. Meanwhile, Aethra must keep silence, lest Aegeus's nephews, the fifty children of Pallas, plotted against her life. The sword was an heirloom from Cecrops.[5]

f. At a place now called Genethlium, on the way from the city to the harbour of Troezen, Aethra gave birth to a boy. Some say that she at once named him Theseus, because the tokens had been *deposited* for him; others, that he afterwards won this name at Athens. He was brought up in Troezen, where his guardian Pittheus discreetly spread the rumour that Poseidon had been his father; and one Connidas, to whom the Athenians still sacrifice a ram on the day before the Thesean Feasts, acted as his pedagogue. But some say that Theseus grew up at Marathon.[6]

g. One day Heracles, dining at Troezen with Pittheus, removed his lion-skin and threw it over a stool. When the palace children came in, they screamed and fled, all except seven-year-old Theseus, who ran to snatch an axe from the woodpile, and returned boldly, prepared to attack a real lion.[7]

h. At the age of sixteen years he visited Delphi, and offered his first manly hair-clippings to Apollo. He shaved, however, only the fore-part of his head, like the Arabians and Mysians, or like the war-like Abantes of Euboea, who thereby deny their enemies any advantage in close combat. This kind of tonsure, and the precinct where he per-formed the ceremony, are both still called Thesean. He was now a strong, intelligent and prudent youth; and Aethra, leading him to the rock underneath which Aegeus had hidden the sword and sandals, told him the story of his birth. He had no difficulty in moving the rock, since called the 'Rock of Theseus', and recovered the tokens. Yet, despite Pittheus's warnings and his mother's entreaties, he would not visit Athens by the safe sea route, but insisted on travelling overland; impelled by a desire to emulate the feats of his cousin-german Heracles, whom he greatly admired.[8]

1. Scholiast on Euripides's *Medea* 668; Apollodorus: iii. 15. 6; Pausanias: i. 14. 6.
2. Euripides: *Medea* 660 ff.; Strabo: viii. 6. 14; Plutarch: *Theseus* 2.
3. Plutarch: *loc. cit.*; Pausanias: ii. 31. 3–4 and 8–9.
4. Pausanias: ii. 31. 12 and 33. 1; Apollodorus: iii. 15. 7; Plutarch: *Theseus* 3; Hyginus: *Fabula* 37.
5. Plutarch: *loc. cit.*; Apollodorus: *loc. cit.*; Pausanias: ii. 32. 7.

6. Pausanias: ii. 32. 8; Plutarch: *Theseus* 4 and 6; Lactantius on Statius's *Thebaid* xii. 194.

7. Pausanias: i. 27. 8.

8. Homer: *Iliad* ii. 542; Pausanias: *loc. cit.* and ii. 32. 7; Plutarch: *Theseus* 5 and 7.

*

1. Pittheus is a masculine form of Pitthea. The names of the towns which he united to form Troezen suggests a matriarchal calendar-triad (see 75. 2), consisting of Anthea ('flowery'), the Goddess of Spring; Hyperea ('being overhead'), the Goddess of Summer, when the sun is at its zenith; and Pitthea ('pine-goddess'), worshipped in autumn when Attis-Adonis (see 79. 1) was sacrificed on his pine. They may be identified with the Triple-goddess Themis, to whom Pittheus raised an altar since the name Troezen is apparently a worn-down form of *trion hezomenon*, '[the city] of the three sitters', which refers to the three white thrones which served 'Pittheus and two others' as seats of justice.

2. Theseus must originally have had a twin, since his mother lay with both a god and a mortal on the same night; the myths of Idas and Lynceus Castor and Polydeuces (see 74. 1), Heracles and Iphicles (see 118. 3), make this certain. Moreover, he wore the lion-skin, like Heracles, and will therefore have been the sacred king, not the tanist. But when, after the Persian Wars, Theseus became the chief national hero of Athens, his paternity at least had to be Athenian, because his mother came from Troezen. The mythographers then decided to have it both ways: he was an Athenian, the son of Aegeus, a mortal; but whenever he needed to claim Poseidon as his father, he could do so (see 98. *j* and 101. *f*). In either case, his mother remained a Troezenian; Athens had important interests there. He was also allowed a honorary twin, Peirithous who, being mortal, could not escape from Tartarus – as Heracles, Polydeuces, and Theseus himself did (see 74. *j*; 103. *d*; and 134. *d*). No efforts were spared to connect Theseus with Heracles, but the Athenians never grew powerful enough to make him into an Olympian god.

3. There seem, however, to have been at least three mythological characters called Theseus: one from Troezen, one from Marathon in Attica, and the third from Lapith territory. These were not unified into a single character until the sixth century B.C., when (as Professor George Thomson suggests) the Butads, a Lapith clan who had become leading aristocrats at Athens and even usurped the native Pelasgian priesthood of Erechtheus, put forward the Athenian Theseus as a rival to Dorian Heracles (see 47. 4). Again, Pittheus was clearly both an Elean and a Troezenian title – also borne by the eponymous hero of an Attic deme belonging to the Cecropian tribe.

4. Aethra's visit to Sphaeria suggests that the ancient custom of self-

prostitution by unmarried girls survived in Athene's temple for some time after the patriarchal system had been introduced. It can hardly have been brought from Crete, since Troezen is not a Mycenaean site; but was perhaps a Canaanite importation, as at Corinth.

5. Sandals and sword are ancient symbols of royalty; the drawing of a sword from a rock seems to have formed part of the Bronze Age coronation ritual (see 81. 2). Odin, Galahad, and Arthur were all in turn required to perform a similar feat; and an immense sword, lion-hilted and plunged into a rock, figures in the sacred marriage scene carved at Hattasus (see 145. 5). Since Aegeus's rock is called both the Altar of Strong Zeus and the Rock of Theseus, it may be assumed that 'Zeus' and 'Theseus' were alternative titles of the sacred king, who was crowned upon it; but the goddess armed him. The 'Apollo' to whom Theseus dedicated his hair will have been Karu ('son of the goddess Car' – see 82. 6 and 86. 2), otherwise known as Car, or Q're, or Carys, the solar king whose locks were annually shorn before his death (see 83. 3), like those of Tyrian Samson and Megarean Nisus (see 91. 1). At a feast called the Comyria ('hair trimming'), young men sacrificed their forelocks in yearly mourning for him, and were afterwards known as Curetes (see 7. 4). This custom, probably of Libyan origin (Herodotus: iv. 194), had spread to Asia Minor and Greece; an injunction against it occurs in *Leviticus* xxi. 5. But, by Plutarch's time, Apollo was worshipped as the immortal Sun-god and, in proof of this, kept his own hair rigorously unshorn.

6. Aetius's division of Troezenia between Troezen, Pittheus, and himself, recalls the arrangement made by Proetus with Melampus and Bias (see 72. *h*). The Pittheus who taught rhetoric and whose treatise survived until Classical times must have been a late historical character.

96

THE LABOURS OF THESEUS

THESEUS set out to free the bandit-ridden coast road which led from Troezen to Athens. He would pick no quarrels but take vengeance on all who dared molest him, making the punishment fit the crime, as was Heracles's way.[1] At Epidaurus, Periphetes the cripple waylaid him. Periphetes, whom some call Poseidon's son, and others the son of Hephaestus and Anticleia, owned a huge brazen club, with which he used to kill wayfarers; hence his nickname Corunetes, or 'cudgel-man'.

Theseus wrenched the club from his hands and battered him to death. Delighted with its size and weight, he proudly carried it about ever afterwards; and though he himself had been able to parry its murderous swing, in his hands it never failed to kill.[2]

b. At the narrowest point of the Isthmus, where both the Corinthian and Saronic Gulfs are visible, lived Sinis, the son of Pemon; or, some say, of Polypemon and Sylea, daughter of Corinthus, who claimed to be Poseidon's bastard.[3] He had been nicknamed Pityocamptes, or 'pinebender', because he was strong enough to bend down the tops of pine-trees until they touched the earth, and would often ask innocent passers-by to help him with this task, but then suddenly release his hold. As the tree sprang upright again, they were hurled high into the air, and killed by the fall. Or he would bend down the tops of two neighbouring trees until they met, and tie one of his victim's arms to each, so that he was torn asunder when the trees were released.[4]

c. Theseus wrestled with Sinis, overpowered him, and served him as he had served others. At this, a beautiful girl ran to hide herself in a thicket of rushes and wild asparagus. He followed her and, after a long search, found her invoking the plants, promising never to burn or destroy them if they hid her safely. When Theseus swore not to do her any violence, she consented to emerge, and proved to be Sinis's daughter Perigune. Perigune fell in love with Theseus at sight, forgiving the murder of her hateful father and, in due course, bore him a son, Melanippus. Afterwards he gave her in marriage to Deioneus the Oechalian. Melanippus's son Ioxus emigrated to Caria, where he became the ancestor of the Ioxids, who burn neither rushes nor wild asparagus, but venerate both.[5]

d. Some, however, say that Theseus killed Sinis many years later, and rededicated the Isthmian Games to him, although they had been founded by Sisyphus in honour of Melicertes, the son of Ino.[6]

e. Next, at Crommyum, he hunted and destroyed a fierce and monstrous wild sow, which had killed so many Crommyonians that they no longer dared plough their fields. This beast, named after the crone who bred it, was said to be the child of Typhon and Echidne.[7]

f. Following the coast road, Theseus came to the precipitous cliffs rising sheer from the sea, which had become a stronghold of the bandit Sciron; some call him a Corinthian, the son of Pelops, or of Poseidon; others, the son of Henioche and Canethus.[8] Sciron used to seat himself upon a rock and force passing travellers to wash his feet: when they stooped to the task he would kick them over the cliff into the sea, where a giant turtle swam about, waiting to devour them. (Turtles closely resemble tortoises, except that they are larger, and have flippers instead of feet.) Theseus, refusing to wash Sciron's feet, lifted him from the rock and flung him into the sea.[9]

g. The Megareans, however, say that the only Sciron with whom Theseus came in conflict was an honest and generous prince of Megara, the father of Endeis, who married Aeacus and bore him Peleus and Telamon; they add, that Theseus killed Sciron after the capture of Eleusis, many years later, and celebrated the Isthmian Games in his honour under the patronage of Poseidon.[10]

h. The cliffs of Sciron rise close to the Molurian Rocks, and over them runs Sciron's footpath, made by him when he commanded the armies of Megara. A violent north-westerly breeze which blows seaward across these heights is called Sciron by the Athenians.[11]

i. Now, *sciron* means 'parasol'; and the month of Scirophorion is so called because at the Women's Festival of Demeter and Core, on the twelfth day of Scirophorion, the priest of Erechtheus carries a white parasol, and a priestess of Athene Sciras carries another in solemn procession from the Acropolis – for on that occasion the goddess's image is daubed with *sciras*, a sort of gypsum, to commemorate the white image which Theseus made of her after he had destroyed the Minotaur.[12]

j. Continuing his journey to Athens, Theseus met Cercyon the Arcadian, whom some call the son of Branchus and the nymph Argiope; others, the son of Hephaestus, or Poseidon.[13] He would challenge passers-by to wrestle with him and then crush them to death in his powerful embrace; but Theseus lifted him up by the knees and, to the delight of Demeter, who witnessed the struggle, dashed him headlong to the ground. Cercyon's death was instantaneous. Theseus did not trust to strength so much as to skill, for he had invented the art of wrestling, the principles of which were not hitherto understood. The Wrestling-ground of Cercyon is still shown near Eleusis, on the road to Megara, close to the grave of his daughter Alope, whom Theseus is said to have ravished.[14]

k. On reaching Attic Corydallus, Theseus slew Sinis's father Polypemon, surnamed Procrustes, who lived beside the road and had two beds in his house, one small the other large. Offering a night's lodging to travellers, he would lay the short men on the large bed, and rack them out to fit it; but the tall men on the small bed, sawing off as much of their legs as projected beyond it. Some say, however, that he used only one bed, and lengthened or shortened his lodgers according to its measure. In either case, Theseus served him as he had served others.[15]

1. Diodorus Siculus: iv. 59; Plutarch: *Theseus* 7 and 11.
2. Hyginus: *Fabula* 38; Apollodorus: iii. 16. 1; Pausanias: ii. 1. 4; Plutarch: *Theseus* 8.
3. Pausanias: *loc. cit.*; Ovid: *Ibis* 507 ff.; Apollodorus: iii. 16. 2; Scholiast on Euripides's *Hippolytus* 977.
4. Ovid: *Metamorphoses* vii. 433 ff.; Apollodorus: *loc. cit.*; Hyginus: *loc. cit.*; Diodorus Siculus: iv. 59; Pausanias: *loc. cit.*
5. Plutarch: *Theseus* 8 and 29.
6. *Parian Marble* 35 ff.; Plutarch: *Theseus* 25.
7. Plutarch: *Theseus* 9; Diodorus Siculus: iv. 59; Ovid: *Metamorphoses* vii. 433 ff.; Apollodorus: *Epitome* i. 1; Hyginus: *Fabula* 38.
8. Strabo: ix. 1. 4; Apollodorus: *Epitome* i. 2; Plutarch: *Theseus* 25.
9. Scholiast on Statius's *Thebaid* i. 339; Pausanias: i. 44. 12; Apollodorus: *Epitome* i. 2–3.
10. Plutarch: *Theseus* 10 and 25.
11. Pausanias: i. 44. 10–12; Strabo: ix. 1. 4.
12. Scholiast on Aristophanes's *Parliament of Women* 18; Aristophanes: *Wasps* 925; *Etymologicum Magnum*: *sub* Scirophorion.
13. Plutarch: *Theseus* 11; Apollodorus: *Epitome* i. 3; Hyginus: *Fabula* 38; Aulus Gellius: xiii. 21.
14. Ovid: *Ibis* 407 ff.; Apollodorus: *loc. cit.*; Pausanias: i. 39. 3; Plutarch: *Theseus* 11 and 29.
15. Diodorus Siculus: iv. 59; Apollodorus: *Epitome* i. 4; Pausanias: i. 38. 5; Hyginus: *Fabula* 38; Plutarch: *Theseus* 11.

*

1. The killing of Periphetes has been invented to account for Theseus's brass-bound club, like the one carried by Heracles (see 120. 5). Periphetes is described as a cripple because he was the son of Daedalus the smith, and smiths were often ritually lamed (see 92. 1).

2. Since the North Wind, which bent the pines, was held to fertilize women, animals, and plants, 'Pityocamptes' is described as the father of Perigune, a cornfield-goddess (see 48. 1). Her descendants' attachment to wild asparagus and rushes suggests that the sacred baskets carried in the Thesmophoria Festival were woven from these, and therefore tabooed for ordinary use. The Crommyonian Sow, *alias* Phaea, is the white Sow-Demeter (see 24. 7 and 74. 4), whose cult was early suppressed in the Peloponnese. That Theseus went out of his way to kill a mere sow troubled the mythographers: Hyginus and Ovid, indeed, make her a boar, and Plutarch describes her as a woman bandit whose disgusting

behaviour earned her the nickname of 'sow'. But she appears in early Welsh myth as the Old White Sow, Hen Wen, tended by the swineherd magician Coll ap Collfrewr, who introduced wheat and bees into Britain; and Demeter's swineherd magician Eubuleus was remembered in the Thesmophoria Festival at Eleusis, when live pigs were flung down a chasm in his honour. Their rotting remains later served to fertilize the seed-corn (Scholiast on Lucian's *Dialogues Between Whores* ii. 1).

3. The stories of Sciron and Cercyon are apparently based on a series of icons which illustrated the ceremony of hurling a sacred king as a *pharmacos* from the White Rock. The first hero who had met his death here was Melicertes (see 70. *h*), namely Heracles Melkarth of Tyre who seems to have been stripped of his royal trappings – club, lion-skin, and buskins – and then provided with wings, live birds, and a parasol to break his fall (see 89. *6*; 92. *3*; and 98. *7*). This is to suggest that Sciron, shown making ready to kick a traveller into the sea, is the *pharmacos* being prepared for his ordeal at the Scirophoria, which was celebrated in the last month of the year, namely at midsummer; and that a second scene, explained as Theseus's wrestling with Cercyon, shows him being lifted off his feet by his successor (as in the terracotta of the Royal Colonnade at Athens – Pausanias: i. 3. 1), while the priestess of the goddess looks on delightedly. This is a common mythological situation: Heracles, for instance, wrestled for a kingdom with Antaeus in Libya (see 133. *h*), and with Eryx in Sicily (see 132. *q*); Odysseus with Philomeleides on Tenedos see 161. *f*). A third scene, taken for Theseus's revenge on Sciron, shows the *pharmacos* hurtling through the air, parasol in hand. In a fourth, he has reached the sea, and his parasol is floating on the waves – the supposed turtle, waiting to devour him, was surely the parasol, since there is no record of an Attic turtle cult. The Second Vatican Mythographer (127) makes Daedalus, not Theseus, kill Sciron, probably because of Daedalus's mythic connexion with the *pharmacos* ritual of the partridge king (see 92. *3*).

4. All these feats of Theseus's seem to be interrelated. Grammarians associate the white parasol with a gypsum image of Athene. This recalls the white *pharmacos* dolls, called 'Argives' ('white men'), thrown into running water once a year at the May purification of temples (see 132. *p*); also the white cakes shaped like pigs, and made of flour mixed with gypsum (Pliny: *Natural History* xvii. 29. 2), which were used in the Thesmophoria to replace the pig remains recovered from Eubuleus's chasm – 'in order not to defraud his sacred serpents', explains the scholiast on Lucian's *Dialogues Between Whores*. The Scirophoria Festival formed part of the Thesmophoria. *Thes* has the same meaning in *Thesmophoria* as in *Theseus*: namely 'tokens deposited' – in the baskets woven of wild asparagus and rush which Perigune sanctified. They were phallic tokens

and the festival was an erotic one: this is justified by Theseus's seduction of Perigune, and also by Hermes's seduction of Herse (see 25. *d*). The priest of Erechtheus carried a parasol, because he was the president of the serpent cult, and the sacred functions of the ancient kings rested with him after the monarchy had been abolished: as they rested at Rome with the Priest of Zeus.

5. Cercyon's name connects him with the pig cult. So does his parentage: Branchus refers to the grunting of pigs, and Argiope is a synonym for Phaea. It will have been Poseidon's son Theseus who ravished Alope: that is to say, suppressed the worship of the Megarean Moon-goddess as Vixen (see 49. *2*).

6. Sinis and Sciron are both described as the hero in whose honour the Isthmian Games were rededicated; Sinis's nickname was Pityocamptes; and Sciron, like Pityocamptes, was a north-westerly wind. But since the Isthmian Games had originally been founded in memory of Heracles Melkarth, the destruction of Pityocamptes seems to record the suppression of the Boreas cult in Athens – which was, however, revived after the Persian Wars (see 48. *4*). In that case, the Isthmian Games are analogous to the Pythian Games, founded in memory of Python, who was both the fertilizing North Wind and the ghost of the sacred king killed by his rival Apollo. Moreover, 'Procrustes', according to Ovid and the scholiast on Euripides's *Hippolytus* (977), was only another nickname for Sinis-Pityocamptes; and Procrustes seems to be a fictional character, invented to account for a familiar icon: the hair of the old king – Samson, Pterelaus (see 89. *7*), Nisus (see 91. *1*), Curoi, Llew Llaw, or whatever he may have been called – is tied to the bedpost by his treacherous bride, while his rival advances, axe in hand, to destroy him. 'Theseus' and his Hellenes abolished the custom of throwing the old king over the Molurian Rock, and rededicated the Games to Poseidon at Ino's expense, Ino being one of Athene's earlier titles.

97

THESEUS AND MEDEA

ARRIVED in Attica, Theseus was met beside the River Cephissus by the sons of Phytalus, who purified him from the blood he had spilled, but especially from that of Sinis, a maternal kinsman of his. The altar of Gracious Zeus, where this ceremony was performed, still stands by the riverside. Afterwards, the Phytalids welcomed Theseus as their guest, which was the first true hospitality he had received since leaving

Troezen. Dressed in a long garment that reached to his feet and with his hair neatly plaited, he entered Athens on the eighth day of the month Cronius, now called Hecatomboeon. As he passed the nearly-completed temple of Apollo the Dolphin, a group of masons working on the roof mistook him for a girl, and impertinently asked why he was allowed to wander about unescorted. Disdaining to reply, Theseus unyoked the oxen from the masons' cart and tossed one of them into the air, high above the temple roof.[1]

b. Now while Theseus was growing up in Troezen, Aegeus had kept his promise to Medea. He gave her shelter in Athens when she fled from Corinth in the celebrated chariot drawn by winged serpents, and married her, rightly confident that her spells would enable him to beget an heir; for he did not yet know that Aethra had borne him Theseus.[2]

c. Medea, however, recognised Theseus as soon as he arrived in the city, and grew jealous on behalf of Medus, her son by Aegeus, who was generally expected to succeed him on the Athenian throne. She therefore persuaded Aegeus that Theseus came as a spy or an assassin, and had him invited to a feast at the Dolphin Temple; Aegeus, who used the temple as his residence, was then to offer him a cup of wine already prepared by her. This cup contained wolfsbane, a poison which she had brought from Bithynian Acherusia, where it first sprang from the deadly foam scattered by Cerberus when Heracles dragged him out of Tartarus; because wolfsbane flourishes on bare rocks, the peasants call it 'aconite'.[3]

d. Some say that when the roast beef was served in the Dolphin Temple, Theseus ostentatiously drew his sword, as if to carve, and thus attracted his father's attention; but others, that he had unsuspectingly raised the cup to his lips before Aegeus noticed the Erechtheid serpents carved on the ivory sword-hilt and dashed the poison to the floor. The spot where the cup fell is still shown, barred off from the rest of the temple.

e. Then followed the greatest rejoicing that Athens had ever known. Aegeus embraced Theseus, summoned a public assembly, and acknowledged him as his son. He lighted fires on every altar and heaped the gods' images with gifts; hecatombs of garlanded oxen were sacrificed and, throughout the palace and the city, nobles and commoners feasted together, and sang of Theseus's glorious deeds that already outnumbered the years of his life.[4]

f. Theseus then went in vengeful pursuit of Medea, who eluded him by casting a magic cloud about herself; and presently left Athens with young Medus, and an escort which Aegeus generously provided. But some say that she fled with Polyxenus, her son by Jason.[5]

g. Pallas and his fifty sons, who even before this had declared that Aegeus was not a true Erechtheid and thus had no right to the throne, broke into open revolt when this footloose stranger threatened to baulk their hopes of ever ruling Athens. They divided their forces: Pallas with twenty-five of his sons and numerous retainers marched against the city from the direction of Sphettus, while the other twenty-five lay in ambush at Gargettus. But Theseus, informed of their plans by a herald named Leos, of the Agnian clan, sprang the ambush and destroyed the entire force. Pallas thereupon disbanded his command, and sued for peace. The Pallantids have never forgotten Leos's treachery, and still will not intermarry with the Agnians nor allow any herald to begin a proclamation with the words '*Akouete leoi!*' ('Hearken, ye people!'), because of the resemblance which *leoi* bears to the name of Leos.[6]

h. This Leos must be distinguished from the other Leos, Orpheus's son, and ancestor of the Athenian Leontids. Once, in a time of famine and plague, Leos obeyed the Delphic Oracle by sacrificing his daughters Theope, Praxithea, and Eubule to save the city. The Athenians set up the Leocorium in their honour.[7]

1. Pausanias: i. 37. 3 and 19. 1; Plutarch: *Theseus* 12.
2. Euripides: *Medea* 660 ff.; Apollodorus: i. 9. 28.
3. Plutarch: *Theseus* 12; Apollodorus: *Epitome* i. 6; Ovid: *Metamorphoses* vii. 402 ff.
4. Plutarch: *loc. cit.*; Ovid: *loc. cit.*
5. Ovid: *loc. cit.*; Apollodorus: *loc. cit.*; Diodorus Siculus: iv. 55. 6; Hellanicus, quoted by Pausanias: ii. 3. 7.
6. Plutarch: *Theseus* 13.
7. Pausanias: i. 5. 2; Suidas *sub* Leos; Aristides: *Panathenian Oration*; Jerome: *Against Jovinianus* p. 185, ed. Mart; Suidas *sub* Leocorium; Aelian: *Varia Historia* xii. 28.

*

1. This artificial romance with its theatrical *dénouement* in the poisoning scene recalls that of Ion (see 44. *a*); and the incident of the ox tossed into the air seems merely a crude imitation of Heracles's feats. The masons' question is anachronistic, because in the heroic age young women

went about unescorted; neither could Theseus have been mistaken for a girl if he had already dedicated his hair to Apollo and become one of the Curetes. Yet the story's weaknesses suggest that it has been deduced from an ancient icon which, since the men on the temple roof were recognizably masons, will have shown a sacrifice performed on the day when the temple was completed (see 84. *1*). It is likely that the figure, taken for Theseus, who unyokes the sacrificial white ox from a cart, is a priestess; and that, because of its dolphin decorations, the temple has been misread as Apollo's, though the dolphin was originally an emblem of the Moongoddess. The beast has not been tossed into the air. It is the deity in whose honour the sacrifice is being offered: either a white moon-cow, the goddess herself, or the white bull of Poseidon (see 88. *c*), who shared a shrine on the Acropolis with Athene and to whom, as Sea-god, dolphins were sacred; Apollo's priests, Plutarch not the least, were always zealous to enhance his power and authority at the expense of other deities. A companion icon, from which the story of the poisoned cup will have been deduced – aconite was a well-known paralysant – probably showed a priest or priestess pouring a libation to the ghosts of the men sacrificed when the foundations were laid, while Persephone and Cerberus stand by. Plutarch describes Aegeus as living in the Dolphin Temple rather than a private house; and this is correct since, as sacred king, he had apartments in the Queen's palace (see 25. *7*).

2. Medea's expulsion first from Corinth, and then from Athens, refers to the Hellenic suppression of the Earth-goddess's cult – her serpent chariot shows her to be a Corinthian Demeter (see 24. *m*). Theseus's defeat of the Pallantids similarly refers to the suppression of the original Athene cult (see 9. *1* and 16. *3*), with its college of fifty priestesses – *pallas* can mean either 'youth' or 'maiden'. Still another version of the same story is the sacrifice of Leos's three daughters, who are really the goddess in triad. The Maiden is Theope ('divine face'), the New Moon; the Nymph is Praxithea ('active goddess'), the Queen-bee. Cecrops's mother bore the same name in Euboea (Apollodorus: iii. 15. *1* and *5*); the Crone is Eubule ('good counsel'), the oracular goddess, whom Eubuleus the swineherd served at Eleusis.

3. That Pallantids and Agnians refrained from inter-marriage may have been a relic of exogamy, with its complex system of group-marriage between phratries, each phratry or sub-phratry consisting of several totem clans: if so, Pallantids and Agnians will have belonged to the same sub-phratry, marriage being permitted only between members of different ones (see 80. *5*). The Pallantid clan probably had a goat for its totem, as the Agnians had a lamb, the Leontids a lion, and the Erechtheids a serpent. Many other totem clans are hinted at in Attic mythology: among them, crow, nightingale, hoopoe, wolf, bear, and owl.

4. To judge from the Theseus and Heracles myths, both Athene's chief priestess at Athens, and Hera's at Argos, belonged to a lion clan, into which they adopted sacred kings; and a gold ring found at Tiryns shows four lion-men offering libation vessels to a seated goddess, who must be Hera, since a cuckoo perches behind her throne (see 12. 4). Despite the absence of lions in Crete, they figured there too as the Goddess's beasts. Athene was not associated with the cuckoo but had several other bird epiphanies, which may be totemistic by origin. In Homer she appears as a sea-eagle (*Odyssey* iii. 371) and a swallow (*ibid*. xxii. 239); in company with Apollo, as a vulture (*Iliad* vii. 58); and in company with Hera, as a dove (*ibid* v. 778). In a small Athenian vase of 500 B.C. she is shown as a lark; and Athene the diver-bird, or gannet, had a shrine near Megara (Pausanias: i. 5. 3. and 41. 6 – see 94. c). But the wise owl was her principal epiphany. The owl clan preserved their ritual until late Classical times: initiates in owl-disguise would perform a ceremony of catching their totem bird (Aelian: *Varia Historia* xv. 28; Pollux: iv. 103; Athenaeus: 391a–b and 629f).

5. Plutarch's story of *Akouete leoi* is plausible enough: it often happened in primitive religions that words were banned because they sounded like the name of a person, object, or animal, which could not be safely mentioned; especially words suggesting the names of dead kinsmen, even if they had come to a natural end.

6. The Pallantids' denial that Aegeus and Theseus were true Erechtheids may reflect a sixth-century protest at Athens against the usurpation of the immigrant Butadae (who refurbished the Theseus legend) of the native Erechtheid priesthood (see 95. 3).

98

THESEUS IN CRETE

It is a matter of dispute whether Medea persuaded Aegeus to send Theseus against Poseidon's ferocious white bull, or whether it was after her expulsion from Athens that he undertook the destruction of this fire-breathing monster, hoping thereby to ingratiate himself further with the Athenians. Brought by Heracles from Crete, let loose on the plain of Argos, and driven thence across the Isthmus to Marathon, the bull had killed men by the hundred between the cities of Probalinthus and Tricorynthus, including (some say) Minos's son Androgeus. Yet Theseus boldly seized those murderous horns and dragged the bull in triumph through the streets of Athens, and up the steep slope of the Acropolis, where he sacrificed it to Athene, or to Apollo.[1]

b. As he approached Marathon, Theseus had been hospitably entertained by a needy old spinster named Hecale, or Hecalene, who vowed a ram to Zeus if he came back safely. But she died before his return, and he instituted the Hecalesian Rites, to honour her and Zeus Hecaleius, which are still performed today. Because Theseus was no more than a boy at this time, Hecale had caressed him with childish endearments, and is therefore commonly called by the diminutive Hecalene, rather than Hecale.[2]

c. In requital for the death of Androgeus, Minos gave orders that the Athenians should send seven youths and seven maidens every ninth year – namely at the close of every Great Year – to the Cretan Labyrinth, where the Minotaur waited to devour them. This Minotaur, whose name was Asterius, or Asterion, was the bull-headed monster which Pasiphaë had borne to the white bull.[3] Soon after Theseus's arrival at Athens the tribute fell due for the third time, and he so deeply pitied those parents whose children were liable to be chosen by lot, that he offered himself as one of the victims, despite Aegeus's earnest attempts at dissuasion. But some say that the lot had fallen on him. According to others, King Minos came in person with a large fleet to choose the victims; his eye lighted on Theseus who, though a native of Troezen, not Athens, volunteered to come on the understanding that if he conquered the Minotaur with his bare hands the tribute would be remitted.[4]

d. On the two previous occasions, the ship which conveyed the fourteen victims had carried black sails, but Theseus was confident that the gods were on his side, and Aegeus therefore gave him a white sail to hoist on return, in signal of success; though some say that it was a red sail, dyed in juice of the kerm-oak berry.[5]

e. When the lots had been cast at the Law Courts, Theseus led his companions to the Dolphin Temple where, on their behalf, he offered Apollo a branch of consecrated olive, bound with white wool. The fourteen mothers brought provisions for the voyage, and told their children fables and heroic tales to hearten them. Theseus, however, replaced two of the maiden victims with a pair of effeminate youths, possessed of unusual courage and presence of mind. These he commanded to take warm baths, avoid the rays of the sun, perfume their hair and bodies with unguent oils, and practise how to talk, gesture, and walk like women. He was thus able to deceive Minos by passing them off as maidens.[6]

f. Phaeax, the ancestor of the Phaeacians, among whom Odysseus fell, stood as pilot at the prow of the thirty-oared ship in which they sailed, because no Athenian as yet knew anything about navigation. Some say that the helmsman was Phereclus; but those who name him Nausitheus are likely to be right, since Theseus on his return raised monuments to Nausitheus and Phaeax at Phalerum, the port of departure; and the local Pilots' Festival is held in their joint honour.[7]

g. The Delphic Oracle had advised Theseus to take Aphrodite for his guide and companion on the voyage. He therefore sacrificed to her on the strand; and lo! the victim, a she-goat, became a he-goat in its death-throes. This prodigy won Aphrodite her title of Epitragia.[8]

h. Theseus sailed on the sixth day of Munychion [April]. Every year on this date the Athenians still send virgins to the Dolphin Temple in propitiation of Apollo, because Theseus had omitted to do so before taking his leave. The god's displeasure was shown in a storm, which forced him to take shelter at Delphi and there offer belated sacrifices.[9]

i. When the ship reached Crete some days afterwards, Minos rode down to the harbour to count the victims. Falling in love with one of the Athenian maidens – whether it was Periboea (who became the mother of Ajax) or Eriboea, or Phereboea, is not agreed, for these three bore confusingly similar names – he would have ravished her then and there, had Theseus not protested that it was his duty as Poseidon's son to defend virgins against outrage by tyrants. Minos, laughing lewdly, replied that Poseidon had never been known to show delicate respect for any virgins who took his fancy.[10]

'Ha!' he cried, 'prove yourself a son of Poseidon, by retrieving this bauble for me!' So saying, he flung his golden signet ring into the sea.

'First prove that you are a son of Zeus!' retorted Theseus.

j. This Minos did. His prayer: 'Father Zeus, hear me!' was at once answered by lightning and a clap of thunder. Without more ado, Theseus dived into the sea, where a large school of dolphins escorted him honourably down to the palace of the Nereids. Some say that Thetis the Nereid then gave him the jewelled crown, her wedding gift from Aphrodite, which Ariadne afterwards wore; others, that Amphitrite the Sea-goddess did so herself, and that she sent the Nereids swimming in every direction to find the golden ring. At all events, when Theseus emerged from the sea, he was carrying both the ring and the crown, as Micon has recorded in his painting on the third wall of Theseus's sanctuary.[11]

k. Aphrodite had indeed accompanied Theseus: for not only did both Periboea and Phereboea invite the chivalrous Theseus to their couches, and were not spurned, but Minos's own daughter Ariadne fell in love with him at first sight. 'I will help you to kill my half-brother, the Minotaur,' she secretly promised him, 'if I may return to Athens with you as your wife.' This offer Theseus gladly accepted, and swore to marry her. Now, before Daedalus left Crete, he had given Ariadne a magic ball of thread, and instructed her how to enter and leave the Labyrinth. She must open the entrance door and tie the loose end of the thread to the lintel; the ball would then roll along, diminishing as it went and making, with devious turns and twists, for the innermost recess where the Minotaur was lodged. This ball Ariadne gave to Theseus, and instructed him to follow it until he reached the sleeping monster, whom he must seize by the hair and sacrifice to Poseidon. He could then find his way back by rolling up the thread into a ball again.[12]

l. That same night Theseus did as he was told; but whether he killed the Minotaur with a sword given him by Ariadne, or with his bare hands, or with his celebrated club, is much disputed. A sculptured frieze at Amyclae shows the Minotaur bound and led in triumph by Theseus to Athens; but this is not the generally accepted story.[13]

m. When Theseus emerged from the labyrinth, spotted with blood, Ariadne embraced him passionately, and guided the whole Athenian party to the harbour. For, in the meantime, the two effeminate-looking youths had killed the guards of the women's quarters, and released the maiden victims. They all stole aboard their ship, where Nausitheus and Phaeax were expecting them, and rowed hastily away. But although Theseus had first stove in the hulls of several Cretan ships, to prevent pursuit, the alarm sounded and he was forced to fight a sea-battle in the harbour, before escaping, fortunately without loss, under cover of darkness.[14]

n. Some days later, after disembarking on the island then named Dia, but now known as Naxos, Theseus left Ariadne asleep on the shore, and sailed away. Why he did so must remain a mystery. Some say that he deserted her in favour of a new mistress, Aegle, daughter of Panopeus; others that, while wind-bound on Dia, he reflected on the scandal which Ariadne's arrival at Athens would cause.[15] Others, again that Dionysus, appearing to Theseus in a dream, threateningly demanded Ariadne for himself, and that, when Theseus awoke to see Dionysus's fleet bearing down on Dia, he weighed anchor in sudden terror; Dionysus having cast a spell which made him forget his promise to Ariadne and even her very existence.[16]

o. Whatever the truth of the matter may be, Dionysus's priests at Athens affirm that when Ariadne found herself alone on the deserted shore, she broke into bitter laments, remembering how she had trembled while Theseus set out to kill her monstrous half-brother; how she had offered silent vows for his success; and how, through love of him, she had deserted her parents and motherland. She now invoked the whole universe for vengeance, and Father Zeus nodded assent. Then, gently and sweetly, Dionysus with his merry train of satyrs and maenads came to Ariadne's rescue. He married her without delay, setting Thetis's crown upon her head, and she bore him many children.[17] Of these only Thoas and Oenopion are sometimes called Theseus's sons. The crown, which Dionysus later set among the stars as the Corona Borealis, was made by Hephaestus of fiery gold and red Indian gems, set in the shape of roses.[18]

p. The Cretans, however, refuse to admit that the Minotaur ever existed, or that Theseus won Ariadne by clandestine means. They describe the Labyrinth as merely a well-guarded prison, where the Athenian youths and maidens were kept in readiness for Androgeus's funeral games. Some were sacrificed at his tomb; others presented to the prizewinners as slaves. It happened that Minos's cruel and arrogant general Taurus had carried all before him, year after year: winning every event in which he competed, much to the disgust of his rivals. He had also forfeited Minos's confidence because he was rumoured to be carrying on an adulterous affair with Pasiphaë, connived at by Daedalus, and one of her twin sons bore a close resemblance to him. Minos, therefore, gladly granted Theseus's request for the privilege of wrestling against Taurus. In ancient Crete, women as well as men attended the games, and Ariadne fell in love with Theseus when, three times in succession, she saw him toss the former champion over his head and pin his shoulders to the ground. The sight afforded Minos almost equal satisfaction: he awarded Theseus the prize, accepted him as his son-in-law, and remitted the cruel tribute.[19]

q. A traditional Bottiaean song confirms this tradition that not all the victims were put to death. It records that the Cretans sent an offering of their first-born to Delphi, for the most part children of Cretanized Athenian slaves. The Delphians, however, could not support these on the resources of their small city, and therefore packed them off to found a colony at Iapygia in Italy. Later, they settled at Bottiaea in Thrace, and the nostalgic cry raised by the Bottiaean maidens: 'O let us return to Athens!', is a constant reminder of their origin.[20]

r. An altogether different account is given by the Cypriots and others. They say that Minos and Theseus agreed on oath that no ship – except the *Argo*, commanded by Jason, who had a commission to clear the sea of pirates – might sail in Greek waters with a crew larger than five. When Daedalus fled from Crete to Athens, Minos broke this pact by pursuing him with warships, and thus earned the anger of Poseidon, who had witnessed the oath, and now raised a storm which drove him to his death in Sicily. Minos's son Deucalion, inheriting the quarrel, threatened that unless the Athenians surrendered Daedalus, he would put to death all the hostages given him by Theseus at the conclusion of the pact. Theseus replied that Daedalus was his blood-relation, and enquired mildly whether some compromise could not be reached. He exchanged several letters on the subject with Deucalion, but meanwhile secretly built warships: some at Thymoetidae, a port off the beaten track, and others at Troezen, where Pittheus had a naval yard about which the Cretans knew nothing. Within a month or two his flotilla set sail, guided by Daedalus and other fugitives from Crete; and the Cretans mistook the approaching ships for part of Minos's lost fleet and gave them a resounding welcome. Theseus therefore seized the harbour without opposition, and made straight for Cnossus, where he cut down Deucalion's guards, and killed Deucalion himself in an inner chamber of the palace. The Cretan throne then passed to Ariadne, with whom Theseus generously came to terms; she surrendered the Athenian hostages, and a treaty of perpetual friendship was concluded between the two nations, sealed by a union of the crowns – in effect, she married Theseus.[21]

s. After long feasting they sailed together for Athens, but were driven to Cyprus by a storm. There Ariadne, already with child by Theseus, and fearing that she might miscarry from sea-sickness, asked to be put ashore at Amathus. This was done, but hardly had Theseus regained his ship when a violent wind forced the whole fleet out to sea again. The women of Amathus treated Ariadne kindly, comforting her with letters which, they pretended, had just arrived from Theseus, who was repairing his ship on the shores of a neighbouring island; and when she died in childbed, gave her a lavish funeral. Ariadne's tomb is still shown at Amathus, in a grove sacred to her as Aridela. Theseus, on his eventual return from the Syrian coast, was deeply grieved to learn that she had died, and endowed her cult with a large sum of money. The Cypriots still celebrate Ariadne's festival on the second day of September, when a youth lies down in her grove and imitates a travailing woman; and worship two small statues of her, one in silver, the other in brass, which Theseus left them. They say that Dionysus, so far from marrying Ariadne, was indignant that she and Theseus had profaned his Naxian grotto, and complained to Artemis, who killed her in childbed with merciless shafts; but some say that she hanged herself for fear of Artemis.[22]

t. To resume the history of Theseus: from Naxos he sailed to Delos, and there sacrificed to Apollo, celebrating athletic games in his honour. It was then that he introduced the novel custom of crowning the victor with palm-leaves, and placing a palm-stem in his right hand. He also prudently dedicated to the god a small wooden image of Aphrodite, the work of Daedalus, which Ariadne had brought from Crete and left aboard his ship – it might have been the subject of cynical comment by the Athenians. This image, still displayed at Delos, rests on a square base instead of feet, and is perpetually garlanded.[23]

u. A horned altar stands beside the round lake of Delos. Apollo himself built it, when he was only four years of age, with the closely compacted horns of countless she-goats killed by Artemis on Mount Cynthus – his first architectural feat. The foundations of the altar, and its enclosing walls, are also made entirely of horns; all taken from the same side of the victims – but whether from the left, or from the right, is disputed.[24] What makes the work rank among the seven marvels of the world is that neither mortar nor any other colligative has been used. It was around this altar – or, according to another version, around an altar of Aphrodite, on which the Daedalic image had been set – that Theseus and his companions danced the Crane, which consists of labyrinthine evolutions, trod with measured steps to the accompaniment of harps. The Delians still perform this dance, which Theseus introduced from Cnossus; Daedalus had built Ariadne a dancing floor there, marked with a maze pattern in white marble relief, copied from the Egyptian Labyrinth. When Theseus and his companions performed the Crane at Cnossus, this was the first occasion on which men and women danced together. Old-fashioned people, especially sailors, keep up much the same dance in many different cities of Greece and Asia Minor; so do children in the Italian countryside, and it is the foundation of the Troy Games.[25]

v. Ariadne was soon revenged on Theseus. Whether in grief for her loss, or in joy at the sight of the Attic coast, from which he had been kept by prolonged winds, he forgot his promise to hoist the white sail.[26] Aegeus, who stood watching for him on the Acropolis, where the Temple of the Wingless Victory now stands, sighted the black sail, swooned, and fell headlong to his death into the valley below. But some say that he deliberately cast himself into the sea, which was thenceforth named the Aegean.[27]

w. Theseus was not informed of this sorrowful accident until he had completed the sacrifices vowed to the gods for his safe return; he then buried Aegeus, and honoured him with a hero-shrine. On the eighth day of Pyanepsion [October], the date of the return from Crete, loyal Athenians flock down to the seashore, with cooking-pots in which they stew different kinds of beans – to remind their children how Theseus, having been obliged to place his crew on very short rations, cooked all his remaining provisions in one pot as soon as he landed, and filled their empty bellies at last. At this same festival a thanksgiving is sung for the end of hunger, and an olive-branch, wreathed in white wool and hung with the season's fruits, is carried to commemorate the one which Theseus dedicated before setting out. Since this was harvest time, Theseus also instituted the Festival of Grape Boughs, either in gratitude to Athene and Dionysus, both of whom appeared to him on Naxos, or in honour of Dionysus and Ariadne. The two bough-bearers represent the youths whom Theseus had taken to Crete disguised as maidens, and who walked beside him in the triumphal procession after his return. Fourteen women carry provisions and take part in this sacrifice; they represent the mothers of the rescued victims, and their task is to tell fables and ancient myths, as these mothers also did before the ship sailed.[28]

x. Theseus dedicated a temple to Saviour Artemis in the market place at Troezen; and his fellow-citizens honoured him with a sanctuary while he was still alive. Such families as had been liable to the Cretan tribute undertook to supply the needful sacrifices; and Theseus awarded his priesthood to the Phytalids, in gratitude for their hospitality. The vessel in which he sailed to Crete has made an annual voyage to Delos and back ever since; but has been so frequently overhauled and refitted that philosophers cite it as a stock instance, when discussing the problem of continuous identity.[29]

1. Apollodorus: *Epitome* i. 5; Servius on Virgil's *Aeneid* viii. 294; First Vatican Mythographer: 47; Pausanias: i. 27. 9; Plutarch: *Theseus* 14; Hesychius *sub* Bolynthos.

2. Plutarch: *loc. cit.*; Callimachus: *Fragment* 40, ed. Bentley; Ovid: *Remedies of Love* 747.

3. Diodorus Siculus: iv. 61; Hyginus: *Fabula* 41; Apollodorus: iii. 1. 4; Pausanias. ii. 31. 1.

4. Plutarch: *Theseus* 17; Apollodorus: *Epitome* i. 7; Scholiast on Homer's *Iliad* xviii. 590; Diodorus Siculus: *loc cit.*; Hellanicus, quoted by Plutarch: *Theseus* 19.

5. Plutarch: *loc. cit.*; Simonides, quoted by Plutarch: *loc. cit.*

6. Plutarch: *Theseus* 18; Demon's *History*, quoted by Plutarch: *Theseus* 23.

7. Philochorus, quoted by Plutarch: *Theseus* 17; Simonides, quoted by Plutarch: *loc. cit.*; Pausanias: i. 1. 2.

8. Plutarch: *Theseus* 18.

9. Plutrach: *loc cit.*; Scholiast on Aristophanes's *Knights* 725.

10. Pausanias: i. 42. 1; Hyginus: *Poetic Astronomy* ii. 5; Plutarch: *Theseus* 29.

11. Pausanias: i. 17. 3; Hyginus: *loc. cit.*

12. Plutarch: *Theseus* 29; Apollodorus: *Epitome* i. 8.

13. Scholiast on Homer's *Odyssey* xi. 322, quoted by Pherecydes; Homer: *Iliad* xviii. 590; Eustathius on Homer's *Odyssey* xi. 320; Apollodorus: *Epitome* i. 9; Ovid: *Heroides* iv. 115; Pausanias: iii. 18. 7.

14. Pausanias: ii. 31. 1; Pherecydes, quoted by Plutarch: *Theseus* 19; Demon, quoted by Plutarch: *loc cit.*

15. Scholiast on Theocritus's *Idylls* ii. 45; Diodorus Siculus: iv. 61. 5; Catullus: lxiv. 50 ff.; Plutarch: *Theseus* 29; Hyginus: *Fabula* 43.

16. Pausanias: x. 29. 2; Diodorus Siculus. v. 51. 4; Scholiast on Theocritus: *loc.cit.*

17. Pausanias: i. 20. 2; Catullus: lxiv. 50 ff.; Hyginus: *Poetic Astronomy* ii. 5.

18. Plutarch: *Theseus* 20; Bacchylides: xvi. 116.

19. Plutarch: *Romulus and Theseus Compared*; Philochorus, quoted by Plutarch: *Theseus* 15; Servius on Virgil's *Aeneid* vi. 14; Philochorus, quoted by Plutarch: *Theseus* 19.

20. Aristotle: *Constitution of the Bottiaeans*, quoted by Plutarch: *Theseus* 16; Plutarch: *Greek Questions* 35.

21. Cleidemus, quoted by Plutarch: *Theseus* 19.

22. Hesychius *sub* Aridela; Paeonius, quoted by Plutarch: *Theseus* 21; *Contest of Homer and Hesiod* 14.

23. Plutarch: *loc. cit.*; Pausanias: viii. 48. 2 and ix. 40. 2; Callimachus: *Hymn to Delos* 312.

24. Callimachus: *Hymn to Apollo* 60 ff.; Plutarch: *loc. cit.* and *Which Animals Are the Craftier?* 35.

25. Plutarch: *Theseus* 21; Callimachus: *Hymn to Delos* 312 ff.; Homer: *Iliad* xviii. 591–2; Pausanias: ix. 40. 2; Pliny: *Natural History* xxxvi. 19; Scholiast on Homer's *Iliad* xviii. 590; Eustathius on Homer's *Iliad* p. 1166; Virgil: *Aeneid* v. 588 ff.

26. Catullus: lxiv. 50 ff.; Apollodorus: *Epitome* i. 10; Plutarch: *Theseus* 22.

27. Catullus: *loc. cit.*; Pausanias: i. 22. 4–5; Plutarch: *loc. cit.* and *Romulus and Theseus Compared*; Hyginus: *Fabula* 43.

28. Pausanias: i. 22. 5; Plutarch: *Theseus* 22 and 23; Proclus: *Chresto-mathy*, quoted by Photius: 989.

29. Pausanias: iii. 31. 1; Plutarch: *loc cit.*

*

1. Greece was Cretanized towards the close of the eighteenth century B.C., probably by an Hellenic aristocracy which had seized power in Crete a generation or two earlier and there initiated a new culture. The straightforward account of Theseus's raid on Cnossus, quoted by Plutarch from Cleidemus, makes reasonable sense. It describes a revolt by the Athenians against a Cretan overlord who had taken hostages for their good behaviour; the secret building of a flotilla; the sack of the unwalled city of Cnossus during the absence of the main Cretan fleet in Sicily; and a subsequent peace treaty ratified by the Athenian king's marriage with Ariadne, the Cretan heiress. These events, which point to about the year 1400 B.C., are paralleled by the mythical account: a tribute of youths and maidens is demanded from Athens in requital for the murder of a Cretan prince. Theseus, by craftily killing the Bull of Minos, or defeating Minos's leading commander in a wrestling match, relieves Athens of this tribute; marries Ariadne, the royal heiress; and makes peace with Minos himself.

2. Theseus's killing of the bull-headed Asterius, called the Minotaur, or 'Bull of Minos'; his wrestling match with Taurus ('bull'); and his capture of the Cretan bull, are all versions of the same event. *Bolynthos*, which gave its name to Attic Probalinthus, was the Cretan name for 'wild bull'. 'Minos' was the title of a Cnossian dynasty, which had a sky-bull for its emblem – 'Asterius' could mean 'of the sun' or 'of the sky' – and it was in bull-form that the king seems to have coupled ritually with the Chief-priestess as Moon-cow (see 88. 7). One element in the forma-tion of the Labyrinth myth may have been that the palace at Cnossus – the house of the *labrys*, or double-axe – was a complex of rooms and corridors, and that the Athenian raiders had difficulty in finding and killing the king when they captured it. But this is not all. An open space in front of the palace was occupied by a dance floor with a maze pattern

used to guide performers of an erotic spring dance (see 92. 4). The origin
of this pattern, now also called a labyrinth, seems to have been the traditional brushwood maze used to decoy partridges towards one of their
own cocks, caged in a central enclosure, which uttered food-calls, love-
calls, and challenges; and the spring dancers will have imitated the ecstatic
hobbling love-dance of the cock-partridges (see 92. 2), whose fate was to
be knocked on the head by the hunter (*Ecclesiasticus* xi. 30).

3. An Etruscan wine-jar from Tragliatella (see 104. 4), showing two
mounted heroes, explains the religious theory of the partridge-dance. The
leader carries a shield with a partridge device and a death-demon perches
behind him; the other hero carries a lance, and a shield with a duck
device. To their rear is a maze of a pattern found not only on certain
Cnossian coins, but in the British turf-cut mazes trodden by school-
children at Easter until the nineteenth century. Love-jealousy lured the
king to his death, the iconographer is explaining, like a partridge in the
brushwood maze, and he was succeeded by his tanist. Only the exceptional hero – a Daedalus, or a Theseus – returned alive; and in this context
the recent discovery near Bosinney in Cornwall of a Cretan maze cut on
a rock-face is of great importance. The ravine where the maze was first
noticed by Dr Renton Green is one of the last haunts of the Cornish
chough; and this bird houses the soul of King Arthur – who harrowed
Hell, and with whom Bosinney is closely associated in legend. A maze
dance seems to have been brought to Britain from the eastern Mediterranean by neolithic agriculturists of the third millennium B.C., since
rough stone mazes, similar to the British turf-cut ones, occur in the
'Beaker B' area of Scandinavia and North-eastern Russia; and ecclesiastic
mazes, once used for penitential purposes, are found in South-eastern
Europe. English turf-mazes are usually known as 'Troy-town', and so
are the Welsh: *Caer-droia*. The Romans probably named them after their
own Troy Game, a labyrinthine dance performed by young aristocrats
in honour of Augustus's ancestor Aeneas the Trojan; though, according
to Pliny, it was also danced by children in the Italian countryside.

4. At Cnossus the sky-bull cult succeeded the partridge cult, and the
circling of the dancers came to represent the annual courses of the heavenly
bodies. If, therefore, seven youths and maidens took part, they may
have represented the seven Titans and Titanesses of the sun, moon, and
five planets (see 1. 3 and 43. 4); although no definite evidence of the Titan
cult has been found in Cretan works of art. It appears that the ancient
Crane Dance of Delos – cranes, too, perform a love dance – was similarly
adapted to a maze pattern. In some mazes the dancers held a cord, which
helped them to keep their proper distance and execute the pattern fault-
lessly; and this may have given rise to the story of the ball of twine (A. B.
Cook: *Journal of Hellenic Studies* xiv. 101 ff., 1949); at Athens, as on

Mount Sipylus, the rope dance was called *cordax* (Aristophanes: *Clouds* 540). The spectacle in the Cretan bull ring consisted of an acrobatic display by young men and girls who in turn seized the horns of the charging bull and turned back-somersaults between them over his shoulders. This was evidently a religious rite: perhaps here also the performers represented planets. It cannot have been nearly so dangerous a sport as most writers on the subject suggest, to judge from the rarity of casualties among *banderilleros* in the Spanish bull ring; and a Cretan fresco shows that a companion was at hand to catch the somersaulter as he or she came to earth.

5. 'Ariadne', which the Greeks understood as 'Ariagne' ('very holy'), will have been a title of the Moon-goddess honoured in the dance, and in the bull ring: 'the high, fruitful Barley-mother', also called Aridela, 'the very manifest one'. The carrying of fruit-laden boughs in Ariadne's honour, and Dionysus's, and her suicide by hanging, 'because she feared Artemis', suggests that Ariadne-dolls were attached to these boughs (see 79. 2). A bell-shaped Boeotian goddess-doll hung in the Louvre, her legs dangling, is Ariadne, or Erigone, or Hanged Artemis; and bronze dolls with detachable limbs have been found in Daedalus's Sardinia. Ariadne's crown made by Hephaestus in the form of a rose-wreath is not a fancy; delicate gold wreaths with gemmed flowers were found in the Mochlos hoard.

6. Theseus's marriage to the Moon-priestess made him lord of Cnossus, and on one Cnossian coin a new moon is set in the centre of a maze. Matrilinear custom, however, deprived an heiress of all claims to her lands if she accompanied a husband overseas; and this explains why Theseus did not bring Ariadne back to Athens, or any farther than Dia, a Cretan island within sight of Cnossus. Cretan Dionysus, represented as a bull – Minos, in fact – was Ariadne's rightful husband; and wine, a Cretan manufacture, will have been served at her orgies. This might account for Dionysus's indignation, reported by Homer, that she and the intruder Theseus had lain together.

7. Many ancient Athenian customs of the Mycenaean period are explained by Plutarch and others in terms of Theseus's visit to Crete: for instance, the ritual prostitution of girls, and ritual sodomy (characteristic of Anatha's worship at Jerusalem (see 61. 1), and the Syrian Goddess's at Hierapolis), which survived vestigially among the Athenians in the propitiation of Apollo with a gift of maidens, and in the carrying of harvest branches by two male inverts. The fruit-laden bough recalls the *lulab* carried at the Jerusalem New Year Feast of Tabernacles, also celebrated in the early autumn. Tabernacles was a vintage festival, and corresponded with the Athenian Oschophoria, or 'carrying of grape clusters'; the principal interest of which lay in a foot race (Proclus: *Chrestomathia* 28).

Originally, the winner became the new sacred king, as at Olympia, and received a fivefold mixture of 'oil, wine, honey, chopped cheese, and meal' – the divine nectar and ambrosia of the gods. Plutarch associates Theseus, the new king, with this festival, by saying that he arrived accidentally while it was in progress, and exculpates him from any part in the death of his predecessor Aegeus. But the new king really wrestled against the old king and flung him, as a *pharmacos*, from the White Rock into the sea (see 96. 3). In the illustrative icon which the mythographer has evidently misread, Theseus's black-sailed ship must have been a boat standing by to rescue the *pharmacos*; it has dark sails, because Mediterranean fishermen usually tan their nets and canvas to prevent the salt water from rotting them. The kerm-berry, or cochineal, provided a scarlet dye to stain the sacred king's face, and was therefore associated with royalty. 'Hecalene', the needy old spinster, is probably a worn-down form of 'Hecate Selene', 'the far-shooting moon', which means Artemis.

8. Bean-eating by men seems to have been prohibited in pre-Hellenic times – the Pythagoreans continued to abstain from beans, on the ground that their ancestors' souls could well be resident in them and that, if a man (as opposed to a woman) ate a bean, he might be robbing an ancestor of his or her chance to be reborn. The popular bean-feast therefore suggests a deliberate Hellenic flouting of the goddess who imposed the taboo; so does Theseus's gift of a male priesthood to the Phytalids ('growers'), the feminine form of whose name is a reminder that fig-culture, like bean-planting, was at first a mystery confined to women (see 24. 13).

9. The Cypriots worshipped Ariadne as the 'Birth-goddess of Amathus', a title belonging to Aphrodite. Her autumn festival celebrated the birth of the New Year; and the young man who sympathetically imitated her pangs will have been her royal lover, Dionysus. This custom, known as *couvade*, is found in many parts of Europe, including some districts of East Anglia.

10. Apollo's horn temple on Delos has recently been excavated. The altar and its foundations are gone, and bull has succeeded goat as the ritual animal in the stone decorations – if it indeed ever was a goat; a Minoan seal shows the goddess standing on an altar made entirely of bulls' horns.

11. Micon's allegorical mural of Thetis presenting a crown and ring to Theseus, while Minos glowers in anger on the shore, will have depicted the passing of the thalassocracy from Cretan to Athenian hands. But it may be that Minos had symbolically married the Sea-goddess by throwing a ring into the sea, as the Doges of Venice did in the middle ages.

12. 'Oenopion and Thoas are sometimes called Theseus's sons' because these were the heroes of Chios and Lemnos (see 88. h), subject allies of the Athenians.

THE FEDERALIZATION OF ATTICA

WHEN Theseus succeeded his father Aegeus on the throne of Athens, he reinforced his sovereignty by executing nearly all his opponents, except Pallas and the remainder of his fifty sons. Some years later he killed these too as a precautionary measure and, when charged with murder in the Court of Apollo the Dolphin, offered the unprecedented plea of 'justifiable homicide', which secured his acquittal. He was purified of their blood at Troezen, where his son Hippolytus now reigned as king, and spent a whole year there. On his return, he suspected a half-brother, also named Pallas, of disaffection, and banished him at once; Pallas then founded Pallantium in Arcadia, though some say that Pallas son of Lycaon had done so shortly after the Deucalionian Flood.[1]

b. Theseus proved to be a law-abiding ruler, and initiated the policy of federalization, which was the basis of Athens' later well-being. Hitherto, Attica had been divided into twelve communities, each managing its own affairs without consulting the Athenian king, except in time of emergency. The Eleusinians had even declared war on Erechtheus, and other internecine quarrels abounded. If these communities were to relinquish their independence, Theseus must approach each clan and family in turn; which he did. He found the yeomen and serfs ready to obey him, and persuaded most of the large landowners to agree with his scheme by promising to abolish the monarchy and substitute democracy for it, though remaining commander-in-chief and supreme judge. Those who remained unconvinced by the arguments he used respected his strength at least.[2]

c. Theseus was thus empowered to dissolve all local governments, after summoning their delegates to Athens, where he provided these with a common Council Hall and Law Court, both of which stand to this day. But he forbore to interfere with the laws of private property. Next, he united the suburbs with the city proper which, until then, had consisted of the Acropolis and its immediate Southern dependencies, including the ancient Temples of Olympian Zeus, Pythian Apollo, Mother Earth, Dionysus of the Marshes, and the Aqueduct of Nine Springs. The Athenians still call the Acropolis 'the City'.

d. He named the sixteenth day of Hecatomboeon [July] 'Federation Day', and made it a public festival in honour of Athene, when a bloodless sacrifice is also offered to Peace.³ By renaming the Athenian Games celebrated on this day 'All-Athenian', he opened it to the whole of Attica; and also introduced the worship of Federal Aphrodite and of Persuasion. Then, resigning the throne, as he had promised, he gave Attica its new constitution, and under the best auspices: for the Delphic Oracle prophesied that Athens would now ride the stormy seas as safely as a pig's bladder.⁴

e. To enlarge the city still further, Theseus invited all worthy strangers to become his fellow-citizens. His heralds, who went throughout Greece, used a formula which is still employed, namely: 'Come hither, all ye people!' Great crowds thereupon flocked into Athens, and he divided the population of Attica into three classes: the Eupatrids, or 'those who deserved well of their fatherland'; the Georges, or 'farmers'; and the Demiurges, or 'artificers'. The Eupatrids took charge of religious affairs, supplied magistrates, interpreted the laws, embodying the highest dignity of all; the Georges tilled the soil and were the backbone of the state; the Demiurges, by far the most numerous class, furnished such various artificers as soothsayers, surgeons, heralds, carpenters, sculptors, and confectioners.⁵ Thus Theseus became the first king to found a commonwealth, which is why Homer, in the Catalogue of Ships, styles only the Athenians a sovereign people – and his constitution remained in force until the tyrants seized power. Some, however, deny the truth of this tradition: they say that Theseus continued to reign as before and that, after the death of King Menestheus, who led the Athenians against Troy, his dynasty persisted for three generations.⁶

f. Theseus, the first Athenian king to mint money, stamped his coins with the image of a bull. It is not known whether this represented Poseidon's bull, or Minos's general Taurus; or whether he was merely encouraging agriculture; but this coinage caused the standard of value to be quoted in terms of 'ten oxen', or 'one hundred oxen', for a considerable time. In emulation of Heracles, who had appointed his father Zeus patron of the Olympic Games, Theseus now appointed his father Poseidon patron of the Isthmian Games. Hitherto the god thus honoured had been Melicertes son of Ino, and the games, which were held at night, had been mysteries rather than a public spectacle. Next, Theseus made good the Athenian claim to the sovereignty of Megara and then, having summoned Peloponnesian delegates to the Isthmus, prevailed upon them to settle a long-standing frontier dispute with their Ionian neighbours. At a place agreed by both parties, he raised the celebrated column marked on its eastern side: 'This is not the Peloponnese, but Ionia!', and on the western: 'This is not Ionia, but the Peloponnese!' He also won Corinthian assent to the Athenians' taking the place of honour at the Isthmian Games; it consisted of as much ground as was covered by the mainsail of the ship that had brought them.[7]

1. Hyginus: *Fabula* 244; Apollodorus: *Epitome* i. 11; Servius on Virgil's *Aeneid* viii. 54; Euripides: *Hippolytus* 34-7; Pausanias: i. 22. 2; i. 28. 10 and viii. 3. 1.
2. Diodorus Siculus: iv. 61; Thucydides: ii. 15; Plutarch: *Theseus* 24.
3. Thucydides: *loc. cit.*; Plutarch: *loc. cit.*; Scholiast on Aristophanes's *Peace* 962.
4. Pausanias: viii. 2.1 and i. 22. 3; Plutarch: *loc cit.*
5. Plutarch: *Theseus* 25; Homer: *Odyssey* 383 ff. and xix. 135; Plato: *Symposium* 188d and *Republic* 529e; Herodotus: vii. 31.
6. Plutarch: *loc. cit.*; Homer: *Iliad* ii. 552 ff.; Pausanias: i. 3. 2.
7. Strabo: ix. 1. 6.

*

1. The mythical element of the Theseus story has here been submerged in what purports to be Athenian constitutional history; but the Federalization of Attica is dated several hundred years too early; and Theseus's democratic reforms are fifth-century propaganda, probably invented by Cleisthenes. Legal reforms made during the late Jewish monarchy were similarly attributed to Moses by the editors of the Pentateuch.

2. Oxen provided the standard of value in ancient Greece, Italy, and Ireland, as they still do among backward pastoral tribes of East Africa, and the Athenians struck no coins until nearly five hundred years after the Trojan War. But it is true that Cretan copper ingots of a fixed weight were officially stamped with a bull's head, or a recumbent calf (Sir Arthur Evans: *Minoan Weights and Mediums of Currency* p. 335); and the Butadae of Athens, who seem to have been largely responsible for the development of the Theseus myth, may have had this tradition in mind when they coined money stamped with the ox-head, their clan-device.

3. The division of Attica into twelve communities is paralleled by a similar arrangement in the Nile Delta and in Etruria, and by the distribution of conquered Canaanite territory among the twelve tribes of Israel; the number may in each case have been chosen to allow for a monthly progress of the monarch from tribe to tribe. Greeks of the heroic age did

not distinguish between murder and manslaughter; in either case a blood-price had to be paid to the victim's clan, and the killer then changed his name and left the city for ever. Thus Telamon and Peleus continued to be highly regarded by the gods after their treacherous murder of Phocus (see 81. *b*); and Medea killed Apsyrtus without antagonizing her new Corinthian subjects (see 153. *a* and 156. *a*). At Athens, however, in the Classical period, wilful murder (*phonos*) carried the death penalty: manslaughter (*akousia*), that of banishment; and the clan was bound by law to prosecute. *Phonos hekousios* (justifiable homicide) and *phonos akousios* (excusable homicide) were later refinements, which Draco probably introduced in the seventh century B.C.; the latter alone demanded expiation by ritual cleansing. The mythographers have not understood that Theseus evaded permanent exile for the murder of the Pallantids only by exterminating the entire clan, as David did with the 'House of Saul'. A year's absence at Troezen sufficed to rid the city of the pollution caused by the murder.

100

THESEUS AND THE AMAZONS

SOME say that Theseus took part in Heracles's successful expedition against the Amazons, and received as his share of the booty their queen Antiope, also called Melanippe; but that this was not so unhappy a fate for her as many thought, because she had betrayed the city of Themiscyra on the river Thermodon to him, in proof of the passion he had already kindled in her heart.[1]

b. Others say that Theseus visited their country some years later, in the company of Peirithous and his comrades; and that the Amazons, delighted at the arrival of so many handsome warriors, offered them no violence. Antiope came to greet Theseus with gifts, but she had hardly climbed aboard his ship, before he weighed anchor and abducted her. Others again say that he stayed for some time in Amazonia, and entertained Antiope as his guest. They add that among his companions were three Athenian brothers, Euneus, Thoas, and Soloön, the last of whom fell in love with Antiope but, not daring to approach her directly, asked Euneus to plead his cause. Antiope rejected these advances, though continuing to treat Soloön no less civilly than before, and it was not until he had thrown himself into the river Thermodon and drowned, that Theseus realized what had been afoot, and became much distressed. Remembering a warning given him by the Delphic Oracle that, if he should ever find himself greatly afflicted in a strange country, he must found a city and leave behind some of his companions to govern it, he built Pythopolis, in honour of Pythian Apollo, and named the near-by river Soloön. There he left Euneus, Thoas, and one Hermus, an Athenian noble, whose former residence in Pythopolis is now mistakenly called 'Hermes's House'. He then sailed away with Antiope.[2]

c. Antiope's sister Oreithyia, mistaken by some for Hippolyte whose girdle Heracles won, swore vengeance on Theseus. She concluded an alliance with the Scythians, and led a large force of Amazons across the ice of the Cimmerian Bosphorus, then crossed the Danube and passed through Thrace, Thessaly, and Boeotia. At Athens she encamped on the Areiopagus and there sacrificed to Ares; an event from which, some say, the hill won its name; but first she ordered a detachment to invade Laconia and discourage the Peloponnesians from reinforcing Theseus by way of the Isthmus.[3]

d. The Athenian forces were already marshalled, but neither side cared to begin hostilities. At last, on the advice of an oracle, Theseus sacrificed to Phobus, son of Ares, and offered battle on the seventh day of Boedromion, the date on which the Boedromia is now celebrated at Athens; though some say the festival had already been founded in honour of the victory which Xuthus won over Eumolpus in the reign of Erechtheus. The Amazons' battle-front stretched between what is now called the Amazonium and the Pnyx Hill near Chrysa. Theseus's right wing moved down from the Museum and fell upon their left wing, but was routed and forced to retire as far as the Temple of the Furies. This incident is recalled by a stone raised to the local commander Chalcodon, in a street lined with the tombs of those who fell, and called after him. The Athenian left wing, however, charged from the Palladium, Mount Ardettus and the Lyceum, and drove the Amazon right wing back to their camp, inflicting heavy casualties.[4]

e. Some say that the Amazons offered peace terms only after four months of hard fighting; the armistice, sworn near the sanctuary of Theseus, is still commemorated in the Amazonian sacrifice on the eve of his festival. But others say that Antiope, now Theseus's wife, fought heroically at his side, until shot dead by one Molpadia, whom Theseus then killed; that Oreithyia with a few followers escaped to Megara, where she died of grief and despair; and that the remaining Amazons, driven from Attica by the victorious Theseus, settled in Scythia.[5]

f. This, at any rate, was the first time that the Athenians repulsed foreign invaders. Some of the Amazons left wounded on the field of battle were sent to Chalcis to be cured. Antiope and Molpadia are buried near the temple of Mother Earth, and an earthen pillar marks Antiope's grave. Others lie in the Amazonium. Those Amazons who fell while crossing Thessaly lie buried between Scotussaea and Cynoscephalae; a few more, near Chaeronaea by the river Haemon. In the Pyrrhichan region of Laconia, shrines mark the place where the Amazons halted their advance and dedicated two wooden images to Artemis and Apollo; and at Troezen a temple of Ares commemorates Theseus's victory over this detachment when it attempted to force the Isthmus on its return.[6]

g. According to one account, the Amazons entered Thrace by way of Phrygia, not Scythia, and founded the sanctuary of Ephesian Artemis as they marched along the coast. According to another, they had taken refuge in this sanctuary on two earlier occasions: namely in their flight from Dionysus, and after Heracles's defeat of Queen Hippolyte; and its true founders were Cresus and Ephesus.[7]

h. The truth about Antiope seems to be that she survived the battle, and that Theseus was eventually compelled to kill her, as the Delphic Oracle had foretold, when he entered into an alliance with King Deucalion the Cretan, and married his sister Phaedra. The jealous Antiope, who was not his legal wife, interrupted the wedding festivities by bursting in, fully armed, and threatening to massacre the guests. Theseus and his companions hastily closed the doors, and despatched her in a grim combat, though she had borne him Hippolytus, also called Demophoön, and never lain with another man.[8]

1. Apollodorus: *Epitome* i. 16; Hegias of Troezen, quoted by Pausanias: i. 2. 1.
2. Pindar, quoted by Pausanias: i. 2. 1; Pherecydes and Bion, quoted by Plutarch: *Theseus* 26; Menecrates, quoted by Plutarch: *loc cit.*
3. Justin: ii. 4; Hellanicus, quoted by Plutarch: *Theseus* 26–7; Diodorus Siculus: iv. 28; Apollodorus: *Epitome* i. 16; Aeschylus: *Eumenides* 680 ff.
4. Plutarch: *Theseus* 27; *Etymologicum Magnum: sub* Boedromia; Euripides: *Ion* 59; Cleidemus, quoted by Plutarch: *loc. cit.*

5. Cleidemus, quoted by Plutarch: *loc. cit.*; Plutarch: *loc. cit.*; Pausanias: i. 41. 7; Diodorus Siculus: iv. 28.

6. Plutarch: *loc cit.*; Pausanias: i. 2. 1; i. 41. 7; iii. 25. 2 and ii. 32. 8.

7. Pindar, quoted by Pausanias: vii. 2. 4.

8. Hyginus: *Fabula* 241; Apollodorus: *Epitome* i. 17; Diodorus Siculus: iv. 62; Ovid: *Heroides* 121 ff.; Pausanias: i. 22. 2; Pindar, quoted by Plutarch: *Theseus* 28.

★

1. 'Amazons', usually derived from *a* and *mazon*, 'without breasts', because they were believed to sear away one breast in order to shoot better (but this notion is fantastic), seems to be an Armenian word, meaning 'moon-women'. Since the priestesses of the Moon-goddess on the South-eastern shores of the Black Sea bore arms, as they also did in the Libyan Gulf of Sirte (see 8. *1*), it appears that the accounts of them which travellers brought back confused the interpretation of certain ancient Athenian icons depicting women warriors, and gave rise to the Attic fable of an Amazonian invasion from the river Thermodon. These icons, which were extant in Classical times on the footstool of Zeus's throne at Olympia (Pausanias: v. 11. 2), at Athens on the central wall of the Painted Colonnade (Pausanias: i. 15. 2), on Athene's shield, in the sanctuary of Theseus, and elsewhere (Pausanias: i. 17. 1), represented either the fight between the pre-Hellenic priestesses of Athene for the office of High-priestess or a Hellenic invasion of Attica and the resistance offered by them. There will also have been armed priestesses at Ephesus – a Minoan colony, as the name of the founder Cresus ('Cretan') suggests – and in all cities where Amazons' graves were shown. Oreithyia, or Hippolyte, is supposed to have gone several hundred miles out of her way through Scythia; probably because the Cimmerian Bosphorus – the Crimea – was the seat of Artemis's savage Taurian cult, where the priestess despatched male victims (see 116. *2*).

2. Antiope's interruption of Phaedra's wedding may have been deduced from an icon which showed the Hellenic conqueror about to violate the High-priestess, after he had killed her companions. Antiope was not Theseus's legal wife, because she belonged to a society which resisted monogamy (see 131. *k*). The names Melanippe and Hippolytus associate the Amazons with the pre-Hellenic horse cult (see 43. *2*). Soloön's name ('egg-shaped weight') may be derived from a weight-tossing event in the funeral games celebrated at the Greek colony of Pythopolis, so called after the oracular serpent of its heroic founder; there seems to have been a practice here of throwing human victims into the river Thermodon. The Boedromia ('running for help') was a festival of Artemis, about which little is known: perhaps armed priestesses took part in it, as in the Argive festival of the Hybristica (see 160. *5*).

101

PHAEDRA AND HIPPOLYTUS

AFTER marrying Phaedra, Theseus sent his bastard son Hippolytus to Pittheus, who adopted him as heir to the throne of Troezen. Thus Hippolytus had no cause to dispute the right of his legitimate brothers Acamas and Demophoön, Phaedra's sons, to reign over Athens.[1]

b. Hippolytus, who had inherited his mother Antiope's exclusive devotion to chaste Artemis, raised a new temple to the goddess at Troezen, not far from the theatre. Thereupon Aphrodite, determined to punish him for what she took as an insult to herself, saw to it that when he attended the Eleusinian Mysteries, Phaedra should fall passionately in love with him. He came dressed in white linen, his hair garlanded, and though his features wore a harsh expression, she thought them admirably severe.[2]

c. Since at that time Theseus was away in Thessaly with Peirithous, or it may have been in Tartarus, Phaedra followed Hippolytus to Troezen. There she built the Temple of Peeping Aphrodite to overlook the gymnasium, and would daily watch unobserved while he kept himself fit by running, leaping, and wrestling, stark naked. An ancient myrtle-tree stands in the Temple enclosure; Phaedra would jab at its leaves, in frustrated passion, with a jewelled hair-pin, and they are still much perforated. When, later, Hippolytus attended the All-Athenian Festival and lodged in Theseus's palace, she used the Temple of Aprodite on the Acropolis for the same purpose.[3]

d. Phaedra disclosed her incestuous desire to no one, but ate little, slept badly, and grew so weak that her old nurse guessed the truth at last, and officiously implored her to send Hippolytus a letter. This Phaedra did: confessing her love, and saying that she was now converted by it to the cult of Artemis, whose two wooden images, brought from Crete, she had just rededicated to the goddess. Would he not come hunting one day? 'We women of the Cretan Royal House,' she wrote, 'are doubtless fated to be dishonoured in love: witness my grandmother Europe, my mother Pasiphaë, and lastly my own sister Ariadne! Ah, wretched Ariadne, deserted by your father, the faithless Theseus, who has since murdered your own royal mother – why have the Furies not punished you for showing such unfilial indifference to her fate? – and must one day murder me! I count on you to revenge yourself on him by paying homage to Aphrodite in my company. Could we not go away and live together, for awhile at least, and make a hunting expedition the excuse? Meanwhile, none can suspect our true feelings for each other. Already we are lodged under the same roof, and our affection will be regarded as innocent, and even praiseworthy.'[4]

e. Hippolytus burned this letter in horror, and came to Phaedra's chamber, loud with reproaches; but she tore her clothes, threw open the chamber doors, and cried out: 'Help, help! I am ravished!' Then she hanged herself from the lintel, and left a note accusing him of monstrous crimes.[5]

f. Theseus, on receiving the note, cursed Hippolytus, and gave orders that he must quit Athens at once, never to return. Later he remembered the three wishes granted him by his father Poseidon, and prayed earnestly that Hippolytus might die that very day. 'Father.' he pleaded, 'send a beast across Hippolytus's path, as he makes for Troezen!'[6]

g. Hippolytus had set out from Athens at full speed. As he drove along the narrow part of the Isthmus a huge wave, which overtopped even the Molurian Rock, rolled roaring shoreward; and from its crest sprang a great dog-seal (or, some say, a white bull), bellowing and spouting water. Hippolytus's four horses swerved towards the cliff, mad with terror, but being an expert charioteer he restrained them from plunging over the edge. The beast then galloped menacingly behind the chariot, and he failed to keep his team on a straight course. Not far from the sanctuary of Saronian Artemis, a wild olive is still shown, called the Twisted Rhachos – the Troezenian term for a barren olive-tree is *rhachos* – and it was on a branch of this tree that a loop of Hippolytus's reins caught. His chariot was flung sideways against a pile of rocks and broken into pieces. Hippolytus, entangled in the reins, and thrown first against the tree-trunk, and then against the rocks, was dragged to death by his horses, while the pursuer vanished.[7]

h. Some, however, relate improbably that Artemis then told Theseus the truth, and rapt him in the twinkling of an eye to Troezen, where he arrived just in time to be reconciled to his dying son; and that she revenged herself on Aphrodite by procuring Adonis's death. For certain, though, she commanded the Troezenians to pay Hippolytus divine honours, and all Troezenian brides henceforth to cut off a lock of their hair, and dedicate it to him. It was Diomedes who dedicated the ancient temple and image of Hippolytus at Troezen, and who first offered him his annual sacrifice. Both Phaedra's and Hippolytus's tombs, the latter a mound of earth, are shown in the enclosure of this temple, near the myrtle-tree with the pricked leaves.

i. The Troezenians themselves deny that Hippolytus was dragged to death by horses, or even that he lies buried in his temple; nor will they reveal the whereabouts of his real tomb. Yet they declare that the gods set him among the stars as the Charioteer.[8]

j. The Athenians raised a barrow in Hippolytus's memory close to the Temple of Themis, because his death had been brought about by curses. Some say that Theseus, accused of his murder, was found guilty, ostracized, and banished to Scyros, where he ended his life in shame and grief. But his downfall is more generally believed to have been caused by an attempted rape of Persephone.[9]

k. Hippolytus's ghost descended to Tartarus, and Artemis, in high indignation, begged Asclepius to revive his corpse. Asclepius opened the doors of his ivory medicine cabinet and took out the herb with which Cretan Glaucus had been revived. With it he thrice touched Hippolytus's breast, repeating certain charms, and at the third touch the dead man raised his head from the ground. But Hades and the Three Fates, scandalized by this breach of privilege, persuaded Zeus to kill Asclepius with a thunderbolt.

l. The Latins relate that Artemis then wrapped Hippolytus in a thick cloud, disguised him as an aged man, and changed his features. After hesitating between Crete and Delos as suitable places of concealment, she brought him to her sacred grove at Italian Aricia.[10] There, with her consent, he married the nymph Egeria, and he still lives beside the lake among dark oak-woods, surrounded by sheer precipices. Lest he should be reminded of his death, Artemis changed his name to Virbius, which means *vir bis*, or 'twice a man'; and no horses are allowed in the vicinity. The priesthood of Arician Artemis is open only to runaway slaves.[11] In her grove grows an ancient oak-tree, the branches of which may not be broken, but if a slave dares do so then the priest, who has himself killed his predecessor and therefore lives in hourly fear of death, must fight him, sword against sword, for the priesthood. The Aricians say that Theseus begged Hippolytus to remain with him at Athens, but he refused.

m. A tablet in Asclepius's Epidaurian sanctuary records that Hippolytus dedicated twenty horses to him, in gratitude for having been revived.[12]

1. Apollodorus: *Epitome* i. 18; Pausanias: i. 22. 2; Ovid: *Heroides* iv. 67 ff.

2. Pausanias: ii. 31. 6; Ovid: *loc. cit.*

3. Ovid: *loc. cit.*; Seneca: *Hippolytus* 835 ff.; Pausanias: ii. 32. 3 and i. 22. 2; Euripides: *Hippolytus* 1 ff.; Diodorus Siculus: iv. 62.

4. Ovid: *loc. cit.*; Pausanias: i. 18. 5.

5. Apollodorus: *Epitome* i. 18; Diodorus Siculus: iv. 62; Hyginus: *Fabula* 47.

6. Plutarch: *Parallel Stories* 34; Servius on Virgil's *Aeneid* vi. 445.

7. Pausanias: ii. 32. 8; Euripides: *Hippolytus* 1193 ff.; Ovid: *Metamorphoses* xv. 506 ff.; Plutarch: *loc. cit.*; Diodorus Siculus: iv. 62.

8. Euripides: *Hippolytus* 1282 ff. and 1423 ff.; Pausanias: ii. 32. 1–2.

9. Pausanias: i. 22. 1; Philostatus: *Life of Apollonius of Tyana* vii. 42; Diodorus Siculus: iv. 62.

10. Ovid: *Metamorphoses* xv. 532 ff. and *Fasti* vi. 745.

11. Virgil: *Aeneid* vii. 775; Ovid: *Fasti* v. 312 and *Metamorphoses* xv. 545; Strabo: iii. 263 ff.; Pausanias: ii. 27. 4.

12. Servius on Virgil's *Aeneid* vi. 136; Strabo: v. 3. 12; Suetonius: *Caligula* 35; Pausanias: *loc cit.*

*

1. The incident of Phaedra's incestuous love for Hippolytus, like that of Potiphar's wife and her adulterous love for Joseph (see 75. *1*), is borrowed either from the Egyptian *Tale of the Two Brothers*, or from a common Canaanite source. Its sequel has been based upon the familiar icon showing the chariot crash at the end of a sacred king's reign (see 71. *1*). If, as in ancient Ireland, a prophetic roaring of the November sea warned the king that his hour was at hand, this warning will have been pictured as a bull, or seal, poised open-mouthed on the creast of a wave. Hippolytus's reins must have caught in the myrtle, rather than in the sinister-looking olive later associated with the crash: the myrtle, in fact, which grew close to his hero shrine, and was famous for its perforated leaves. Myrtle symbolized the last month of the king's reign: as appears in the story of Oenomaus's chariot crash (see 109. *j*); whereas wild olive symbolized the first month of his successor's reign. *Vir bis* is a false derivation of Virbius, which seems to represent the Greek *hierobios*, 'holy life' – the *h* often becoming *v*: as in *Hestia* and *Vesta*, or *Hesperos* and *Vesper*. In the *Golden Bough* Sir James Frazer has shown that the branch which the priest guarded so jealously was mistletoe; and it is likely that Glaucus son of Minos (see 90. *c*), who has been confused with Glaucus son of Sisyphus (see 71. *a*), was revived by mistletoe. Though the pre-Hellenic mistletoe and oak cult had been suppressed in Greece (see 50. *2*), a refugee priesthood from the Isthmus may well have brought it to

Aricia. Egeria's name shows that she was a death-goddess, living in a grove of black poplars (see 51. 7 and 170. *l*).

2. Hippolytus's perquisite of the bride's lock must be a patriarchal innovation, designed perhaps to deprive women of the magical power resident in their hair, as Mohammedan women are shaved on marriage.

3. The concealment of Hippolytus's tomb is parallelled in the stories of Sisyphus and Neleus (see 67. 3), which suggests that he was buried at some strategic point of the Isthmus.

102

LAPITHS AND CENTAURS

SOME say that Peirithous the Lapith was the son of Ixion and Dia, daughter of Eioneus; others, that he was the son of Zeus who, disguised as a stallion, coursed around Dia before seducing her.[1]

b. Almost incredible reports of Theseus's strength and valour had reached Peirithous, who ruled over the Magnetes, at the mouth of the river Peneus; and one day he resolved to test them by raiding Attica and driving away a herd of cattle that were grazing at Marathon. When Theseus at once went in pursuit, Peirithous boldly turned about to face him; but each was filled with such admiration for the other's nobility of appearance that the cattle were forgotten, and they swore an oath of everlasting friendship.[2]

c. Peirithous married Hippodameia, or Deidameia, daughter of Butes – or, some say, of Adrastus – and invited all the Olympians to his wedding, except Ares and Eris; he remembered the mischief which Eris had caused at the marriage of Peleus and Thetis. Since more feasters came to Peirithous's palace than it could contain, his cousins the Centaurs, together with Nestor, Caeneus, and other Thessalian princes, were seated at tables in a vast, tree-shaded cave near by.

d. The Centaurs, however, were unused to wine and, when they smelled its fragrance, pushed away the sour milk which was set before them, and ran to fill their silver horns from the wine-skins. In their ignorance they swilled the strong liquor unmixed with water, becoming so drunk that when the bride was escorted into the cavern to greet them, Eurytus, or Eurytion, leaped from his stool, overturned the table, and dragged her away by the hair. At once the other Centaurs followed his disgraceful example, lecherously straddling the nearest women and boys.[3]

e. Peirithous and his paranymph Theseus sprang to Hippodameia's rescue, cut off Eurytion's ears and nose and, with the help of the Lapiths, threw him out of the cavern. The ensuring fight, in the course of which Caeneus the Lapith was killed, lasted until nightfall; and thus began the long feud between the Centaurs and their Lapith neighbours, engineered by Ares and Eris in revenge for the slight offered them.[4]

f. On this occasion the Centaurs suffered a serious reverse, and Theseus drove them from their ancient hunting grounds on Mount Pelion to the land of the Aethices near Mount Pindus. But it was not an easy task to subdue the Centaurs, who had already disputed Ixion's kingdom with Peirithous, and who now, rallying their forces, invaded Lapith territory. They surprised and slaughtered the main Lapith army, and when the survivors fled to Pholoë in Elis, the vengeful Centaurs expelled them and converted Pholoë into a bandit stronghold of their own. Finally the Lapiths settled in Malea.

g. It was during Theseus's campaign against the Centaurs that he met Heracles again for the first time since his childhood; and presently initiated him into the Mysteries of Demeter at Eleusis.[5]

1. Diodorus Siculus: iv. 70; Eustathius on Homer p. 101.
2. Strabo: *Fragment* 14; *Vatican Epitome*; Plutarch: *Theseus* 30.
3. Apollodorus: *Epitome* i. 21; Diodorus Siculus: iv. 70; Hyginus: *Fabula* 33; Servius on Virgil's *Aeneid* vii. 304.
4. Pindar: *Fragment* 166f, quoted by Athenaeus: xi. 476b; Apollodorus: *loc. cit.*; Ovid: *Metamorphoses* xii. 210 ff.; Homer *Odyssey* xxi. 295; Pausanias: v. 10. 2.
5. Plutarch: *loc. cit.*; Homer: *Iliad* ii. 470 ff.; Diodorus Siculus: *loc. cit.*; Herodotus, quoted by Plutarch: *loc. cit.*

*

1. Both Lapiths and Centaurs claimed descent from Ixion, an oak-hero, and had a horse cult in common (see 63. *a* and *d*). They were primitive mountain tribes in Northern Greece, of whose ancient rivalry the Hellenes took advantage by allying themselves first with one, and then with the other (see 35. 2; 78. 1; and 81. 3). *Centaur* and *Lapith* may be Italic words: *centuria*, 'war-band of one hundred', and *lapicidae*, 'flint-chippers'. (The usual Classical etymology is, respectively, from *cent-tauroi*, 'those who spear bulls', and *lapizein*, 'to swagger'.) These mountaineers seem to have had erotic orgies, and thus won a reputation for

promiscuity among the monogamous Hellenes; members of this neo-lithic race survived in the Arcadian mountains, and on Mount Pindus, until Classical times, and vestiges of their pre-Hellenic language are to be found in modern Albania.

2. It is, however, unlikely that the battle between Lapiths and Centaurs – depicted on the gable of Zeus's temple at Olympia (Pausanias: v. 10. 2); at Athens in the sanctuary of Theseus (Pausanias: i. 17. 2); and on Athene's aegis (Pausanias: i. 28. 2) – recorded a mere struggle between frontier tribes. Being connected with a royal wedding feast, divinely patronized, at which Theseus in his lion-skin assisted, it will have depicted a ritual event of intimate concern to all Hellenes. Lion-skinned Heracles also fought the Centaurs on a similarly festive occasion (see 126. 2). Homer calls them 'shaggy wild beasts', and since they are not differentiated from satyrs in early Greek vase-paintings, the icon probably shows a newly-installed king – it does not matter who – battling with dancers disguised as animals: an event which A. C. Hocart in his *Kingship* proves to have been an integral part of the ancient coronation ceremony. Eurytion is playing the classical part of interloper (see 142. 5).

3. Whether Ixion or Zeus was Peirithous's father depended on Ixion's right to style himself Zeus. The myth of his parentage has evidently been deduced from an icon which showed a priestess of Thetis – Dia, daughter of Eioneus, 'the divine daughter of the seashore' – halter in hand, encour-aging the candidate for kingship to master the wild horse (see 75. 3). Hippodameia's name ('horse-tamer') refers to the same icon. Zeus, dis-guised as stallion, 'coursed around' Dia, because that is the meaning of the name Peirithous; and Ixion, as the Sun-god, spread-eagled to his wheel, coursed around the heavens (see 63. 2).

103

THESEUS IN TARTARUS

AFTER Hippodameia's death Peirithous persuaded Theseus, whose wife Phaedra had recently hanged herself, to visit Sparta in his company and carry away Helen, a sister of Castor and Polydeuces, the Dioscuri, with whom they were both ambitious to be connected by marriage. Where the sanctuary of Serapis now stands at Athens, they swore to stand by each other in this perilous enterprise; to draw lots for Helen when they had won her; and then to carry off another of Zeus's daughters for the loser, whatever the danger might be.[1]

b. This decided, they led an army into Lacedaemon; then, riding ahead of the main body, seized Helen while she was offering a sacrifice in the Temple of Upright Artemis at Sparta, and galloped away with her. They soon outdistanced their pursuers, shaking them off at Tegea where, as had been agreed, lots were drawn for Helen; and Theseus proved the winner.[2] He foresaw, however, that the Athenians would by no means approve of his having thus picked a quarrel with the redoubtable Dioscuri, and therefore sent Helen, who was not yet nubile – being a twelve-year-old child or, some say, even younger – to the Attic village of Aphidnae, where he charged his friend Aphidnus to guard her with the greatest attention and secrecy. Aethra, Theseus's mother, accompanied Helen and cared well for her. Some try to exculpate Theseus by recording that it was Idas and Lynceus who stole Helen, and then entrusted her to the protection of Theseus, in revenge for the Dioscuri's abduction of the Leucippides. Others record that Helen's father Tyndareus himself entrusted her to Theseus, on learning that his nephew Enarephorus, son of Hippocoön, was planning to abduct her.[3]

c. Some years passed and, when Helen was old enough for Theseus to marry her, Peirithous reminded him of their pact. Together they consulted an oracle of Zeus, whom they had called upon to witness their oath, and his ironical response was: 'Why not visit Tartarus and demand Persephone, the wife of Hades, as a bride for Peirithous? She is the noblest of my daughters.' Theseus was outraged when Peirithous, who took this suggestion seriously, held him to his oath; but he dared not refuse to go, and presently they descended, sword in hand, to Tartarus. Avoiding the ferry-passage across Lethe, they chose the back way, the entrance to which is in a cavern of Laconian Taenarus, and were soon knocking at the gates of Hades's palace. Hades listened calmly to their impudent request and, feigning hospitality, invited them to be seated. Unsuspectingly they took the settee he offered, which proved to be the Chair of Forgetfulness and at once became part of their flesh, so that they could not rise again without self-mutilation. Coiled serpents hissed all about them, and they were well lashed by the Furies and mauled by Cerberus's teeth, while Hades looked on, smiling grimly.[4]

d. Thus they remained in torment for four full years, until Heracles, coming at Eurystheus's command to fetch up Cerberus, recognized them as they mutely stretched out their hands, pleading for his help. Persephone received Heracles like a brother, graciously permitting him to release the evil-doers and take them back to the upper air, if he could.[5] Heracles thereupon grasped Theseus by both hands and heaved with gigantic strength until, with a rending noise, he was torn free; but a great part of his flesh remained sticking to the rock, which is why Theseus's Athenian descendants are all so absurdly small-buttocked. Next, he seized hold of Peirithous's hands, but the earth quaked warningly, and he desisted; Peirithous had, after all, been the leading spirit in this blasphemous enterprise.[6]

e. According to some accounts, however, Heracles released Peirithous as well as Theseus; while, according to others, he released neither, but left Theseus chained for ever to a fiery chair, and Peirithous reclining beside Ixion on a golden couch – before their famished gaze rise magnificent banquets which the Eldest of the Furies constantly snatches away. It has even been said that Theseus and Peirithous never raided Tartarus at all, but only a Thesprotian or Molossian city named Cichyrus, whose king Aidoneus, finding that Peirithous intended to carry off his wife, threw him to a pack of hounds, and confined Theseus in a dungeon, from which Heracles eventually rescued him.[7]

1. Diodorus Siculus: iv. 63; Pindar, quoted by Pausanias: i. 18. 5; Pausanias: i. 41. 5.
2. Diodorus Siculus: *loc. cit.*; Hyginus: *Fabula* 79; Plutarch: *Theseus* 31.
3. Apollodorus: *Epitome* i. 24; Tzetzes: *On Lycophron* 143; Eustathius on Homer's *Iliad* p. 215; Plutarch: *loc. cit.*
4. Hyginus: *Fabula* 79; Diodorus Siculus: *loc. cit.*; Horace: *Odes* iv. 7. 27; Panyasis, quoted by Pausanias: x. 29. 4; Apollodorus: *Epitome* i. 24.
5. Seneca: *Hippolytus* 835 ff.; Apollodorus: ii. 5. 12; Diodorus Siculus iv.: 26; Euripides: *Madness of Heracles* 619; Hyginus: *loc. cit.*
6. Apollodorus: *loc. cit.*; Suidas *sub* Lispoi; Scholiast on Aristophanes's *Knights* 1368.
7. Diodorus Siculus: iv. 63; Virgil: *Aeneid* vi. 601–19; Aelian: *Varia Historia* iv. 5; Plutarch: *Theseus* 31.

*

1. Leading heroes in several mythologies are said to have harrowed Hell: Theseus, Heracles (see 134. *c*), Dionysus (see 170. *m*), and Orpheus (see 28. *c*) in Greece; Bel and Marduk in Babylonia (see 71. *1*); Aeneas in Italy; Cuchulain in Ireland; Arthur, Gwydion, and Amathaon in Britain; Ogier le Danois in Brittany. The origin of the myth seems to be a tem-

porary death which the sacred king pretended to undergo at the close of his normal reign, while a boy *interrex* took his place for a single day, thus circumventing the law which forbade him to extend his term beyond the thirteen months of a solar year (see 7. *1*; 41. *1*; 123. *4*, etc.).

2. Bel and his successor Marduk, spent their period of demise in battle with the marine monster Tiamat, an embodiment of the Sea-goddess Ishtar who sent the Deluge (see 73. *7*); like ancient Irish kings, who are reported to have gone out to do battle with the Atlantic breakers, they seem to have ceremonially drowned. An Etruscan vase shows the moribund king, whose name is given as Jason (see 148. *4*), in the jaws of a sea-monster: an icon from which the moral anecdote of Jonah and the Whale has apparently been deduced, Jonah being Marduk.

3. Athenian mythographers have succeeded in disguising the bitter rivalry between Theseus and his acting-twin Peirithous (see 95. *2*) for the favours of the Goddess of Death-in-Life – who appears in the myth as both Helen (see 62. *3*) and Persephone – by presenting them as a devoted royal pair who, like Castor and Polydeuces, made an amatory raid on a neighbouring city (see 74. *c*), and one of whom was excused death because he could claim divine birth. Idas and Lynceus, a similar pair of twins, have been introduced into the story to emphasize this point. But Peirithous's name, 'he who turns about', suggests that he was a sacred king in his own right, and on vase-paintings from Lower Italy he is shown ascending to the upper air and saying farewell to Theseus, who remains beside the Goddess of Justice, as though Theseus were merely his tanist.

4. Helen's abduction during a sacrifice recalls that of Oreithyia by Boreas (see 48. *a*), and may have been deduced from the same icon showing erotic orgies at the Athenian Thesmophoria. It is possible, of course, that a shrine of the Attic goddess Helen at Aphidnae contained an image or other cult object stolen by the Athenians from her Laconian counterpart – if the visit to Tartarus is a doublet of the story, they may have made a sea-raid on Taenarus – and that this was subsequently recovered by the Spartans.

5. The four years of Theseus's stay in Tartarus are the usual period during which a sacred king made room for his tanist; a new sacred king, Theseus *redivivus*, would then be installed. An attempt was made by the Athenians to raise their national hero to the status of an Olympian god, like Dionysus and Heracles, by asserting that he had escaped from death; but their Peloponnesian enemies successfully opposed this claim. Some insisted that he had never escaped, but was punished eternally for his insolence, like Ixion and Sisyphus. Others rationalized the story by saying that he raided Cichyrus, not Tartarus; and took the trouble to explain that Peirithous had not been mauled by Cerberus, but by Molos-

sian hounds, the largest and fiercest breed in Greece. The most generous
concession made to Athenian myth was that Theseus, released on bail
after a humiliating session in the Chair of Forgetfulness (see 37. 2), had
apologetically transferred most of his temples and sanctuaries to Heracles
the Rescuer, whose labours and sufferings he aped.

6. Yet Theseus was a hero of some importance, and must be given the
credit of having harrowed Hell, in the sense that he penetrated to the
centre of the Cretan maze, where Death was waiting, and came safely
out again. Had the Athenians been as strong on land as they were at sea,
he would doubtless have become an Olympian or, at least, a national
demi-god. The central source of this hostility towards Theseus is probably Delphi, where Apollo's Oracles was notoriously subservient to the
Spartans in their struggle against Athens.

104

THE DEATH OF THESEUS

DURING Theseus's absence in Tartarus the Dioscuri assembled an
army of Laconians and Arcadians, marched against Athens, and demanded the return of Helen. When the Athenians denied that they
were sheltering her, or had the least notion where she might be, the
Dioscuri proceeded to ravage Attica, until the inhabitants of Deceleia,
who disapproved of Theseus's conduct, guided them to Aphidnae,
where they found and rescued their sister. The Dioscuri then razed
Aphidnae to the ground; but the Deceleians are still immune from all
Spartan taxes and entitled to seats of honour at Spartan festivals – their
lands alone were spared in the Peloponnesian War, when the invading
Spartans laid Attica waste.[1]

b. Others say that the revealer of Helen's hiding-place was one
Academus, or Echedemus, an Arcadian, who had come to Attica on
Theseus's invitation. The Spartans certainly treated him with great
honour while he was alive and, in their later invasions, spared his small
estate on the river Cephissus, six stadia distant from Athens. This is
now called the Academia: a beautiful, well-watered garden, where
philosophers meet and express their irreligious views on the nature of
the gods.[2]

c. Marathus led the Arcadian contingent of the Dioscuri's army and,
in obedience to an oracle, offered himself for sacrifice at the head of

his men. Some say that it was he, not Marathon the father of Sicyon and Corinthus, who gave his name to the city of Marathon.[3]

d. Now, Peteos son of Orneus and grandson of Erechtheus had been banished by Aegeus, and the Dioscuri, to spite Theseus, brought back his son Menestheus from exile, and made him regent of Athens. This Menestheus was the first demagogue. During Theseus's absence in Tartarus he ingratiated himself with the people by reminding the nobles of the power which they had forfeited through Federalization, and by telling the poor that they were being robbed of country and religion, and had become subject to an adventurer of obscure origin – who, however, had now vacated the throne and was rumoured dead.[4]

e. When Aphidnae fell, and Athens was in danger, Menestheus persuaded the people to welcome the Dioscuri into the city as their benefactors and deliverers. They did indeed behave most correctly, and asked only to be admitted to the Eleusinian Mysteries, as Heracles had been. This request was granted, and the Dioscuri became honorary citizens of Athens. Aphidnus was their adoptive father, as Pylius had been Heracles's on a similar occasion. Divine honours were thereafter paid them at the rising of their constellation, in gratitude for the clemency which they had shown to the common people; and they cheerfully brought Helen back to Sparta, with Theseus's mother Aethra and a sister of Peirithous as her bond-woman. Some say that they found Helen still a virgin; others, that Theseus had got her with child and that at Argos, on the way home, she gave birth to a girl, Iphigeneia, and dedicated a sanctuary to Artemis in gratitude for her safe delivery.[5]

f. Theseus, who returned from Tartarus soon afterwards, at once raised an altar to Heracles the Saviour, and reconsecrated to him all but four of his own temples and groves. However, he had been greatly weakened by his tortures, and found Athens so sadly corrupted by faction and sedition that he was no longer able to maintain order.[6] First smuggling his children out of the city to Euboea, where Elpenor son of Chalcodon sheltered them – but some say that they had fled there before his return – and then solemnly cursing the people of Athens from Mount Gargettus, he sailed for Crete, where Deucalion had promised to shelter him.

g. A storm blew the ship off her course, and his first landfall was the island of Scyros, near Euboea, where King Lycomedes, though a close friend of Menestheus, received him with all the splendour due to his fame and lineage. Theseus, who had inherited an estate on Scyros, asked permission to settle there. But Lycomedes had long regarded this estate as his own and, under the pretence of showing Theseus its boundaries, inveigled him to the top of a high cliff, pushed him over, and then gave out that he had fallen accidentally while taking a drunken, post-prandial stroll.[7]

h. Menestheus, now left in undisturbed possession of the throne, was among Helen's suitors, and led the Athenian forces to Troy, where he won great fame as a strategist but was killed in battle. The sons of Theseus succeeded him.[8]

i. Theseus is said to have forcibly abducted Anaxo of Troezen; and to have lain with Iope, daughter of Tirynthian Iphicles. His love-affairs caused the Athenians such frequent embarrassment that they were slow to appreciate his true worth even for several generations after he had died. At the Battle of Marathon, however, his spirit rose from the earth to hearten them, bearing down fully armed upon the Persians; and when victory had been secured, the Delphic Oracle gave orders that his bones should be brought home. The people of Athens had suffered from the Scyrians' contumely for many years, and the Oracle announced that this would continue so long as they retained the bones.[9] But to recover them was a difficult task, because the Scyrians were no less surly than fierce and, when Cimon captured the island, would not reveal the whereabouts of Theseus's grave. However, Cimon observed a she-eagle on a hill-top, tearing up the soil with her talons. Acclaiming this as a sign from Heaven, he seized a mattock, hastened to the hole made by the eagle, and began to enlarge it. Almost at once the mattock struck a stone coffin, inside which he found a tall skeleton, armed with a bronze lance and a sword; it could only be that of Theseus. The skeleton was reverently brought to Athens, and re-interred amid great ceremony in Theseus's sanctuary near the Gymnasium.[10]

j. Theseus was a skilled lyre-player and has now become joint-patron with Heracles and Hermes of every gymnasium and wrestling school in Greece. His resemblance to Heracles is proverbial. He took part in the Calydonian Hunt; avenged the champions who fell at Thebes; and only failed to be one of the Argonauts through being detained in Tartarus when they sailed for Colchis. The first war between the Peloponnesians and the Athenians was caused by his abduction of Helen, and the second by his refusal to surrender Heracles's sons to King Eurystheus.[11]

k. Ill-treated slaves and labourers, whose ancestors looked to him for protection against their oppressors, now seek refuge in his sanctuary, where sacrifices are offered to him on the eighth day of every month. This day may have been chosen because he first arrived at Athens from Troezen on the eighth of Hecatomboeon, and returned from Crete on the eighth day of Pyanepsion. Or perhaps because he was a son of Poseidon: for Poseidon's feasts are also observed on that day of the month, since eight, being the first cube of an even number, represents Poseidon's unshakeable power.[12]

1. Apollodorus: *Epitome* i. 23; Hereas, quoted by Plutarch: *Theseus* 32; Herodotus: ix. 73.
2. Dicaearchus, quoted by Plutarch: *loc. cit.*; Diogenes Laertius: iii. 1. 9; Plutarch: *Cimon* 13.
3. Dicaearchus, quoted by Plutarch: *Theseus* 32; Pausanias: ii. 1. 1.
4. Pausanias: x. 35. 5; Apollodorus: *Epitome* i. 23; Plutarch: *loc. cit.*
5. Plutarch: *Theseus* 33; Hyginus: *Fabula* 79; Pausanias: ii. 22. 7.
6. Aelian: *Varia Historia* iv. 5; Philochorus, quoted by Plutarch: *Theseus* 35; Plutarch: *loc. cit.*
7. Pausanias: i. 17. 6; Plutarch: *loc. cit.*
8. Plutarch: *loc. cit.*; Apollodorus: iii. 10. 8.
9. Plutarch: *Theseus* 29 and 36; Pausanias: i. 15. 4; and iii. 3. 6.
10. Pausanias: i. 17. 6; Plutarch: *loc. cit.*
11. Pausanias: v. 19. 1; iv. 32. 1 and i. 32. 5; Plutarch: *Theseus* 29 and 36; Apollonius Rhodius: i. 101.
12. Plutarch: *Theseus* 36.

*

1. Menestheus the Erechtheid, who is praised in *Iliad* ii. 552 ff. for his outstanding military skill, and reigned at Athens during Theseus's four years' absence in Tartarus, seems to have been his mortal twin and co-king, the Athenian counterpart of Peirithous the Lapith. Here he appears as a prototype of the Athenian demagogues who, throughout the Peloponnesian War, favoured peace with Sparta at any price; but the mythographer, while deploring his tactics, is careful not to offend the Dioscuri, to whom Athenian sailors prayed for succour when overtaken by storms.

2. The theme of the feathered *pharmacos* reappears in the names of Menestheus's father and grandfather, and in the death of Theseus himself. This took place on the island of Scyros ('stony'), also spelled *Sciros*; which suggests that, in the icon from which the story has been deduced, the word *scir* (an abbreviated form of Scirophoria, explaining why the king is being flung from a cliff) has been mistaken for the name of the island. If so, Lycomedes will have been the victim; his was a common

Athenian name. Originally, it seems, sacrifices were offered to the Moon-goddess on the eighth day of each lunation, when she entered her second phase, this being the right time of the month for planting; but when Poseidon married her, and appropriated her cult, the month became a solar period, no longer linked with the moon.

3. The mythic importance of Marathus ('fennel') lay in the use made of fennel stalks for carrying the new sacred fire from a central hearth to private ones (see 39. *g*), after their annual extinction (see 149. 3).

4. Before closing the story of Theseus, let me here add a further note to the Tragliatella vase (see 98. 3), which shows the sacred king and his tanist escaping from a maze. I have now seen the picture on the other side of this vase, which is of extraordinary interest as the prologue to this escape: a sunwise procession on foot led by the unarmed sacred king. Seven men escort him, each armed with three javelins and a shield with a boar device, the spear-armed tanist bringing up the rear. These seven men evidently represent the seven months ruled by the tanist, which fall between the apple harvest and Easter - the boar being his household badge (see 18. 7). The scene takes place on the day of the king's ritual death, and the Moon-queen (Pasiphaë - see 88. 7) has come to meet him: a terrible robed figure with one arm threateningly akimbo. With the outstretched other arm she is offering him an apple, which is his passport to Paradise; and the three spears that each man carries spell death. Yet the king is being guided by a small female figure robed like the other - we may call her the princess Ariadne (see 98. *k*), who helped Theseus to escape from the death-maze at Cnossos. And he is boldly displaying, as a counter-charm to the apple, an Easter-egg, the egg of resurrection. Easter was the season when the Troy-town dances were performed in the turf-cut mazes of Britain, and Etruria too. An Etruscan sacred egg of polished black trachite, found at Perugia, with an arrow in relief running around it, is this same holy egg.

MAP OF THE GREEK WORLD